THE ROUGH GUIDE to

Shopping
with a
Conscience

Duncan Clark &
Richie Unterberger

www.roughguides.com

Credits

The Rough Guide to Shopping with a Conscience

Editor: Sean Mahoney
Design & layout: Duncan Clark & Link Hall
Proofreading: Lisa Grzan
Production: Aimee Hampson
& Katherine Owers

Rough Guides Reference

Series editor: Mark Ellingham
Editors: Peter Buckley,
Duncan Clark, Matthew Milton,
Ruth Tidball, Tracy Hopkins,
Joe Staines, Sean Mahoney
Director: Andrew Lockett

Publishing information

This first edition published January 2007 by Rough Guides Ltd,
375 Hudson Street, New York 10014
80 Strand, London WC2R 0RL
www.roughguides.com

Distributed by the Penguin Group

Penguin Putnam, Inc., 375 Hudson Street, NY 10014, USA
Penguin Books Ltd, 80 Strand, London WC2R 0RL
Penguin Group (Australia), 250 Camberwell Road, Camberwell, Victoria 3124, Australia
Penguin Books Canada Ltd, 90 Eglinton Avenue East, Toronto, Ontario, Canada M4P 2YE
Penguin Group (New Zealand), 67 Apollo Drive, Mairongi Bay, Auckland 1310, New Zealand

Printed in USA by Lake Book Manufacturing Inc

Typeset in Din, Minion and Myriad

352 pages; includes index

A catalogue record for this book is available from the British Library

ISBN 13: 978-1-84353-724-3
ISBN 10: 1-84353-724-9

3 5 7 9 8 6 4 2

Contents

CONTENTS

Part III: Find out more

Acknowledgements

Duncan Clark would like to thank the scores of people who have contributed interviews, emails, images and advice for this book. These include, in no particular order: Harriet Lamb, Abi Murray and Diana Gayle at the Fairtrade Foundation; Mike Brady at Baby Milk Action; Beverly Mirando at Nestlé; Becky Price at Genewatch; Professor Michael Wilson from Horticulture Research International; Nina Smith at RUGMARK Foundation; Anne Lally at the Fair Labor Association; Mil Niepold at Verité; Wendy Higgins at BUAV; Bernadette Clark at the Marine Conservation Society; Jon Entine; Shelley Simmons at The Body Shop; Oliver Knowles at Greenpeace; Matthew Criddle at Naturesave Insurance; Paul Garrod at Chandni Chowk; Meagan Tudge at Ethically Me; Richard Young at the Soil Association; Sam Maher from Labour Behind the Label; Frances Galvanoni from the Energy Saving Trust; Greg Valerio at CRED; Scott McAusland at EIRIS; Elanor Gordon at *Ethical Consumer*; Kat Alexander at the Ethical Company Organization; Daniel Blackburn at Veg Oil Motoring; Christine Miles at *The Chichester Observer*; the Garstang Courierand; and Rick Mills. Thanks also to everyone at Rough Guides: Jonathan Buckley and Mark Ellingham for believing such an off-the-wall Rough Guide could be a runner; Andy Dickson for persuading me to write a proposal; Andrew Lockett for signing off this US version; Matt Milton for great editorial input; Joe Staines for years of press cuttings; and Peter Buckley for diagrams.

Richie Unterberger would like to thank Andrew Lockett, editor Sean Mahoney, and agent Robert Shepard for helping to initiate this book and guide it to completion. Also thanks to the following people for information and advice: Emily Alpert of Oxfam America; Anthony Chaba; Tom Doskow; Ruth Kildall; Charlie Milgrim; Professor Jules Pretty from the Department of Biological Sciences, University of Essex; Professor Laura Raynolds from the Department of Sociology, Colorado State University; Tomek Rondio; Janet Rosen; Kristie Stoick of Physicians Committee for Responsible Medicine; John Wasik; and Tim West.

Introduction

Socially responsible shopping—and ethical consumerism in general—is about taking responsibility for your day-to-day impact upon the world. It doesn't mean deluding yourself into thinking that shopping with a conscience can solve all the world's problems, or that the check-out is the new ballot box. And it doesn't mean following a prescriptive list of evil companies and countries that need to be boycotted. It means taking the time to learn a little about how your lifestyle affects people, planet and animals, and making your own decisions about what constitutes an ethical or unethical purchase.

The case for making the effort—laid out further in chapter one—is strong. After all, the things we buy involve us in just about all the pressing issues in the world: from the immense threat of global warming to the world's dwindling fish stocks; from sweatshop labor to the funding of presidential election campaigns; from deforestation to ecologically harmful intensive farming. That's not to say all these problems are our fault, of course, or that consumers are in a position to solve them. But we live in an increasingly integrated world, and the implications of our purchases reach far further than we might think.

Where do you start?

Once you start thinking about all the positive and negative implications of what you buy and use, it quickly becomes clear that there's no one-size-fits-all approach—no simple list of moral checks and crosses. For one thing, there are always conflicting priorities. Is it better, for instance, to support the local independent café round the corner, or buy a fairly traded cup from the global chain across the road? Is it "ethical" to favor local products—doing your bit to limit environmentally harmful transportation—or does that mean harming impoverished countries that are eager to export? Should we boycott goods from countries run by oppressive regimes, or will economic isolation just cause their people even more suffering—perhaps even helping the regime stay in power?

It's also difficult to know whose information to trust. Facts get muddled and distorted, and views are thrown at us from such highly partisan sources as transnational companies and transnational single-issue pressure groups (which, some say, have as much interest in exaggerating stories as the big companies have in playing them down). So should we take it seriously when we hear of child slaves assembling our sneakers, banks lending our money to arms manufacturers, or passenger planes frying the climate? Should we trust companies who tell us, "don't worry about it, we have a code of conduct." And what about the arguments that "ethical" shopping may do more harm than good?

All these unanswered questions are enough to make many people think that basing purchases on a code of ethics is just too much work, and that no choice is really "ethical" if you scrutinize it hard enough. True, we're always going to be compromised by incomplete information, conflicting priorities and the time we have available to think about it all. But an ever growing number of people *are* attempting to be more conscientious in the things they buy and use—at least that's what every new study seems to show. And that's why we've published this book.

About this book

Though it certainly won't provide all the answers, this Rough Guide should help you navigate the often confusing and contradictory world of shopping with a conscience, also known as "ethical consumerism". If you're after a list of every major brand name with columns for the various types of bad behavior they're up to, then you'll need to look elsewhere (such as the magazines and books listed in chapter 10). If, however, you want a balanced assessment of issues ranging from organic food to fair-trade clothes, and pointers to companies that have put moral standards at the heart of their operations, then you should find this book useful.

Part I looks at ethical consumerism as a whole: the arguments for and against it, and the various different approaches. Part II focuses in on specific products and services, in each case looking at the issues, the debates and the ethical (or supposedly ethical) options. Finally, Part III provides some pointers to where you can read more, and includes tips on doing your own research into a company's practices.

But before moving on to all that, a brief note about the book's title. "Shopping" is used here in the broadest sense: to mean anything you can "shop" for. So expect to find sections on vacation travel, financial services and electricity supplies—not just all those things you can put in a cart.

Part I

Issues

- Ethical consumerism
- Five approaches
- Should we buy from ...

Ethical consumerism

Should we shop ethically?
The cases for and against

Most of this book is concerned with the social and environmental implications of specific products, companies, labels (such as organic or Fair Trade) and approaches to ethically minded shopping. But first of all it's worth asking something more fundamental: **is ethical consumerism a good idea?** This may sound like a silly question. But, though very few people suggest we should deliberately ignore ethical issues when choosing what to buy, many do claim that focusing on them too much is a waste of time—or even counterproductive. Here are the main arguments for and against ethical shopping.

Arguments for

The basic case for ethical shopping, socially responsible consumerism, shopping with a conscience or whatever you want to call it, is very simple—that now more than ever, the things we buy and consume link us to a huge range of social, economic, political and environmental issues. We can choose to ignore this fact if we like, but there's really no denying it.

It's not that you have to be vindictive to "shop unethically." After all, it won't say on the label if an item of clothing has been made in a factory that denies workers the basic right to join a union and bargain for decent pay and conditions. Nor will it say if a piece of furniture is made from wood logged from Indonesia's swiftly disappearing rainforests. But

// We have to accept that we're born consumers, and the only rational course open to us is responsible, accountable consumerism. **//**

Anita Roddick

// Buying ethical products sends support directly to progressive companies ... while at the same time depriving others that abuse for profit. **//**

Ethical Consumer magazine

the fact remains: if we buy such products, we support the companies in question and the way they produce their goods. Likewise, if we buy products from the firms which fund politicians—which many of them do (see p.67)—we effectively endorse whichever party they're bankrolling.

However, it's not all about the negative impacts we make on the world. As most people in the ethical consumerism movement are keen to point out, shopping ethically can make a positive difference, too. By supporting progressive businesses, or products bearing labels that testify to their social and environmental credentials, we may help bring about deeper change. CRED jewelry, for example, is a small British fair-trade supplier, but it has been integral to the slow ethical awakening of the whole jewelry industry. Pax World Fund was the only socially responsible mutual fund in the US when it was founded in 1971; today, more than one out of every nine dollars under professional management in the US is tied to socially responsible investing. Similarly, companies specializing in renewable electricity, "green" paints or electric cars are likely to be actively involved in the research and development of eco-friendly products that may gradually enter the mainstream.

Or think of the **Fair Trade** labeling system, which aims to ensure that marginalized producers in poor countries—cocoa farmers in West Africa, say—get a bigger proportion of the price we pay for their goods, as well as up-front payments and other benefits. This model is entirely consumer driven, yet many of its principles are starting to crop up in the policy ideas of governments, companies and radical political writers alike. This doesn't mean that ideals of equity and partnership will soon come to be embedded in all global trade (and some people doubt whether that would be a good idea anyway—more on that later), but it does show that ethical consumers have influenced thinkers of all kinds.

Furthermore, buying socially or environmentally focused products can **raise the profile of issues** that might otherwise be ignored. The very availability of an "ethical" option inevitably gets people thinking, whether it's about the real costs of fossil fuels (in the case of a solar roof) or the environmental and animal-right impacts of intensive agriculture (in the case of organic food).

Finally, on a less ambitious level, considering the implications of what we buy may simply allow us to align our beliefs with our actions—a purely personal aim, but there's nothing wrong with that.

Arguments against (and the arguments against them)

Arguments against the "moralization" of consumerism come from both the reactionary right and the radical left, as well as semantic pedants and good old-fashioned miserable conservatives (who simply grumble that it's all "political correctness gone mad"). The following few pages take a look at the most common objections. Arguments for and against approaches to ethical shopping about specific industries, or types of product, are discussed throughout this book, in the relevant sections.

Nothing's truly "ethical," so why bother?

The argument that no consumer—let alone a producer or product—can be truly, 100%, categorically "ethical" is often given as a reason for not bothering with ethically minded shopping. After all, if it's ethical to, say, choose a car with lower greenhouse emissions, it must be even more ethical to walk instead of drive, to take the stairs rather than an elevator, or to only eat raw food to save wasting the energy used in cooking. The logical conclusion, skeptics sometimes revel in pointing out, would be to minimize your negative impact on the world by stopping breathing altogether.

The "e" word is without a shadow of a doubt **subjective**, morally loaded and often problematic. And it's easy to make ethical consumerism sound laughable by taking it to its apparently absurd logical conclusions. But, while you could spend hours arguing over the subjectivity of it all, semantic nit-picking is not really very good grounds for ignoring the effects we have on the rest of the world. And, while we all have our own specific ideas of what should and shouldn't count as accepted standards, it's probably fair to say that we all aspire to some common ideals. For example: *no* to unnecessarily harming people or the environment; *yes* to the provision of safe, dignified conditions for workers; *no* to hiding the social and environmental implications of a product from the person buying it. It's surely more constructive to ask how these standards can be achieved than to argue over whether or not ethical shopping is an oxymoron.

That said, it's true that you should treat ethical claims with a certain degree of caution until you know exactly what it is they refer to—especially when someone's trying to make money out of them.

A distraction from the real problems?

Ethical consumerism has a love-hate relationship with **the radical left**. Though many dutifully buy their fairly traded bananas, others worry that it is, in its own, well-meaning way, potentially dangerous. After all, while it is usually seen as a progressive, essentially left-wing movement, ethical shopping is still all about buying things. It's a form of **consumer power** and it may act as a distraction from engagement with real politics and **the big issues**—such as national and international legislation on tax, equality, climate change and labor and environmental standards enforced by governments and international bodies such as the UN. Writer and activist George Monbiot, for example, claims that this problem has been apparent for years. The greatest failure of the green movement in the 1980s, he once wrote, was the misconception that "we could buy our way out of trouble."

But it's not as if anyone who thinks about ethical shopping is somehow using up all their intellectual energy and will give up engaging in real politics—especially when you consider that many organizations involved in ethical consumerism spend considerable effort raising awareness of broader political issues and campaigning for global, structural change. Socially responsible mutual investment funds, for example, make it a priority not only to invest their shareholders' money in an ethical manner, but also to pressure major corporations to become more environmentally responsible, and are now increasingly plowing their resources into projects benefiting low-income communities (see p. 213).

That said, some of ethical shopping's advocates do like to hint at the goal of a new **consumer democracy** that can deliver where

// 'Light' green business tends to merely perpetuate the colonization of the mind, sapping our visions of an alternative and giving the idea that our salvation can be gained through shopping rather than through social struggle. **//**

Christopher and Judith Plant, *Green Business: Hope or Hoax?*

// Because ethical consumerism is based *wholly* on market solutions ... it is incapable even of recognizing the *root* cause of that crisis, namely the atomizing nature of market society. **//**

Anarchist FAQ Webpage

state and social activism has failed. In this model, the checkout is the new ballot box and **commercial disobedience** is the new *civil* disobedience. British writer Noreena Hertz, for example, has written that, "In a world in which power increasingly lies in the hands of corporations rather than governments, the most effective way to be political is not to cast one's vote at the ballot box but to do so at the supermarket or at a shareholders meeting."

Such statements (which, it should be said, do not fully reflect Hertz's views), are dangerous—not just because they might discourage political engagement, but also because they're based on a skewed concept of democracy that's heavily weighted in favor of the wealthy. Political democracy is based on the principle of one person one vote, but in a consumer democracy you **vote in hard currency**.

For all this, the sensible response is not to dismiss ethical consumerism; rather, we should simply make sure that we are always aware of its limits and not let it take the place of politics. Some have put it like this: be **ethical citizens** first, and ethical consumers second.

Letting governments off the hook

Another view from the left is that, by pressuring companies rather than politicians, ethical shoppers make it easier for governments to avoid legislating for legally enforceable, across-the-board change. This doesn't apply to to fair-trade companies and other "ethical specialists," but if consumers manage to persuade big firms to introduce **voluntary codes of conduct**, for example, or join **ethical trade bodies**, then politicians can say "we don't need to introduce any new laws or regulations … the corporate sector is already dealing with the problems."

This argument is entirely valid (politicians have indeed sometimes taken this line) but it's not entirely persuasive. For one thing, it's just as logical to suppose that progressive, responsible companies will catalyze new laws and new regulations—by showing that good corporate practice is achievable—than deter them. After all, once a company has committed, say, to only selling wood from

> // The purpose of corporate social responsibility is to avoid regulation. It permits governments and the public to believe that compulsory rules are unnecessary, as the same objectives are being met by other means. Of course, the great advantage of voluntary rules is that you can break them whenever they turn out to be inconvenient. //
>
> George Monbiot

sustainable sources, then a law making this a general requirement would actually be in its interest, since the company's competitors would then be forced to play catch-up. So supporting big companies that make voluntary improvements may weaken, rather than strengthen, anti-regulation corporate lobbying.

Furthermore, in reality, **laws can often only go so far**. Much, perhaps most, of the world's labor abuse and environmental damage is already illegal, but it still goes on regardless. That's why an increasing number of charities and non-governmental organizations (NGOs) now agree that problems ranging from safety in diamond mines to working hours in clothes factories can only be really solved when governments, NGOs *and* companies are all genuinely committed to change. And companies will never become committed without pressure from consumers.

Hurting the poor

From the opposite side of the political spectrum comes the opposite criticism: not that ethical consumerism may deter new laws and regulations, but that it might in itself be almost *too much* of a regulation. This argument is based on a strong belief in the **free market**—that if you let **supply and demand** do their thing, it will be in everyone's interest, and anti-market ethical meddling, however well meaning, will simply get in the way.

For example, if coffee prices are low due to oversupply, then we must let the market do its work and force down the number of coffee growers: propping up an unsustainable system via the Fair Trade label is just dragging the problem out. Likewise, if Western consumers demand higher labor standards for workers in poor countries, this will force up the cost of producing in the developing world, reducing the number of companies moving their facilities there, and denying people naively described as "exploited" the very jobs they desperately want and need.

Furthermore, the argument goes, if we have patience, the "invisible hand" of the market will eventually improve working conditions: once enough sweatshops and export farms open up in a country, unemployment will drop, the workforce will get better off, and soon the employers will be competing with each other to raise standards and attract staff.

There is certainly some truth in all this but, again, it's not a wholly convincing case. For one thing, it makes little sense to criticize ethical consumerism as being "anti-market." It is, after all, about people making free choices about what they do and don't want, and using their spending power in the marketplace to implement those decisions—practically a textbook definition of how a free market should work. Second, there's quite clearly no such thing as a genuinely free market: all markets exist within a framework of laws (covering everything from monopolies and the minimum wage, to slavery and toxic dumping) and ethical shopping, like voting, is a perfectly valid way of taking a stand about what these laws should be. Third, on the ground level, and especially in poor countries, "free" markets are often in practice hugely distorted, with political corruption and violent threats having far more sway than supply and demand. In many cases, ethical consumerism is helping to limit, not add to, these market distortions—by giving us the option to buy direct from producers, for example.

// The adoption of Western standards would mean that the cost of production in the developing countries increases manifold; this would take away their entire competitive edge. //

Ranvir Nayar, *The Indian Express*

Despite all this theory, however, it's still a valid question to ask whether well-meaning ethical shoppers may end up doing more harm than good in relation to specific issues, such as third-world labor standards and Fair Trade coffee. These questions are dealt with in the sections on sweatshops (p.45) and Fair Trade (p.20).

Why not ethical thrift?

One argument against certain areas of ethical shopping is that they mean **spending extra money** that could be better used elsewhere. Granted, buying organic food lets us support a more responsible farming system that is better both for wildlife, soil fertility and animal welfare—undoubtedly worthy causes. But the problems they address are arguably far less acute than—to pick a random example—the lack of food and essential medicines at any number of the world's refugee camps. As such, how can we justify spending an extra $35 or so each week buying organic food "on ethical grounds," instead of hunting down bargains and giving the money saved to Oxfam or Médecins Sans Frontières? Can conventional agriculture really be so bad that we'll prioritize it over appalling human misery?

Some would say that the answer is that ethical shopping allows us to deal with the structural problems rather than just the symptoms. And that's a fair point—the world needs social and environmental justice as well as charity. But could it also be partly that conscientious consumerism gives us greater "guilt relief" than charity, as it makes us feel at ease with our comparative wealth?

From fringe to mainstream
How big is ethical consumerism?

The impact of ethical shopping is largely down to how many people get involved, so "How many ethical shoppers are there?" is an obvious question to ask. However, this is actually something that's very hard to measure. We can keep tabs on how much people are spending on explicitly "ethical" goods, such as those carrying the Fair Trade label (more than $400 million worldwide annually at the time of writing, according to the Fair Trade Federation, and rising fast). But it's not so easy to work out what people *aren't* buying on ethical grounds—through **consumer boycotts**—or whether they are favoring some mainstream shops or brands because they suspect they're more ethical than the others.

The only way to gauge it is by asking people, and, as social scientists tend to agree, people often give the answer they feel the questioner wants to hear; or one which reflects their ideals, even though they might rarely actually act on them. According to the Hartman Group, a research firm specializing in the health marketplace, 63% of consumers say they will pay more for products that demonstrate a positive environmental impact. LOHAS (Lifestyles of Health and Sustainability), an organization that tracks green economic trends, has found that about 30% of US adults are "LOHAS consumers," i.e. ones who (as defined on its website, www.lohas.com) consume "goods and services focused on health, the environment, social justice, personal development and sustainable living." Yet ethical sales numbers simply don't support such claims. Countless reports have suggested that consumers are adamantly against animal-testing for cosmetics, yet most products bearing the Coalition for Consumer Information on Cosmetics white-rabbit logo still account for a dramatically lower percentage of the US market than their large, "inhumane" counterparts.

Even when people are buying "ethical" goods, it's easy to read too much into the figures. Consumers choosing energy-efficient washing machines, say, might be doing it to save money rather than save the planet; or favoring local stores because they're nearer (rather

US ethical consumerism in figures

Consumer attitudes/practice

$230 billion ▶ the value of the LOHAS market in 2000

68 million ▶ the number of Americans who are LOHAS consumers

76-86% ▶ the percentage of consumers who say they are willing to pay more for items that are made under good working conditions

26% ▶ the percentage of consumers who bought an item labeled as being produced under good working conditions even when it cost more than an identical non-labeled item

Green consumption

$7.8 billion ▶ the amount spent on organic food in 2005

$36 billion ▶ sales of natural products, including food and personal care products, in 2002

205,749 ▶ the number of hybrid automobiles sold in 2005

1.2% ▶ percentage of total automobiles sold in the US in 2005 that were hybrids

Fair Trade

20% ▶ the percentage of Americans that are aware of Fair Trade certified products

12% ▶ the percentage of coffee consumers who are aware of Fair Trade labels

79% ▶ the percentage of college students that would purchase Fair Trade items if they were available on campus

49% ▶ the percentage of college students that would pay more for Fair Trade items if they were available on campus

1.8% ▶ the proportion of the US coffee market that is Fair Trade in 2004

80% ▶ the proportion of people who say that corporate support of causes wins their trust in that company

73% ▶ the percentage of people who would boycott a company's products if they have behaved illegally or unethically

90% ▶ the percentage of people who would switch product brands in response to unethical or illegal corporate behavior

86% ▶ the percentage of people who would switch to a brand associated with a cause in selecting between products of similar price and quality

80% ▶ the percentage of Americans who can name a company that stands out in their mind as a strong corporate citizen

Compiled by the Center for Fair and Alternative Trade Studies, Colorado State University; see its website, http://www.colostate.edu/Depts/Sociology/cfats/index.html, for full citations of sources for the above figures.

// In order to make an ethical choice, consumers wanted the full facts about the make-up of the different products on offer. But three quarters (76 per cent) said they were being kept in the dark ... they were hungry for information. //

Cooperative group,
Shopping with Attitude

than because they want to take a stand against the supermarkets' oligopolistic control of the food chain). Similarly, millions have said they want to avoid genetically engineered foods, and the supermarkets' quick decision to stop selling them is often held up as an example of the power of ethical shoppers. But, arguably, most GE boycotters have done so mainly on the grounds of a perceived health risk, rather than for the wider ethical implications (see p.93).

But if there's one thing we can say for certain, it's that conscientious consumerism as a whole just keeps on growing. Though the ethical share of the total US market is still quite small, and occasionally something suggests a slow-down (such as the recent decisions by major automobile companies to virtually abandon manufacturing electric cars for the US market), nearly every pointer suggests a clear upward trend. Like all such figures, none of these stats (or the ones cited in the box on p.11 "US Ethical Consumerism Figures") should be treated as concrete. But they do provide a broad-brush impression of the ethical consumer's increasing influence.

Another observation made by just about every relevant survey and poll is that people would *like* to be more active ethical shoppers than they are, but feel held back by a lack of information. Considering that as morally minded consumerism grows more information is becoming available, this suggests a possible snowball-effect growth for ethical shopping in the not-too-distant future.

Five approaches

Every consumer area has its own "ethical approaches," from investment screening in financial services to organics in the world of food. There are scores of similar examples, most of which you'll find discussed in the relevant sections of this book. However, there are also more general approaches that cut across the whole field of ethical shopping: concepts such as "fair trade," boycotts and simply buying less. This chapter takes a look at five of the most important.

#1: Going green
Buying less & reducing your footprint

While trying to support ethical brands or products is all well and good, many in the environmental movement point out that it doesn't take account of a more fundamental issue: that we Westerners consume too much. A fairly traded T-shirt is laudable enough, they'd say, but the most ethical approach to shopping would involve simply **buying as little as possible**—in addition to opting for the products whose manufacture, transport and use results in minimum energy consumption.

There are many prongs of reasoning here, beyond the argument that buying too much stuff turns us all into super-materialist consumption machines. First, there is only so much stuff in the world, and so buying more of it must somewhere down the line mean **depriving others** of their fair share. According to the UN's *Human Development Report 2003*, the richest 20% of the world's population consume 88% of the world's goods and services, while the poorest fifth consume only 3.3%. Such staggering inequality won't be solved, of course, by ethically minded consumers buying less. But for as long as the comparatively wealthy people in the world spend all their money on buying things—as opposed to giving to charity, say—it's unlikely to change.

Second, our consumption habits are ultimately **unsustainable**, and we'd do well to remedy this before the end of the oil age turns the situation into a global crisis. With easily accessible reserves quickly becoming exhausted, it seems very likely that, within a few decades, oil production will be on the decline. As the inevitable worldwide recession kicks in, we're bound to look back with dismay on our massive consumption of everything from petrol to plastic bottles at a time when cheap, abundant oil could have been used in the development of alternative energy sources.

But perhaps the most widely stated argument for buying less and favoring greener products is that our consumption habits are a driving force behind much of the devastation that humans are wreaking on the planet. The most obvious and worrying example is **climate change** ...

We're buying, the climate's frying

There isn't space here for a full discussion of the science and potential impacts of climate change, but it's worth quickly spelling out a few key facts. Despite a handful of remaining skeptics (their voices amplified by corporate-funded think tanks), there is now a solid scientific consensus that humans have measurably changed the climate in the last century. We've done this by releasing huge volumes of so-called **greenhouse gases** into the atmosphere. The most important greenhouse gas—carbon dioxide or CO_2—is released primarily by the burning of fossil fuels such as coal, oil and natural gas to create electricity, power vehicles and machines or heat buildings. Others, such as methane and nitrous oxides, are released mainly by farming and industrial processes.

As sunlight reaches Earth, it's converted into infrared energy and emitted back through the atmosphere and into space. Greenhouse gases absorb some of this energy, reducing the amount that is lost to space and hence warming the atmosphere. There have always been greenhouse gases in the air (if there were none, our planet would be a freezing, lifeless chunk of rock), but in the last century and a half, we've increased their levels with remarkable speed.

It's true, of course, that the world's climate has always been in a state of flux: ice ages have come and gone, and in the really long run the Sun will grow to 250 times its current size, boil the oceans, kill all life and cause "iron rain and silicon snow" to fall on Earth, as described in *New Scientist*. Unlike this unavoidable, natural climate change, however, our emissions of greenhouse gases threaten humans and other species now—rather than at some unimaginably distant point in the future.

Indeed, some serious impacts are already observable. The World Health Organization estimates that in 2000 alone, more than 150,000 people died as a result of direct and indirect climate-change impacts such as the widening reach of **malaria** and **dengue fever**, the seemingly paradoxical increase in both **drought** and **flooding**, and a rise in the intensity of **heat waves** and **hurricanes**.

Looking forward, the potential changes are terrifying. A study published in science journal *Nature* in January 2004 concluded that, if mid-range predictions for greenhouse emissions and the climate's sensitivity to them prove correct, 15–37% of the world's plant and animal species will be "committed to extinction" by 2050. By the end of the century, a combination of warming oceans and melting Arctic and Antarctic ice could raise sea levels by as much as 3 ft, devastating low-lying regions such as Bangladesh through loss of land and higher-reaching storm surges. A couple of centuries further on, the sea-level rise could be many times greater, displacing billions of people and destroying many of the world's great cities, London and New York included.

Of course, a different climate may also have some benefits, but the costs are likely to be incomparably greater and will be felt most acutely by people who are least financially able to adapt (the same people who are least responsible for the problem in the first place). As for the US, climate change may take the edge off our cold winters, but it looks set to bring increased rainfall and flooding too. It may even intensify the

Paani Laupepa of the low-lying nation of Tuvalu looks out at the rising ocean that is expected to cover his country within decades. "The question is not if but when we'll be drowned."

weather patterns known as El Niño and La Niña—two parts of the same ocean-atmosphere cycle that spans a third of the globe from Ecuador to Indonesia. If this happens, the chances of powerful, destructive hurricanes rising out of the Atlantic Ocean will increase significantly.

For a comprehensive overview of climate change science, see *The Rough Guide to Climate Change.*

Solutions great & small

As individuals, we can attempt to tackle climate change both directly—by seeking to reduce the greenhouse-gas emissions that we're personally responsible for—and by lobbying our political representatives to put the issue toward the top of the national and international agendas. We can also consider paying a carbon offset company to invest in projects that will counteract some or all of our emissions (see p.300).

When focusing on the personal level, the first step is to take stock of your personal **carbon footprint**—the total amount of CO_2 emissions that you are directly or indirectly responsible for. A good start is to play with a carbon calculator. These simple online tools allow you to calculate how much carbon each activity in your life generates and how your total compares to those of the people around you and elsewhere in the world. The carbon-offset companies all offer calculators for specific activities, but to quickly assess your overall carbon footprint, visit:

Ecological Footprint Quiz www.myfootprint.org
BP www.bp.com/environment

These sites, though useful, tend to focus on our most obvious carbon-intensive activities, such as flying and driving. A more comprehensive analysis should include less obvious emissions sources such as the production and transport of all the goods we buy. The following charts, based on figures from Best Foot Forward (www.bestfootforward.com), break down the carbon footprint of the average US resident, with an average figure for Africa provided for comparison. They include aviation and the manufacture of imported goods, both of which are usually excluded from official per-capita emissions statistics.

As the chart shows, over half of the average US citizen's emissions are accounted for by home energy (heating and electricity) and travel (road, air and sea). So these are sensible areas to focus on. Later in this book you'll find lots of tips to get started – see p.239 for household energy and p.281 for travel. But what about the other half of our emissions? These are

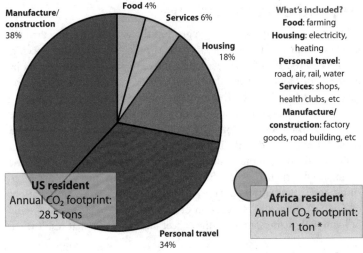

Food 4%

Services 6%

Housing 18%

Manufacture/
construction
38%

What's included?
Food: farming
Housing: electricity,
heating
Personal travel:
road, air, rail, water
Services: shops,
health clubs, etc
**Manufacture/
construction**: factory
goods, road building, etc

US resident
Annual CO_2 footprint:
28.5 tons

Africa resident
Annual CO_2 footprint:
1 ton *

Personal travel
34%

* Excludes aviation and imported goods

caused by the production and transportation of the food and goods we buy, the construction of our homes, offices and roads, and the services we use. Some of these emissions are completely beyond our control. But we can reduce them somewhat by recycling, avoiding unnecessary purchases and favoring locally produced food (see p.89).

Another approach is to favor brands, shops and services that have sought to reduce their own emissions, and avoid those which have lobbied against mandated cuts in greenhouse-gas emissions. Until fairly recently, the latter category included most of the mainstream business community, especially in the US. In May 2001, for example, Thomas J. Donohue, CEO of the Chamber of Commerce of the United States of America, which speaks on behalf of "three million businesses," wrote a letter to President George W. Bush claiming that "global warming is an important issue that must be addressed—but the Kyoto Protocol is a flawed treaty that is not in the US interest." Today, however, many companies have managed to reduce their emissions considerably—or have at least ended their membership of industry lobby groups such as the Global Climate Coalition, which was once enormously influential in derailing climate protection measures.

Given President Bush's rejection of the Kyoto Protocol, there's also a decent case for avoiding any company that has bankrolled his election campaigns (see p.68).

Beyond climate change

Climate change may be the single greatest threat to the world's environments but our consumer choices can harm the planet in more specific, localized ways. **Rainforest clearance**, for example, is driven mainly by demand for wood and the desire for land to grow crops such as soya (mainly used as feed for the meat and milk industries) and palm oil (which is found in everything from soap to biscuits). Such clearances have been responsible for many of the estimated 300,000 species that have been rendered extinct in the last fifty years.

But it's not just animals and plants that feel the effect of local-level ecological destruction: when the environment suffers, people also tend to suffer, and that usually means the poor. There are countless manifestations of this fact, from the persecution of indigenous people that goes hand in hand with deforestation, to the cancer and blindness that result when

Ecological footprints

The concept of a carbon footprint grew out of a longer-established and broader idea: the **ecological footprint**. This is a measure of our consumption levels in terms of the total area of the Earth's surface needed to support our individual existence. This area—measured in hectares of average productivity—includes the space for growing crops, grazing animals, harvesting timber, catching fish, accommodating infrastructure and absorbing carbon dioxide emissions. The icons below give some sense of the inequality in the footprints of people around the world.

To calculate your own ecological footprint (and find out how many planets we'd need if everyone lived just like you) see www.myfootprint.org, or, for more on the ecological footprint system, visit:

Redefining Progress www.redefiningprogress.org

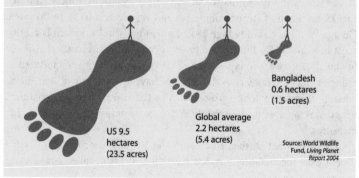

Bangladesh
0.6 hectares
(1.5 acres)

US 9.5
hectares
(23.5 acres)

Global average
2.2 hectares
(5.4 acres)

Source: World Wildlife
Fund, *Living Planet
Report 2004*

industrial effluent is pumped untreated into rivers used for water supplies, such as has happened around Bangladeshi leather tanneries (see p.172). Local-level environmental problems have also forced millions of people from their homes. Though **environmental refugees** are not specifically recognized by the Geneva Convention, there may now be more of them than political refugees: 25 million compared with 22 million, according to analysis by the environmental ecologist Norman Myers. And this figure is set to rocket as climate change kicks in.

The typical response of environmentalists to all this is to advocate buying and consuming as little as possible, but many exponents of globalization have a different view. They claim that people only start to care for their local environment when they reach a certain level of material wealth (two academics from Princeton University put the threshold at an annual average income of $50,000). That explains, the argument goes, why air and water quality are generally going up in rich countries and down in poor countries. Since many poor countries rely on exporting goods to Western markets, then cutting back on consumerism could end up harming developing economies. The only way people there are likely to become rich enough to be able to pay heed to environmental issues, we're told, is through more trade—which necessarily involves people buying and consuming more.

But, even if it's true, there's at least one serious problem with this line of reasoning. Rich countries may have fewer local environmental problems, but they are incomparably worse when it comes to global warming.

Started in 1993 by members of Adbusters (see p.54), Buy Nothing Day embodies the "buy less" approach to ethical consumerism—and it has become a global event. The challenge is to go 24 hours without buying anything. It's a commitment to consuming less, recycling more and challenging corporations to clean up and be fair. "Culture jammers" take the opportunity to stage pranks and protests in shopping malls, or start a Saturday job timed specifically to get fired from it (for refusing to sell anything on Buy Nothing Day, of course) and generally raise awareness of one's ecological footprint. Buy Nothing Day is "celebrated" on different late November days in different countries, but always takes place in North America the day after Thanksgiving, the biggest shopping day of the year. In 2006 Adbusters began a new phase in their Buy Nothing campaign, with the introduction of Buy Nothing Christmas.

#2: Fair trade

How does it work? How "fair" is it?

There are various approaches to fair trade, and even more various terms to describe them. For instance, "fair" is sometimes substituted with "**alternative,**" "**responsible**" or "**ethical**"—perhaps on the grounds that no business arrangement between rich consumers and poor producers can ever be entirely fair. And then there are different levels of formality, from officially certified products bearing the Fair Trade Certified label, to uncertified goods whose ethical credentials are based mainly on trust (more on these two systems below).

But, for all this, the basic idea remains the same: a business model that aims to **improve the livelihoods of poor and marginalized workers** in the developing world. As most consumers understand it, this simply means paying producers—whether they be farmers, plantation workers, manufacturers or craftspeople—more money for their goods. And it's true that dealing directly with suppliers and paying them a decent price for their work is a key fair trade principle. But this isn't the end of the story. Fair trade also aims to **empower producers** by—among other things—encouraging them to form democratically run cooperatives. And it means making **up-front payments** and **long-term trading arrangements**, to save producers relying on potentially crippling loans and to enable them to plan ahead.

In return, the suppliers are expected to produce goods of a very high **quality** and ensure that the **environment** is properly cared for. All in all, the exchange is based on partnership and cooperation, rather than straightforward buying power.

As well as making a direct difference to producers, the fair trade movement also aims to improve things beyond its immediate sphere of influence. And this seems to work. You wonder, for example, whether without fair trade's existence, company-specific initiatives (such as Chiquita's "Better Banana" initiative and Starbucks' "Commitment to Origins"), however imperfect they may be, would ever have happened at all.

What's wrong with "normal trade"?

The fair trade movement aims to reconnect producers with consumers, and ensure a better deal for the former. There are a whole host of reasons why this is necessary, but one of them is that under current world trade

Fair trade defined

The closest thing to an official definition of fair trade has come from FINE, an association of four international organizations:

F ▶ **Fairtrade Labelling Organizations International** www.fairtrade.net

I ▶ **International Federation for Alternative Trade** www.ifat.org

N ▶ **Network of European World Shops** www.worldshops.org

E ▶ **European Fair Trade Association** www.eftafairtrades.org

The definition

"Fair trade is a trading partnership, based on dialogue, transparency and respect, which seeks greater equity in international trade. It contributes to sustainable development by offering better trading conditions to, and securing the rights of, marginalised producers and workers—especially in the South. Fair-trade organizations (backed by consumers) are engaged actively in supporting producers, awareness raising and in campaigning for changes in the rules and practices of conventional international trade."

The goals

▶ **To improve the livelihoods** and well-being of producers by improving market access, strengthening producer organizations, paying a better price and providing continuity in the trading relationship.

▶ **To promote development** opportunities for disadvantaged producers, especially women and indigenous people and to protect children from exploitation in the production process.

▶ **To raise awareness** among consumers of the negative effects on producers of international trade so that they exercise their purchasing power positively.

▶ **To set an example** of partnership in trade through dialogue, transparency and respect.

▶ **To campaign for changes** in the rules and practice of conventional international trade.

▶ **To protect human rights** by promoting social justice, sound environmental practices and economic security.

rules, things often seem distinctly skewed in favor of rich countries. This is what organizations such as Oxfam (with their "Make Trade Fair" campaign) have been trying to publicize over the last few years.

One issue is **import tariffs**. At the moment, for a poor producer to sell their goods in the US, they often face duties that are much higher than those paid by producers in rich countries. According to Oxfam, for instance, "the average US tariff for all imports is 1.6 percent, but this

// Proper economic prices should be fixed not at the lowest possible level, but at a level sufficient to provide producers with proper nutritional and other standards. **//**

John Maynard Keynes, 1944

rises to 14-15 percent for LDCs (least developed countries) such as Bangladesh, Nepal and Cambodia. As a result, in 2004, the US Treasury collected roughly the same amount in tariff revenue on imports from Bangladesh ($329 million) as on imports from France ($354 million), even though France exports 15 times as much to the USA." Such practices are estimated by trade justice campaigners to cost poor nations around twice as much as they receive in aid: $100 billion annually. And, in the agricultural sector, the tariffs are usually higher on "processed" goods (canned fruit, say, rather than fresh fruit), which locks poor producers into selling raw commodities while the West benefits from lucrative processing, where most of the profit is made.

A second problem is **Western farm subsidies**. In the US, the issue revolves primarily around our massive domestic cotton subsidies, adding up to $4 billion a year. Paying our own farmers to grow so much cotton, activists argue, leads to overproduction and **"dumping"** of the surplus on the world market, at a price point that developing countries can't meet. Oxfam estimates that dumping has caused losses of almost $400 million for the ten million cotton farmers of West and Central Africa between 2001 and 2003 alone. Such practices aren't limited to the US: the EU spends around half its total budget—tens of billions of pounds—subsidizing its own farmers to produce and export agricultural goods, likewise making it very difficult for poor countries to compete. Take sugar: though few people realize it, British farmers are subsidized to grow sugar in Yorkshire and East Anglia, while poor African and Caribbean farmers are desperate to sell the UK their crops. After numerous wranglings at the World Trade Organization, Western farm subsidies are now due to be phased out, but at the time of writing no timetable for this has been agreed upon.

One aim of fair trade, then, is to help producers in the developing world overcome these kinds of barriers.

The Fair Trade Certified label

Though the concept of fair trade has been around much longer than the formal **labeling and certification system**—which first emerged in Holland in the 1980s, in response to plummeting international coffee prices—this "official" system now dominates the fair trade world.

So how does it work? Basically, any product bearing the "Fair Trade Certified™" label has been traded according to a set of **internationally agreed standards** (more on these below) and the supply chain has been **audited** to make sure that the rules are being stuck to. It's important to note that Fair Trade is **not a brand or a company**, but a certification system, with different labels (or "marks," as they're sometimes also called) administered by various organizations in several areas of the world, though the concept of what they stand for is consistent.

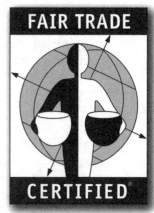

The Fair Trade Certified label, administered in the US by TransFair USA.

Unlike many comparable programs, the Fair Trade system isn't primarily funded by the producers. Other than a small percentage, the cost of administration and certification is passed on to the licensee of the logo—the specific coffee brand, for instance—which ultimately passes it on to the consumer or absorbs it in reduced profits. This system allows the economically marginalized to get involved without much up-front capital.

Fair trade, both as an understood concept and a concrete label, was considerably slower to get off the ground in the US than it was in Europe. It wasn't until 1999 that Transfair USA certified its first product (coffee), while the first product bearing the UK's Fairtrade Mark appeared in 1994. And it might be some time before the Fair Trade label becomes part of mainstream American culture, as it is in Britain, where two in five adults know it on sight. Still, US awareness is growing rapidly. According to the National Coffee Association, consumption of Fair Trade coffee—easily the most popular fair trade product—doubled between 2003 and 2005. Too, although Fair Trade coffee now accounts for only 2% of the overall $22 billion domestic retail coffee market, it's seen a tenfold increase in just the last five years, with the percentage expected to triple by 2010. While the fair trade concept is not quite a household term in the US yet, it should be emphasized that its recognition is hardly limited to the counterculture. No less a figure than former president Jimmy Carter endorsed it in a 2005 letter to the Fair Trade Futures Conference, declaring his Carter Center human rights organization as proud supporters of "the growing fair trade movement, which uplifts the basic principles of human rights and human dignity and takes positive, concrete steps towards poverty reduction."

At the other end of the chain, more than a million producers and their dependents, in more than 60 countries, are benefiting from the system, and though food and drink is still the focus (exclusively so in the US), there is an ever-growing range of products available. There were even fair trade Resolutions passed by the cities of New York and San Francisco in 2005, and "**Fairtrade towns**" are proudly being declared all over the UK.

The standards

Unlike with organic foods, say, where the "rules" are very general, each new product certified under the Fair Trade system gets its own specific criteria, since each raises a different mix of problems and priorities. But there are certain core ideas that apply to all products. Fair Trade traders must:

▶ Pay a price to producers that covers the costs of **sustainable production and living**

▶ Pay a "premium" that producers can invest in **development**

▶ Make partial **advance payments** when requested by producers

▶ Sign **contracts** that allow for long-term planning and sustainable production practices

Behind these core ideas there are two underlying sets of standards. One covers crops such as coffee and cocoa, mostly grown by **small-scale independent producers**, and is primarily concerned with ensuring that farmers in "democratic and participative" cooperatives receive a decent and stable minimum price for their crops, rather than being left to ruthless middlemen and the fluctuating prices of the world commodity markets. The other set of standards is for crops such as tea, which are largely produced on estates; it focuses mainly on issues such as the **pay and conditions** of the workers, the right to form unions, health and safety, child labor, and so on.

As well as these minimum trading requirements, Fair Trade bodies also have a set of so-called **progress requirements**, which are implemented if and when a producer receives enough Fair Trade revenues. Through this system, producers are encouraged to invest continuously in improving environmental sustainability, social provision, working conditions and business efficiency.

Who's in charge?

After having grown independently in different countries, the Fair Trade system became internationally unified in the late 1990s, with the establishment of the **Fairtrade Labelling Organizations International** (FLO). This body is now ultimately responsible for defining the standards and for certifying that accredited products really are produced in accordance with them. To do this, it works "with a network of independent inspectors that regularly visit all producer organizations," and implements a trade auditing system which "checks that every Fairtrade-labeled product

Fair trade resolutions

While the United States might still be a long way from implementing fair trade as federal policy, some towns and cities have acted as boosters for the movement by passing **fair trade resolutions** at their local level. It needs be said that a resolution is not the same thing as a law, or enforceable policy. It's more a symbolic gesture, intended to bolster awareness of fair trade and encourage such practices at a municipal level. Still, it's a significant step into public visibility, considering that a decade or so ago, hardly anyone in the country knew what fair trade was bar a few progressive activists.

The most prominent fair-trade resolutions by far were those passed in 2005 by San Francisco and New York City. The New York City Council's resolution encouraged city agencies and food service venues to purchase Fair Trade Certified Coffee, and recognized the efforts of local organizations doing their part for the fair-trade cause. Bolder was the resolution passed by the City and County of San Francisco the same year, aimed toward maximizing purchase of all Fair Trade Certified products, not just coffee. It also gave the city's Department of the Environment a specific task of looking into how this could be done, the goal being for the Bay Area Fair Trade Coalition to work with municipal officials to see those recommendations through to completion. The same year, the city's Board of Supervisors passed a resolution making May 8th **Fair Trade Day** in San Francisco—though cynics who view the ultra-liberal Bay Area as something of a sovereign city-state might contend that it's the only large city in the nation where such a resolution could have stood a chance. For info on how such resolutions are crafted and passed, download Global Exchange's *Fair Trade Zone Packet* (www.globalexchange.org/campaigns/ftzone/FTZonePacket. pdf) or Oxfam America's *Just Add Justice* (www. oxfamamerica.org).

It hasn't caught on here, but more than 100 cites in the UK have become Fairtrade towns. If you're interested in seeing how this was done, or even in getting ideas for how it might be done on this side of the ocean, download the *Fairtrade Town Goals and Action Guide* from: www.fairtrade.org.uk

FAIR TRADE DAY
BAY AREA WORLD MARKET

sold to a consumer has indeed been produced by a certified producer organisation."

Based in Bonn (Germany is very much at the heart of ethical consumerism), the FLO comprises a membership of so-called National Initiatives—eighteen at the time of writing—which implement the FLO system on the country level. The US's body is the Oakland, California-based **TransFair USA**, a nonprofit organization that began operations in the late 1990s.

For more info on the organizations, standards and so on, see:

FLO International www.fairtrade.net
TransFair USA www.transfairusa.org

Beyond food

Though "unofficial" fair trade covers a wide range of goods, you'll currently find the official Fair Trade label only on foods (see p.143 to get an idea of the range of products available), though a few other products such as cotton goods and, bizarrely enough, **soccer balls** and **roses** are available abroad. The reason for the focus on food and drinks is partly historical—as already mentioned, the labeling system was set up as a response to the coffee crisis—but it's also practical. While it's relatively easy to define a set of clear criteria for a specific crop, the same isn't true of many other goods. The supply chain for an item of clothing, for example, is highly convoluted, taking in cotton or wool farmers, synthetic fabric and thread factories, weavers, dyers, various levels of subcontracted cutters and garment-workers, and a whole host of people distributing between these groups.

Despite all this (and despite the US still having some catching up to do on even matching the range of Fair Trade foods already certified elsewhere), we can expect to see the Fair Trade label on many more non-food goods in the not-too-distant future. Handicrafts, precious metals and stones are all possibilities. Considering the problems that exist in the rubber industry, the head of the Fairtrade Foundation told Rough Guides, at some stage we might even see **Fair Trade condoms**.

Beyond the third world?

Despite the fact that the Fair Trade label is appearing on an ever-wider selection of goods, one parameter likely to remain is the focus on products from the developing world. The organizers recognize that some small-scale producers and farmers in **rich countries** suffer many of the same problems as those in the third world, but they have decided—after consultation with Fair Trade consumers—that the system should focus on "absolute poverty" rather than the "relative poverty" found in countries in the West. This was the reason why the idea—floated back in 2003—to market Fair Trade **organic food** grown in the UK never took off, though the newly formed Organic Farmers & Gardeners Union (OFGU) organization wants to unite Fair Trade and organic practices (see p.85).

Fair trade without the label

Unlike those bearing the Fair Trade Certified label, these goods are not necessarily certified or traded according to any single set of standards. So anyone can theoretically slap "fairly traded" on their products without adhering to any specific international code. As such, it sometimes all seems to be entirely based on trust. In the promotional literature of such companies, it's not uncommon to read variations on phrases such as "we carefully examine the standards of our suppliers to make sure they are in line with fair trade criteria," or more euphemistically, "the clothing was made by workers in (fill-in-the-blank developing nation) who are paid fair wages, and manufactured with sensitivity to environmentally sustainable practices."

Not only is such wording sometimes used by sellers of items (such as clothes) that are not yet sold with official Fair Trade Certified labels—it's sometimes used by companies that don't even belong to the Fair Trade Federation, the organization of online/mail-order/retail shops specializing in fair-trade items. Such assurances, though admirable in their intentions, don't wholeheartedly inspire confidence in the integrity of unlabeled fair trade. Indeed, they seem oddly similar to the ethical assertions of most transnational companies such as Nike—which, though never calling itself a fair trade company, claims to ensure all its workers receive a "fair wage." So can we trust a self-declared "fairly traded" item to be what it says it is?

The Fair Trade Federation

If you're uneasy about fair trade claims on non-TransFair USA-certified products (particularly non-food items, which aren't yet covered by that program), you might consider patronizing businesses that are members of the **Fair Trade Federation**. This association of companies (including producers and wholesalers) that sell via retail, mail-order and online sites are required to adhere to the FTF's criteria for membership (see p. 316), paying annual dues on a sliding scale based on their gross earnings. While the stringency isn't comparable to the standards that TransFair USA applies to the products it certifies, membership at least supplies some evidence that the organizations' committment to fair trade is sincere (for a list of FTF shops, see pp. 315–322).

In any case, some of the importing and selling is done by trusted groups who are not only FTF members, but have been around for longer than the Fair Trade Certified label and were, in fact, central to its establishment. Perhaps the best-known example is **Global Exchange**, founded in 1988 as a human rights organization, which now sells both Fair Trade Certified

Better left to the market?

Few people argue against the aims of fair trade, but some free-marketeers have made a case against one aspect of the system. They claim that, by offering a minimum-price guarantee to, say, coffee and cocoa farmers, fair traders are interfering with the market, and this, they claim, may do more harm than good. So is this true?

As touched on in chapter one, the idea that fair trade is anti-market is on one level quite odd: no one is forcing the consumers, traders or suppliers to play by these rules; no one is manipulating fair-trade supply and demand. Indeed, in many ways you could see this as less of a distorted free market than the equivalent non-fair-trade goods: there is almost no fair-trade **advertising**, and the direct links with producers aim to cut out middlemen who can genuinely distort the operation of a fair market by exploiting a monopoly over delivery equipment—or even the straightforward use of force. What the people who make this case are promoting, then, is not exactly a free market, but a specific (and rather "unfree") version of it in which low price is the only consideration consumers are allowed to consider important.

That said, the argument does raise a legitimate question: if people buy a "fairly trad-ed" product, might this not reduce the demand for the non-fair-trade alternative, depressing prices and forcing uncertified producers to plumb even lower depths of bad working conditions to stay afloat?

In a market where supply and demand are pretty much balanced, this argument simply doesn't stand up: if half the shoppers start purchasing fairly traded mangos, and half the producers start producing them, then the remaining half of the market still has the same balance of supply and demand as before, and hence the price they receive shouldn't be affected. However, things are different for products where sup-ply *does* exceed demand, such as the market for coffee. As discussed on p.137, the most serious problem currently faced by coffee farmers is low price caused by mas-sive **oversupply**. Ultimately, if there is oversupply, the free-marketeers argue, there must be too many producers. So, unless consumers start altruistically doubling their caffeine intake, the problem will only really be resolved when some coffee farmers stop producing and start diversifying into other crops. Fair trade, they claim, can only get in the way of this essential market mechanism by propping up the inefficient producers.

goods and non-food fair trade items through its website and retail stores. As an additional boost to its credibility, another member of the FTF is **Equal Exchange**, founded in 1986, which is the oldest and largest non-profit Fair Trade company in the US.

Groups producing, importing, and selling unlabeled fair-trade goods may also be members of other respected fair-trade organizations, the most important being **IFAT**: the **International Federation for Alternative Trade**.

As usual, the issues are not quite as simple as the free-market fundamentalists make out. True, it's essential that more coffee farmers diversify into other crops to reduce oversupply. But which farmers are best equipped to do this? According to the Harriet Lamb of the Fairtrade Foundation (which administers the Fairtrade label or "mark" in the UK), diversification is often easier for those currently supplying Fair Trade coffee than for those who aren't: after all, they are likely to have access to more **capital, advice and support**. Furthermore, for as long as farmers are getting paid very low amounts for their products, the only response open to them will be to try and produce even more than before—hence fanning the flames of oversupply—until their reserves of money and energy are exhausted, at which point diversification may be less likely than starvation. And, indeed, many thousands of farmers and their children have died as a result of being left to the free market.

There are ways, of course, to support marginalized farmers and encourage diversification without "interfering with the market"—namely through financial and other types of **support from governments** and individuals. But all these things require people to be aware of the issues, and there can be little doubt that the fair trade movement has done a pretty amazing job at getting Western consumers thinking about something as far removed from their lives as the plight of equatorial coffee farmers.

But even if this were not the case, there would be a more fundamental question: if some farmers are going to have to go out of business, which of them should we do our best to save from this unfortunate fate? Or, put another way, which trade model do we want to survive? The first one (non-fair-trade) offers the potential for the lowest price and cheapest production, but might mean poor wages and substandard health and safety for farmers and farm workers; child labor and even slave labor (such as the 1000 enslaved coffee farmers set free in Brazil in 2003); environmental and therefore also economic sustainability sacrificed to short-term crop maximization; and large companies winning over smaller players as their deep pockets allow them to support their operations through the economic winter. The other option is a system in which the market is allowed to play out but within a set of minimum standards: small farmers paid a minimum price upfront, allowing them to invest without relying on debt; importers audited to ensure no bullying or malpractice is going on; transparency and redistribution ensured; and the environment cared for. Fair Trade provides consumers with a free-market-style choice between these two options.

To join IFAT, producer groups have to undertake an extensive self-assessment program according to the core IFAT principles and be open to random spot-checks to ensure they are sticking to their plan. Importers have to undergo a similar process and must have fair trade as their primary focus. Membership in IFAT, however, is far more widespread among other countries than in the US, where less than a dozen organizations are members, one of them being Equal Exchange.

If you do wonder about the legitimacy of a "fairly traded" product that doesn't bear the Fair Trade Certified label, try asking the retailer whether the store, catalog or site is a member of FTF. If they can give you an informed response (or if you see them using the trademarked Fair Trade Federation logo of two encircled hands, which members have a right to use), then there's no need to worry. After all, fair-trade "scams" are pretty well unheard of—there are easier ways to make a fast buck than trying to con ethical consumers. For more on FTF or IFAT, see:

FTF www.fairtradefederation.com
IFAT www.ifat.org

#3: Boycotts
Bashing the bad guys

The idea of punitively refusing to do business with a particular person, company or country is nothing new. The term dates from the late nineteenth century (**Charles C. Boycott** was a land agent in Ireland who, after ignoring calls for lower rents, found himself shunned by mailmen, servants, shopkeepers and others) and boycott organizers since then have included the likes of **Mahatma Gandhi,** whose *swadeshi* campaign encouraged the rejection of British goods in favor of local self-sufficiency. However, the idea of shoppers taking part in national or worldwide boycotts in response to problems which don't affect them directly is a more recent phenomenon. It first really took off in the 1970s and 1980s with calls for consumers to avoid companies doing business in apartheid **South Africa,** and **Nestlé** for its irresponsible promotion of baby milk products in the third world.

Today, boycotts are perhaps the most widely understood approach to ethical consumerism, aimed not just at companies and countries but also at types of products, such as shrimp, mahogany and GE food (all discussed later in this book). Though it's impossible to accurately measure, the value of goods and services boycotted on ethical grounds can add up to huge sums—according to EarthRights International, for instance, a boycott of Wells Fargo launched by the AFL-CIO in 1998 has cost the bank almost $1.5 billion in closed accounts.

Do boycotts work?

People would probably still want to boycott companies, governments and products they find morally reprehensible even if they doubted they could make much of a difference. But, in theory at least, a boycott can be a powerful force for change if enough people get involved: the moment a company thinks that improving its behavior is more profitable than not doing so, it will opt for reform. After all, directors have a legal duty to their shareholders to take the path of maximum profits, even if it means swallowing their pride. And, in an era of "brand value," companies are so eager to avoid negative publicity that they might capitulate even if a boycott isn't currently making much difference to their bottom line.

In practice, of course, it's actually very difficult to tell how effective boycotts are. For one thing, rather like the invariably wildly contrasting attendance numbers given by police and organizers after a political demonstration, the targets and practitioners of consumer boycotts tend to have very different views on their impact. A case in point is the **StopEsso** campaign (see p.283), directed at the overseas Esso branch of ExxonMobil. The organizers' website claims that one million people in the UK don't buy Esso petrol on ethical grounds, but, as *The Observer* reported, the oil giant disagrees: "The Stop Esso campaign ... has not affected our fuel sales." The company does seem to have gradually shifted its position on global warming since the boycott kicked in, though they deny this has had anything to do with the boycott.

Likewise with **Nestlé**, who for more than a quarter of a century have suffered a high-profile international boycott on the grounds of their alleged advertising of formula milk in the developing world (see p.148 for more details on this particular case). While the campaigners claim that the company has still not cleaned up its act, they acknowledge that

things have improved. But the extent to which this has anything to do with the boycott is debated. Nestlé claims that any changes in its behavior are due entirely to it proactively responding to new regulation and health research. But then they also told Rough Guides that the boycott has had no effect on their sales, which—since it's clear some people do avoid Nestlé goods—cannot be true. Their evidence was simply that sales have kept rising rather than falling: not the same point at all. That said, if Nestlé thought the boycott was costing them as much in lost sales as their developing-world formula milk brings in (and that's reported to be less than 1% of their total turnover) you might think they'd stop selling formula milk in poor countries, which they haven't done.

The campaigners, for their part, claim that the boycott has hit sales, with some product lines down by 3% in the UK after the Church of England started advocating avoiding Nestlé, forcing the company to up their advertising budget to counteract negative press. Furthermore, the negative publicity has hurt the company in other ways, making it hard for them to get stand space at graduate recruitment fairs, for instance.

Of course, boycotts are usually only one part of a wider campaign, so even when a company does capitulate, it's very difficult to work out how much of this is down to consumers withholding their custom and how much is down to the inconvenience and embarrassment of having hardcore **activists** invading and picketing their stores, offices or gas stations. Activists and ethical shoppers may be two sides of the same coin, but we shouldn't credit consumers for all the hard work of committed campaigners.

However, consumers' boycotts, and the public debate they help generate, can be very effective. One case often given as an example is the international boycott of Shell in 1995 against the proposed dumping of the **Brent Spar** oil platform into the North Sea. Many people now think that the environmental arguments against the dumping were factually flawed—and hence describe the result as a mixed success—but the boycott certainly seemed to work. Sales were reported to drop below half in some stations and Shell eventually backed down (though here, too, pressure didn't only come from consumers: the issue became so high profile that German chancellor Helmut Kohl is said to have personally requested prime minister John Major do something about it).

Another good example is the numerous companies that stopped doing business in South Africa after consumer boycotts of their products, with about 100 publicly traded US firms with operations in the country—including such big names as Coca-Cola and General Motors—pulling out between

Greenpeace activists at Shell's Brent Spa oil platform, the subject of a high-profile consumer boycott in 1995 that forced Shell to abandon plans to sink the disused rig into the North Sea.

the late 1970s and late 1980s. Similarly, the Rainforest Action Network stopped a nine-year boycott against Mitsubishi's paper manufacturing concerns only when the company pledged to stop using old-growth timber, and implement a variety of other environmental-friendly policies. More recently, a four-year boycott of Taco Bell led by the Coalition of Immokalee Workers ended when the fast-food giant undertook several efforts to improve conditions for laborers on Florida tomato farms. The tuna fishing industry taking measures to stop killing dolphins is another success.

Furthermore, regardless of their *direct* impact, boycotts—like fair trade—can still be useful in simply raising the profile of important issues. Even if you believe the Nestlé line on the ineffectiveness of the boycott against them, it's difficult to deny that it has massively raised people's awareness of a problem linked to tens of thousands of unnecessary deaths each year (see p.148). The same goes for the Esso/Exxon boycott and what it has revealed of the short-sighted corporate response to global warm-

Who's boycotting whom?

Following are some of the high-profile boycotts under way at the time of writing—some serious, some less so. Please note that inclusion of a campaign here doesn't suggest endorsement from Rough Guides.

Drugs www.huumeboikotti.org
We might rail about oil firms and trainers companies, but, according to this Finnish campaign, the illicit drugs industry is probably the least ethical of all. Cocaine, especially, has led to countless deaths in Columbia, but all drug production and distribution is "firmly in the hands of organized crime [and] goes hand in hand with corruption and money-laundering."

George W Bush donors www.boycottbush.net
You'd be amazed who bankrolls the US's simplest-ever president. See the box on pp.68–69 for a list of companies.

Nestlé www.babymilkaction.org
International Baby Food Action Network promotes the ongoing boycott of Nestlé's armada of products for allegedly irresponsible marketing of breast-milk substitutes in the developing world. For more on this issue and a list of brands, see pp.144 and 148.

ExxonMobil www.exposeexxon.com
A major campaign to encourage consumers to avoid the oil company that "has acted consistently to move our country backward on energy policy by opposing efforts to stop global warming, lobbying to drill in America's most pristine wilderness areas, and failing to promote renewable energy and fuel efficiency." For more on the Exxon boycott, see p.283.

Companies doing business in Burma www.burmacampaign.org.uk
Appeals to consumers to boycott all the companies who still do business in Burma, despite calls from the pro-democracy groups within the country for them to pull out (for more on the situation in Burma see p.307). Although geared toward UK consumers, it includes numerous American and foreign companies doing business in the US. A more comprehensive list, including many foreign companies you've probably never heard of, can be found at: www.global-unions.org/burma

Companies doing business in Israel www.bigcampaign.org
More controversial than most consumer campaigns are the calls—now relatively widespread—for consumers to boycott goods produced in Israel. Some of the pressure from Europe has subsided since Israel bowed to EU requests to stop labeling items which have been grown or manufactured in the Occupied Territories as "produce of," or "made in," Israel. But the bigger issues are still driving on many consumer campaigns, such as this website and product list maintained by the Palestine

Solidarity Campaign, which targets "Israel's refusal to abide by UN Resolutions, International Humanitarian law and the Fourth Geneva Convention."The controversy is heightened by the Israeli claim that if people stop importing Israeli produce, then their goods will be consumed domestically, which will ultimately hurt the Palestinian producers who rely primarily on export to the Israeli market.

Companies doing business in China

www.boycottmadeinchina.org
A collection of "loose-knit groups and individuals" are behind this campaign to boycott Chinese goods. The campaign is a response to the full range of human rights abuse by the Chinese government and its refusal to recognize independent trade unions, but it focuses primarily on the occupation of Tibet. Note that not all human-rights activists think that a China boycott is a good idea, for the reasons discussed on pp.66.

Companies doing business in the US

Calls to boycott the US—in response to everything from the invasion of Iraq to the financing of the Turkish military—are nothing new. But George W. Bush's tearing up of international initiatives on climate change and the International Criminal Court has provoked more bad feeling than ever. There are many groups suggesting US boycotts, though as Boycott the USA (www.stopusa.org) acknowledges, "to boycott all US products when living in the US is not possible or practical."

There are scores of other boycotts under way, from **tropical timber** (see p.261) and **tiger shrimp** (see p.126) to **Janet Jackson**, for duetting with Beenie Man, a ragga deejay whose lyrics, some maintain, advocate the murder of homosexuals. Also on lists are **Gillette**, for using "spy chips" to stop shoplifters making off with their Mach 3 razorblades (see www.boycottgillette. com); **Canada**, for the mass slaughter of seals (see www.boycott-canada.com); **Gap**, for its owners' felling of old-growth forest in the US (see www.gapsucks.org); **Bacardi**, for allegedly attempting to have Fidel Castro overthrown while continuing to use Cuban imagery to promote its products (www.ratb.org.uk); and **Adidas**, for using kangaroo skin in its football boots (www.viva.org.uk).

To stay up to speed with boycott news, check the Boycott News section of *The Co-Op America Quarterly* (back issues downloadable online from www.coopamerica.org), and look at the AFL-CIO's boycott list on www.unionlabel.org. And while the **Ethical Consumer Boycotts List** (www.ethicalconsumer.org/boycotts/boycotts.htm) primarily focuses on issues affecting consumers in the UK, it also lists many multinational companies that are based in and/or do business in the US.

ing. And while boycotts of high-profile clothes and footwear brands have been contentious—since non-name-brand clothes are arguably at least as bad (see p.53)—the consumer debate has pushed the issue of third-world workers' rights into the public eye like never before.

Regardless of how much or little impact consumer boycotts have at the moment, one thing we can certainly say is that they are less effective than they should be. That's because most boycotters don't take the time to tell the company that they are actually boycotting them, which in many cases renders their action ineffectual (more on this in the next section).

What about the workers?

When it comes to developing-world factories, some commentators—including many of the most vocal trade unions and campaigning groups—take the line that boycotting companies may be counterproductive. If workers are being treated badly, we should demand better treatment for them, but if we actually boycott their employer, we'll **reduce demand** for the goods they're producing, putting their jobs at risk—hurting the very people we're trying to help.

It's certainly true that an uninformed, knee-jerk reaction from the public might have a negative effect: a big Western company pulling out of a factory or region after child labor is discovered may mean catastrophic loss of jobs in a poor area. However, a few things are worth bearing in mind here. For one thing, most boycotts relating to sweatshops and child labor are called when a Western company *pulls out* of a factory rather than staying put and cleaning up its act.

Secondly, it's unlikely that a company will change its ways unless "requests" for it to reform are backed up by a credible threat of force—in this case reduced sales. Companies follow the most profitable business model they can come up with, and unless their profits are threatened they won't change it—even if the directors actually think, deep down, that their practices are immoral. Company bosses have a **fiduciary duty** to act in the interests of their shareholders. To follow their moral instincts—or moral requests from consumers—without a financial motive would be to breach the terms of their contract.

So, even if it's possible that a boycott might harm workers now, this has to be weighed against the potential for creating long-term change. And that's not necessarily unattainable: even the commentators (such as Philippe Legrain, author of *Open World*) who write about Nike being far more ethically progressive than unbranded clothes producers admit that actual or threatened boycotts have been integral in raising Nike's standards.

Thirdly, while there's a theoretical possibility that we might be jeopardizing the jobs of the people we're trying to support, this has to be balanced against **supporting decent jobs elsewhere**. Unless boycotting a company means that you're actually going to stop buying something full stop—which usually isn't the case—then, by taking your custom somewhere else, you're probably going to be supporting the same number of jobs, only decent ones rather than bad ones. True, we each need to decide where to draw the line about what constitutes "decent" standards: boycotting any company that pays low wages by Western standards, for example, would mean boycotting all companies who produce in the developing world, which would hurt the poorest people (for more on the question of employment and exploitation of the poor world, see p.45). But boycotting sweatshops in favor of ethically sourced goods from the same countries can hardly be a bad thing overall for workers there.

//** When you threaten to boycott a company that buys stock from a shady supplier, the company's immediate reaction is to cancel orders and turn to another supplier who is not necessarily any better ... So boycotts should only be used as a last resort, but we should not rule it out entirely as an option, because we should have at least one weapon we can use to fight against those who refuse to cooperate in any way. **//

Neil Kearney, General Secretary of the International Textile, Garment and Leather Workers' Federation

As for boycotting whole countries in favor of other countries, that's a different, and rather more complex, matter (see p.61).

#4: Selective shopping
Shop by shop, brand by brand

While products from ethical specialists and labels like Fair Trade Certified are great when they're available, and while boycotts are fine for taking a stance against exploitative companies or countries, these approaches only cover a small proportion of what we buy, at opposite ends of the spectrum: the very good and the very bad. So what about the **chain stores and major brands** that account for the vast majority of our

Barcodes: the future of ethical shopping?

Books, magazines and websites are OK for getting the ethical lowdown on companies. But with single supermarkets stocking more than 50,000 items, and companies endlessly changing ownership and practices, you'd need a great deal of time to check every item you might want to buy. The future of conscientious shopping, then, will surely include some means by which we can get information about any product at any time.

Enter the Corporate Fallout Detector (CFD). Created by American "interaction designer" James Patten, the CFD combines a barcode scanner with the ECRA Corporate Critic database (see p.326), and another database of US polluters. When a product is swiped, the device makes a geigercounter-style clicking in proportion to the nastiness of the company in question. Just "swipe and gripe."

OK, it's early days. The CFD is a big, cumbersome box with limited information inside it—as Mr. Patten is well aware. But the idea is a good one. There's no reason why, in a few years, we shouldn't have barcode scanners in our mobile phones, say, which would be able to provide all sorts of product info, including the ethical standards of the company in question. They might even be able to send an email to each company that has been scanned but not passed the test, to let them know that they've "just been boycotted."

Obviously, any system of ranking companies automatically is rife with problems of methodology and standards. But there's no reason why we couldn't each set out our own ethical criteria. For more info (and videos) on the CFD, go to: www.jamespatten.com/cfd.

The devil's in the barcode: James Patten armed with his Corporate Fallout Detector, ready to "swipe and gripe" in the supermarket aisle purchasing, the companies which don't feature on boycott lists yet, but are not exactly known for being all that sound. Should we bother—where possible, or perhaps just when convenient—making ethical discriminations between familiar names such as, say, Safeway and Albertsons, or Philips and Samsung?

Considering that companies like these account for most of what we buy, it would be odd not to include them in our ethical-shopping efforts. Getting them to improve standards, even in a small way, would arguably have a bigger effect than anything else we might achieve. Either way, it's nearly impossible to avoid big companies, so we might as well give our money to the most responsible ones, even if very few of them are really all that conscientious. And it's getting easier to find information comparing the ethical "performance" of companies. Many examples are explored in this book, and more comprehensive information can be gleaned from both online and paper sources (see p.325). Co-op America's Retailer Scorecard, for example, makes it clear that shopping at Target is a more socially responsible choice than going to Wal-Mart, even if neither of those "big box" stores are very ethical operations per se.

But does this kind of picking and choosing between company A and company B actually make any difference? As always, it's hard to measure the exact effect. But one thing that seems clear is that it won't make much difference unless you tell the stores or brands what you're doing: if you don't, there's absolutely no reason to believe they'll even realize you're shunning them.

Words speak louder than actions

In free-market theory, **supply and demand** naturally work their way toward a happy equilibrium: if people don't want something, it will stop being produced; if people want more of something, more will be supplied. This is, of course, just as true of ethical shopping: the more demand there is for socially responsible companies, the more socially responsible companies there will be.

But economists (some of them at least) understand that such elegant market mechanisms don't work when buyers and sellers don't have access to the same information: so-called **information asymmetry** stops supply and demand from functioning properly. And so it is with ethical shoppers: *you* might know why you're avoiding one shop and favoring another, but *they* don't. As such, it's even possible that your decision may have the opposite effect from the one you intended.

If a clothes shop, for example, notices that sales are down in a season, it will probably assume (and their assumption will probably be correct) that this is mainly because consumers were unhappy with the season's styles or prices. Unless the shop operates an unusually comprehensive market-research strategy, they will probably never realize that a small percentage of that loss might have been people going elsewhere on ethical grounds. To quote George Monbiot again: "the signal they are trying to send becomes lost in the general market noise." And if that market noise is demanding, say, lower prices, the quiet ethical shopper may be unwittingly contributing towards a price-slashing drive, in which the store leans even more heavily on its suppliers to produce more goods for less money: not good news for workers' rights.

That's the irony about selective ethical shopping: you'll probably make a bigger difference **expressing concerns** to a store's assistant manager as you hand over your credit card than you will by simply not going in. Indeed, for anyone who likes the idea of trying to favor the more progressive of the big brands but ultimately always caves in to the lowest price or best design, maybe a useful rule of thumb would be this: shop anywhere you like, but whenever you buy from a business you don't trust, make up for it by writing to them pretending you just boycotted them on ethical grounds.

Of course, you'll make the *most* difference (putting aside the option of campaigning naked outside the shop) by both voting with your wallet *and* making your views known to the businesses in question. Some within the ethical shopping movement understand this well. Co-Op America's Responsible Shopper website, for example, not only lists the names and addresses of each company it reviews—it also provides a "Quick Mail" form encouraging readers to email those companies with specific comments, supplying a few suggested "alerts" (criticisms of their ethical policies) and "positive items" (praise of progress they've made in their corporate responsibility) to include in the message. Check out the site:

Responsible Shopper www.responsibleshopper.org

#5: Buy local
Thinking small

The idea of "buying local" whenever possible is often thought of as a core tenet of ethical shopping. Proponents of this strategy accept that trade is an essential and potentially beneficial part of life, but claim that it'll be more of a force for good if trading networks are local, creating **accountability** (people are less likely to rip off or exploit their neighbors) and **collaboration** (everyone sharing the goal of furthering the well-being of the community). On an international scale, they argue, vast distances and powerful financial interests come between the parties engaged in the "real" exchange—the producers and the consumers—and wealthy countries and companies have the political and economic clout to determine the terms of trade. Hence poor-country workers end up with little for their efforts except bad pay, appalling working conditions and exported natural resources.

Furthermore, localizers point out, global trade is inherently eco-unfriendly, both directly—as it relies on the burning of a vast quantity of **transport fuel**, contributing to climate change—and indirectly, since it separates consumers from the mess their goods are making, removing any pressure on them to act responsibly. The environmental impact is compounded by the fact that world trade is inherently tied up with a corporate-driven consumerism which encourages us all to buy and use as much as possible. And, as mentioned later on, there's the question of **food security**: our long-term ability to feed ourselves. As we become ever-more reliant on transporting food from abroad, the oil that facilitates that transport gets closer to being exhausted.

For all these reasons, the argument goes, as well as numerous others, the best way forward is a new era of "**localization**," which shoppers can help realize by favoring local goods and services wherever possible. Obviously, there will always be some national trade (it wouldn't make sense for every town to make its own buses, say) and some international trade (not every country has the minerals and metals necessary to make buses, nor the climate to grow coffee). But whenever home-

> **//** Localization ... has the potential to increase community cohesion, reduce poverty and inequality, improve livelihoods, social provision and environmental protection and provide the all-important sense of security. **//**
>
> Colin Hines, author of *Localization: A Global Manifesto*

produced is available—in agriculture, clothes production or whatever—a conscientious effort to select those goods can help strengthen the community on numerous levels.

Overall, localization might mean that we'd end up **producing and consuming less**, the argument continues, but that's not a bad thing, since, as we've already seen, the world simply cannot sustain the West's ever-rising level of consumption. Moreover, our food would be fresher; local engagement with politics and environmental problems would be stimulated; perhaps we'd even be happier. **Poor countries** would in theory also benefit: no longer reliant on cash-crop and manufacturing exports, they'd be able to grow their own food, protect their environments, shape their own development and benefit from processing and using their own natural resources.

One step forward or three steps back?

Most progressive writers and thinkers agree that a move towards localization for **fresh foods** would be a good idea on the environmental level. This may not *always* be the case—sometimes the efficiency of foreign growers may more than offset the environmental costs of transportation. But no one can deny that **air-freighting** out-of-season grapes from the southern hemisphere to a US supermarket is a heavy and unnecessary burden on the environment; or that locally farmed vegetables are a better option, in terms of minimizing climate change, than those trucked from the opposite coast. (For more on food transport, see p.87.)

(For more on food transport, see p.87.)

But when it comes to the bigger aims—favoring locally produced dried foods, clothes, shoes and other goods with an aim to winding down global trade completely—the proponents of localization are increasingly standing on their own. For a start, these kinds of goods are usually shipped, not flown, so the environmental costs, though certainly not negligible, are as much as fifty times lower per kilogram than the aforementioned fruit. But the point where most people part company with the localizer is the claim that a reduction in international trade would be good for the developing world.

// The problem with localization is that it would trap the poorest economies in their current subordinate relationship to the rest of the world, and would require a whole new coercive apparatus to impose it. It is a backward-looking and reactionary reformism. //

Paul Hampton, Workers' Liberty

Will it really help Bangladesh if we produce our clothes in Los Angeles?

❚❚ 30 years ago, South Korea was as poor as Ghana. Today, thanks to trade-led growth, it is as rich as Portugal. ❚❚

Mike Moore, ex-Director of the World Trade Organization

Clearly there are many problems with the current system of globalization, such as the gung-ho opening of financial and capital markets that the International Monetary Fund has forced on many poor countries as a condition of borrowing money. Or the patent laws which stop life-saving drugs getting to dying people in the poorest countries. But does that make global trade a bad thing? Not according to groups like **Oxfam**, which have spent the last few years campaigning hard to get *more* access to world markets for producers in poor countries (for example, by ending US cotton subsidies).

And it's not just Oxfam. Numerous anti-poverty groups and left-wing political writers have expressed concern that, without trade, poor countries can only get hard cash via **aid**—which is not only insufficient, but puts recipient countries under the thumbs of the donors and is no kind of long-term solution anyway. Without hard cash, these critics of localization claim, poor countries won't be able to invest in home production and they'll end up being locked into their current position of exporting raw commodities, such as minerals and cash crops, with all the lucrative processing and manufacturing—the creation of the actual finished product—done elsewhere.

Certainly, increased international trade can cause problems in the developing world, the argument goes, from poor labor and environmental conditions to the eroding of local cultures and, in some cases, unemployment. And, certainly, trade in itself is no immediate answer to poverty: a 2004 report by the United Nations Conference on Trade and Development (UNCTAD) pointed out that the world's least developed countries have opened their markets to external trade during the last few years but have gained very little—or even lost out. But, overall, there are more cases of countries becoming rich through embracing international trade—such as the "Tiger" economies of East Asia—than there are of those which have avoided it.

On a broader—and more controversial level—there's also the argument that global trade, for all its many current problems, is catalyzing the kind of multilateral, rules-based system of **international integration** that will be essential if the world is ever to combat global-scale issues such as climate change effectively. The **World Trade Organization** (WTO), via

II **Trade is the fuel for growth but not the engine ... we need development-led trade policies.** *II*

Michael Herrmann, UNCTAD specialist in least developed countries

which international trade rules are negotiated and disputes are settled, has rightfully been attacked for—among other things—its lack of transparency and accountability. Most deals are brokered behind closed doors, where the coercion of poor countries by rich countries seems almost inevitable; and the judges in the dispute procedures are accountable to no one.

But, for all its numerous problems, the WTO is a forum in which poor countries *can* combine forces and demand a better deal, as happened at the 2003 meeting in Cancun, which saw the emergence of the "G21" group of developing countries. In 2004, the practices of both the EU (for its sugar export subsidies) and the US (for its cotton subsidies) were even declared illegal at the WTO after objections by Brazil. These kinds of developments would have been unimaginable before the existence of the rules-based system brought about by world trade. That said, human-rights/aid/labor organizations worldwide were disappointed by the results of the WTO meeting in Hong Kong in late 2005, Oxfam International characterizing the negotiations as "a betrayal of development promises by rich countries, whose interests have prevailed yet again."

So, once again, a simple approach—buying local—turns out to be less straightforward than people sometimes suggest. Whether favoring local goods is "more ethical" depends on the individual product and transport method as well as your individual views on the impact of world trade on everything from poverty to **labor rights** (see p. 45) and **oppressive governments** (see p.61).

Should we buy from ...

Sweatshops, etc.
Made in the third world: exploitation or opportunity?

One of the most hotly debated consumer issues is whether, with the current world order being what it is, buying goods produced in poor countries is good or bad for the people in those countries—not to mention for workers at home. Though it's rarely posed in such stark terms, this is the question that people end up asking themselves after hearing reports of **sweatshop labor** in Far Eastern garment factories or the **appropriation of water and land** for the growing of cash crops in Africa. In the case of some specific countries, there's also the further question of whether we're supporting an oppressive regime (a related but separate issue, discussed on p.61) but for the rest it's mainly a matter of whether buying goods produced in poor countries amounts to the exploitation of poverty or the provision of an opportunity out of poverty.

In fact, about two-thirds of what we consume in the US is still produced at home. But as globalization rolls onwards, a growing chunk of our goods come from the developing world, where **wages** are low and **labor and environmental regulations** tend to be slack, or at least not properly enforced. Sweatshop-produced sneakers, toys and footballs have garnered most of the media attention in the area of worker exploitation and child labor, but really this issue covers everything from cut flowers to car parts, bananas to silk, tobacco to electronic equipment. A report by the New York-based National Labor Committee, for example, found serious abuses in Chinese export factories manufacturing products ranging from bicycles (15-hour shifts, 7 days a week with no overtime pay) to handbags (guards beating the workers for being late).

The question of whether or not sourcing goods from cheap factories and farms in the third world is ethical could (and does) fill many books on subjects ranging from economics to cultural imperialism. The following few pages can only serve to briefly outline the debate.

The problems

Few people would deny that labor conditions in poor countries are generally very low when judged by Western standards. Some of these issues are widely discussed, such as the hours worked and wages received in sweatshop-style export factories and farms in Asia, Latin America and Africa. Countless reports—not just investigative exposés, but studies from the Western companies using third-world suppliers—have shown that manufacturers in Asia and Latin America often demand truly incredible working weeks of 120 hours or more. In many cases, up to half of the hours worked count as unpaid overtime, and for each "official" hour worked, the pay can be as little as twenty cents—hence the shocking **wage inequality** reflected in much-quoted statistics, such as the supposed fact that it would take a Bangladeshi garment worker sewing Disney clothes more than 200 years to earn what the company's CEO get each hour. According to sweatshop campaigners, common phenomena include workers suffering injuries due to tiredness and even pregnant women miscarrying due to overwork.

To compound the problem, workers are commonly not paid on time, or have **wages deducted** for making mistakes or for being a few minutes late; 2003 figures from the Department of Labor and Employment in the Philippines, for instance, showed that nearly half the companies inspected that year had failed to pay workers properly—and those are just the official figures. And, importantly, in this era of "flexible" labor, **job security** is an increasingly rare phenomenon: millions of workers have no contract, and even those who do have one can be dismissed for being ill, late or pregnant—or simply because a factory has become financially unsustainable after a big company has placed its orders elsewhere. This may be against the law, or against a company's policy, but this doesn't seem to stop it happening.

Less discussed, but just as important, is **health and safety**. A staggering number of workers—more than two million—die every year due to work-related accidents or illnesses, according to the UN's International Labour Organization (ILO). This is an international problem, but poor countries bear the brunt of it: the rate of fatal workplace accidents in developing countries in Asia, for example, is four times higher than in the industrialized world. The same can presumably be said for the hundreds of millions more affected annually by non-fatal health problems, such as the three million farmers around the world who (according to World Health Organization estimates) suffer acute **agrochemical poisonings** each year.

Less dangerous but equally demeaning conditions include unsanitary toilets available only at certain times of day, round-the-clock surveillance, and crowded, dark dormitories. Sometimes humiliation tactics appear to be a deliberate policy: according to Oxfam Community Aid Abroad, for example, Indonesian women working in some export factories don't take their entitlement of two unpaid days of menstrual leave per month, since to qualify they have to remove their underwear in front of (female) factory doctors to prove that they are indeed menstruating. Even more seriously, **verbal and physical abuse** is widely reported, ranging from minor offenses to serious sexual assault.

Perhaps most significant of all is the fact that collective bargaining for better terms and conditions through **unions** and other groups—something recognized by the ILO as a fundamental worker right—is often impossible. In some countries only a state-controlled union is allowed (such as the All-China Federation of Trade Unions, which is so much a tool of the state that it has reportedly turned down offers of increased wages from foreign companies, to help keep China cheap and business friendly). In others, free unions are legal but rarely tolerated in reality: organizers are usually simply fired, but in many cases they're harassed, beaten, jailed or even killed. According to the International Confederation of Free Trade Unions (ICFTU), 213 trade unionists were assassinated or "disappeared" worldwide in 2002 alone.

> **//** Globalization has the potential to bring prosperity to people across the world, but today crude free market globalization is pushing standards down and leading to massive exploitation. **//**
>
> Guy Ryder, General Secretary, International Confederation of Free Trade Unions

Buy "Western" instead?

Reports of these kinds of conditions have caused a minor uproar in the West since the mid-1990s, but the question remains as to how we should respond. For many people, who feel that benefiting materially from such harsh conditions is unacceptable, the obvious conclusion is that we should where possible support "decent" jobs by favoring goods produced in, say, Europe or America, and avoiding goods imported from countries where the poor are exploited and the environment polluted.

But the idea of helping third-world workers by simply shunning their products is obviously problematic since, for one thing, these jobs are clearly in big demand. True, even some of the more ethically aware Western brands have found themselves in court for using sweatshops that exploit **indentured labor** (whereby workers are conned into signing away a large proportion of their wages in return for securing the job, putting

Child labor

With more than 350 million children aged 5–17 classed as "economically active" by the International Labor Organization, children account for a substantial proportion of the global workforce. Around half of this total is considered to be acceptable: 15- and 16-year-olds working full time in safe conditions, or younger children doing a few hours after school. But much of the rest, in the ILO's words, "is not jobs for kids … it is adults exploiting the young, naive, innocent, weak, vulnerable and insecure for personal profit."

While the issue is widely associated in the West with stitching footballs and sports shoes, in reality the problem is much more diverse, the most widely affected industries including **silk**, **carpet weaving**, **brassware** and **glassware**, **precious stone cutting**, **mining**, **leather tanneries** and **farming**. A frightening 170 million children are involved in work classified as hazardous, and of these more than a third—roughly an equivalent number to the entire population of California and Texas combined—are aged eleven and under. At the most shocking end of the spectrum, at least eight million children are stuck in what the ILO describes as the "unconditional worst forms of child labor": armed conflict, forced and bonded labor, prostitution, pornography and illegal activities.

While (nearly) everyone agrees that it's imperative to end all dangerous and degrading forms of child labor, there's no consensus on the best response to the hundreds of millions who are working in safe, or at least relatively safe, conditions. Studies by the ILO have shown that if all child workers were put through **education** instead of working, the result would be an enormous boost not only to the children's quality of life, but also to the economy of their countries. However, in most cases, no one is offering to pay for these children to be educated and, until someone does, a clampdown may simply exacerbate the problems, forcing it underground and further marginalizing and impoverishing the children involved. After all, child labor tends to be primarily a **symptom of poverty** (though interestingly it appears to be more common in households which own land), and banning it is unlikely to help reduce this poverty.

So where does all this leave the concerned shopper? One thing worth noting is that the vast majority—probably around 95%—of child laborers are not working in the formal economy creating goods for export to the West. They're working

them in a vicious cycle of debt and making it impossible to leave). But this is the exception rather than the rule—the vast majority of workers are taking these jobs by choice.

And no wonder, globalization advocates argue, since jobs in the export sector are usually the best thing going. According to right-leaning think tanks such as the Institute for International Economics, American and European firms in poor countries pay on average around twice what equivalent local firms offer. Of course, these wages still sound shockingly low to those in the West, but the alternative for a worker is either even

largely for a local or domestic market on **subsistence farms**, or producing silk, bricks, cigarettes or matches; a large number are also working in "domestic service." As such, some people say that the best way forward is to encourage more global trade—since child labor is a symptom of poverty, and world trade, they argue, is the best way to make countries richer. Others claim that it's none of our business—it's a cultural issue and we shouldn't meddle. This debate is bound to run and run.

But what about the 5% of children—still a number in the millions—who *are* producing goods for the West, making clothes, carpets, shoes and furniture, tanning leather and mining and polishing gems? Should we demand that all our goods are "child labor free"?

For **factory-produced goods**, at least, the obvious answer is yes. If global trade, as its advocates claim, is providing valuable and in-demand jobs in the poor world, then surely it would make sense for these jobs to go to poor adults rather than poor children (not least as the adults may then be able to afford to send their children to school). But in other areas, such as more **craft-based industries**, there's an argument to say that an unqualified demand for child-labor-free goods may add up to refusing to do business with the poorest people, hence worsening their position.

Partly, it all depends on who's in charge and what other opportunities—if any—will be offered to children who currently *are* working. A faceless directive from a corporate headquarters to stamp out all child labor—or to pull out from regions where child labor is widespread—may do more harm than good, with desperate children left with no option but to turn to dangerous work, crime or even prostitution. According to Oxfam, this is exactly what happened in Pakistan, where large numbers of child laborers were found to be making Western soccer balls a few years ago.

But local programs set up specifically to deal with the problem—such as the RUGMARK label for South Asian rugs (see p.272)—have shown that with appropriate monitoring and focus it's possible to reduce child labor constructively, using labeling both to inform Western consumers and fund education for ex-child laborers.

A billboard promotes a private "EPZ" in Ho Chi Minh City, Vietnam. These special no- or low-tax areas are designed to attract foreign business, and they're associated with the worst type of sweatshop abuse.

worse pay from a domestic firm, or rural work. The latter, despite Western middle-class idealization of "simple" countryside living, usually involves grinding poverty and hard labor—hence the tens of millions of **subsistence farmers** voluntarily leaving home each year to head for the cities and factories. (Furthermore, converting third-world wages into Western currency can slightly exaggerate the inequality, because in countries where, say, fifty cents per hour is a standard wage, fifty cents tends to buy a lot more than it would in the US, a fact that backpackers on six-month trips around Asia are well aware of.) And it's not just wages that are better in export jobs, pro-globalizers claim. Other problems such as health and safety risks and child labor—widely associated in Western eyes with, say, Gap clothes factories—are actually most problematic in areas where Western companies aren't involved, such as artisan mining and small-scale farming (see pp.48–49 for more on child labor).

The same people also argue that sweatshop-style jobs can be an important part of **economic development**, pointing out that in the 1960s the West's shoe sweatshops were in **Japan**, which is now almost as big an economic power as the US, and has strict labor and environmental legislation. In the 1970s and 1980s, they were in **Taiwan** and **South Korea**, which have since become specialists in microelectronics and are among the richest countries in Asia. By the same token, what we now call sweatshop conditions were standard in Europe and the US a century ago. Industrialization may not be very pretty in its early stages, but every country wealthy today, we're told, has been through this process—and only once people become wealthier will they be able to demand better environmental and labor conditions.

Things aren't quite this simple, of course. For a start, it would be naive to think that everyone is pleased to work under such harsh conditions. **Strikes** are not uncommon in export factories (at least in areas where unions aren't suppressed) and there is no shortage of outspoken workers complaining about the labor abuses. Similarly, despite the fact that some multinationals might pay *relatively* high wages, many have successfully lobbied governments for exemption from having to match the minimum wage. They also frequently choose to use factories based in the notorious **export processing zones**, or **EPZs**, where labor law is even slacker than elsewhere.

In the words of the ICFTU, EPZs "have become a symbol of crude free market globalization, where workers are made to take amphetamines to get them to work harder and faster, where violence and abuse are a daily reality for thousands upon thousands of workers, and where attempts to form unions and bargain collectively for a fair deal are often met with reprisals, sackings [firings] and even death threats."

Furthermore, while Taiwan and South Korea may have become richer through sweatshop-style manufacturing, they did so at a time when there was less global trade, and hence much less **competition between poor nations**. Today, poor countries struggling to make money through sweatshops have to deal with the fact that other poor countries can try and undercut them on price (and labor conditions), hence slowing development down. Today, it's a "race to the bottom," campaigners claim, with real-terms minimum wages in some areas of China (the leader of the "race") having fallen in the last ten years. According to many campaigners, even where higher wages are *officially* paid, they are sometimes simply balanced out by forced unpaid overtime (more on this in the next chapter).

Also, you cannot isolate this discussion from a whole range of bigger issues. The poverty of many poor countries is inextricably linked to a whole host of factors: the unsustainable **debt** foisted on them decades ago by the West; colonial and post-colonial **wars**; the rich world's **farm subsidies** that erode poor-country agricultural societies; currency instability helped along by Western banks and speculators and the International Monetary Fund's strong-arm opening of poor-world financial markets. And so on.

So when ex-farmers "voluntarily" take 14-hours-per-day shifts producing lampshades for Britain, or green beans for the US, they may be doing it "out of choice," but that choice may have been shaped by an unjust global order which has made their previous life impossible. And even if export factories and farms are comparatively high for those people who choose to work in them, they may bring nothing but misery to others, such as villagers who find their water is being drained by a nearby plantation, or their air and rivers being polluted by factory effluent (third world environmental regulation and enforcement is incomparably less strict than that in the West).

Still, even with all these evident problems in mind, the case for trying to help third world workers by simply avoiding third-world goods is clearly problematic—as we've already seen (see p.42).

Demanding better standards

If shunning third-world goods is unconstructive, how about using our power as consumers to demand that companies improve conditions throughout their supply chains? Certainly this seems like a more sensible strategy, though—as ever—not everyone is convinced it's a good idea. Free-marketeers claim that, while it's laudable to desire better standards and wages for third-world workers, their "cheapness" is exactly what allows them to undercut the West and create jobs and wealth—it's their **comparative advantage**, to use the economics jargon. If Western consumers demand better labor and environmental standards, they risk limiting this advantage, thereby reducing the incentive for companies to invest in, and provide jobs in, developing countries. Hence the fact that, in international trade negotiations with the West, governments of poor countries have often objected to the idea of making trade deals conditional on the enforcement of better labor or welfare conditions—they claim the main beneficiaries of this would be workers in Europe or the US, as it would increase the cost of doing business in poor countries.

However, the argument that consumer pressure for better standards is likely to harm third-world workers isn't very convincing. For one thing, to those who believe in the free market, it ought to be clear that the improvements that could be made—such as clamping down on abusive managers and ending humiliating restrictions on when workers can visit the toilet, two problems that have been reported everywhere from Mexico to China—don't cost much economically. Indeed, they may end up saving money, since, as numerous recent studies have shown, workers treated with respect are more productive than those who aren't (no surprise there).

Another thing that costs very little—at least if the companies have got nothing to hide—is **transparency**. Hardly any big companies that make use of cheap developing-world manufacturing reveal exactly where their products are made, which means that it's difficult for anyone other than investigative journalists to get an independent view of conditions. As Labour Behind the Label told Rough Guides, "no company produces a complete map of its supply chain." Usually, the excuse is not wanting to give away valuable business secrets to competitors—it would be "a little like giving your playbook to the opposing team before a game," as the Nike website once said. But, in an interesting turn, Nike has since revealed the names and locations of more than 700 factories where their products are manufactured (see p.181). But it's hard to believe that big businesses operating in the same countries, and sometimes the same factories, cannot find out where their competitors' goods are produced.

Even those improvements which will cost money, such as better **health and safety**, and ensuring that **wages** are high enough to provide a decent standard of living, are likely to be small costs in comparison with the money saved by sourcing from poor countries in the first place. Indeed, labor costs are as much as fifty times lower in poor countries than rich countries, so, even when you factor in transport and import costs, it's likely that there is plenty of room for improvement before it becomes economically unviable for companies to source from the developing world—as many fair-trade suppliers have already shown.

Big brands, big business
No logo, pro logo & CSR

In general, the bigger, more visible and more strongly "brand-name" a company is, the more it's disliked by those who describe themselves as ethical shoppers or consumer activists. This is due to widespread distrust both of transnational companies themselves, and the logos, advertising and chain-store outlets associated with them.

Anti-corporate, anti-advertising sentiment is nothing new, of course, but it's been running at an all-time high since the 1990s, and especially since the publication of **Naomi Klein**'s bestseller—*No Logo*—which

> **//** Quite simply, every company with a powerful brand is attempting to develop a relationship with consumers that resonates so completely with their sense of self that they will aspire, or at least consent, to be serfs under these feudal brandlords. **//**
>
> Naomi Klein, *No Logo*

catapulted modern branding strategies and global supply chains firmly into the public consciousness. Klein made the case that big companies are getting bigger, and that their focus is shifting away from real-world activities such as employing staff and manufacturing products (which they increasingly "outsource" to exploitative contractors in the developing world) and towards the insidious process of branding: using logos and advertising to make people think that their products "mean" something. This has inherent problems, she argued, but it's especially ugly when you consider that the companies constantly appropriate people's icons and aspirations for their advertising and logos, which they force ever further into our public spaces—from concert halls to classrooms.

Though Klein has never really been an advocate of ethical shopping (she tends to be far more concerned with political issues such as the deals brokered at the World Trade Organization and the International Monetary Fund), her arguments have undoubtedly entered the ethical consumerism debate. The heavily branded companies she criticized—such as Starbucks, McDonald's, Nike and Gap—may not ever have been popular among ethically minded shoppers, but since *No Logo* they're at the top of most people's list of companies to avoid.

All this raises an important, though rarely asked, question: are the big brands—indeed, big companies in general—less or more ethical than the rest? How do they compare with manufacturers of **non-name-brand** goods, or less high-profile retailers?

No group better sums up the anti-brand ethos than Adbusters, a self-proclaimed "global network of artists, activists, writers, pranksters, students, educators and entrepreneurs who want to advance the new social activist movement of the information age." It's best known for the striking, witty series of spoof ads it designs, which often adorn the cover of Adbusters magazine, its print outlet for ecological, anti-corporate and anti-brand comment. But it also runs PowerShift, an "advocacy advertising agency," which helps like-minded organizations to promote their cause visually. And though commercial television networks refused to sell Adbusters airtime for its 15-second public-health broadcast about the fat content of Big Macs, you can view it online at www.adbusters.org/videos

ave as good a coffee sourcing policy as that of Starbucks (see

se, the argument continues, the big companies are a very long
perfect. As already discussed, many of them refuse to publish
of developing-world suppliers. And, inevitably, some of their
licies are overblown PR efforts—in a recent case, Nike settled
urt after exaggerating its ethical standards (see box on p.181).
y their efforts are better than nothing? Surely a code of conduct
n of factory auditors is better than the code-free, no-promises
of the faceless companies that supply bargain stores and street

economist from the Bank of England put it, while we might
global *regulation*, in the meantime we can at least have global
. And without reverting to small-scale localization (see p.41),
you might know the individuals who grew your food and sewed
irt, that reputation is most precious to the bigger, more visible
d retailers.

nd gives, the other takes away ...

us conclusion to the above case is, sure, avoid big brands and
ou think that advertising is inherently distasteful, that global
chain stores are destroying cultural diversity and homogenizing
ce, and that big firms are draining money from local economies.
try and fool yourself into thinking that the no-name alternative
ter in terms of workers' rights or environmental awareness—in
ility it's considerably worse.

r point. As ever, though, it's not quite so simple. For one thing,
cessarily true that the big, visible companies are the most ethi-
ghtened. The world's biggest chain retailer, **Wal-Mart**, is often
n example of exactly how ethical businesses *shouldn't* behave.
ow has a code of conduct, but at the time of writing it is "silent
nion rights," according to Oxfam. The right to organize is a fun-
ILO right, but one which Wal-Mart famously doesn't recognize
55).

r, even if you're prepared to accept, for the sake of argument,
visible companies *are* more likely to be ethically accountable
smaller, no-name rivals, there remains a case for saying that—
—their whole way of doing business may still be contributing
labor and environmental standards. This view has been put

CSR: ethical big business?

One of the defining business buzzwords of the last decade has been CSR, or **corporate social responsibility**. There's no single definition of what this means, although the International Organization for Standardization is developing a voluntary International Standard of guidelines, to be published in 2008. But it usually involves a company "aligning its business operations with social values" by drawing up codes of conduct and "reporting," which refers to companies publishing public, self-penned documents assessing their social and environmental "performance."

This issue splits those in the ethical shopping movement down the middle. While most people agree that a company prepared to acknowledge ethical issues is better than one which is not, some see CSR as primarily "greenwash": a cheap smokescreen to satisfy ethically minded consumers, get rid of annoying protesters, and to persuade governments that there's no need for the thing that big companies really fear: laws and regulations that *force* them to behave well all the time.

It's certainly true that CSR contains a fundamental limitation, at least in the case of companies owned by shareholders—it can only include things that are likely to increase profits. Doing anything else would violate the basic obligations of company directors to their shareholders: to maximize returns. So while a company's CSR report may talk about wanting to be a "good corporate citizen," this can only go so far. If it can be shown, for example, that improving conditions for workers will raise productivity, avoid the cost of strikes or high staff turnover, or reduce the chance of a consumer boycott, then changes will probably be made—and the company will make a proud public statement about its solid commitment to its workforce. But if it looks set to harm profits, then things will stay as they are.

And can CSR claims be believed? According to many anti-poverty NGOs, the answer is often no. "Corporate practices do not match ethical policies," wrote Oxfam recently about the sportswear industry.

At almost the same time, Christian Aid examined the ethical claims of some high-profile companies such as British American Tobacco (on worker health and safety in their developing-world plantations), Coca-Cola (on their promises not to harm local communities by extracting too much groundwater) and Shell (on its social impact on communities in Nigeria and elsewhere). They concluded that in each case the claims were not reflected on the ground and that in general CSR was proving "a completely inadequate response to the sometimes devastating impact that multinational companies can have in an ever-more globalized world—and that it is actually used to mask that impact."

To try and prove that their codes of conduct are enforced, many of the more progressive companies employ **independent monitors**—professional auditors examining labor rights in Chinese supplier factories, for example. But even "independent" auditors can be contentious: while some companies employ expert, nonprofit monitors such as Verité (www.verite.org) in interviewing staff about violations, others employ companies that may sometimes have a financial interest in not uncovering all the problems (exactly the kind of conflict of interest that lay behind the Enron scandal).

CSR's defenders claim that all this criticism and skepticism is unhelpful. They claim that this ethical approach to running a big business has already yielded some very positive results, and that it is sowing the seeds of wider change in a much more effective way than enforceable regulation could ever achieve.

A protester outside the US supreme court takes a stand against what many see as our "brand new world," on the day of Nike vs. Kasky (see box on p.181). But how do the corporate giants compare to smaller, non-name-brand companies?

Branding as accountability?

Klein's critics, as exemplified by the "Pro Logo" writers at *The Economist*, say that she has it all wrong. In practice, they claim, the more heavily branded a company is, the more visible it is, and the more accountable to consumers it becomes. One foot wrong from a famous global brand and consumers can take revenge within hours. "Even mighty Coca-Cola has been humbled," they point out: "Told of a contamination incident in Belgium, its then-boss, Doug Ivester, is said to have dismissed it with the comment: 'Where the fuck is Belgium?' A few months later, after a mishandled public-relations exercise that cost Coke sales across Europe, he was fired."

Indeed, *The Economist* writers continue, branding is "an effective weapon for holding even the largest global corporations to account." And this accountability extends to ethical matters, so that when Klein and others attack heavily branded companies for, say, exploiting sweatshops, these companies fear a consumer boycott and are forced to clean up their

act. Nike has been forced to "revamp its whole st such a fear, they point out—but only because its b name and swoosh logo) makes it such an easy unbranded, no-name products, it wouldn't have consumer pressure. In fact, it probably would nev writers visiting its factories in the first place.

Commentators who take this line admit that contradictions between, say, the inclusive, one-' used in a big sportswear company's marketing ca of its factories. But surely, they argue, the impor good or bad the working conditions are, not whe a few Western adverts, which everyone knows claptrap anyway.

Few people would disagree with that last p brands and retailers *really* more conscientious than the non-name-brand equivalents? Well, it as a group—and especially those with high-prof targeted by activists—big companies have issue and introduced more **codes of conduct** than Indeed, the field of **CSR**, or **corporate social re** now thriving—there's a corporate social respor (www.csrwire.com), and as an after-effect of th government has been taking steps toward ensur match their quarterly reports and press releases

Take clothing manufacturers and retailers. Nu panies have signed up to the Fair Labor Asso aims to ensure good labor practices in their d But you won't find your local fabric store or ta involved in the social and environmental aud factories treat it as a given that conditions are w dominated, non-name-brand garment sectors, consumer pressure is non-existent and camp seen. One person who works for an auditing "it's common knowledge ... that non-name-feeders."

Even the most despised big firms may be be small-scale rivals. McDonald's uses free-range that have been injected with the controversial **growth hormone**, and doesn't use eco-unfrien aging. Can your local burger joint say the sar

forward by numerous pressure groups such as Oxfam, and holds that, once a brand or retailer has grown big enough, it can exert extraordinary leverage over its suppliers, forcing them to produce faster, more cheaply and more "flexibly" (being able to turn around big orders very quickly, for example).

Once that leverage is available, critics of corporations maintain, a company will invariably exercise it, no matter how many factory auditors it employs or CSR reports it publishes. This allows the brands and shops to pass savings on to consumers and shareholders. But the cost is shouldered by the suppliers, who—in order to meet their ambitious production targets and stay on good terms with the big buyers—have to cut corners. The result, for workers, is very often more overtime, less job security, frozen wages, less spending on health and safety in the workplace, and poor environmental standards.

While decent codes of conduct are to be welcomed, says Oxfam, they may be ignored on the ground, because the big brands' "supply-chain purchasing practices are undermining the very labor standards that they claim to support." A 2003 World Bank document seemed to agree, pointing to a frequent and unresolved "tension among price, quality and delivery time on the one hand, and CSR requirements on the other."

On a different level, there's also a fundamental limitation with thinking of corporate size and visibility as a form of accountability: most branded products are made from virtually **untraceable commodity** supply chains over which brands have no ethical control. For instance, even if a big clothes company is relatively "ethical" in its factories, its codes are unlikely to cover the farmers growing the cotton they use. Likewise, even the most ethically enlightened electronics brand can't claim to know the provenance of the bauxite or coltan used in its new laptop series. This might all seem a touch pedantic, were it not for the fact that extraction of coltan—a black, tar-like mineral used in mobile phone and computer circuit boards—has for years been funding murderous civil war in central Africa. Besides, minerals mining is overall one of the most dangerous, exploitative and ecologically damaging of all industries (faceless mining conglomerates don't feature much in the mainstream press, but they do crop up in reports on human rights and the environment).

According to many campaigners, what these "invisible" commodity sectors need is a clear and strict **international legal framework** to enforce decent standards and hold companies that behave badly to account. But big business is not often in favor of this. Indeed, the same mega-brands who claim to be ethical trailblazers are often major players

In the Democratic Republic of the Congo, a Rwanda-backed rebel group, the Congolese Union for Democracy, controls most of the country's coltan mines. Using peasants and prisoners for labor, they systematically strip the land of its mineral wealth and use the profits to gear armies of local children in a quest to maintain control over the highly valued resource.

in the corporate lobby groups which spend millions lobbying *against* any across-the-board enforceable regulations. The UN's proposed **Human Rights Norms For Business** are a good recent example: they have met fierce resistance from big-business-dominated trade groups such as the International Chamber of Commerce. Furthermore, as discussed below, in many cases big business bolsters its lobbying case by giving money to politicians. Even where they are making positive developments in their own supply chains, then, companies may be having a negative effect elsewhere.

So, once again, there are no simple answers for ethically minded shoppers. Big brands and retailers do generally have more developed ethical policies than those producing no-name goods, but their codes only go so far, and arguably their aggressive buying practices, lobbying and political donations (not to mention their invasive advertising, fat-cat pay and other corporate trappings) offset the good they do with their moral efforts. Thankfully, however, in a growing number of cases, we can get the best of both worlds by favoring ethical specialists and formal certification programs such as, for food, Fair Trade Certified or, for wooden products, the Forest Stewardship Council (see p.264). Many such firms and programs are listed throughout the rest of this book.

Oppressive regimes
To trade or not to trade?

As mentioned in chapter two, some of the first well-known boycotts of companies were primarily a means of boycotting a government—that of South Africa—in protest at the apartheid regime. People still debate the degree to which Western consumers contributed towards apartheid's eventual fall (they were just one of many political and economic pressures applied), but most agree that they did help. That success triggered a new approach to ethical shopping: avoiding products—and services, in the case of vacations—from countries with oppressive governments.

The logic is straightforward. A government always benefits from its country's exports—via corporation tax, export tariffs and the like. So when we buy goods imported from a country where the regime in power is oppressing its own people, we may be adding to the government's coffers and tightening its grip on power. Likewise if we give our custom to any multinational company that does business in the country in question.

If, on the other hand, we avoid all goods from oppressed countries (and the big businesses operating in them), we shoppers can help to isolate the governments economically, cutting off their much-needed cash supplies, weakening their grip on power and giving their people a better chance to rid themselves of their tyrants. Even Western governments seem to acknowledge the potential power of such a tactic. In a bid to stabilize corporate agendas with government policy, the US Department of Commerce's Bureau of Industry and Security maintains the Office of Antiboycott Compliance, which aims to "encourage, and in specified cases, require US firms to refuse to participate in foreign boycotts that the United States does not sanction."

But boycotting countries is always going to be a thorny issue. For one thing, it's difficult to know which countries to avoid. There is, after all, no single and uncontroversial measure of the "oppressiveness" of a country. And where should we draw the line? If we're going to boycott oppressive regimes, then shouldn't we really also be boycotting the Western countries that fund, or otherwise support, such regimes? This would certainly seem the logical conclusion, but if we're taking foreign policy into account (not to mention crimes against the global environment), then not many countries would be left on the thumbs-up list. What about the US, for instance? Considering that the current administration has, among other things, fought a war of questionable legality in Iraq and

Activists of the Tibetan Youth Congress shout anti-China slogans during a rally in New Delhi. Campaigners such as these call on Western consumers to avoid Chinese goods until China stops human rights abuses among its own people and the people of Tibet.

been hell-bent on derailing the international response to climate change, should ethically minded American consumers boycott goods from their own country?

Unintended consequences

Besides these conundrums about moral consistency, there's also the risk that boycotting oppressive regimes may actually be counterproductive. While hitting a government where it hurts is fine in principle, inevitably it also means harming the population—at least in the short term. Oppressed countries are also usually poor, and have a terribly unequal distribution of wealth, so if Western consumers refuse to buy goods from such countries, it may well hit factory and agricultural workers much harder than the government itself. If so, the effect could be a double whammy: the poor will go hungry and also find themselves *even more* reliant on the regime in question than before, leaving them less able to do anything about it.

No single boycott of a country has ever been big enough (and independent of other international pressures) for us to know whether this argument stands up. But we can perhaps get a sense of the effects of a boycott on a country's people by looking at what happens when *states* impose trade sanctions on each other. Take Iraq, which was subject to around a decade of international sanctions (imposed by the UN but driven by the US and UK) to "contain" the military capabilities of dictator Saddam Hussein. This case was unusual in that it involved an "Oil for Food" program (through which Iraqi oil could be exchanged for humanitarian goods), in theory ensuring that the poor of the country didn't feel the brunt of the sanctions. And yet by all accounts the results were still a human catastrophe. Denis Halliday, former UN humanitarian coordinator in Iraq, described the sanctions as "genocidal," pointing to "the death of some 5–6,000 children a month" through malnutrition, disease resulting from damaged water infrastructure and so on. It seems that the sanctions were bad for nearly the whole population, except perhaps Hussein, whose government seemed only to tighten its grip.

True, this is an extreme case. And it's worth remembering that a similar argument was initially used by Margaret Thatcher and Ronald Reagan to try to discourage people boycotting South Africa. But it demonstrates that the effects of economic isolation are not necessarily positive. A very different but equally useful example is Cuba, which since October 1960 has faced a trade embargo from the US. Critics of the embargo regularly and rightly point to the fact that the negative effects are felt not by the government but by the Cuban people. (Curiously, many of these critics also rail against the increase in world trade brought about by globalization.)

Trade as Trojan horse?

A more controversial argument against consumers shunning oppressive regimes and the companies doing business in them is the claim that even if international trade may help a bad government in the short term, it may ultimately be the best way to "open up" a repressed country—especially when big foreign businesses are involved. After all, global trade encourages communication, transparency, clear property laws and other factors which those on the right tend to see as likely to bring about democracy and respect for human rights.

On one level, such an argument is patently absurd; there have been countless examples of oppressive and corrupt governments feeding off international trade while their people get nothing except pollution, further oppression and increasing inequality. Just think of **Nigeria**, where infamous dictator General Abacha

// The rise of democracy in South Korea and Taiwan attests to the power of the market in generating political liberalization. Both countries have moved from closed, authoritarian regimes to open-market democracies without bloody revolutions and without the threat of economic sanctions ... will China follow? **//**

James A. Dorn, *The Cato Journal*

// We have reached the point where the most ardent defenders of Chinese communism are US capitalists. **//**

Trade unionist Mark Anderson in 1996, on the US's decision not to make China's "most favored nation" trade status conditional on human rights improvements

personally embezzled a staggering amount of public money (an estimated $4 billion) in the 1990s, almost all of it from oil sales to the West.

And yet, despite a few notable exceptions, measures of economic "openness"—such as the Index of Economic Freedom compiled by the right-wing combo of The Heritage Foundation thinktank and *The Wall Street Journal*—do tend to equate roughly with measures of political freedom. And foreign trade often encourages this kind of economic openness.

Oppressive regimes lists

There is no definitive list of oppressive regimes, but there is a huge amount of research available as to how the various countries of the world compare on **human rights** issues, political openness and other such criteria. Much of this research is carried out by non-governmental organizations such as Amnesty International, Human Rights Watch and Freedom House. Governments also sometimes release surveys of this kind of information.

A number of organizations concerned with ethical consumerism use this data to maintain their own lists of oppressive regimes, which shoppers and investors can choose to take into account if they so desire. Following are two examples of lists from respected groups: the Ethical Investment Research Service and ECRA—the research body behind Ethical Consumer magazine (see p.329).

Such lists are always **controversial**—not just inherently, but because, in practice, they're very prone to going out of date, since they're time-consuming to compile and rely on third-party, on-the-ground research. The following may have been updated by the time you read this.

Ethical Investment Research Service oppressive regimes list

Category A (the worst offenders)

▶ Afghanistan	▶ Congo (DRC)	▶ North Korea	▶ Tunisia
▶ Algeria	▶ Egypt	▶ Oman	▶ United Arab
▶ Angola	▶ Iran	▶ Pakistan	Emirates
▶ Brunei	▶ Iraq	▶ Rwanda	▶ Vietnam
▶ Burma	▶ Ivory Coast	▶ Saudi Arabia	▶ Zimbabwe
▶ Cameroon	▶ Kazakhstan	▶ Somalia	
▶ China	▶ Lebanon	▶ Sudan	
▶ Colombia	▶ Libya	▶ Syria	

Category B

▶ Azerbaijan	▶ Central African	▶ Equatorial	▶ Haiti
▶ Bahrain	Republic	Guinea	▶ India
▶ Belarus	▶ Chad	▶ Eritrea	▶ Indonesia
▶ Bhutan	▶ Cuba	▶ Ethiopia	▶ Israel
▶ Burundi	▶ Congo (People's	▶ Guinea	▶ Kenya
▶ Cambodia	Republic of)	▶ Guinea-Bissau	▶ Kyrgyzstan

CSR: ethical big business?

One of the defining business buzzwords of the last decade has been CSR, or **corporate social responsibility**. There's no single definition of what this means, although the International Organization for Standardization is developing a voluntary International Standard of guidelines, to be published in 2008. But it usually involves a company "aligning its business operations with social values" by drawing up codes of conduct and "reporting," which refers to companies publishing public, self-penned documents assessing their social and environmental "performance."

This issue splits those in the ethical shopping movement down the middle. While most people agree that a company prepared to acknowledge ethical issues is better than one which is not, some see CSR as primarily "greenwash": a cheap smokescreen to satisfy ethically minded consumers, get rid of annoying protesters, and to persuade governments that there's no need for the thing that big companies really fear: laws and regulations that *force* them to behave well all the time.

It's certainly true that CSR contains a fundamental limitation, at least in the case of companies owned by shareholders—it can only include things that are likely to increase profits. Doing anything else would violate the basic obligations of company directors to their shareholders: to maximize returns. So while a company's CSR report may talk about wanting to be a "good corporate citizen," this can only go so far. If it can be shown, for example, that improving conditions for workers will raise productivity, avoid the cost of strikes or high staff turnover, or reduce the chance of a consumer boycott, then changes will probably be made—and the company will make a proud public statement about its solid commitment to its workforce. But if it looks set to harm profits, then things will stay as they are.

And can CSR claims be believed? According to many anti-poverty NGOs, the answer is often no. "Corporate practices do not match ethical policies," wrote Oxfam recently about the sportswear industry.

At almost the same time, Christian Aid examined the ethical claims of some high-profile companies such as British American Tobacco (on worker health and safety in their developing-world plantations), Coca-Cola (on their promises not to harm local communities by extracting too much groundwater) and Shell (on its social impact on communities in Nigeria and elsewhere). They concluded that in each case the claims were not reflected on the ground and that in general CSR was proving "a completely inadequate response to the sometimes devastating impact that multinational companies can have in an ever-more globalized world—and that it is actually used to mask that impact."

To try and prove that their codes of conduct are enforced, many of the more progressive companies employ **independent monitors**—professional auditors examining labor rights in Chinese supplier factories, for example. But even "independent" auditors can be contentious: while some companies employ expert, nonprofit monitors such as Verité (www.verite.org) in interviewing staff about violations, others employ companies that may sometimes have a financial interest in not uncovering all the problems (exactly the kind of conflict of interest that lay behind the Enron scandal).

CSR's defenders claim that all this criticism and skepticism is unhelpful. They claim that this ethical approach to running a big business has already yielded some very positive results, and that it is sowing the seeds of wider change in a much more effective way than enforceable regulation could ever achieve.

A protester outside the US supreme court takes a stand against what many see as our "brand new world," on the day of Nike vs. Kasky (see box on p.181). But how do the corporate giants compare to smaller, non-name-brand companies?

Branding as accountability?

Klein's critics, as exemplified by the "Pro Logo" writers at *The Economist*, say that she has it all wrong. In practice, they claim, the more heavily branded a company is, the more visible it is, and the more accountable to consumers it becomes. One foot wrong from a famous global brand and consumers can take revenge within hours. "Even mighty Coca-Cola has been humbled," they point out: "Told of a contamination incident in Belgium, its then-boss, Doug Ivester, is said to have dismissed it with the comment: 'Where the fuck is Belgium?' A few months later, after a mishandled public-relations exercise that cost Coke sales across Europe, he was fired."

Indeed, *The Economist* writers continue, branding is "an effective weapon for holding even the largest global corporations to account." And this accountability extends to ethical matters, so that when Klein and others attack heavily branded companies for, say, exploiting sweatshops, these companies fear a consumer boycott and are forced to clean up their act. Nike has been forced to "revamp its whole supply chain" due to just such a fear, they point out—but only because its branding (the ubiquitous name and swoosh logo) makes it such an easy target. Had it produced unbranded, no-name products, it wouldn't have been so vulnerable to consumer pressure. In fact, it probably would never have had investigative writers visiting its factories in the first place.

Commentators who take this line admit that there are clearly jarring contradictions between, say, the inclusive, one-world imagery cynically used in a big sportswear company's marketing campaigns, and the reality of its factories. But surely, they argue, the important issue is simply how good or bad the working conditions are, not whether they're at odds with a few Western adverts, which everyone knows are a load of marketing claptrap anyway.

Few people would disagree with that last point. But are big, visible brands and retailers *really* more conscientious and good for the world than the non-name-brand equivalents? Well, it's undoubtedly true that as a group—and especially those with high-profile brands that have been targeted by activists—big companies have issued more ethical statements and introduced more **codes of conduct** than less visible companies. Indeed, the field of **CSR**, or **corporate social responsibility** (see p.55), is now thriving—there's a corporate social responsibility newswire service (www.csrwire.com), and as an after-effect of the Enron scandal, the US government has been taking steps toward ensuring that corporate actions match their quarterly reports and press releases.

Take clothing manufacturers and retailers. Numerous big garment companies have signed up to the Fair Labor Association (see p.182), which aims to ensure good labor practices in their developing-world suppliers. But you won't find your local fabric store or tailor on the list, and many involved in the social and environmental auditing of developing-world factories treat it as a given that conditions are worse in the small-business-dominated, non-name-brand garment sectors, where margins are tighter, consumer pressure is non-existent and campaigners are nowhere to be seen. One person who works for an auditing body told Rough Guides, "it's common knowledge ... that non-name-brands tend to be bottom feeders."

Even the most despised big firms may be better in many ways that their small-scale rivals. McDonald's uses free-range eggs, shuns milk from cows that have been injected with the controversial protein known as **bovine growth hormone**, and doesn't use eco-unfriendly polystyrene in its packaging. Can your local burger joint say the same? And can your local café claim to have as good a coffee sourcing policy as that of Starbucks (see p.140)?

Of course, the argument continues, the big companies are a very long way from perfect. As already discussed, many of them refuse to publish their list of developing-world suppliers. And, inevitably, some of their ethical policies are overblown PR efforts—in a recent case, Nike settled out of court after exaggerating its ethical standards (see box on p.181). Still, surely their efforts are better than nothing? Surely a code of conduct and a team of factory auditors is better than the code-free, no-promises approach of the faceless companies that supply bargain stores and street markets?

As one economist from the Bank of England put it, while we might push for global *regulation*, in the meantime we can at least have global *reputation*. And without reverting to small-scale localization (see p.41), in which you might know the individuals who grew your food and sewed your T-shirt, that reputation is most precious to the bigger, more visible brands and retailers.

One hand gives, the other takes away ...

The obvious conclusion to the above case is, sure, avoid big brands and shops if you think that advertising is inherently distasteful, that global logos and chain stores are destroying cultural diversity and homogenizing public space, and that big firms are draining money from local economies. But don't try and fool yourself into thinking that the no-name alternative is any better in terms of workers' rights or environmental awareness—in all probability it's considerably worse.

It's a fair point. As ever, though, it's not quite so simple. For one thing, it's not necessarily true that the big, visible companies are the most ethically enlightened. The world's biggest chain retailer, **Wal-Mart**, is often given as an example of exactly how ethical businesses *shouldn't* behave. True, it now has a code of conduct, but at the time of writing it is "silent on trade union rights," according to Oxfam. The right to organize is a fundamental ILO right, but one which Wal-Mart famously doesn't recognize (see pp. 155).

However, even if you're prepared to accept, for the sake of argument, that big, visible companies *are* more likely to be ethically accountable than their smaller, no-name rivals, there remains a case for saying that—very often—their whole way of doing business may still be contributing to lower labor and environmental standards. This view has been put forward by numerous pressure groups such as Oxfam, and holds that, once a brand or retailer has grown big enough, it can exert extraordinary leverage over its suppliers, forcing them to produce faster, more cheaply and more "flexibly" (being able to turn around big orders very quickly, for example).

Once that leverage is available, critics of corporations maintain, a company will invariably exercise it, no matter how many factory auditors it employs or CSR reports it publishes. This allows the brands and shops to pass savings on to consumers and shareholders. But the cost is shouldered by the suppliers, who—in order to meet their ambitious production targets and stay on good terms with the big buyers—have to cut corners. The result, for workers, is very often more overtime, less job security, frozen wages, less spending on health and safety in the workplace, and poor environmental standards.

While decent codes of conduct are to be welcomed, says Oxfam, they may be ignored on the ground, because the big brands' "supply-chain purchasing practices are undermining the very labor standards that they claim to support." A 2003 World Bank document seemed to agree, pointing to a frequent and unresolved "tension among price, quality and delivery time on the one hand, and CSR requirements on the other."

On a different level, there's also a fundamental limitation with thinking of corporate size and visibility as a form of accountability: most branded products are made from virtually **untraceable commodity** supply chains over which brands have no ethical control. For instance, even if a big clothes company is relatively "ethical" in its factories, its codes are unlikely to cover the farmers growing the cotton they use. Likewise, even the most ethically enlightened electronics brand can't claim to know the provenance of the bauxite or coltan used in its new laptop series. This might all seem a touch pedantic, were it not for the fact that extraction of coltan—a black, tar-like mineral used in mobile phone and computer circuit boards—has for years been funding murderous civil war in central Africa. Besides, minerals mining is overall one of the most dangerous, exploitative and ecologically damaging of all industries (faceless mining conglomerates don't feature much in the mainstream press, but they do crop up in reports on human rights and the environment).

According to many campaigners, what these "invisible" commodity sectors need is a clear and strict **international legal framework** to enforce decent standards and hold companies that behave badly to account. But big business is not often in favor of this. Indeed, the same mega-brands who claim to be ethical trailblazers are often major players

In the Democratic Republic of the Congo, a Rwanda-backed rebel group, the Congolese Union for Democracy, controls most of the country's coltan mines. Using peasants and prisoners for labor, they systematically strip the land of its mineral wealth and use the profits to gear armies of local children in a quest to maintain control over the highly valued resource.

in the corporate lobby groups which spend millions lobbying *against* any across-the-board enforceable regulations. The UN's proposed **Human Rights Norms For Business** are a good recent example: they have met fierce resistance from big-business-dominated trade groups such as the International Chamber of Commerce. Furthermore, as discussed below, in many cases big business bolsters its lobbying case by giving money to politicians. Even where they are making positive developments in their own supply chains, then, companies may be having a negative effect elsewhere.

So, once again, there are no simple answers for ethically minded shoppers. Big brands and retailers do generally have more developed ethical policies than those producing no-name goods, but their codes only go so far, and arguably their aggressive buying practices, lobbying and political donations (not to mention their invasive advertising, fat-cat pay and other corporate trappings) offset the good they do with their moral efforts. Thankfully, however, in a growing number of cases, we can get the best of both worlds by favoring ethical specialists and formal certification programs such as, for food, Fair Trade Certified or, for wooden products, the Forest Stewardship Council (see p.264). Many such firms and programs are listed throughout the rest of this book.

Oppressive regimes
To trade or not to trade?

As mentioned in chapter two, some of the first well-known boycotts of companies were primarily a means of boycotting a government—that of South Africa—in protest at the apartheid regime. People still debate the degree to which Western consumers contributed towards apartheid's eventual fall (they were just one of many political and economic pressures applied), but most agree that they did help. That success triggered a new approach to ethical shopping: avoiding products—and services, in the case of vacations—from countries with oppressive governments.

The logic is straightforward. A government always benefits from its country's exports—via corporation tax, export tariffs and the like. So when we buy goods imported from a country where the regime in power is oppressing its own people, we may be adding to the government's coffers and tightening its grip on power. Likewise if we give our custom to any multinational company that does business in the country in question.

If, on the other hand, we avoid all goods from oppressed countries (and the big businesses operating in them), we shoppers can help to isolate the governments economically, cutting off their much-needed cash supplies, weakening their grip on power and giving their people a better chance to rid themselves of their tyrants. Even Western governments seem to acknowledge the potential power of such a tactic. In a bid to stabilize corporate agendas with government policy, the US Department of Commerce's Bureau of Industry and Security maintains the Office of Antiboycott Compliance, which aims to "encourage, and in specified cases, require US firms to refuse to participate in foreign boycotts that the United States does not sanction."

But boycotting countries is always going to be a thorny issue. For one thing, it's difficult to know which countries to avoid. There is, after all, no single and uncontroversial measure of the "oppressiveness" of a country. And where should we draw the line? If we're going to boycott oppressive regimes, then shouldn't we really also be boycotting the Western countries that fund, or otherwise support, such regimes? This would certainly seem the logical conclusion, but if we're taking foreign policy into account (not to mention crimes against the global environment), then not many countries would be left on the thumbs-up list. What about the US, for instance? Considering that the current administration has, among other things, fought a war of questionable legality in Iraq and

Activists of the Tibetan Youth Congress shout anti-China slogans during a rally in New Delhi. Campaigners such as these call on Western consumers to avoid Chinese goods until China stops human rights abuses among its own people and the people of Tibet.

been hell-bent on derailing the international response to climate change, should ethically minded American consumers boycott goods from their own country?

Unintended consequences

Besides these conundrums about moral consistency, there's also the risk that boycotting oppressive regimes may actually be counterproductive. While hitting a government where it hurts is fine in principle, inevitably it also means harming the population—at least in the short term. Oppressed countries are also usually poor, and have a terribly unequal distribution of wealth, so if Western consumers refuse to buy goods from such countries, it may well hit factory and agricultural workers much harder than the government itself. If so, the effect could be a double whammy: the poor will go hungry and also find themselves *even more* reliant on the regime in question than before, leaving them less able to do anything about it.

No single boycott of a country has ever been big enough (and independent of other international pressures) for us to know whether this argument stands up. But we can perhaps get a sense of the effects of a boycott on a country's people by looking at what happens when *states* impose trade sanctions on each other. Take Iraq, which was subject to around a decade of international sanctions (imposed by the UN but driven by the US and UK) to "contain" the military capabilities of dictator Saddam Hussein. This case was unusual in that it involved an "Oil for Food" program (through which Iraqi oil could be exchanged for humanitarian goods), in theory ensuring that the poor of the country didn't feel the brunt of the sanctions. And yet by all accounts the results were still a human catastrophe. Denis Halliday, former UN humanitarian coordinator in Iraq, described the sanctions as "genocidal," pointing to "the death of some 5–6,000 children a month" through malnutrition, disease resulting from damaged water infrastructure and so on. It seems that the sanctions were bad for nearly the whole population, except perhaps Hussein, whose government seemed only to tighten its grip.

True, this is an extreme case. And it's worth remembering that a similar argument was initially used by Margaret Thatcher and Ronald Reagan to try to discourage people boycotting South Africa. But it demonstrates that the effects of economic isolation are not necessarily positive. A very different but equally useful example is Cuba, which since October 1960 has faced a trade embargo from the US. Critics of the embargo regularly and rightly point to the fact that the negative effects are felt not by the government but by the Cuban people. (Curiously, many of these critics also rail against the increase in world trade brought about by globalization.)

Trade as Trojan horse?

A more controversial argument against consumers shunning oppressive regimes and the companies doing business in them is the claim that even if international trade may help a bad government in the short term, it may ultimately be the best way to "open up" a repressed country—especially when big foreign businesses are involved. After all, global trade encourages communication, transparency, clear property laws and other factors which those on the right tend to see as likely to bring about democracy and respect for human rights.

On one level, such an argument is patently absurd; there have been countless examples of oppressive and corrupt governments feeding off international trade while their people get nothing except pollution, further oppression and increasing inequality. Just think of **Nigeria**, where infamous dictator General Abacha

// The rise of democracy in South Korea and Taiwan attests to the power of the market in generating political liberalization. Both countries have moved from closed, authoritarian regimes to open-market democracies without bloody revolutions and without the threat of economic sanctions ... will China follow? **//**

James A. Dorn, *The Cato Journal*

// We have reached the point where the most ardent defenders of Chinese communism are US capitalists. **//**

Trade unionist Mark Anderson in 1996, on the US's decision not to make China's "most favored nation" trade status conditional on human rights improvements

personally embezzled a staggering amount of public money (an estimated $4 billion) in the 1990s, almost all of it from oil sales to the West.

And yet, despite a few notable exceptions, measures of economic "openness"—such as the Index of Economic Freedom compiled by the rightwing combo of The Heritage Foundation thinktank and *The Wall Street Journal*—do tend to equate roughly with measures of political freedom. And foreign trade often encourages this kind of economic openness.

Oppressive regimes lists

There is no definitive list of oppressive regimes, but there is a huge amount of research available as to how the various countries of the world compare on **human rights** issues, political openness and other such criteria. Much of this research is carried out by non-governmental organizations such as Amnesty International, Human Rights Watch and Freedom House. Governments also sometimes release surveys of this kind of information.

A number of organizations concerned with ethical consumerism use this data to maintain their own lists of oppressive regimes, which shoppers and investors can choose to take into account if they so desire. Following are two examples of lists from respected groups: the Ethical Investment Research Service and ECRA—the research body behind Ethical Consumer magazine (see p.329).

Such lists are always **controversial**—not just inherently, but because, in practice, they're very prone to going out of date, since they're time-consuming to compile and rely on third-party, on-the-ground research. The following may have been updated by the time you read this.

Ethical Investment Research Service oppressive regimes list

Category A (the worst offenders)

▶ Afghanistan	▶ Congo (DRC)	▶ North Korea	▶ Tunisia
▶ Algeria	▶ Egypt	▶ Oman	▶ United Arab
▶ Angola	▶ Iran	▶ Pakistan	Emirates
▶ Brunei	▶ Iraq	▶ Rwanda	▶ Vietnam
▶ Burma	▶ Ivory Coast	▶ Saudi Arabia	▶ Zimbabwe
▶ Cameroon	▶ Kazakhstan	▶ Somalia	
▶ China	▶ Lebanon	▶ Sudan	
▶ Colombia	▶ Libya	▶ Syria	

Category B

▶ Azerbaijan	▶ Central African	▶ Equatorial	▶ Haiti
▶ Bahrain	Republic	Guinea	▶ India
▶ Belarus	▶ Chad	▶ Eritrea	▶ Indonesia
▶ Bhutan	▶ Cuba	▶ Ethiopia	▶ Israel
▶ Burundi	▶ Congo (People's	▶ Guinea	▶ Kenya
▶ Cambodia	Republic of)	▶ Guinea-Bissau	▶ Kyrgyzstan

This is a wide and heated debate. Take **China**, for example, which is swiftly becoming the "factory of the world", and which features high up on every list of oppressive states thanks to its appalling record on torture, deaths in custody, prisoners of conscience, unfair trials, detention without charge or trial, and executions, among other things. Some human rights campaigners claim that increased foreign trade is gradually helping to make China's government more open, less oppressive and more vulnerable

▶ Maldives	▶ Russia	▶ Tajikistan	▶ Uzbekistan
▶ Mauritania	▶ Serbia and	▶ Tanzania	▶ Venezuela
▶ Morocco	Montenegro	▶ Togo	▶ Yemen
▶ Nepal	▶ Sierra Leone	▶ Turkey	
▶ Nigeria	▶ Sri Lanka	▶ Turkmenistan	
▶ Qatar	▶ Swaziland	▶ Uganda	

ECRA Oppressive Regimes Category

ECRA make no distinction between bad and *really* bad. For the most up-to-date version see: www.ethicalconsumer.org/magazine/buyers/categories.htm

▶ Afghanistan	Guinea	▶ Lebanon	▶ Sudan
▶ Algeria	▶ Eritrea	▶ Liberia	▶ Swaziland
▶ Belarus	▶ Ethiopia	▶ Libya	▶ Tanzania
▶ Brazil	▶ Fiji	▶ Malaysia	▶ Thailand
▶ Burma	▶ Guatemala	▶ Mexico	▶ Togo
▶ Burundi	▶ Indonesia	▶ Nigeria	▶ Tunisia
▶ Central African	▶ Iran	▶ Pakistan	▶ Turkey
Republic	▶ Iraq	▶ Qatar	▶ United Arab
▶ Chad	▶ Israel	▶ Russian	Emirates
▶ China	▶ Jordan	Federation	▶ Uzbekistan
▶ Congo (DRC)	▶ Kazakhstan	▶ Rwanda	▶ Vietnam
▶ Cote d'Ivoire	▶ Kenya	▶ Saudi Arabia	▶ Zimbabwe
▶ Egypt	▶ Kuwait	▶ Senegal	
▶ Equatorial	▶ Laos	▶ Somalia	

If you'd rather go straight to the source and get information about specific countries, try:

Amnesty International Library www.amnesty.org/library
Human Rights Watch www.hrw.org
Freedom House www.freedomhouse.org

Or read the out-of-date but nonetheless informative *Observer Human Rights Index 1999*, available online at www.guardian.co.uk

to pressure from the rest of the world (for example through the World Trade Organization, which China recently joined). But the regime's human rights standards are still extremely bad, and many critics, not least those in the Free Tibet movement, are calling for the international community—consumers included—to use a trade boycott as a way of putting pressure on the Chinese government to make much more radical improvements.

So what can you do?

There's no golden rule that says whether trade will be a blessing or a curse for the people living under an oppressive government. It depends on the specific regime, and the specific circumstances, such as the products being exported (natural resources, for example, seem to spell much more trouble than manufacturing). And it depends on the speed with which an economy opens up to international trade: a recent study by Israeli academics suggested that the faster the transition, the greater the amount of corruption it creates.

If a boycott is called for from within the country itself, by opposition groups which represent the majority of the population, then there can be little question that it's the right thing to do. This was the case in South Africa, and at the time of writing is the case with **Myanmar** (Burma). There, pro-democracy leaders won free elections by a landslide nearly 15 years ago, but have been prevented from taking office by a brutal military regime. They are calling on the world's companies, shoppers and travelers to boycott the country (see p.307).

But in most other cases the picture is less clear, and citizens of the countries in question are sometimes shocked and offended to find their homeland—including all the companies their friends and families work for—on an international boycott list. Ask people from Venezuela, China and elsewhere whether they support Western consumers boycotting all big companies that operate in their country, and you're unlikely to get a very positive response.

So, once again it's a matter of making your own decisions, and once again it's true that making your views known politically is arguably far more important than simply buying or not buying. If you do decide that shunning certain countries is the way to go, the box on pp.64–65 shows the governments that certain organizations define as being oppressive; pp.34–35 list a few current high-profile country boycotts.

Political donors
Voting with your wallet—literally

Though we might get upset about what certain politicians are up to, most of us continue to fund those same politicians via the companies we support (as well as the unions we're members of, but that's outside the scope of this book). This issue affects many countries, but it's perhaps most pressing in the US, where campaign contributions are huge and where the politicians influenced by these donations have more influence on the world than anyone else. So, for example, we might lament George W. Bush's stance on climate change and the International Criminal Court, to pick just two of many possible objections, but we continue to buy from the huge list of companies which support him and his party (see box on pp.68–69).

Financial contributors don't determine the outcome of every decision made in Washington, of course, and a causal link between contributions and policy decisions is extremely difficult to prove. However, as with advertising, we can be sure that companies only spend money on political donations when they expect something in return. And research by organizations like the Center for Responsive Politics certainly suggests that there is a very real link between contributions and voting patterns. Anyhow, altruism doesn't seem like a very likely motive, nor does ideology, considering that many companies—such as Microsoft and AOL—are associated with donating heavily to any candidate with a chance of being elected.

Some people claim that political donations from companies are not a bad thing—the necessary counterbalance to equivalent donations from trade unions. But even if you agree with that, it doesn't change the fact that as consumers we have a choice: we can either buy goods from companies giving money to politicians we dislike, or we can shop elsewhere. The only problem is that it can be hard to pin down exactly who's giving what to whom, not least because the political funding may not come from the company itself, but from individual directors or from **PACs**—political action committees. Luckily, however, there are a number of websites that will help you navigate the murky world of political giving:

Center for Responsive Politics (US donations) www.opensecrets.org
PoliticalMoneyLine (US donations) www.tray.com
Party Watch (UK donations) www.new-politics.com/partywatch

Who elected George W. Bush? You did!

Maintained by *Ethical Consumer* magazine and drawing on research from OpenSecrets.org, the Boycott Bush website encourages consumers to shun companies who have donated the most to George W. Bush's election campaigns. The project was launched on Bush's rejection of the Kyoto treaty, but also objects to his "illegal invasion of Iraq and other regressive steps such as opposing weapons proliferation treaties." Following is their list of the top-25 corporate donors to the Republican Party at the time of writing, along with the amount of money they donated between 1999-2004 and their most prominent brands:

▶ **Altria ($6.9 million):** Marlboro, Virginia Slims, Chesterfield, Kool-Aid, Tang, General Foods, Maxwell House, Sanka, Cool Whip, Jell-O, Cream of Wheat, Golden Crisp, Grape-Nuts, Honeycomb, Raisin Bran, Shredded Wheat, Waffle Crisp, Barnum's Animals, Kraft Cheese Nips, Chips Ahoy!, Newton's, Oreo, Triscuit, Wheat Thins, Planter's Nuts, Milk-Bone, Altoids, Life Savers, Cheez Whiz, Cracker Barrel, Breakstone's sour cream and cottage cheese, Knudsen sour cream and cottage cheese, Shake 'N Bake, Louis Rich, Oscar Mayer, Boca, Claussen

▶ **Microsoft ($6.2 million):** Windows operating system, Xbox 360

▶ **United Parcel Services ($5.8 million)**

▶ **AT&T ($5.4 million)**

▶ **MBNA ($5.3 million)**

▶ **Citigroup ($5.0 million):** Citibank, 80% of the Student Loans Corporation

▶ **Pfizer ($4.7 million):** Benadryl, BENGAY, Cortizone, Emetrol, Listerine, Listermint, Luden's, Progaine, Rogaine, Rolaids

▶ **FedEx ($4.4 million)**

▶ **Wal-Mart ($3.6 million)**

▶ **Bristol-Myers ($3.6 million):** Exedrin, Boost, ChoiceDM, Enfamil

▶ **GlaxoSmithKline ($3.5 million):** Abeva, Alluna, Aquafresh, Citrocel, Contac, Ecotrin, Gaviscon, Nicorette, Os-Cal, Tagament, Tums

▶ **ExxonMobil ($3.1 million)**

▶ **Anheuser Busch ($2.9 million):** Budweiser, Michelob, ZiegenBock, Busch, Hurricane Malt Liquor, Busch Gardens (theme park), SeaWorld (theme park)

▶ **Time Warner ($2.5 million):** AOL, Netscape Navigator, HBO, Cinemax, Warner Bros., CNN, Cartoon Network, Hanna-Barbera, Castle Rock Entertainment, Little, Brown & Co., Warner Books, Time, DC Comics, IPC magazines

▶ **ChevonTexaco ($2.5 million)**

▶ **PepsiCo ($2.1 million):** Pepsi, Mountain Dew, Sierra Mist, Lipton Iced Tea, Quaker, Sugar Puffs

▶ **Schering Plough ($1.9 million):** A+D, Afrin, Claritin, Coricidin HPB, Correctol, Drixoral, GyneLotrimin, Dr. Scholl's, Coppertone

▶ **Wyeth ($1.9 million):** Advil, Alavert, Anbesol, Caltratre, Centrum, Chap Stick, Dimetapp, FiberCon, Freelax, Preparation H, Primatene, Robitussin

▶ **Ford ($1.9 million):** Lincoln, Mercury, Mazda, Volvo, Jaguar, Land Rover, Aston Martin, Hertz

▶ **Alticor Inc. ($1.8 million):** Quixtar, Body Series, Artistry, Satinique, Glister

▶ **Archer Daniels Midland ($1.8 million):** Novasoy, NutriSoy, Soy7, Natural Source

▶ **AMR Corp ($1.8 million):** American Airlines

▶ **General Motors ($1.46 million):** Buick, Cadillac, Chevrolet, GMC, Holden, Hummer, Isuzu, Oldsmobile, Opel, Pontiac, Saab, Saturn, Subaru, Suzuki, Vauxhall

▶ **BP plc ($1.44 million):** Amoco, ARCO

▶ **Disney ($1.4 million)**

Note that, technically speaking, it's not necessarily the companies that make the donations: due to US political contribution laws, it's very often organizations "affiliated" with the company, or their employees who funnel the cash. But the effect is the same. Also note that some of the businesses listed above (such as AOL) have given more money to the Democrats than to the Republicans—not that trying to buy influence with all the candidates is much better. Finally, be aware that this list looks at the period from 1999–2004, and at least one company listed—BP—has since promised to stop all political donations.

For the most up-to-date list, methodology and background on the campaign (and, on the Boycott Bush site, some suggested alternative brands to patronize), go straight to the sources:

Boycott Bush www.boycottbush.net
Open Secrets www.opensecrets.org

Beyond donations: lobby groups and think tanks

Even when companies aren't donating directly to politicians, they may be having an even greater—and even less transparent—impact on government policy and media content through their contributions to corporate lobby groups and think tanks. We've already seen how even the most mainstream business groups—such as the US Chamber of Commerce—have taken a firm stance against the Kyoto Treaty and the UN's Human Rights Norms for Businesses. A number of similar examples crop up elsewhere in this book.

However, more sinister than these giant groups are the small but highly influential think tanks—many of them funded largely or entirely by corporations—which exist solely to push for big-business-friendly agendas on everything from animal testing to nuclear power. It's beyond the scope of this book to look into this area—not least because accurate information about which companies are giving to which think tanks is very difficult to come by. But if you fancy exploring the issue, check out SourceWatch. You'll never look at big companies (or right-wing politicians) in the same way again.

SourceWatch www.sourcewatch.org

Part II

Products & companies

- Food & drink
- Clothes, cosmetics & jewelry
- Finance
- Household
- Transport & travel
- General fair trade shops

Food & drink

No consumer area is so politically charged as food, which is at the center of debates ranging from farmer exploitation, animal welfare and unfair international trade rules, to public health, biotechnology and environmental degradation. Some of these issues are discussed in general terms in the first section of this book, but this chapter looks in more depth at the wider implications of the food and drink we buy. It covers some general topics—intensive farming, organics, food miles, GE (genetic engineering), and the environmental burden of meat production—before focusing on specific foods and drinks (from p.109) and the pros and cons of different places to shop (see p.152).

"Cheap" food vs. organics
Is organic food and drink more ethical?

Agriculture has undergone a remarkable transition in the last sixty years. In the aftermath of World War II, the drive to produce as much as possible as quickly as possible saw massive government **subsidies** awarded to the biggest, most industrialized farms. Small producers that relied heavily on manpower and produced a range of crops and animal products were gradually eclipsed by larger businesses that focused on just one or two crops or meats and relied primarily on **technology, economies of scale** and large quantities of **agrochemicals** (such as fertilizers and pesticides).

One impact of this process of industrialization has been a massive decrease in the number of farm workers. Roughly four million farm jobs have been lost in the last 40 years. Small farms have been especially

The wonders of soil

Soil may not seem like the most interesting thing in the world, but earth is pretty amazing stuff, and it's at the center of debates about organic and industrial farming. Despite its dull appearance, soil is absolutely packed full of life. The UN's Global Biodiversity Assessment suggested that a single gram of soil "could contain 10,000 million individual cells comprising 4,000–5,000 bacterial types, of which less than 10% have been isolated and are known to science," and that's before you consider snails, earthworms, termites, mites and other invertebrates. But soil not only contains life, it also gives it: without fertile earth, there'd be no plants, no animals and no humans.

The world is covered by an extremely thin and delicate skin of this fertile dirt, just a few feet deep. Yet humans have been rather cavalier in their treatment of it: battering it with intensive, chemical-heavy agriculture, urbanization, and deforestation. According to a report by the UK's Royal Commission on Environmental Pollution, around 10% of the world's total soil has been lost through human-induced causes. Even more amazingly, in just the last 40 years, nearly a third of the world's arable crop land has been abandoned due to soil erosion. Considering that it takes around 500 years to form just a few centimeters of soil suitable for agricultural conditions, we're clearly losing our life-giving earth far more quickly that it can be replaced, in the process endangering the future world's ability to feed itself.

It was precisely these worries that led to the establishment of the organic movement; hence the fact that its longest-standing organization (founded in the UK) is known as the Soil Association.

Source: All facts cited in "Human Nature: Agricultural Biodiversity and Farm-based Food Security," a 1997 study commissioned by the United Nations Food & Agriculture Organization.

hard hit, with nearly 40,000 closures between 1995 and 2002 alone. A prominent factor in this slide has been the increased "efficiency" allowed by technology and chemicals, though the amount of food we import has a played its part as well. Depending on who you ask, this **reduction of the farm workforce** is either a disaster (as family traditions have been destroyed and thousands of workers have lost their jobs) or a good thing (since fewer people are subjected to back-breaking work in rainy fields).

Another impact of subsidized industrial agriculture has been **a fall in the price of the food in our shops**. The average US household is now estimated to spend only about one-tenth of its total budget on food. This compares with around one-fifth just fifty years ago, and that's despite the fact that we're eating posher, more "exotic" ingredients than ever before. Of course, much of this drop in how much of our money we spend on food is from increasing wages and the fact that prices are kept artificially low by our tax-funded subsidies. But even taking these factors into account, food has become significantly less expensive as farming has become more industrialized.

Most people would agree that cheaper food is a good thing (despite the worsening problem of obesity in the US). However, according to a growing number of commentators, we're not getting something for nothing. The hidden costs of industrial farming—to **human health**, the **environment** and long-term **food security**—are big, and getting bigger.

In the words of the staff writers at *Nature* (a peer-reviewed science journal, not a bastion of eco-warriors), "Mainstream agronomists now acknowledge ... that intensive farming reduces biodiversity, encourages irreversible soil erosion and generates run-off that is awash with harmful chemicals—including nitrates from fertilizers that can devastate aquatic ecosystems." In other words, soil and food experts are worried that intensive agriculture is wasting irreplaceable soil, reducing the number of animals, birds, insects and plants in farming areas, and killing fish and plants in nearby streams and rivers. And that's before you consider the impact on **animal welfare**, and the massive wastefulness that accompanies intensive animal farming (more on this later).

Some saw these problems coming right from the beginning. As agricultural industrialization took off, a small bunch of philosophically minded farmers, worried primarily about the potentially damaging effect on soil, planted the seeds of the **organic movement**, which, after decades on the fringe, has seen an amazing boom recently, with annual sales expected to reach $30.7 billion by 2007 in the US alone.

Organic questions and answers

What *is* organic food?

It wasn't until 1990 that the Organic Foods Production Act spurred the creation of the National Organic Program, a sub-department of the United States Department of Agriculture (USDA). It took another twelve years for the USDA Organic label to take effect on products on the shelves. While many organic activists feel there's still much work to be done in defining (and often tightening) regulations, any product labelled as organic—wherever it was produced—must have been grown or raised according to a set of minimum National Organic Program (NOP) standards, and certified by a USDA-accredited agent.

As most people are aware, at the core of the organic movement is a policy that shuns synthetic **fertilizers, pesticides, herbicides, fungicides** and other man-made inputs. Instead of these, organic farmers rely on a mixture of special growing techniques and natural alternatives. In place of chemical fertilizers, for example, soil fertility is maintained by using **animal manure** and through **crop rotation**.

Crop rotation is a farming technique in which the same field is used for growing different crops in successive months or years, to "fix" nitrogen (using plants that can take nitrogen from the air and put it into the soil) and ensure that the nutrients some crops take from the earth are put back by others. It can also reduce the need for pesticides and herbicides, though other techniques are usually also necessary. These range from manual weeding to the introduction of predatory insects to a crop (to eat the pests) or the use of "natural" pesticides such as the *Bt*, derived from a type of beetle.

Organic rules also ban artificial **sweeteners, colors, preservatives, flavorings** and **genetically modified ingredients**, and the process for producing hydrogenated fats generally doesn't meet the standard. But this doesn't tell us the whole story. The organic "idea" is more a whole agricultural philosophy, taking in **animal welfare** and **social justice** as well as environmental and health concerns (see box on pp. 78–79).

In the case of prepared foods, to bear an organic label they must contain at least **95% organic ingredients**. The rest, where applicable, may be non-organic, but only from a list of approved ingredients, all of which must be proven to be unavailable in an organic form before they can be used.

Who enforces the rules?

In order for a product to be labeled "organic," a USDA certifier annually inspects the farm where the food is grown to confirm that the farmer is following all the rules necessary for meeting the organization's standards. The same goes for companies that handle or process organic food before it's sold in supermarkets or restaurants. In the US, there are currently 56 domestic certifying agents and 43 foreign ones, though the scope of what they certify can differ. As a reflection of the geographic imbalance of organic farming's popularity in the US, there are eleven in California alone, where the tremendous variety of crops that can be grown helped produce far more organic farms than are found in the midwest, the bastion of vast, single-crop fields. However, the rest of the country is catching up, with 37 of the 50 states (as well as the District of Columbia) having at least one certifying agent. A list of the agents can be found at www.ams.usda.gov/nop/CertifyingAgents/Accredited.html.

If a product bears the USDA Organic seal and/or the certifying agent's seal it's at least 95% organic. Fruit, vegetables, packages of meat, cartons of dairy products, and other single-ingredient foods will have a small sticker version of the seal; it can also appear on a sign above an organic produce display.

Certification becomes more complicated for packaged foods with more than one ingredient. The USDA labels still signify 95-100% organic content, and if it's 100%, that can be noted on the package. Products with 70-95% organic ingredients can't use the USDA label, but can note some of them on the front of the packaging as long as they also adhere to the strict restrictions on non-organic content (including no GE). Items failing to reach the 70% mark can only list organic ingredients on the side panel. The name and address of the certifier appears on all packaged products with at least 70% organic ingredients.

While the mere existence of a USDA organic standard is seen as a significant victory in numerous eco-conscious quarters, others feel it doesn't raise the bar high enough, and that current gains are continually subject

The organic charter

Though the exact details of organic rules vary around the world, the general principles remain the same. These principles are far more holistic than most consumers realize, covering animal welfare and even social justice, as well as the use of chemicals. The International Federation of Organic Movements (www.ifoam.org) defines four fundamental tenets:

▶ Health: **Organic agriculture should sustain and enhance the health of soil, plant, animal, human and planet as one and indivisible**. While the health of humans consuming organic food (not to mention the potential financial savings if one considers organics preventive health care agents) is a forefront concern of the organic movement, the benefits to the ecosystems and organisms, down to (in the IFOAM's own words) "the smallest in the soil," are also considered vitally important. In grittier terms, this mission statement specifically urges avoiding the use of fertilizers, pesticides, animal drugs and food additives that may be harmful to the health of all life, not just human life. Besides eliminating synthetic agrochemicals, this involves minimizing water waste and pollution; using reusable and recycled substances wherever possible; taking care of the soil; and encouraging biodiversity. Wherever possible, closed-system, self-sufficient farming is favored, so manure from cows, for example, will be used as fertilizer for crops grown on the same farm. This limits pollution both directly and by reducing the need for polluting and energy-guzzling transport.

▶ Ecology: **Organic agriculture should be based on living ecological systems and cycles, work with them, emulate them, and help sustain them**. This aims to promote environmental sustainability through recycling, conserving resources, and maintaining and promoting the well-being of the soil, farm ecosystems and the aquatic environment. In a variation of the "think globally, act locally" paradigm, a sensitivity to local conditions and ecology—as well as local culture—is seen not just as a good idea, but a must.

▶ Fairness: **Organic agriculture should build on relationships that ensure fairness with regard to the common environment and life opportunities**.

to eased restrictions depending upon the political climate. Indeed, in late 2005, a pending Agricultural Appropriations Bill would have allowed for the use of various synthetic food additives and processing aids in organic foods, as well as okaying the treatment of young dairy cows with antibiotics, and permitting them to be raised on genetically engineered feed until they were converted to organic production—unacceptable modifications in the view of many champions of the organic movement.

Just because a product doesn't bear the USDA seal, incidentally, doesn't necessarily mean it *isn't* 95% or even 100% organic, as using the seal is voluntary. In turn, the absence of the seal doesn't necessarily mean a product is "less" organic than those with the sticker; it might well mean

Though less widely publicized, social considerations are taken seriously by the organic movement—at least on the theoretical level. The IFOAM guiding principles, for example, state that "those involved in organic agriculture should conduct human relationships in a manner that ensures fairness at all levels and to all parties—farmers, workers, processors, distributors, traders and consumers." What's "fair" might differ from one person (not to say one culture) to another, and an earlier version of the principles listed a more comprehensive set of standards that many involved in the organic movement would heartily second, such as prohibiting forced or non-voluntary labor; asserting employees and contractors must "have the freedom to associate, the right to organize, and the right to bargain collectively" and be provided with "equal opportunity and treatment"; and recommending any children employed by organic operators "shall be provided with educational opportunities." In addition, humane treatment of animals that "accord with their physiology, natural behavior and well-being" is insisted upon. Like "fairness" this might be subject to interpretation, but most (if not virtually all) organic farmers would agree this means ample space and good conditions; refraining from cruel practices; ruling out routine use of antibiotics and other drugs intended to push animals beyond their "natural" limits of productivity; and seeing that feed is free from geneticaly modified crops and the remains of other farm animals (no feeding chicken to cows, for instance, or for that matter feeding ground cows to other cows, which was a suspected manner of passing Mad Cow disease in the UK).

▶ **Care: Organic agriculture should be managed in a precautionary and responsible manner to protect the health and well-being of current and future generations and the environment.** More specifically, this reflects a wariness regarding implementing potentially harmful technologies, and indeed endorses "rejecting unpredictable ones, such as genetic engineering." Like the fairness principle above, social justice is also implicit here, with a call for a decision-making process on new practices that is "transparent and participatory."

that the product adheres to even stricter rules than the USDA applies. For example, Knoll Farms of Redmond, California—which has been an organic farm for nearly 30 years, and sells to, among other elite customers, Chez Panisse, an internationally esteemed restaurant—opted out of the certification program in 2002, feeling the standards were too lax. If you have questions about the organic content of anything missing the USDA label, it's best to ask the seller—preferably a staffer at a trusted specialist health food store or farmer's market stall.

Finally, don't confuse the word "natural" with "organic." The USDA makes a point of emphasizing that "natural and organic are not interchangeable," and while some foods billed as "natural" are indeed healthy and sometimes even organic, others are not considered organic by USDA standards, and are not especially natural either (or even healthy for that matter). By the same token, be aware that not all organic food companies are independently operated; some are owned by large corporations that consumers might want to think twice about before supporting, an issue of increasing concern to those who want their dollars to fund both healthy food farming and socially conscious companies (see p.150). It can also be contended that buying organic—and hence supporting farms that don't get much or anything in the way of subsidies—is implicitly anti-corporate, as some of the biggest agricultural subsidies are awarded to companies such as Chevron, DuPont and John Hancock Mutual Life Insurance.

Is organic food definitely better for the environment?

There's no single, definitive answer to this question, because environmental impact can be measured in so many different ways, and because the research into it is a long way from comprehensive. However, according to most non-partisan commentators—including a recent summary of the scientific evidence in *Nature*—organic farms are certainly more environmentally friendly in a number of ways.

Compared with conventional farms they tend to **encourage greater biodiversity**, such as insects, birds and other wildlife (because of the absence of pesticides and the fertility of the soil). They also tend to **use less energy** and create less global-warming CO_2 per pound of produce (in part because man-made fertilizers are so energy-intensive to produce) and they **generate less waste** (such as fertilizer packaging). In some areas, such as phosphorous run-off into streams and the all-important question of retaining soil quality, a lack of many long-term comparative studies make the benefits difficult to prove beyond doubt, but, according to *Nature*, "many studies" suggest that organic production lives up to its promises.

The United Nations Food and Agriculture Organization (FAO) seems even more convinced, claiming that, "If organic agriculture is given the consideration it merits, it has the potential to transform agriculture as the main tool for nature conservation. Reconciling biodiversity conservation and food production depends upon a societal commitment to supporting organic agriculture." They also noted that organic farming "encourages both spatial and temporal biodiversity ... conserves soil and water resources and builds soil organic matter and biological processes."

That's not to say that organic is *necessarily* the most eco-friendly farming system in the world—for now or for the future. A growing number of scientists advocate a middle ground that builds on organic concepts but doesn't rule out all synthetic inputs or GE processes—some of which, they claim, are less harmful (both to the environment and health) than their "natural" alternatives. Still, this middle ground isn't something that's being adopted and it's not something that we're offered in the shops, although the Agricultural Appropriations bill referred to above might be perceived, for better or worse, as a step in that direction (p.78). For now, the choice is basically between the produce of "conventional" or organic farms, and the latter are indeed better environmentally.

Still, even if organic *farms* are a good thing for the environment, that doesn't necessarily mean the same can be said of organic *food*. At least, not according to two arguments often made by critics of the organic movement.

The first is that a huge amount of organic produce is **flown or shipped** into the US from the other side of the world or Latin America. This contributes unnecessarily to climate change, via the CO_2 emissions of the planes and boats that transport them. It's a fair point—North America and Europe account for practically all organic food sales, yet around half of total organic food production takes place in Asia, Australia and Latin America. But it's also perhaps irrelevant: a criticism of food imports as a whole, not organic farming. If we grew more organic food at home, there's be less need to import it.

The second argument is that organic farms tend to produce **less food per acre** than their more industrial counterparts. Therefore, if everyone went organic we'd either not have enough food, or we'd have to reclaim more land to use for farming by cutting down vast areas of forest, which of course would have terrible environmental consequences ...

So organic farming couldn't feed the world?

No one knows exactly how much food an exclusively organic world could grow, but by most estimates it would be substantially less than the amount currently produced. Even such keen organic exponents as Lord Melchett (former director of Greenpeace UK and himself an organic farmer) admit that it's an unknown quantity. However, any question of feeding the world has to accurately evaluate how much food the human population actually

How cheap is cheap food?

Supporters of organic and other "alternative" agricultural systems claim that, while organic food is undeniably more expensive, this is partly because the price we pay for conventionally farmed goods at the supermarket check-out doesn't reflect their true cost. As Erin M. Tegtmeier and Michael D. Duffy write in a 2004 study for the International Journal of Agricultural Sustainability, "many in the United States pride themselves on our 'cheap' food. But … consumers pay for food well beyond the grocery store checkout. We pay for food in our utility bills and taxes and in our declining environmental and personal health."

Here are some of the "external" costs—beyond the barcode price on the package—that we, or others, pay for elsewhere.

▶ **The financial cost** The industrial agriculture machine needs financial oiling at many points. In the US, this happens most demonstrably via billions of dollars' worth of direct subsidies, the majority of which go to the biggest, most intensive farms (though, to be fair, some also go to organic farms). However, the taxpayer also bails out industrial farming in less direct ways, such as cleaning up the massive environmental damage it causes. According to a 2004 study by the International Journal of Agricultural Sustainability, these extra costs—such as dealing with the damage done to the environment and to human health—amount to between $5.7 and $16.9 billion a year ($20-60 per person). Sadly, consumers who buy organic, opting out of the industrial farming system, still have to pay for all these extras.

▶ **The human cost** People debate the health risks posed by agrochemical residues on and in our foods (see p.131). However, less widely discussed is the more measurable impact on farm and plantation workers who apply the stuff. Figures from the World Health Organization (www.who.int) and the World Resources Institute (www.wri.org) suggest that there are between 3.5 and 5 million acute pesticide poisonings annually, tens of thousands of which result in death. And the impact is particularly bad in the developing world, from where a significant proportion of our produce now comes: according to one study published in the *World Health Statistic Quarterly*, 99% of pesticide fatalities occur in poor countries, despite the fact that they only account for a minority of the world's pesticide use. The drive to make food ever cheaper has also arguably exacerbated the problem of child labor. An estimated 70% of the world's child laborers work in agriculture, especially on plantations growing coffee, tea and sugar (as well as tobacco and cotton).

▶ **The cost to animal welfare** When it comes to animal products, intensive farming is generally very bad news for livestock. And though things are slowly improving—veal crates and the worst battery farm cages are on their way out, for example—the conditions that many farm animals are subjected to are still atrocious. As described later in this chapter, they are often treated as mere commodities, living their short existences in chronically over-crowded sheds, never seeing natural light until being packed into a truck on slaughter day.

To this list we could also add the potential cost to human health of routine antibiotic use for livestock (see p.106) and the environmental cost of intensive meat farms (see p.104).

needs. After all, much of what we currently produce ends up squandered in the rearing of **cheap meat**. Indeed, as discussed later in this chapter, the world's rainforests *are* already being chopped down to make way for more farmland. But this isn't to grow organic carrots; the crop of choice is intensively farmed soybeans (much of it GE), the vast majority of which is used in the inefficient and environmentally burdensome process of feeding cattle.

On these grounds, some in the organic movement claim that if we gave up our desire for cheap, intensively farmed meat (which we would *have* to, since huge monocrop soybean farms aren't exactly suited to good old crop rotation), an exclusively organic world could indeed feed itself.

Others aren't convinced we'd even need to change our diet very much. Several food economists have pointed out that many small farmers in poor countries have massively *increased* their yields by adopting organic practices. As Nadia Scialabba wrote in a report for the FAO, "In developing countries ... properly managed organic agriculture systems can increase agricultural productivity and restore the natural resource base."

Furthermore, it's clear that solving world hunger is as much a matter of **increasing political will** and **reducing waste** as of producing more. Even according to the cautious figures of the US Department of Agriculture (www.usda.gov), one-fourth of America's food ends up in the trash—enough to feed the people who starve around the world each year twice over.

Still, even if a completely organic world could feed itself now, it may struggle in the future. After all, the global population is predicted to rise to at least ten billion by 2050, according to the UN. The main sticking point is the fact that organic rules currently ban the use of man-made fertilizers, which have been central to boosting world food productivity in the last few decades, and which—though they can cause serious environmental problems when applied irresponsibly—are not necessarily all that bad when used carefully.

Hence it is sometimes said that green-minded consumers should certainly support organic farming, but that they should accept that, in the long run, the rules may need to be made slightly more flexible, to allow, for example, a certain amount of carefully regulated synthetic fertilizer.

Why is organic food so expensive?

There's no way of avoiding it: organic food is more expensive. And, largely because of the higher labor costs, it looks likely that this will never change.

However, it's pretty clear that the "real" difference in price isn't quite as great as it currently appears, for two main reasons. First, conventional non-organic farming comes with a number of "external" costs that our taxes pay for, from subsidies given to farmers to the clearing up of their environmental mess (see box on p.82)—not that organic shoppers are excluded from paying these costs, of course. Second, organic foods are usually treated as "premium products" by supermarkets, which means they charge a larger mark-up on them.

Whether organic food is worth the money is for each shopper to decide. But bear in mind that you can always **be selective**. Just because you have no intention, or lack the cash, to turn yourself into a 100% organic-only zone, it needn't stop you from just buying, say, organic animal products— which score a hat-trick in terms of animal welfare, antibiotics and pollution issues (all of which are discussed later on in this chapter). Also, bear in mind that organic produce can very often be found at sub-supermarket prices via produce and health food stores, farmers' markets (see p.159), and even online sites that will deliver boxes to your door.

Is it better for the farmers?

Organic farming can certainly offer some advantages to farm owners and workers. For example, it removes the considerable **health risks** associated with over-exposure to agrochemicals—a huge issue on developing-world plantations, especially (see pp.132–133). It also means that small farmers are less likely to find themselves getting caught up in a spiral of **debt** driven by the cost of chemical inputs. This is a common problem since, as soil quality goes down and chemical-resistant pests develop, farmers can find they need to spend more on inputs each year. As the UN has reported, "the conventional food production model ties farmers into conditions of dependence on large corporations to buy agricultural inputs (seeds, fertilizers, pesticides) and to sell their produce."

That said, it's certainly not the case that life is rosy for all farmers and workers growing organic produce. Though the organic codes on worker welfare are much better than nothing, the organic food we import from the third world still generally comes from farms where the employees see little reward for the fruits of their labour. And, in the US, too, while some farmers have profited from converting to organic, many others have struggled to make a decent income from their produce. Some blame the supermarkets for taking too big a slice of the organic pie, others the subsidies and other external costs already described that allow conventional farming to appear cheaper than it really is.

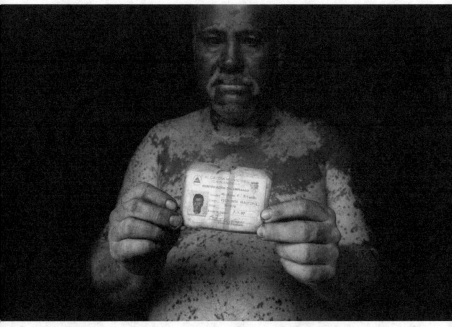

An ex-banana-plantation worker from the Chinandega (a farming area of Nicaragua) where widespread genetic illnesses, ranging from skin disorders to deformed babies, are blamed on decades of heavy pesticide use. Shocking pictures such as this aren't typical of non-organic farming, of course, and many of the worst agrochemicals are no longer in use. However, around 20,000 farmers are still killed each year—and literally millions poisoned—by the ingestion of pesticides.

Whatever the truth, there's a ever-increasing amount of organic **Fair Trade** products available—and these certainly offer farmers a better deal. The recently formed nonprofit Organic Farmers & Gardeners Union (OFGU) has made uniting Fair Trade and organic practices one of its prime goals, though years will likely pass before its effectiveness can be measured.

Is organic food healthier?

Organic foods are widely marketed as safer and healthier, but the benefits are not universally accepted. The claims fall into two separate categories, the first of which relates to the potentially harmful effects of **pesticide residues** in our food. Unsurprisingly, organic foods carry incomparably fewer of these residues, and no one denies that this is a good thing. However, toxicologists aren't universally convinced that the levels of pesticide residues in conventional food—even those that exceed the official safety limits—are a serious cause for concern (for more on this topic, see p.131).

The second issue is whether organic foods are more **nutritious**. There have been studies showing organic food to be higher in levels of vitamin C, essential minerals, cancer-preventing phytonutrients and other beneficial elements. But the differences tend to be slight, and there's a possibility that organic food may bring risks, too, such as—according to at least one study—a higher proportion of certain microrganisms in chicken meat.

Where to buy organic food & drink

Though the supermarkets now stock a pretty wide range of organic foods, there remains a strained relationship between organic farmers and the retail giants where most of their produce is sold. One point of contention is the issue of profit margins: like all farmers, organic producers feel that supermarkets' near-monopoly powers give them the ability to demand unreasonably low prices while making massive profits.

But beyond this, supermarkets also have various habits that many feel are the very antithesis of the organic philosophy: flying in produce from abroad, even when US stock is available; packing fruit and vegetables in completely unnecessary plastic packaging; and contributing to the corporatization of the organic movement itself by favoring large organic suppliers rather than independent local farms.

For these reasons—and various others (see p.152)—you might prefer to buy your organic food via farmers markets, food co-ops, and specialist health food stores. To find them, turn to Where To Shop (see p.152). Or, for organic views and news, see:

Organic Consumers Association www.organicconsumers.org
Organic Trade Association www.ota.com
Organic.org www.organic.org
USDA National Organics Program www.ams.usda.gov/hop

Alternative organic

While the USDA certification program is the one most widely adopted by organic farmers, it's not the only one. The nonprofit Certified Naturally Grown, while using many of the same standards as the National Organic Program, is specifically designed for small, diversified organic family farms that grow many different varieties of crops, who may find it difficult to afford the higher bureaucratic costs necessary to maintain USDA certification. The label is only made available to small farmers whose produce is distributed locally and directly via farmer's markets, co-ops, independent grocery stores, and other outlets much smaller in scale than supermarkets or chains. The New York State-based nonprofit organization has more than 400 participating farms in most of the 50 states, is free to join, and run on a voluntary basis, and its annual inspections are done by fellow farmers in the program.

Food Alliance is a third-party certifier of environmentally friendly and socially responsible agriculture products. Its standards are different and broader than organic ones, allowing for the use of pesticides, for example, but only when natural solutions are ineffective. As they do ban GE foods and embrace soil and water conservation, fair working conditions, and humane treatment of animals, they're an alternative for both farmers who (for financial or other reasons) don't go totally organic, and consumers who want to be socially conscious to at least some degree. More than 200 producers in 16 states are part of the program, though all but a couple of the participants are based in the northwest and midwest.

Certified Naturally Grown www.naturallygrown.org
Food Alliance www.foodalliance.org

Local food vs. imports
Meals & miles

The US has been importing food and drink from far and wide for centuries—tea from China, spices from India, coffee from Brazil. But the globalization of modern food markets is on a completely different scale. These days we fly in fruit from the global South when it's **out of season** in the North, and we ship in goods that we could grow in the US, but which can be **sourced more cheaply** from elsewhere.

Though only a small proportion of the food produced in the world is traded internationally—probably around 90% is consumed in the country where it's grown—the food we put on our plates in the US typically travels between 1500 and 2500 miles, an increase of as much as 25% since 1980.

Today, the contents of an average shopping basket of goods—including organic foods—can be the result of tens of thousands of miles journeying, by road, sea and increasingly air.

For **food grown in the US** the distance from "farm to fork" is bigger than ever, not least because most fresh fruits and vegetables grown domestically are shipped from the far-flung states of Florida, California, and Washington. As supermarket systems rely on everything being delivered to the store via massive distribution centers often located in different regions of the country, long truck journeys are inevitable. As one study by Matthew Hora of the Capitol Area Food Bank pointed out, if a farmer near Atlanta wants to sell lettuce to a Safeway there, it first has to be shipped 620 miles to Maryland for inspection at the corporation's giant mid-Atlantic distribution center—and then be shipped all the way back to Georgia.

The most obvious problem with extra "food miles" is their **environmental impact**, especially in terms of global warming. Goods transport is one of the fastest-growing sources of greenhouse gases, and—in the case of air freight—there is no mechanism by which the importers and exporters pay in full for the environmental damage caused. Gas used to transport food in trucks or tractor trailers at least has a tax payable on it, but aviation fuel—used, for example, to import out-of-season peaches from Chile to the US, and sometimes fraudulently purchased for diesel truck shipping—is taxed at a rate that's 2.5 cents lower per gallon. What's more, Congess has recently considered suspending the aviation fuel tax (as well as the 7.5% federal ticket tax), and in many countries, jet fuel isn't taxed at all. Yet, ironically, if global warming really kicks in, one of its most disastrous symptoms may be an impact on agriculture, in turn perhaps necessitating even more food transport—potentially a very vicious cycle.

It may not always be the case that local food is more eco-friendly. As economist Philippe Legrain argues, "growing Kiwi fruit in heated greenhouses in England gobbles up more energy than transporting them from New Zealand." This may be true, as long as they are shipped rather than flown. But the point only relates to "exotic" produce that is hard to grow in the UK—not the majority of food imports. Even for food grown and consumed within the US, there's no doubt that buying local cuts down on the environmental costs—according to a study by the Leopold Center for Sustainable Agriculture, fresh produce transported to Iowans under conventional systems not only traveled longer distances, but used four to seventeen times more fuel, and released five to seventeen times more CO_2, than produce conveyed in a local or Iowa-based regional food system (see box opposite).

Long-distance dining

In a 2003 study comparing "food miles" for local vs. conventional produce sales to Iowa food institutions, the Leopold Center for Sustainable Agriculture found drastic differences in the WASD (Weighted Average Source Distance) miles traveled:

Produce Type	Locally grown WASD (miles)	Conventional source estimation WASD (miles)
Apples	61	1726
Beans	65	1313
Broccoli	20	1846
Cabbage	50	719
Carrots	27	1838
Corn, Sweet	20	1426
Garlic	31	1811
Lettuce	43	1823
Onions	35	1759
Peppers	44	1589
Potatoes	75	1155
Spinach	36	1815
Squash	52	1277
Strawberries	56	1830
Tomatoes	60	1569
Average	45	1566
Total	675	23,496

For the full report, see: http://www.leopold.iastate.edu/pubs/staff/files/food_travel072103.pdf

Additionally, in a study titled *Food, Fuel and Freeways*, the Leopold Center calculated the average distance traveled by truck by various forms of produce in 1998 to Chicago Terminal Market:

Produce type	Miles traveled	States supplying item	% of total from Mexico
Grapes	2143	1	7
Broccoli	2095	3	3
Asparagus	1671	5	37
Apples	1555	8	0
Sweet Corn	813	16	7
Squash	781	12	43
Pumpkins	233	5	0

The average distance traveled by produce in this manner was 1518 miles, a 22% increase from the 1245 average miles traveled in 1981.

Environmental damage isn't the only criticism that local-food advocates make of our increasingly long-distance dining. In the case of shipping live animals, longer-than-necessary distances raise the likelihood not only of animal welfare abuses but also of the **spreading of diseases** such as foot and mouth. And these can end up costing astronomical sums of money: the total bill for the UK's foot-and-mouth crisis of 2001–2002, including lost tourism revenue, is estimated to be around £10 billion ($17.5 billion).

In the case of fruit and vegetables, there's also the possibility of food losing **nutrients** en route. Studies by the Austrian Consumers Association, for example, found that "fresh" out-of-season fruit and vegetables are often significantly lower in vitamins and higher in harmful nitrates than genuinely fresh ones (or, indeed, frozen ones, which are usually put in the freezer within hours of being picked).

Poor-country imports

While the impact on climate change of unnecessary food miles is quite clear-cut, the effects on workers and local environments are more complex. First of all, there's the question already raised in chapter three (p.45): how much the people in the countries exporting food to us—whether it's beans from East Africa or chicken from East Asia—are benefiting or suffering as a result of this trade.

There's no doubt that many export farms are far from model workplaces—they are very often large, intensively run, monocrop operations which cause considerable environmental harm and which offer workers **wages and conditions** equivalent to manufacturing sweatshops. In many cases, the majority of the profits end up in the hands of a few rich owners, hence driving up **inequality**, and large plantations can put enormous pressure on already stretched sources of water and other resources. In some parts of Kenya, for example, cash-crop growing has been causally linked to the starvation of local people.

On the other hand, export farming can clearly provide **jobs and investment** in areas where they're badly needed. Hence it's not just big business and WTO advocates that are campaigning for increased international agricultural trade, but also many anti-poverty NGOs. In countries such as "Uganda and Vietnam, where smallholder production dominates, agricultural export growth in the 1990s contributed to rapid rural poverty reduction," wrote Oxfam senior policy advisor Kevin Watkins in a debate for *The Ecologist* magazine. He acknowledged that increased global food trade can cause environmental damage and, in some cases, raise inequality, and that

Let's play swap!

Regardless of what you think about the potential costs and benefits of our increasingly globalized food industry, the international trade in food is unquestionably more wasteful and environmentally damaging than it needs to be. For such is the weird and wonderful world of global commodity markets that countries often end up exchanging exactly the same products. Local specialties changing hands, you might think, or seasonal rotation between the hemispheres. But no: even such "generic" products as milk are exchanged. Here are just a few examples, from the UN's FAO Food Balance Sheets:

▶ In 2002 the US imported 2.92 million tons of potatoes while exporting 1.93 million.

▶ In the same year the US exported 2.11 million tons of milk while importing 4.98 million.

▶ We also imported 540,000 tons of pig meat and exported 734,000.

these problems "have to be addressed." But he believes that "making common cause with protectionist lobbies and right-wing populists to exclude poor countries from rich country markets in the interests of 'self-reliance' is a prescription for mass poverty and inequality."

Then, of course, there's the impact of food imports on **US farmers**, many of whom have been forced out of their jobs by foreign competition. The number of major tomato farms in Florida, for example, dwindled from about 300 in 1993 to barely more than a dozen in 2001. Even the long-standing pineapple industry in Hawaii is now under threat. In 2006, Del Monte, the largest pineapple grower in the world, decided to wind down its operations in the state, and transfer them to Thailand and the Phillipines, where the fruit can be produced much more cheaply. Imports aren't the only driver behind this kind of trend (some would say poor financial planning by US farmers is another significant factor) but they have certainly played an important role.

The implications of this are hotly debated. Farming groups tend to claim that, beside the pain felt by farmers forced from their land, we all lose through a disintegration of our national traditions and compromised long-term food security—since the price of imports depends on oil prices, an oil crisis could seriously jeopardize the availability of foods we depend on.

However, you can also look on the bright side: The US currently has a low unemployment rate, and fewer people are in the kind of farm-labor jobs that most of us simply don't want to do (though much of that has been delegated to migrant workers who are not legal US residents). As for food security, it's probably fair to say that we could easily revive fallow US farms, if oil prices or other factors necessitated it.

The ethical choice?

The environmental case for buying local food is very strong and—for anyone who prefers small independents over giant businesses—farmer's markets, food co-ops and specialist health food stores provide the ideal way to do this (see p.156). However, we shouldn't convince ourselves that avoiding the produce of poor countries is somehow doing them a favor. For all the inequalities of pay and the labour abuse that goes on within the international trade in food, unions in poor countries, as well as global anti-poverty groups working with them, are demanding more access to North American markets.

The ideal solution would be to support global trade in food but demand that workers are treated well, resources are ethically managed, international trade rules are fair, and that the consumer (via regulation of producers) bears any environmental costs of the things they buy. This will only happen with political—rather than just consumer—pressure, but in the meantime we can at least buy fair-trade imports wherever possible (see pp.162–163).

"Local" in supermarket-speak

If you do want to buy local food, be cautious of **supermarkets**, which often seem have their own peculiar definitions of the term. Friends of the Earth showed that most supermarkets use "local" to mean "produced in the US" or produced as part of "a local traditional"—regardless of where that tradition is based. And, as already mentioned, even when food is genuinely produced locally, supermarket distribution systems can mean that the food has still spent a considerable amount of time travelling.

According to critics such as George Monbiot, the supermarkets are also guilty of causing **extra animal transport** to take place purely in the name of fooling their customers. "Scotch beef" and "Welsh lamb," Monbiot has written, "now come from animals pastured in Scotland or Wales for just two weeks. They are trucked all over the United Kingdom so that the stores can change their designation and thus raise the price of their meat." This is not only profoundly wasteful and misleading, it's also cruel to animals and adds unnecessarily to the risk of spreading farm diseases.

To find more genuinely local food, see pp. 158-164.

Genetically engineered food
To buy or to boycott?

Whatever your position on genetically engineered foods, if you've lived in North America during the last ten years, it's likely you've consumed them in some form. The US grows about two-thirds of the world's commercially genetically engineered crops, with Canada one of the leading five nations in this category as well. It's estimated that around 70% of food in North American grocery stores contains GE ingredients. Even if you make a determined effort to exclude them from your diet, it's hard to avoid them altogether, particularly as labeling GE foods is not mandatory in the US.

The US Food and Drug Administration determined in 1992 that GE foods were not significantly different from products grown by traditional methods, clearing the way for their entry into the commercial market-place shortly afterward. There have been periodic waves of concern about the wisdom of GE products since then, particularly after scientist **Árpád**

GE food: what, when, where?

Genetic modification is a kind of **biotechnology** in which the DNA of an organism, most commonly a crop, is altered. This can be done either by changing an existing part of the DNA or by adding a new gene from elsewhere—usually from a bacteria, a virus or another plant—allowing scientists to "cross" two organisms that 'are highly unlikely to cross in nature. GE has been a theoretical possibility ever since the discovery of DNA in 1953, but it was in the early 1980s that the techniques were actually developed, and in the 1990s that GE foods became a commercial reality.

Though the potential applications are very wide ranging, the only commercially available GE food crops at the time of writing are **soybean, maize, cotton,** and **canola** (with wheat probably on the way soon). The majority of current modified plants are engineered to be **herbicide tolerant**—capable of dealing with special herbicides that would kill normal crops. The rest have been made **insect resistant**, with their cells modified to produce an insecticide known as Bt toxin. Some GE crops are both herbicide tolerant and insect resistant.

GE planting has halted in many parts of the world, but there's been no such hold up in North America or in developing countries in South America and Asia. At the time of writing there are around six million farmers growing GE crops on roughly 185 million acres (that's approximately twice the land space that makes up the entire United Kingdon). By 2009, it's expected that there will be around ten million farmers growing GE crops on roughly 250 million acres (approximately one-ninth the land space of the US). **Monsanto** soy products account for the majority of these crops, with most of the planted area being in the US and Argentina, followed by Canada and China.

Anti-GE food protesters ripping up biotech crops in Banbury, Oxfordshire.

Pusztai caused an outcry in 1999 by claiming to show that young rats fed GE potatoes were showing signs of ill health. Pusztai's experiments are now widely accepted to have been "irrevocably flawed," as *New Scientist* put it, but did fuel debate that's helped lead to the mandatory labeling of GE foods in the EU, Japan, Australia, New Zealand, and several other countries. While the introduction of GE foods hasn't been nearly as much of a hot-button issue here, there are indications that public opinion heavily favors a federally mandated labeling policy, at the very least. Over time, the arguments have broadened from questions concerning the safety and ethics of "tampering with nature" to claims that, by shunning GE crops, Western shoppers are inadvertently harming both the **environment** and people in the **third world**.

The following pages outline the cases for and against "biotech" food, before looking at how to avoid GE in the shops.

Health

There is nothing concrete to suggest that the current generation of GE food is more harmful or less healthy than any other foods, and the American population, as the biotech industry is always keen to remind us, has been eating it for years with no measurable side effects. However, critics such as **Michael Meacher**—the Environment Minister fired by Tony Blair after expressing scepticism about GE—claim that this isn't enough proof of their safety, pointing out that there have been no proper "human feeding trials," in the US or elsewhere, to rigorously screen the health of GE consumers.

Furthermore, not all scientists are convinced that the current laws, which require biotech firms to show that their crops are "substantially equivalent" to their non-GE counterparts, are enough to rule out potential increases in the levels of plant toxins or reductions in the levels of nutrients. Tests that have been done have been largely carried out by the GE companies themselves, and have been, according to Meacher, "scientifically vacuous."

Overall, the scientific consensus seems to be that the risk of serious damage to human health is low. But if a danger were found at some point down the road—by which time the GE crop in question would probably have widely cross-pollinated with its conventional cousins—it could be almost impossible to solve.

Environmental impact

Environmental groups are leading the campaign against GE, but biotech advocates say they are shooting themselves in the foot, since GE technology could offer considerable environmental benefits. Their claims are numerous. Insect-resistant plants—with "natural" pest resistance built in—can mean **less pesticide** being pumped into fields, hence improving soil fertility and reducing both pollution and poisoning of farmers. Herbicide-resistant crops, meanwhile, allow for special "designer" weedkillers that are safe to use and quick to break down in the soil, and which make it easier for farmers to adopt **non-tillage** (plough-free) techniques, which reduce soil erosion and degradation.

GE could also make higher-yield crops possible or crops able to grow in soil that's been left saline by irrigation (pumping water onto crops often results in salty groundwater rising up and damaging the soil). Both these technologies could help the world meet its ever-increasing demands for food without having to cut down forests to claim new farmland. And the applications aren't limited to food: biotechnology is already being used to research ecologically sound replacements for products such as bleach and formaldehyde.

The green movement is largely unconvinced by these claims. After all, in the case of herbicide-resistant crops, there's as much evidence to suggest they end up **increasing weedkiller use and harming wildlife** as there is to suggest the opposite. In parts of Argentina, for example, the development of weeds resistant to the "designer" herbicides has led to huge amounts of other herbicide being used, harming local peoples' health and crops. There's also the concern that different herbicide-resistant GE crops will cross-pollinate with each other, resulting in "**super-weeds**" resistant to multiple herbicides. Even the British government's **farm-scale evaluations** of three GE varieties suggested that two could be harmful to wildlife, and that was in comparison to their equivalents from conventional intensive farms; a more meaningful study might compare GE crops to organically grown produce.

As for increasing the world's food supply, the greens argue that's also a red herring. Most GE crops are simply supplying feed for the intensive livestock industry, the land for which is now one of the most important drivers of the disastrous clearance of Amazon rainforest (see p.105). Hence we should be looking to consume less meat and redistribute more, not simply increase production (more on this later).

There is one area where some GE critics concede that biotechnology may have proved environmentally beneficial. Pest-resistant crops—such as cotton plants engineered to produce **Bt toxin**, the pesticide based on a naturally occurring bacterium, and used by many organic farmers—are widely recognized to have helped reduce pesticide use in China and elsewhere.

The question remains, can we release GE crops into the wild with absolute certainty that they won't cause environmental or health problems? After all, **contamination** (or "cross-pollination," depending on who you're talking to) is inevitable, as farmers in the US and Canada have already discovered. And even if this doesn't prove dangerous, it limits consumer choice and risks the livelihoods of **organic farmers**, since no GE-tainted crop can be sold as organic.

Some GE advocates, such as molecular biologist Conrad Lichtenstein, claim that organic farmers should simply embrace biotechnology: "GE technology … is by definition a very organic technology," he once wrote. "There is no contradiction between organic and GE." But organic farmers and consumers beg to differ.

Corporate control of the food chain

No part of the GE debate is as heated as the claims about the potential benefits for the world's poor. The biotech industry and the US government talk of **high-yield crops** able to resist harsh winters or droughts, which could reduce hunger and increase food security in regions struck by problematic climates and soils. Special nutritionally improved staples have already been designed to help farmers and their children get the vitamins and nutrients they are currently lacking.

These have so far failed to live up to their creators' promises. So-called **golden rice**, for example, aimed at combating the vitamin A deficiency which blinds and kills thousands of children in poor countries every week, needs to be consumed in vast quantities to have the desired effect. Still, it's "much better than nothing," GE scientist Michael Wilson told Rough Guides, and we should remember that this is only "first-genera-tion" technology. At some stage, life-saving and environmentally benefi-cial GE crops are inevitably going to become reality and, by shunning biotechnology as shoppers, we risk being the "GE Jeremiahs"—in the words of the *Guardian* columnist Nick Cohen—who slow this essential process down.

It's a contentious case, made all the more contentious by the fact that many leaders of poor countries, as well as most anti-poverty groups, have spoken out against GE. In 1998, for example, a group of African delegates to the UN issued a joint statement saying that they "strongly object that the image of the poor and hungry from our countries is being used by giant multinational corporations to push a technology that is neither safe, environmentally friendly nor economically beneficial to us." ActionAid, meanwhile, considers GE crops to be currently "largely irrelevant for the poorest farming communities—only 1% of GE research is aimed at crops used by poor people—and they may pose a threat to their livelihoods." Indeed, as already mentioned, the vast majority of biotech crops are mainly serving to supply intensive meat farms, which, you might argue, are the single biggest threat to world food security (see p.102).

Even when pro-poor GE crops do evolve, some argue they will become yet another patchwork fix misdirecting us from the underlying problems. In *So Shall We Reap*, Colin Tudge writes that Vitamin A rice is the "heroic, Western high-tech solution to the disaster that Western commercial high-tech has itself created," pointing out that vitamin A deficiency doesn't exist "so long as people have horticulture," which has always been part of "traditional farming." The problem isn't low-tech rice, he claims, but a global agricultural ideology based on "obsessive mono-culture" and global trade.

But the main concern of ActionAid is that "four multinationals domi-nate GE technology—giving them unprecedented control over their GE seeds and the chemicals that go with them." The companies in question are Monsanto, Syngenta, Bayer CropScience and Dupont, whose family trees can be traced at:

CorporateWatch archive.corporatewatch.org/genetics/
familytree/familytree_click.htm

Like many other GE skeptics, ActionAid worry that near-monopolies on **seed distribution**, combined with a lack of education in some countries about the legal implications of using GE seeds (for example, the requirement to buy new seeds each year), allows the big companies to effectively force their products on farmers, who will then find themselves taking on otherwise avoidable debt.

Furthermore, the big companies are registering ever more **patents**, giving them the sole rights to perform certain types of genetic manipulation on certain plants. So even if public-sector organizations stumble across potentially positive GE crop developments, they are likely to find them all wrapped up in legal red tape.

The biotech companies tell us not to worry, and that they are out to create a better world. Yet they tend to behave in a way that suggests consumers would be right to be skeptical of such claims. For example, the firms spend millions on **political donations and lobbying**. According to the Center for Responsive Politics, by 2003 biotech firms have received close to $26 million in individual, political action committee (PAC) and soft money contributions since 1989. Along with the Biotechnology Industry Organization (their main trade group), they also spent nearly $143 million to lobby Congress, the White House and the Food and Drug Administration between 1998 and 2002; $18.5 million was spent from 1999-2004 just by Monsanto, who at one point had nine Washington lobbyists on its payroll. And that's only the start of it, according to campaigners. For full critical resumés of these companies, check out www. corpwatch.org.

In the short term at least, some farmers are already benefiting from GE technologies—or thousands of them wouldn't be voluntarily choosing biotech crops in Argentina, China, India and elsewhere. And, in the longer term, it's quite possible that GE could be part of a solution for a better world. Certainly the UN Food and Agriculture Organization thinks so: "biotechnology is capable of benefiting small, resource-poor farmers" was one conclusion of their latest *State of Food and Agriculture* report.

But whether the world *needs* GE crops, whether they're part of the solution or the problem, and whether it's the industry or consumers who are holding up any potential positive benefits, is highly questionable. After all, if crops truly beneficial to the world's poor are proved to be effective and safe, and offered at reasonable prices and terms, it will surely take more than a few concerned voices about modified cornflakes to stop them being taken up around the world.

GE foods: what's in the shops?

The FDA has imposed no labeling requirements for GE foods on the market, though that shouldn't be taken to mean that the American public has given a unanimous thumbs-up to that policy. The FDA has been targeted with petitions and legal action calling for mandatory testing and labeling from numerous organizations, scientists and religious leaders. Some mainstream opinion polls have found the public in favor of labeling, sometimes heavily so—a 2001 poll by ABC News revealed that 93% of Americans wanted some form of labeling to be clearly presented on GE products. ABC News further observed that "such near-unanimity in public opinion is rare."

Recently a few California counties have even banned GE cultivation, though some agricultural-rich counties in the state passed resolutions endorsing their production as well. Vermont is also at the forefront of anti-GE sentiment; the state's Senate recently passed a Farmer Protection Act holding biotech corporations accountable for contamination by genetically engineered crops. On the national level, congressman and former Democratic presidential candidate (and vegan) Dennis Kucinich introduced legislation to label GE foods in July 2003.

Nonetheless, dozens of genetically engineered crops are allowed in the US food supply, and while voluntary labeling is permitted, no company has stepped forward to take advantage of that privilege. It's also been charged that the FDA has made it difficult for companies to label products as non-GE. Pressure from the private sector has helped squash some efforts to institute labeling at the regional level; a Monsanto lawsuit forced a Maine dairy to add qualifying language to its "no artificial growth hormone used" label, and the same corporation spent $6 million to defeat an Oregon ballot proposition to require labels on GE food. All of which makes it hard to avoid GE foods completely, unless you're prepared to go totally organic (see "Going GE-free" on p.100).

Steering clear of GE foods isn't as simple as avoiding any of the crops that are permitted to be grown with the technology, including non-organic squash, sugar beet, and papaya, as well as several varieties of potatoes. GE canola, corn, cotton, and soy derivatives can be found in many packaged foods, while the recombinant bovine growth hormone might be found in dairy products. All food with animal products, in fact, is suspect since animal feed often contains GE foodstuffs. Even some items commonly thought of as health food, like veggie burgers and tofu dogs, might contain GE soy derivatives.

Given the massive space already used for GE crops in the US, and the heavy presence of GE foods in the shops, it might be argued that even mandatory, rigorous labeling and testing policies would not be effective in curbing their manufacture and distribution. Mandatory labeling, however, has been crucial to halting the spread of GE foods abroad, and not just in the shops. GE labels have certainly ensured the virtual elimination of a market for GE foods in Europe—which, in turn, has made it virtually impossible, logistically and politically to grow GE crops there (though some companies, such as Kellogg's, have managed to have it both ways, pledging to eliminate GE from their European products while continuing to sell GE food in the US and Canada). There's reason for purists to be wary of using foreign GE bans as a model, however. As strict as the EU is (relative to North America), it doesn't require labeling on meat, fish, eggs or dairy products that come from farm animals fed GE crops.

Similar rules apply in cafés and restaurants. Owners aren't obliged to specify GE ingredients on the menu but the staff must—in theory at least—be able to inform you, if asked, of any dishes that would require a label if sold in a shop.

Going GE-free

As explained above, most people in the US find it hard to avoid buying or consuming GE foods in at least some quantities. But if you'd rather be consuming none at all, you may want to check out the True Food Network's comprehensive online shopping guide. It gives thumbs up or down to hundreds of products, as well as listing supermarkets carrying store brand products likely to be GE foods. Note that it excludes almost every product made from or by animals, as the way US grain is pooled, and the lack of labeling or tracking requirements, makes it very difficult to know whether animals are being fed GE grains:

The True Food Shopping Guide www.truefoodnow.org/shoppersguide

Alternatively, buy organic, since the organic rules ban all use of GE technologies. Even this won't completely remove all traces of modification from your diet, since accidental contamination of organic food by GE crops has already been spotted. Investigations of the 2000 harvest found that virtually all seed corn in the US, including the organic variety, was contaminated with at least a trace of GE material. Once intermixing gets started, it can be all but impossible to completely eradicate; when Iowa farmers planted 1% of their corn crop with GE StarLink seed that same year, about half the crop was found to have been contaminated at harvest time. Still, buying organic is about as close as you can get to sidestepping GE. As there are currently no GE grasses being grown, 100% grass-fed meat also avoids GE feed, though this could change if Monsanto's GE Alfalfa enters the market, because alfafa is a big part of the diet of both dairy and beef cows.

Staying GE-free when eating out, incidentally, isn't any easier, at least if you want an official seal of approval. Under NOP standards, restaurants and retailers aren't required to obtain certification. Eating establishments can seek certification voluntarily, which entitles them to display the USDA sticker, but at the beginning of 2004, there were only three such certified organic restaurants in the entire country.

GE links

To read more about the GE issues from various different perspectives, try the following websites:

Biotechnology Industry Organization www.bio.org
Council for Responsible Genetics www.gene-watch.org
Food and Drug Administration www.fda.gov
Friends of the Earth www.foe.org
Genewatch www.genewatch.org
The True Food Network www.truefoodnow.org
Union of Concerned Scientists www.ucsusa.org

Eating animals

Waste, pollution & the ethics of meat

Beyond animal welfare concerns and the standard moral questions that surround killing animals for food, there are some serious **ecological problems** with our consumption of animal products—especially those that come from intensive farms.

The ethics of vegetarianism & veganism

Shopping for "ethical" meat is all well and good, but many would say the idea of being nice to an animal before unnecessarily electrocuting or slitting its throat is odd, to say the least. Most of us would be bothered by the idea of eating free-range cat and dog meat, after all, yet there's little difference between this and "ethically reared" meat from intelligent animals such as pigs. Why are we prepared to kill certain animals and not others? And is it really justifiable to kill any animals simply so we can have the pleasure of eating them?

This must be one of the longest-running of all ethical consumerism debates: exclusively non-animal diets have been relatively common in Asia since the development of ancient religions such as **Jainism**, and Europe first grappled with the concept just as long ago. **Pythagoras**, **Plato**, **Socrates** and **Ovid** all expressed doubts about meat. However, Western vegetarianism as we know it today didn't really take off until the beginning of the 19th century, when the tireless campaigning of the appropriately named **William Cowherd**, a reverend from Salford, started the ball rolling. The term itself was coined in 1847 by the UK's newly formed **Vegetarian Society**, which made a point of deriving it from *vegetus*, Latin for lively, rather than vegetable (though this seems a bit academic considering that both words come from the same Latin root). Numbers have grown ever since (though it wasn't until 1927 that the first comparable US organization, the Vegetarian Society of the District of Columbia, was formed), and today surveys suggest that about 3% of the US population describe themselves as vegetarian, with many more consciously limiting their meat intake.

Besides individual views about killing animals unnecessarily, numerous more objective arguments can be made for vegetarianism. The two most convincing are the facts that most meat and farmed fish is **wasteful** to produce (as discussed in this section), and that **animal welfare** standards are usually very low (more on this later). Organic and other non-intensive meat and fish is available, of course, but it's more expensive, harder to find in restaurants and still ultimately more wasteful than non-animal foods.

Some other arguments, however, such as the idea that we're evolutionarily herbivore by design, are flawed. People disagree about the exact diets of our ancestors, but it's actually pretty clear that early humans, like the chimps they evolved from, ate at least some meat when it was available. As for claims of better **health**, vegetarians do tend to live longer and suffer fewer serious problems, but it's difficult to work out how much of this is due to a meat-free diet, and how much of it is down to other attributes that,

Many of the problems stem from the fact that most animal products are very **inefficient to produce**. Take beef, for instance. There's no single definitive figure, but producing a single pound of intensively farmed beef typically takes around 10 pounds of grain for feed. Beef is among the worst culprits, but similar problems apply to most meats, farmed fish and, to a slightly lesser extent, dairy and eggs. Obviously all these foods have relatively high energy and protein levels, so a pound of feed is not directly comparable to a pound of meat. But even taking this into

according to the stats, happen to be common to most vegetarians, such as a wealthy class background and general health consciousness. Still, whatever the reasons, most vegetarian diets do tend to be very healthy.

But what about **eggs and dairy products**? Produced intensively, these too fall into the ecologically damaging category. The rearing of egg-laying chickens (p.116) and dairy cows (p.112) is associated with animal-welfare problems at least as great as those of the meat trade. Egg-laying chickens are killed after only weeks of life, ending up as meat in pet food, while dairy products rely on a constant stream of calves being born, most of which are slaughtered for meat (if they weren't, we'd end up with an ever-growing bovine population). So "lacto" vegetarians still kill animals, you might argue, and intensively farmed milk and eggs are not necessarily morally superior to, for example, organic, free-range chicken.

These contradictions lie behind the small but growing number of people going **vegan**—abstaining from all animal products, including dairy, eggs and even honey. Veganism grew out of the vegetarian movement in the first half of the twentieth century, and it generally sees itself as the logical conclusion of that movement, as is implied by the term "vegan": the beginning and the end of the word vegetarian. It is a much bigger commitment than vegetarianism, ruling out many foods and guaranteeing a considerable degree of inconvenience when eating out or traveling. But it's ultimately a more coherent ideology, at least from the animal-welfare and ecological perspectives.

Still, even veganism isn't enough for some, who ask why should we draw the line at plants? **Fruitarians** only eat foods—such as fruits, berries, olives, tomatoes—that can be eaten without deliberately harming any organism, and also save energy by eliminating the need for cooking, refrigeration or even washing up. This is one branch of ethical shopping that is hard to see ever really taking off.

For more information, visit:

Vegetarian Society www.vegsoc.org
Vegan Society www.vegansociety.com
International Vegetarian Union www.ivu.org
The Fruitarian Site www.fruitarian.com
Beyond Vegetarianism www.beyondveg.com

account, the simple fact remains: we get far less food out of most animals than we put in.

Animal produce *can* be made far more efficiently on **mixed, closed-system farms** of the type often favored by organic growers. Chickens and some other animals can be fed on scraps that might otherwise go to waste. In some cases animals graze on land that would be no good for crops, with a diet largely consisting of grasses, perhaps supplemented with crop **by-products**. For these reasons, the most efficient food production systems *do* actually include some animal products. But in reality, the

Making meat

The exact quantity of feed required to make each pound of meat or fish varies between breed and farming method—and there are also great differences between the figures favored by campaigners, on the one hand, and the meat industry, on the other. The following "middle-of-the-road" estimates come from the non-partisan Council for Agricultural Science and Technology.

Pounds of feed required to produce 1 pound of food

Farmed fish	1.5–2.0	
Poultry meat	2.1–3.0	
Pork	4.0–5.5	
Beef	10	

The amount of water required to produce certain meats is also often very high (though naturally the relevance of this varies from country to country). According to a study by D. Pimentel, and published in *Bioscience*:

Gallons of water required to produce 1 pound of food

Potatoes	60	
Wheat	110	
Maize	170	
Rice	230	
Soya beans	240	
Chicken	420	
Beef	12,000	... and 180 more

majority of farmed animals consume feed that could be more effectively used elsewhere.

This is no minor issue. Global meat consumption has increased by around 500% since 1950—the world today contains around **twice as many chickens as humans,** plus 1 billion pigs, roughly 1.3 billion cows and 1.8 billion sheep and goats—and there is no sign of this slowing down. According to agricultural commentator Colin Tudge, if the current growth rate of animal-product consumption continues, by 2050, livestock will consume as much food as the entire human population did in 1970.

This rising demand for animal feed has a number of implications, one of which is a growing demand for farmland to grow feed crops such as soy. This is already resulting in the clearing of **rainforests** in the Amazon and elsewhere, and looks set to become one of the worst threats to the world's biodiversity (not to mention the other environmental and human problems caused by deforestation).

A second implication, in the slightly longer term, is a threat to the **food security** of the world's poorest people. Unless rainforest clearance and/or a revolution in farm technology manages to keep up both with rising meat consumption and rising global population, we'll soon get to the point where there won't be enough crops to feed all the people and all the farm animals. At this point, demand will outstrip supply and the price of crops will rise. The price of meat will go up even more, of course (since meat farmers will have to pay more for feed). But such is global inequality that those who consume animal products will probably be able to absorb this rise in price far more easily than those in poor countries, who already struggle to buy enough basic crops to feed themselves and their families.

The environmental burden

Even if rainforests weren't at risk, the intensive production of animal products would create a range of serious environmental burdens. For one thing, the production of feed crops and the farming of animals uses up an astonishing amount of **water**. It can take 12,000 gallons of water to make a single pound of beef (see box "Making meat"). This isn't usually a big problem in the US and many other rainy countries. But considering that fresh water stocks are already close to being exhausted in much of the developing world, it's a massive issue when the meat is produced there.

Secondly, the world's livestock produce more than 10 billion tons of **mineral-rich effluent** each year. While manure adds to soil fertility in closed-system, mixed farms, it can be a major polluter in intensive farms, finding its way into rivers and groundwater, and raising nitrogen and phosphorous levels higher than aquatic species can survive. Its **ammonia** content can also contribute to acid rain.

And then there's **global warming**. Astonishingly, farm animals are thought to account for around 10% of the world's greenhouse-gas emissions. Part of this contribution is due to the fact that meat production uses a lot of oil—to power farm machines, make fertilizer for feed crops, transport feed and animals, and so on. All told, meat requires around 10–30 times the total energy input per ton than corn or soy. But it is also because cows and other livestock annually burp and fart out an astonishing 80 million tons of **methane**, which is a particularly problematic greenhouse gas.

The antibiotics issue

Along with their diet, many animals in intensive farms—especially pigs and poultry, but also cattle and fish—routinely receive drugs. These are mostly **antibiotics**, both to stimulate growth and to prevent against the diseases that thrive in overcrowded conditions. Animal welfare campaigners object to this because growth promoters are thought to cause health problems and because they push animals beyond their natural limits. Equally troubling is the potential threat to human health via the growth of **antibiotic resistance**. As "super-bugs" in hospitals have shown, resistance to our most useful drugs is on the up. For instance, a significant proportion of cases of the biggest source of food poisoning in the US, campylobacter, are now untreatable by antibiotics. Though not all scientists agree, many microbiologists think we're sitting on a time bomb.

Over-prescription in humans is certainly part of the problem—perhaps even the biggest part—but intensive farming is now widely accepted as a potential breeding ground for resistant bugs, which, once developed, may be passed on to humans via meat, milk or even possibly crops grown from animal fertilizer. The Union of Concerned Scientists, in fact, estimates that 70% of antibiotics purchased in the US are fed to farm animals. Bipartisan legislation to phase out the use of seven antibiotics classes in animal feed has failed several times to pass through Congress, though it was reintroduced for consideration in 2005. Drugging animals also raises the question of carcinogenic or otherwise harmful **drug residues** in our meat or milk. Strict regulations setting out periods of "withdrawal" for animals given drugs theoretically avoids this, but various studies have shown residues far in excess of the legal maximums, suggesting farmers don't always observe the rules.

If you want to avoid routinely administered antibiotics, buy organic or look for products with the USDA-approved labels "raised without antibiotics" and "no subtherapeutic antibiotics administered." The Eat Well Consumer Guide (www.eatwellguide. org) lists retail outlets, restaurants and producers selling meat and poultry raised without the routine use of antibiotics.

The solution?

Something is clearly going to have to be done about our excessive and rising consumption of intensively farmed animal products, and various groups claim they have the solution. **Vegetarians** (see p.102) advocate simply cutting out meat from our diet; **localizers** (see p.87) argue that we should move away from a global free market in food, encouraging countries to focus on self-sufficiency through ecologically friendly "mixed" farms; **GE exponents** (see p.93) look to biotechnology as a means of increasing crop productivity and therefore increasing supply to match demand; and some food economists have even suggested the implementation of a global "food-chain tax," to add to the cost of meat.

As for what individual ethical shoppers can do, the basic choice is simple enough: if you really want to reduce your environmental footprint—in terms of climate change, pollution, water use and deforestation—try to consume fewer animal products, especially those from intensive farms.

Animal welfare labels
What do they mean?

Even if intensive meat production wasn't so problematic environmentally and economically, there are serious issues regarding the conditions to which most animals are subjected. Specific welfare concerns and the non-intensive alternatives are dealt with in the following sections on red meat (p.109), poultry and eggs (p.113), dairy (p.119) and fish (p.121). But first here's a quick look at a few programs that claim to guarantee better levels of welfare, all devised by organizations specifically devoted in part or whole to the humane treatment of farm animals.

Free Farmed & Certified Humane

Administered by the American Humane Association (founded in 1877 to advocate child and animal welfare), **Free Farmed** is a voluntary, fee-based service of inspection, labeling and certification of animal products. The standards stress

healthy food and water access, sufficient shelter and enough space for natural movement. In 2003, its Scientific Advisory Committee of Farm Animal Services left to start **Certified Humane** as part of the nonprofit Humane Farm Animal Care (HFAC), advocating much the same policies. Several dozen companies use the label, as do several dozen restaurants (though all but one of those are based on the East Coast).

Animal Welfare Institute

The **Animal Welfare Institute** certifies products from animals that haven't been denied any of the basic "five freedoms" first laid out  in a scientific report to the British government in 1965: freedom from **fear and distress**, freedom from **hunger and thirst**, freedom from **discomfort**, freedom from **pain, injury and disease**, and freedom to express **normal behavior**. Unlike the previous two programs, the AWI does not offer a label, but gives producers the right to use its name in their mar-

Like a lamb to slaughter: animal transport

Farm animals are often transported long distances by truck between farms, auctions, stockyards and slaughterhouses, but there are no regulations in place to impose a maximum journey time. Although there is a federal law that prohibits transporting animals for more than 28 consecutive hours without unloading them for a minimum of five hours feed and rest time, according to the USDA it only applies to rail shipments, the most common method of animal transport when the law was passed in the 1870s. Trucks surpassed trains for animal shipping in the mid-twentieth century and are now used to transport more than 95% of our farmed animals, but the statute clearly hasn't kept up with the times.

In the summer of 2005, investigators for Compassion Over Killing found that farm animals were often overcrowded onto trucks for journeys exceeding 28 hours without food, water, rest or adequate protection from the elements. COK also reported in-transit injuries, illness and even dead animals left on-board for more than 30 hours among live ones. The conditions might have a direct human cost as well. According to Dr. Michael Greger, the Humane Society's director of Public Health and Animal Agriculture, "transporting farm animals long distances greatly increases the risk that these animals will harbor life-threatening pathogens." The Humane Society, COK, Farm Sanctuary, and Animals' Angels filed a legal petition in October 2005 calling on the USDA to apply the 28-hour law to trucks as well as trains.

keting if they abide by its standards. It also limits participants to family farms, and—unlike Certified Humane, Free Farm, and, for that matter, the National Organic Program—does not allow farmers to produce both certified and non-certified products.

Farm Sanctuary

There's usually agreement that each of these programs does much to ensure a quality of animal welfare considerably above the average industry guidelines, with Certified Humane endorsed by mainstream animal rights groups such as the ASPCA and the Humane Society, but critics have cited serious shortcomings as well. **Farm Sanctuary**, the largest American farm animal rescue and protection organization, points out that Certified Humane and Free Farmed don't require outdoor access for pigs, meat chickens, or laying hens, and allows debeaking of hens and tail-docking of pigs under some circumstances. Its 2005 research report also criticized Free Farmed for having only one animal welfare expert on its advisory committee, and AWI for lacking a formal process for auditing compliance. Producers certified by the USDA as organic, by the way, aren't prohibited from debeaking and tail-docking either, and as NOP regulations allow some animals to be temporarily confined under specific circumstances, it's been charged that some agents have stretched this loophole to keep birds indoors most or all of the time.

Animal Welfare Institute www.awionline.org
Certified Humane www.certifiedhumane.com
Farm Sanctuary www.farmsanctuary.org
Free Farmed www.americanhumane.org

Red meat
Pigs, cows & sheep

Pork products

Of the commonly available red meats, those from pigs pose the most pressing questions in terms of animal welfare. These are **highly intelligent** social animals—usually compared to dogs in the animal IQ stakes—often reared with no respect for their wellbeing. Pig farming techniques have become increasingly industrial over the past few decades. Farms are growing to epic sizes—in the US, there are now individual farms with more than a million swine—and the standard sow has been transformed into a meat-making machine. Relatively recently, female pigs would give birth to around five piglets a year, but 25 is not uncommon today. This is thanks to a mixture of **intensive breeding** programs and the technique of removing piglets from their mothers very early, to maximize the number of possible pregnancies per year.

In the US, many pigs still spend their whole lives in **gestation crates**— tiny barren cages, usually so small that the pig cannot even turn around— or chained to the floor using **tethers**. "Docking" of tail without anesthesia, clipping of teeth, and notching of ears are also routine, all to avoid the pigs biting each other—something they generally do only in cramped, agitating conditions. Most of them are kept in barren, indoor environments, often on slippery concrete and slatted floors that can trap their hooves, causing lameness and other health problems as well as preventing normal rutting and roaming behavior. **Farrowing crates**—small stalls into which sows are put for a week or two either side of giving birth—are still the norm. The industry claims these are needed to protect the piglets from being crushed to death, but organic pig farmers have shown that with good husbandry this isn't necessary.

There are no federal anti-cruelty regulations for farmed pigs in the US, and while individual states can pass anti-cruelty legislation, only Florida has done so, approving a ballot initiative in 2002 that protects female pigs from confinement and tethering during a pregnancy. In contrast, most of the techniques detailed above are due to be made illegal across the EU, though not until 2013.

Besides welfare issues, food buffs are quick to point out that intensively farmed pork is nearly always floppy, watery and tasteless.

What can you do?

Look out for pork meat marked **free range** (the term **free roaming** is also used). With a lack of legal definitions, this doesn't always mean the same thing—it's largely down to individual farmers—but in most cases it implies a considerable improvement to the prevailing standards. At minimum, you'll know the pigs aren't kept permanently indoors. There are USDA free range standards, incidentally, but these only apply to poultry (see p. 115), not pork. The USDA did consider labeling free range (as well as grass-fed) livestock, but withdrew from the rule-making process in

Two extremes of pig farming: the best of organic (left) and the worst of intensive (right).

2003, in part because many farmers and public interest groups feared the standards would be too diluted, as well as confusingly inconsistent with those applied to poultry.

Organic pig meat is likely to offer further improvements. Though NOP livestock standards don't specifically regulate conditions such as crates and surfaces, they do require maintainance of preventive health practices that include freedom of movement "as appropriate to species," physical alterations only as needed to promote the animal's welfare with a minimum of pain, outdoors access, and other measures "which accommodate the health and natural behavior of animals." There have been complaints that the rules are too vague and too vaguely enforced, and even subject to circumvention that allows for some abusive practices, but organic pork is still far more likely to have been produced in a more humane manner. If you can't find free-range or organic pork in your supermarket, or if you want to buy directly from farmers, see pp. 158–159 for pointers.

You might also see pork products marked with the **Certified Humane** or **Free Farmed** logos, or marketed with the blessing of the **Animal Welfare Institute**. These offer some basic animal welfare guarantees, though fewer than organic.

Beef & veal

Meat from cows ranges widely, both in terms of animal welfare and its wastefulness (as already discussed, intensive beef farming requires remarkable quantities of water and crops). Many feel, at least relatively speaking, that cattle have it better than pigs or dairy cows as they're often able to spend at least a few months of their short lives on the range, and are usually not weaned for at least six months. Others point out that they're also often left to forage for themselves on the range without adequate protection from the elements or disease; that they suffer stress during transportation; and that their last months are often spent in overcrowded, disease-prone feedlots where they're given growth hormones and unnatural diets in an effort to fatten them up as much as possible before slaughter.

There's also reason to be wary of beef from **intensive farms.** Stocked with excess calves from the dairy industry (most of which were removed from their mothers on day one), these farms keep their cows almost entirely indoors, usually in barren and over-crowded concrete sheds, with no chance to exercise or graze. As with most intensive farming, this increases the chances of the cows contracting bovine illnesses, which in turn increases the need for **antibiotics** and other drugs.

Veal

Eating veal is not inherently very different, ethically speaking, from eating lamb or any other young animal, but the way much of it is produced is cause for serious concern. Animal rights groups are most troubled by **formula-fed** (also called **milk-fed**) veal calves, which are reared in **crates** intended to keep them completely imobile. They suffer great distress, are very susceptible to disease—hence preventative antibiotics are often used—and are fed a poor **all-liquid diet** deliberately lacking in certain nutrients in order to create a white-colored meat. US veal consumption has dropped to less than a pound per capita after anti-veal campaigns in the last two decades, but over a million create-reared calves still find their way to market each year. Though a ban should see an end to crate use in the EU sometime in 2007, no such legislation is close to passing here.

What to buy

Free-range beef obviously makes for a more ethical choice, and is growing in availability (though it still accounts for less than 5% of the market), so look out for labels or ask your butcher. Better still is buying **organic,**

which ensures strict animal-welfare standards, rules out routine antibiotics and shuns animal and fish products in the feed. Organic beef is widely available, and organic veal from calves which are fed with their mothers' milk, and given outdoor/pasture access, is also available, though less ubiquitous; for pointers to suppliers, see pp.154–164.

Lamb

In terms of animal welfare, sheep get a pretty good deal compared to most farm animals. The overwhelming majority spend their lives freely grazing over extensive pastures, being brought inside only when the weather demands it. This is largely because, as yet, no one has worked out a way to make intensive sheep farming viable. But that's not to say the situation is perfect. There are some serious problems with how many sheep and lambs are transported and slaughtered, and neglect by some farmers means that around 1 in 10 lambs die of **cold or hunger**. Many are also castrated without anaesthetic.

To ensure the best guarantee of animal welfare, as well as respect for the environment, go for **organic** lamb, or buy directly from local farmers whom you can question about welfare issues.

Poultry & eggs
Factory fowl

The chicken industry is perhaps the most extreme example of modern farming methods. Governed by technology and market forces, this is a whole sector of farming carried out almost entirely behind closed doors, and mostly by large firms. Amazingly, just three companies—Aviagen, Cobb-Vantress and Hybro—provide nearly all the world's chicks, both for meat and egg-laying birds, which, during the last half decade, have been engineered into completely separate creatures. The chick companies are proud of their scientific approach, and make no back-to-nature pretence. Visit one of their websites—such as www.aviagen.com—and you'll be invited to check out the "features and benefits" or a "technical data sheet" for each of their "products." If this sounds more like marketing for cars than hens, the names of the breeds—such as the **Hybro PG+** and **Cobb 500**—won't convince you otherwise.

Broilers—meat chickens

Conditions for egg-laying hens are very gradually improving (see pp.116-119), but the same cannot be said for meat chickens, or **broilers** as they're called. Like so many other foods, chicken meat was thought of as a luxury food until relatively recently, when intensive farming methods allowed prices to be slashed. Unfortunately this happened at the expense of animal welfare.

A brave new chicken

The whole idea of a chicken bred solely for meat is only around fifty years old, but today intensive broiler farms in the US account for nearly all of the roughly 8 billion chickens we consume each year—around thirty for each person in the country. To achieve this remarkable turnover, farms use chicks that have been specially bred to grow in the shortest possible time: a modern broiler can get to slaughter weight in just over **forty days**, twice as quickly as a few decades ago. With breeding technology still in its youth—some industry visionaries expect thirty day's growth before slaughter a realistic norm in the near future.

Regrettably for the birds, while their breasts grow unnaturally quickly, the rest of the body cannot keep up, and millions of broilers each year develop painful **leg disorders** or die of **heart failure**. Indeed, the genetic selection is so rigorous that chickens kept for breeding broilers have to be severely underfed; if they weren't, their super-efficient weight-gaining ability would crush them before they reached egg-laying age. But animal welfare is never really going to be a priority while the leading chick suppliers make such proud claims as "output of meat per breeder placed is the ultimate measure of performance."

It's not just breeding process that focuses on a need for speed. Every other element of a broiler's life is controlled by the same bottom line, from its sleep patterns (amounts of time in total darkness is kept to an absolute minimum as a sleeping bird won't eat) to its feed: maximum weight-gain, minimum-excrement pellets.

Chickenshit

Most broilers live in flocks of tens of thousands in giant, windowless sheds, each bird getting little more space than would contain a telephone book. With such dense stocking, clearing out the **litter floor** is only possible once the birds are taken to slaughter, so the birds spend their short lives standing and sitting in their own filth, often leading to **ulcerous feet** and **skin disease**. Evidence of the latter was found in two percent of the chicken meat examined in a recent sample by *Which?*, the UK's best-known consumer magazine.

When their days are up, the birds are transported by crowded truck to a slaughterhouse and processing plant, many of which can cope with more than 10,000 chickens per hour. After being hung upside-down by their feet, the birds have their heads dipped into an electrified pool and their throats cut by a spinning blade. A couple of hours, miles of conveyor belt and numerous machines later, they'll come out plucked, gutted, wrapped and packed—perhaps even marinated (or, more accurately, injected)—and ready for the restaurant cooler or supermarket shelf. For both broiler chickens and egg-laying hens, the journey to the slaughterhouse is itself often perilous, the birds jammed into crates stacked on trucks without access to food, water or protection from the elements.

There are no specific laws governing the chicken farming industry, despite considerable pressure from animal rights groups and celebrities for some kind of guidelines to be set in place. People for the Ethical Treatment of Animals (PETA) has engaged in a long-running campaign against Kentucky Fried Chicken, the world's largest chicken restaurant chain, joined by not only organizations such as the Humane Society and United Poultry Concerns, but even Paul McCartney, who put an open letter to the CEO of KFC's parent company in his 2005 US tour program. Though KFC did at one point establish an Animal Welfare Council and pledge to improve its practices, the council's recommendations have yet to be implemented. For more information about broilers, see the campaign sites of ChickenIndustry.com (www.chickenindustry.com) or the Humane Society (www.husus.org).

As well as animal welfare concerns, industrially produced chicken is said by those in the know to be disastrous for taste and quality. The lack of exercise, poor diet and absorption of water during processing creates, according to none other than Delia Smith (the UK's most popular cook-book author/television chef), "a coarse-grained, watery, limp chicken that has no flavor."

How free is free range?

Some types of chicken—and other poultry—that guarantee better welfare standards (and taste) are now widely available in the US, but the labeling isn't as simple or strict as you might expect. Under USDA standards for

free range poultry, free range chickens (still comprising less than 1% of the chickens produced in the US annually) have at least some outdoor access. The standards are vague, however, only requiring "an undetermined period each day." Critics charge that, in theory, a coop or stall door could be opened for five minutes a day to satisfy such minimal requirements. It's still probable that chicken with the free range label enjoys more, and sometimes quite a bit more, outdoor time than that, but it's also true the label doesn't offer any such guarantees.

Organic, once again, is the best option. Organic standards require welfare at least as good as free range, but outline far smaller flock sizes and a diet consisting of mainly organic feed free from animal proteins. Even if free-range chicken isn't available, look out for the **Certified Humane** or **Free Farmed** labels, and avoid fresh chickens with brown "hock burn" marks near the knee joints—these often imply that welfare standards have been low.

Eggs

According to Humane Society estimates, more than 95% of the roughly 300 million laying hens in the US are kept in cramped **battery cages**, stacked up high in vast buildings with little or no natural light. In most cases the hens have so little space they cannot even turn around or stretch their wings, let alone follow their instincts to preen properly and "dustbathe." The cages lead not just to discomfort, but to **foot injury** and **weak bones**, so that by the end of their productive lives—usually about one year and a few hundred eggs—almost a third of the birds have broken bones, according to animal-welfare groups. And the other two-thirds are in such poor condition that after slaughter they are only used for processing and animal food.

An egg-layer's **diet** contains not only amounts of grains, soy and nutrients, but often also fish products and even (in an odd twist on the chicken-and-egg question) waste chicken extracts. The hens are also given colorants, both artificial and natural, to ensure the consumer isn't faced with a perfectly harmless variety in yolk color, and antibiotics are routinely administered. A study by the Soil Association showed that a large proportion of eggs contain traces of the toxic medicine lasalocid, known to be harmful to mammals but never tested on humans.

One advantage of cages is that it makes it harder for crowded birds to peck each other, meaning that they don't necessarily need to be **debeaked** (the trimming of chicks' beaks with a red-hot blade). However, many battery hens are debeaked anyway, and many claim that careful and minimal debeaking is less cruel than battery conditions. Either way, the practice isn't necessary with a small flock size in better conditions, as is typical of hens which produce organic eggs.

A good egg?

Battery farming still accounts for the vast majority of US egg production, but things are starting to change. There are now various non-battery options and some food retailers have committed to selling cage-free eggs. Although some eggs are billed as **free range** on the carton, US regulations for free-range products apply only to meat chickens, not egg-laying hens. For that reason, animal welfare groups such as United Poultry Concerns have dismissed the billing as virtually meaningless. Consumers insistent

Free-range may be better than battery or barn-reared, but—as this image from a modern farm in Rotterdam shows—it's a long way from the traditional farmyard scene pictured on many egg boxes.

on a definition will need to contact manufacturers of the specific products, and criteria is certain to vary widely from company to company.

That's not to say that at no eggs are laid by hens with access to comfortable space and freedom of movement, but there's no guarantee that such has been the case, nor any government or third-party bodies to hold companies accountable. Even though **Certified Humane** and **Free Farmed**'s standards, for instance, rule out the battery cage, they do not ban crowded barns or debeaking, and don't require outdoor access. And a few years ago, the United Egg Producers trade organization introduced an animal welfare certification program in which participants could use the seal "Animal Care Certified" on their cartons, but seeing as the program did little more than justify the current cage and debeaking practices, this was ruled misleading by the Federal Trade Commission, sparking the creation of the essentially meaningless "United Egg Producers Certified" seal.

Again, **organic** eggs, which have become much easier to find in recent years, are the best option. Birds must have outdoor access, be fed largely on organic food and be kept in smaller flocks; routine antibiotics are banned, and physical alterations only performed to promote welfare, with a minimum of pain and stress.

As in several other areas of animal welfare currently unaddressed by US legislation, the EU has taken some initiative to improve conditions for laying hens, issuing a directive to replace the worst cages by 2012 with marginally more spacious "**enriched cages**," with a nest, perching space and scratching area. These developments are still a long way from ruling out cruel practices entirely, but they are at least a step in the right direction.

In the absence of such US regulation, much of the pressure upon the industry to adopt at least rudimentary guidelines for egg-laying hens is exerted by public interest groups. The Humane Society's No Battery Eggs campaign has scored some recent success on this front, influencing the large health food retail chains Whole Foods and Wild Oats (as well as the

Non-chicken poultry & eggs

Most poultry—including **turkey** and **duck**—are intensively farmed in a similar way to chicken, so look out for better alternatives, particularly organic ones. One exception is **geese**, which (so far at least) have not been able to survive the rigours of industrial farming, so are necessarily free-range. As for eggs, duck and geese eggs are generally not produced intensively, and so will mostly be from small-scale farms where animal welfare conditions are likely to be relatively high.

smaller regional health food chains Earth Fare and Jimbo's…Naturally) to implement "cage-free" policies, as well as helping convince the rapidly expanding health food-oriented chain Trader Joe's to convert its house-brand eggs to the cage-free variety. Shopping at these outlets for eggs is another option, then, though there are plenty of smaller-profile independent food stores carrying "cage-free" and organic eggs as well. The Humane Society also filed a federal lawsuit challenging the USDA's standards (and lack thereof) for fowl in general; for updates on their campaigns, check its website, www.hsus.org. (Throwing another wrench in the fight to gain more space for poultry, as this book went to press, mounting concerns over the spread of avian flu were leading to some speculation that farmers raising free-range birds might be pressured to limit the territory of their charges.)

Dairy products
It's a cow's life

Vegetarians sometimes take the moral high ground on issues of animal welfare. But those who eat and drink dairy products are possibly speaking too soon. The milk trade not only props up the **veal industry** (see p.112), but is also sometimes responsible for animal suffering itself. Dairy cows could easily live for two decades, but such is the strain put on them by modern breeding and milk production techniques that most are slaughtered before they're five years old—exhausted, ill and, in the harsh light of profit margins, economically inefficient.

Modern dairy cows have been **intensively bred** to yield the maximum quantities of milk. While a calf would naturally suckle a few liters a day from its mother, milking machines now extract up to fifty liters. The cows often have oversized udders, which according to animal-rights groups create spinal problems, lameness and other damage. A significant proportion of dairy cows also develop mastitis, a painful infection of the udder. Breeding (mainly through artificial insemination and embryo transfer) has been so intense in the last few decades that the cows have grown too big for older milking parlors.

As with beef farms, dairy farms range from "free-range" setups, where the cows spend most of their time eating grass in fields, and more intensive operations, where the herds are often kept inside for far more of the year than necessary, often in cramped and uncomfortable conditions. Besides the animal welfare issues, more intensive farms are also more ecologically problematic (for the reasons discussed on pp.102–107) and more likely to rely on preventative antibiotics.

And as for the calves …

To keep them milking, dairy cows are usually made to have calves each year, so for most of the year they're both pregnant and lactating. Newborn calves are taken from their mothers almost immediately—often within hours of birth—which is widely reported to cause great distress to both. Females wait in turn to replace their mothers, often spending their first few months in a cramped individual pen. Males are usually taken straight to the market to be sold for veal (see p.112) or are moved to intensive farms to be fattened up for low-quality beef.

Ethical dairy

The best way to guarantee your milk and cheese have been produced with a high standard of animal welfare, and have generated a minimum amount of pollution in the process, is to buy **organic**. In organic farms, cows get a better diet and living conditions, spend more time outside and have a lower incidence of lameness. Preventative antibiotics are banned. NOP standards, oddly, don't address a minimum weaning age, though it's five weeks in the otherwise less stringent Certified Humane and Free Farmed programs.

Organic dairy products are in no short supply. By 2000, in fact, about twice as much organic milk was sold through conventional grocery stores as through natural food supermarkets. But if you're having difficulty finding a specific organic dairy product, see the specialist directories listed on pp.156–164.

A program of note in the UK that as of yet has no US counterpart marks milk—organic or non-organic—**White & Wild**. This program aims to increase farmland wildlife and also give environmentally conscientious farmers a better deal. As intensive techniques have driven down the wholesale price of milk, many smaller, non-intensive farmers have been struggling to get a price for their milk that even covers the cost of production. The White & Wild program gives them a small premium in return for committing to conservation plans—designating a tenth of their farms to the sole aim of maintaining wildlife habitats. A premium also goes to The Wildlife Trusts. White & Wild's nonprofit company Tree Appeal includes tree planting as a major part of its environmental contribution, and as of this writing was looking for partner companies and expansion into the United States is part of its long-term plan. See:

White & Wild www.whiteandwild.co.uk

Fish & seafood
Plenty more in the sea?

The World Resources Institute estimates that fish consumption has risen by more than fivefold in the last half century. In some ways this is a positive thing: fish provide a very healthy and important protein source for hundreds of millions of people around the world, and—unlike livestock—they don't require vast areas of crop land for feed. However, the massive global increase in fish consumption, which shows no sign of slowing down, has been made possible by two developments—**industrial fishing** and intensive **fish farming**, or "aquaculture"—both of which have come with serious environmental, and in some cases social, costs. This section looks briefly at the issues surrounding caught and farmed fish, and then looks at the ethical options (see p.127).

Sea-caught fish: tuna, cod, swordfish et al.

As fishing vessels have grown from small wooden boats to giant factory ships, the world's waters have been reaped so heavily that the proverb "plenty more fish in the sea" is starting to look distinctly tenuous. By the time industrial fishing came of age in the early 1980s, the global catch in two years was equivalent to all the fish caught in the nineteenth century. And today, according to UN figures, a quarter of the world's fisheries are either **over-exploited or depleted**, while another half are being fished to maximum safe levels. The best-known example is **cod**—which in some areas have gone from being richly plentiful to basically extinct—but this certainly isn't the only species to have suffered.

People have long argued about the extent and implications of over-fishing, but a recent groundbreaking study published in *Nature* suggested that the problem may be far worse than was previously expected. By scrutinizing early fishing records, Canadian academics reached the staggering

"The one and only pure ocean machine, unflawed, navigating the waters of death," wrote Pablo Neruda about the bluefin tuna. But, like nearly all the great carnivores of the sea, its numbers have been decimated by high-tech fishing—both legal and illegal—and it's now critically endangered. Bluefin is most widely used in sushi, though it's also often served in steaks.

conclusion that in the last half century 90% of all large fish—including **halibut**, **marlin**, **swordfish**, **sharks** and **tuna**—have been wiped out. And those that are left are tiny compared with their relatively recent ancestors.

The implications could be far reaching, as over-fishing not only knocks out the target fish but also causes havoc in the wider food chain (partly indirectly, and partly because large numbers of non-target fish and other sea creatures are regularly also killed in the nets). If these trends continue, the effect could be a "complete re-organization of ocean ecosystems, with unknown global consequences," in the words of one of the *Nature* report's authors. And global warming may compound the problem, since changing sea temperatures are also starting to have an effect on marine eco-systems.

Currently, many of the most over-fished areas are around Europe and North America. Around the US, Pacific salmon, Gulf of Mexico red snapper, Gulf of Maine cod, and swordfish have been particularly hard hit. Congress has put ten national standards in place to protect the nation's fish populations and promote healthy ocean ecosystems, with one specifically addressing overfishing by requiring fishery councils to prevent fishermen from catching fish faster than they can replenish stocks, and to rebuild stocks that have been overfished. That's in danger of dilution, however, as in 2005 the Bush administration was heavily criticized by environmental groups for proposing regulations that would change how overfishing is calculated, as well as for one that would allow fish farms in federal waters up to 200 miles offshore, a drastic expansion from the current three-mile limit.

Europe has implemented a quota system to limit the damage and allow replenishment. But even if this is sufficient (which many experts doubt) and the rules are implemented properly (which so far they haven't been, according to the European Commission), other areas are feeling the pressure in the meantime. The EU, for example, has already purchased fishing rights from a number of African countries. This may provide short-term income for countries that definitely need it, but many predict that a lack of regulation will soon see stocks in these regions depleted, resulting in dwindling catches for local people who actually rely on fishing to survive.

By catch and sea-bed damage

Fishermen have always hauled in a certain amount of "by catch"—non-target fish and other marine life. But as fishing has become more industrial, the problem has become much more serious. The relationship between tuna fishing and dead **dolphins** is relatively common knowledge (see box overleaf), but the problem actually is much wider, with **turtles**, **sea birds**, **seals**, **whales** and **sharks** routinely getting caught, not to mention huge quantities of small fish, which are very often just thrown back dead. Driftnets, used to catch **tuna**, **swordfish**, **sardines**, **herring**, **albacore** and other species are one major culprit—despite recent legislation, these are

Tuna & dolphins

The various species of tuna sold in the US are all being very heavily fished, some—such as the giant **bluefin**, which is often used in sushi—near to the point of extinction. **Skipjack** and **yellowfin,** which dominate the canned market, are not in such a bad way, but their catching sometimes involves the killing of **dolphins**. The controversy relates primarily to yellowfin, which live in the Eastern Pacific and swim in large schools underneath groups of dolphins. Since around 1950 fishermen have exploited this relationship: find a group of the easily visible dolphins, surround them with large purse-seine nets, and pull in the tuna underneath, usually along with the dolphins, which are thrown back dead. This practice is thought to have killed many millions of dolphins, seriously damaging their numbers, which have not recovered since. **Driftnets** and other tuna-fishing techniques are also responsible for killing dolphins.

The issue came to the US public eye in the 1980s, resulting in a consumer boy-cott, improved fishing techniques, tighter regulations (in some countries) and the "**Dolphin Safe**" label from the Earth Island Institute (www.earthisland.org). All this has made an enormous difference and, though dolphins continue to die in tuna nets, only a small amount of the tuna on the US market now comes from so-called dolphin-deadly fisheries, mostly from Mexico. All major US tuna companies adopted the Dolphin Safe label in the early 1990s, and in 1994 the entire US tuna fleet became Dolphin Safe. The government, however, has in recent years tried to weaken the label. In the eyes of some environmental groups safeguarding the standard, this relaxing of rules is being done principally to appease our Mexican trading partners rather than because dolphins have become inherently "safer."

Still, the issues aren't quite cut and dried, because some tuna-fishing methods that avoid dolphins altogether—attracting them with floating logs or using baited hooks hanging off mile-long floating lines—can be problematic in other ways. They may be better for dolphins but worse for **sharks, turtles** and **non-target fish,** and they may risk damaging tuna stocks by snaring younger fish that haven't yet reproduced. Further, some claim that the inspection system is very weak and the tuna supply chain so convoluted that it's almost impossible to know where your fish has actually come from.

While tuna has got most of the attention, other species such as sea bass and sword-fish are also widely associated with dolphin deaths.

often many miles long and have earned the nickname "walls of death" for good reason. But **bottom trawling,** which entails dragging a fine net over the sea bed, can be even worse. This technique—widely used for shrimp, scallops, plaice, clam, snapper and other species—can result both in incomparably more by catch than target, and can also cause serious dam-age to the sea bed. In biologically diverse underwater "seamounts," *New Scientist* recently reported, trawling is wiping out scores of species before they can even be identified.

Farmed fish: salmon, plaice, trout et al.

With the seas suffering from depleted stocks, fish farming seems like the obvious solution. And, indeed, an increasing proportion of our fish is reared in farms—around a third of the global total—making aquaculture the **fastest growing of all food sectors**. For years the lochs of Scotland and the fjords of Norway have been gradually filling up with the **salmon** industry's giant plastic nets, with farms accounting for nearly 100% of the Scotch salmon for sale. **Trout** is also widely farmed and, with stock numbers low and financial potential high, the farming of **cod, sea bass** and **bream** is also on the rise. Fish farming in the US is currently limited to areas within three miles of our shoes, and dominated by freshwater fish like catfish, as well as some ocean farms raising mussels, clams, oysters, shrimp and salmon. That could change, though, if a bill initiated by the Bush administration allowing fish farming up to 200 miles off the coast passes. We're already consuming a lot of farmed fish, however, as the US imports 70% of the seafood it consumes, with 40% of that number coming from overseas fish farms.

Farms certainly get around the problem of bycatch and satisfy consumer demand for cheap fish, but instead of alleviating the over-exploitation of the sea they very often actually exacerbate it. After all, to farm carnivorous fish like salmon, cod and haddock, you need to catch a huge quantity of smaller fish to feed them. For each pound of salmon you buy in a shop, for example, up to five pounds of fish will have been caught—sometimes on the other side of the world—transported and turned into fish food. By the end of this decade, some estimate, around 90% of the world's fish oil will be used to make aquaculture feed.

And the problems of fish farming can go beyond this wastefulness: green and anti-poverty groups claim the farms can also be problematic in terms of **pollution, animal welfare** and—in the case of tropical shrimp (see box overleaf)—**human rights**.

Environmental impacts

Probably the most pressing of the accusations made against intensive fish farms is the environmental impact. Millions of fish churn out a lot of **mineral-rich feces.** Scottish salmon, for example, excrete twice as much phosphorus as the country's human population according to the World Wildlife Fund.

This goes straight into the surrounding waters, suffocating sea-bed life and possibly creating the **toxic algal blooms** that have left much

Shrimp: no small issue

Shrimp fall into two categories. There are the small cold-water ones frequently used in sandwiches, and the larger tropical ones—also known as "tiger" or "king" shrimp—which have become favorites in restaurants and supermarkets in the last decade or so. According to many environmental and anti-poverty groups, tiger shrimp are about as unethical a crustacean as you can consume, their cultivation involving the very worst practices of both farmed and caught seafood, linked to terrible abuses of people and the environment.

The majority of tigers have been intensively farmed in developing countries such as **Bangladesh, Thailand, Ecuador** and **Honduras**. Tropical shrimp farming has a long history as a sustainable aquaculture, but the large-scale modern methods—if campaign groups are to be believed—are an example of destructive and short-term food production at its worst. According to critics such as Christian Aid and the Environmental Justice Foundation, the shrimp farms' man-made pools drain local water sources, requiring an estimated 6000 gallons of water for each pound of shrimp produced, and become a major source of pollution. **Salt** is added to the water in large quantities, as well as fishmeal food, antibiotics to limit the risks of overcrowding, growth stimulants to make the process faster, and lime to regulate the acidity. This saline cocktail inevitably filters back into nearby **agricultural land**, rendering it unproductive, and pollutes local drinking water sources.

Nearby fishing areas also get hit, both by direct pollution and by aggressive industrial fishing for potential shrimp-feed: like salmon, shrimp consume far more food than they produce. And, furthermore, the farms are responsible for massive destruction of **mangrove swamps**, which are essential to tropical coastal ecosystems. Amazingly, around 25% of the mangrove forest lost each year is due to shrimp farming, according to the Marine Stewardship Council.

In many cases the ponds end up so toxic or virus-ridden that they have simply to be abandoned, the companies that own them moving on to new locations and leaving local people with impure water, a damaged ability to feed themselves and few, if any, real benefits. There have even been numerous reports of people being **violently displaced** from prospective pond sites, as well as murder and rape in some extreme cases. However, despite all these problems, intensive shrimp farming makes quick and serious money—at least for some people. For this reason, the World Bank and other international agencies have encouraged the growth of the industry, and it is increasingly popping up around the coasts of Africa and South America.

Not all tiger shrimp are farmed: others are **sea-caught**. But these aren't necessarily any better, since shrimp trawlers are associated with as much environmental destruction as the farms. The technique used—dragging a fine net over the sea-bed—is as effective as it is unselective. As well as seriously damaging the sea-bed itself, the nets bring in, by weight, as much as **twenty times more by catch than shrimp**, endangering turtle and other sea life and diminishing the catch of subsistence fishermen. According to the Environmental Justice Foundation, shrimp trawling accounts for a third of the world's bycatch but produces only a fiftieth of its seafood.

For more information on the tiger shrimp issue, see:

Christian Aid www.christian-aid.org.uk
Environmental Justice Foundation www.ejfoundation.org

of Scotland closed to shellfishing. Besides minerals, the waste—not to mention the fish—also contains a cocktail of **antibiotics**, uneaten food and dyes (farmed salmon would be gray, not pink, if dye wasn't added). Various illegal chemicals and hormones, banned for their environmental and health impact, have also often shown up in spot checks.

Another potential affect of fish farms is a reduction in **wild stocks** nearby. Sometimes this happens through the inevitable spreading of the diseases and lice that thrive in intensive farms, but there may also be a more sinister mechanism at play. Farmed salmon, for example, regularly escape in huge numbers (the WWF estimates that 630,000 salmon escaped from Norwegian farms in 2002 alone) and if these fish, not adapted for life in the natural world, breed with wild salmon, a kind of **negative evolution** takes place, with wild fish becoming less and less able to cope with their natural conditions.

Finally there are the issues of animal welfare. Few people find it easy to empathize with fish, but keeping creatures that are naturally migratory and/or solitary in incredibly cramped spaces with 50,000 others is surely beyond the pale. And so are practices such as allowing fish to suffocate as a way of killing them, and stocking them in such high density that their fins are regularly damaged—two things reported to be common practice on trout farms.

Ethical fish

The problems described above are serious, but they don't necessarily mean that we should stop eating fish and seafood. There are various measures you can take to minimize the negative impacts of what you buy. One option is to look out for the **Marine Stewardship Council logo** (see box on p.128). However, as yet supplies aren't huge and the range is small—a good sign for the integrity of the program, perhaps, but not great for the shopper.

Another option is to **be picky** about which types of fish and seafood you choose. The quandaries of tropical shrimp, farmed salmon and sea-caught cod have

MSC-certified New Zealand Hoki

The Marine Stewardship Council

Any seafood bearing this blue tick/fish label has been caught according to sustainable criteria set out by the UK-based **Marine Stewardship Council** (MSC). Initially set up by Unilever (the world's largest seafood buyer) and the WWF, but now an independent organization, the MSC both promotes a responsible approach to fishing and monitors practices. To be awarded the mark, fisheries need to be able to demonstrate their commitment to:

▶ The maintenance and re-establishment of **healthy populations** of targeted species, and the integrity of ecosystems.

▶ **Effective management systems**, considering biological, technological, economic, social, environmental and commercial aspects.

▶ Following relevant local, national and international **laws, standards, understandings and agreements**.

A small but growing number of fisheries are now accredited and stocked in a few US supermarkets, health food chains, and on-line retail sites, including **Alaskan salmon**, **New Zealand hoki**, and **Western Australian rock lobster** (pictured). For more information, including where to buy, visit: www.msc.org

already been discussed, but there are many other species endangered by over-fishing or caught in destructive ways, and others still which are relatively unproblematic. For an in-depth view, get *The Good Fish Guide*, a book by Bernadette Clarke of the Marine Conservational Society. You can order it directly from their FishOnline site (www.fishonline.org), but a taster is provided opposite in the form of the Society's top species for consumers to avoid or eat with a clear conscience. Also, as a rule, try to avoid young, undersized fish, as catching these can exacerbate pressure on stocks.

Do eat...

Alaska or walleye pollock

Bib or pouting (line-caught)

Black bream or porgy or seabream (line-caught)

Clams (sustainably harvested)

Cockle (MSC certified or sustainably harvested)

Coley or saithe (from North Sea)

Common dolphinfish (line-caught)

Cuttlefish (trap-caught)

Dab (line-caught or seine netted)

Dover sole (from Eastern channel)

Dublin Bay prawn (MSC certified or pot- or creel-caught)

Flounder

Grey gurnard

Herring or sild (MSC certified or line-caught from North Sea)

Hoki (MSC certified)

King scallop (sustainably harvested)

Lythe or pollack (line-caught)

Mackerel (MSC certified or line-caught)

Mussels (sustainably harvested)

Oysters (farmed Native & Pacific)

Pacific halibut (line-caught)

Pacific salmon (MSC certified)

Red gurnard

Red mullet

Salmon (from organic or Freedom Food-certified farms)

Spider crab

Sprat (from the North Sea, dolphin-friendly)

Whiting (from the English Channel)

Winkle (sustainably harvested)

Witch (line-caught)

Don't eat...

Alfonsinos or golden eye perch

American plaice

Silver smelt (Argentine or greater)

Cod (except from Iceland)

Atlantic halibut

Atlantic salmon (wild-caught)

Blue ling

Chilean seabass or Patagonian toothfish

Dogfish (inc. catshark, nursehound)

European Hake

Greater forkbeard

Grouper

Haddock (except from North Sea, West of Scotland, Skaggerak, Kattegat and Iceland)

Ling

Marlin (blue, Indo-Pacific & white)

Monkfish

Orange roughy

Plaice (except from Irish Sea)

Rat or rabbit fish

Red or blackspot seabream

Redfish or ocean perch

Roundnose grenadier

Seabass (trawl-caught only)

Shark

Skates & rays

Snapper

Sturgeon

Swordfish

Tiger shrimp (except organic)

Tuna (except dolphin-friendly, pole- and line-caught yellowfin and skipjack)

Tusk

Wolfish

Buying **organic** fish in the US is not just a tricky business, but nearly impossible if you're a stickler for official standards. While the demand is growing here for organic fish (as it is for all organic products), as of this writing there are no organic standards in this country for seafood. A few shrimp farms in Florida have received USDA organic certification using livestock rules—and even that decision has been challenged. Until the USDA develops standards for organic fish (which it's been given authority for and has assembled a task force to do, under pressure from Alaskan legislators), the only option is to buy seafood that's been certified organic in Europe and other countries. But standards in those countries can vary, and even the senior scientist for Environmental Defense, Becky Goldburg, has expressed concern that imported fish may have been fed on diets relatively high in contaminants, like PCBs and dioxin. "The upshot is," she told National Public Radio's environmental program *Living on Earth* in 2005, "that when consumers in this country buy seafood that is labeled organic in a grocery store, they really don't know what they are getting."

Fruit & vegetables
What to buy, where to buy

The ethical considerations involved in buying fruit and vegetables relate to many of the issues discussed at the beginning of this chapter and the first section of this book. First, there's the effect of the growing techniques on the **environment**—everything from the impact on wildlife of pesticides running off into streams, to soil erosion caused by over-industrial techniques. There's also the environmental question of **food miles** (see p.87): can it ever be ethically sound to buy fruit and vegetables from the other side of the world when equivalent products are available from local sources? As already discussed, our fresh produce is traveling farther than ever, and the fuel used in food transport is an ever-growing source of the greenhouse gases that are already thought to be killing tens of thousands people every year (see p.14).

Another consideration is whether the workers are receiving decent **pay and conditions.** Are they being subjected to exploitative terms, denied union bargaining power or being exposed to dangerous agrochemicals and other risks? The "sweatshop" issues of inhumanly long hours and other types of labor abuse are just as common, if not more so, in the agricultural sector.

The most shocking labor abuse in the fruit and vegetable sector has occurred in the developing world, such as on the **banana plantations** of Central and South America (see overleaf). However, **migrant workers**

Pesticide residues

With thousands of farm workers killed every year by poisoning, and wildlife and the environment suffering in numerous ways, pesticides unequivocally pose certain threats to people and planet. But what about the residues on our fruit and vegetables? Green campaigners link pesticide residues to skin and eye irritation, mental and nervous problems, breast cancer and other conditions, and point out that little is known about the long-term effects of many of these substances (some of which are hormone disrupters), especially their combined "cocktail effect."

But most toxicologists seem less convinced that the quantities in question are big enough to be a worry. A 2003 FDA study tested more than 2000 fruit and vegetable samples and found that while around 60% were residue-free, about 2% contained "violative residues" (pesticide residues that don't meet EPA regulations), with the remaining 38% or so falling somewhere in between. Environmentalists were up in arms about the 2%, yet the testers concluded that "results in this and earlier reports continue to demonstrate that levels of pesticide residues in the US food supply are well below established safety standards." Still, those who are concerned about pesticide residues—especially people who don't feel that they can justify the expense of buying organic for all their fresh produce—may be interested to know which produce tends to contain higher residues than others. The following lists of fruit and vegetables at the top and bottom of the pesticide residue scales were prepared by the US Environmental Working Group. They relate specifically to the levels of residues found in food as typically prepared for consumption—*not the amount used during growing*. So the banana, for example, because of its thick, inedible skin, lands on the low-residues list despite being associated with massive pesticide use and worker exploitation. These lists, then, are not equivalent to the "most ethical" fruit and vegetables.

Highest levels

▶ Apple ▶ Cherry ▶ Peach ▶ Raspberry
▶ Bell Pepper ▶ Grapes ▶ Pear ▶ Spinach
▶ Celery ▶ Nectarines ▶ Potato ▶ Strawberry

Lowest levels

▶ Asparagus ▶ Broccoli ▶ Kiwi ▶ Papaya
▶ Avocado ▶ Cauliflower ▶ Mango ▶ Pea
▶ Banana ▶ Sweet corn ▶ Onion ▶ Pineapple

For more information, and methodology, see www.foodnews.org. Or to read more about the pesticide issue, see:

Pesticide Action Network www.panna.org

from Mexico and Central America—many of them children—often endure harsh conditions within the US, including substandard housing, failure to get paid after being lured over the border with false promises, and even getting charged fees for social security cards. In 2005, a few such laborers filed a complaint with the Mexican government contending they were denied rights guaranteed to them by the North American Trade Agreement, though

Bananas: globalization in a slippery skin

The world's most widely consumed fruit provides a perfect illustration of many of the most pressing and heated debates about world trade and intensive farming. There are hundreds of varieties of banana grown around the world, most of them in India and other countries where they are cultivated for domestic consumption. But the export market, almost entirely driven by the US and Europe, is largely dominated by just one variety and a handful of giant companies. Roughly 60% of banana exports are controlled by just three multinationals—**Chiquita, Dole Food** and **Del Monte**—which produce primarily in Central and South America, the world of the so-called dollar banana.

Banana farming has always been a big-business sector. It was once dominated by the **United Fruit Company**, which controlled much of Central America and was instrumental in bringing about the 1954 CIA-orchestrated coup in Guatemala, which overthrew the country's elected government and led to half a century of conflict and bloodshed. Today, the big banana firms don't stand accused of starting "real" wars, but they were behind the trade war which saw the US, Ecuador and various South American countries battling with the EU at the World Trade Organization in the late 1990s. The point in question was the legality of EU's banana import policy, which to a certain extent shunned "dollar bananas" in favor of those grown in ex-European colonies in the so-called **ACP** (African, Caribbean and Pacific) countries.

Pro-free-trade commentators claimed that Ecuador and other poor dollar-banana countries were suffering due to their restricted access to European markets. But the EU claimed that small ACP family farms—and in some cases whole countries' economies—would be unable to survive without preferential treatment, so the human consequences of leaving everything to the free market would be huge. Anti-globalization protesters agreed, describing the situation as a classic case of big companies trying to use global trade rules to profit from a "race to the bottom." They pointed out that the Latin American producers were only able to undercut small farmers in the ACP countries because their plantations depended on terrible exploitation of workers and the environment.

It's certainly true that the big banana producers have long been dogged by allegations about their lack of ethical standards. First, there's the question of wages—in the dollar-banana plantations, the workers who actually grow the bananas receive only 1–3% of the final price, or, put another way, as little as a dollar a day, in return for twelve or more hours of hard labour (according to figures from the Fairtrade Foundation). But it seems unlikely either the US or Mexico will clamp down hard on such practices in the near future. And labor abuses in the Western World aren't limited to the US, as a number of recent exposés, such as those in Felicity Lawrence's book, *Not On The Label*, have shown that many European farms rely on temporary, non-resident workers subcontracted through "gangmasters" and paid sub-minimum-wage rates.

that's only one issue. Child labor has been shown to be widespread, as has the **intimidation, firing** or even **murder** of would-be union organizers. And health and safety has often been seriously compromised by the use of **agrochemicals**.

Required in vast quantities due to the single-crop nature of the plantations, fungicides and other pesticides are often sprayed from planes, and though there are theoretically rules to ensure that workers are not put in danger, these have not always been observed. As well as directly breathing in the chemicals, the workers, many of whom live on or next to the plantations, have often ended up drinking and bathing in contaminated water, with sometimes catastrophic results. In the last few decades thousand of workers have died, been made seriously ill or given birth to deformed babies. According to a Fairtrade Foundation report from 2000, "some 20% of the male banana workers in Costa Rica were left sterile after handling toxic chemicals," while women working in the pack houses had twice the normal incidence of leukemia. The ecological damage of the big plantations has also been severe, including soil degradation, lost biodiversity, toxic run-off and forest clearance. None of this was deemed relevant to the WTO case, however, since international trade rules don't currently take social and environmental issues into account.

Partly as a result of the "banana wars"—which the EU eventually lost—two things happened. The first was the extension of the **Fair Trade labelng program** to bananas. Sourced from small-producer cooperatives in the ACP countries, Fair Trade bananas provide all the standard ethical guarantees of the Fair Trade label (see p.21), including improved health and safety and a higher proportion of the price going to the farmers.

The second was that the big banana firms started trying to redefine themselves as "socially responsible" companies, publishing codes of conduct relating to health and safety, pesticide use and union representation. Chiquita even launched a partnership with the Rainforest Alliance and signed an agreement with the International Union of Foodworkers to respect worker rights. As with all such big-business initiatives, however, the degree to which these aims are benefiting the workers on the ground is an open, and much-debated, question. For more on the banana trade, see:

Banana Link www.bananalink.org.uk
US/Labor Education in the Americas Project www.usleap.org

Then there's the question of where we should buy our fruit and vegetables. The **supermarkets** (see p.152), which have become the unrivalled superpowers of the fresh-produce supply chain, are regularly accused of using their size to squeeze suppliers—both at home and abroad—so hard that it becomes almost impossible for them to stick to any serious labor and environmental standards. In the case of fruit and vegetables, they are also resented for causing so much waste, and increased agrochemical use, by refusing to accept anything that doesn't fulfill their infamously strict specifications of size, shape and color. The degree of conformity required—with carrot length, for example, specified in millimeters—would be entertaining were it not so disturbing.

Another matter that often crops up in discussions about the ethics of the fruit and vegetable industry is the dwindling number of varieties on offer. Though we're now offered kiwis and guava at every turn, green commentators often lament the loss—some permanently—of the literally thousands of varieties of apples, potatoes, squashes and other produce which once flourished in the US and around the world. As Andrew Kimbrell wrote in *The Ecologist,* "monoculture industrial agriculture not only limits what we can eat today, it also reduces the choices of future generations ... the UN Food and Agriculture Organization (FAO) estimates that more than three quarters of agricultural genetic diversity was lost in this past century." Again, the blame for this is usually jointly pinned onto industrial farming and the supermarkets, which farmers and the green movement accuse of favoring shelf life and profit margins over and above everything else.

Ethical fruit & vegetables

For all the above reasons, the most common ethical advice is, first, to favor **organic** produce, which offers a range of environmental benefits (see p.76). And, second, to avoid supermarkets and use **seasonal**, **locally produced** fruit and vegetables from alternative outlets such as **health food stores** and **farmers' markets**—for more on these, see pp.156–160.

Fair Trade fresh fruit

The success of the Fair Trade banana has led to an ever-growing range of Fair Trade fruit. Like all products bearing the Fair Trade label, these are sourced from the developing world, according to rules which guarantee that the producers receive a higher proportion of the price we pay for their

Sorting mangoes in a Fair Trade-certified plantation in Chacras, Ecuador.

crops, a premium for social and environmental improvement, advance payment opportunities, and reliable long-term trading relationships. For more on how the Fair Trade program works, see p.20.

At the time of going to press, the Fair Trade range includes grapes, mangoes and pineapples. But each item is only available from certain supermarkets and some independents (see overleaf), according to **seasonal availability**.

As of this writing, 27 of the 50 states had stores carrying Fair Trade Certified fruit, mostly through health food stores and food co-ops, though a few supermarkets were participating. Even within this spectrum, the geographic dispersion of these outlets was uneven: few stores in Illinois, Southern California, the Northwest, and most of the southern states were involved, for instance, and none were in Florida. Yet at the same time, there were quite a few throughout the Northeast and Northern California. The Wild Oats national health food chain was carrying Fair Trade bananas in all of its stores (except in Florida), and one supermarket chain (Andronico's) was carrying Fair Trade fruit in all its California stores, but the big retailers have yet to jump aboard in appreciable numbers. In part it's because the program's still quite young, fruit only having been introduced into TransFair USA's certification program in early 2004.

But for the time being, you'll need to go online to check for the Fair Trade fruit carrier nearest you, or to verify whether there's even one in your locality at all. For the most up-to-date list of products and retailers, see:

TransFair USA www.transfairusa.org

Fair Trade vs. local

The first Fair Trade fruits were bananas and pineapples originating in the tropics. But as the range expands to include products that can also be grown more widely at home, a slight tension may emerge between the fair trade movement, on the one hand, and environmentalists, "localists" and US farmers on the other. Such a situation arose in the UK, where the range of Fair Trade fruit also includes lemons, ranges, pears, plums, green beans and peppers, with South African apples added to the list in 2003. Surely it's crazy, farmers argue, regardless of the good intentions, to fly in apples from the Southern Hemisphere when the bumper crops from Britain's own famously good orchards are rotting in the fields, their owners unable to match the price of imports. As well as the significant environmental costs of flying or shipping the goods 10,000 miles, they argue, imports are leading to poverty and depression at home, where orchards—and ways of life—are being abandoned every week.

On the other hand, the apples from South Africa not only support the poor (and grinding poverty is undoubtedly a more pressing issue in Southern Africa than it is in the UK), but also support a number of positive initiatives and "empowerment projects" including creating opportunities for landless workers to "become co-owners of fruit farms," a scheme recently praised by Nelson Mandela among others. Once again, there's no obvious answer for the ethically minded shopper; a similar choice sometimes has to be made between organic and Fair Trade foods, and organic and local foods.

Fair Trade & organic

Just as organic food (particularly if it's imported from the third world) doesn't necessarily meet Fair Trade standards, neither is all or even most food labeled Fair Trade organic. Less than half of Fair Trade products are certified organic, and the newly-founded **Organic Farmers & Gardeners Union** has made uniting the two concepts one of its goals. They should go hand-in-hand, OFGU contends, not only because both programs emphasize sustainable agricultural and economic development, but also use similar inspection criteria and could save labor by working together. **OFGU** was founded with the help of the **Organic Consumers Organization**, which in turn is involved in campaigns to support and spread fair trade in the US and other countries.

It's not high on the agenda of most activists, but there's a case to be made that at least some organic foods produced within the US could benefit from the Fair Trade label, as growers frequently struggle to cover the cost of production even in comparatively wealthy countries. For a brief while it looked as if the Fair Trade program was going to start being applied within the UK to certain British-grown organic foods. Eventually, the idea was dropped, because Fair Trade consumers tended to believe the program should prioritize the extreme poverty of the developing world.

Organic Farmers & Gardeners Union www.organicconsumers.org/ofgu

Coffee & tea
... and other Fair Trade products

Coffee

The ethics of the coffee trade are perhaps more widely discussed than those of any other sector. And it's not hard to understand why. First, there's the sheer scale of the industry. Literally billions of cups of coffee are consumed around the world every day, a colossal demand that has made coffee, in terms of total value, the **most traded commodity in the world after oil and illegal drugs**. The US is the largest consumer of the product, consuming one-fifth of it. It's thought that around 100 million people work in the coffee trade—more than half the entire working population of the US—including more than 20 million farmers, the vast majority of whom are small-scale growers with less than 10 acres of land.

The second reason we hear so much about coffee is that the world is in the midst of a so-called **coffee crisis**, with the prices received by farmers having dropped to their lowest levels in decades. Coffee farmers

Growing coffee

The coffee "tree" is an evergreen tropical shrub that only flourishes within a couple of thousand miles of the Equator. Especially in the case of the high-quality **Arabica** species—as opposed to the **Robusta** or **Liberica** used for lower quality and instant coffees—it's an incredibly high-maintenance crop. After an initial four or five years bearing no fruit, each bush produces a few thousand "beans" (actually the seeds of the cherry-like fruit)—enough for only around two pounds of roasted coffee. The plants require constant attention, and the cherries usually have to be picked by hand, as they ripen at different times. Much highland coffee is grown on slopes so steep and remote that horses or mules, let alone motor vehicles, cannot be used.

have never been a wealthy bunch. For reasons ranging from their lack of capital to Western trade rules that slap huge import tariffs on processed goods, the vast majority of the profits from each jar of coffee we buy goes to the retailers and packagers—with the farmers receiving as little as two percent.

But as farm-gate prices have plummeted, millions have been pushed into desperate poverty. This has resulted in massive suffering in many areas, and has been especially catastrophic in countries such as Ethiopia and Burundi, where coffee is central to the wider economy. As wages have dropped many farmers have had to take their children out of school, forego medical treatment or accumulate unpayable debt just to maintain their daily existence. Others have abandoned coffee growing completely, in some cases finding themselves with no viable option but to turn to the production of illegal crops such as **coca** and **marijuana**. In some countries, such as Nicaragua, thousands of children are **starving** as a result of the crisis, according to the United Nations World Food Program.

The coffee crisis—what happened?

The main cause of the price crisis faced by millions of coffee growers is massive **oversupply**: there's simply far more coffee being produced than consumers want to drink. On and off until 1989, coffee production and prices were regulated by quotas set by the **International Coffee Organization**—a group of producer and consumer countries that aimed to keep supply and demand in line with each other.

However, at the end of the 1980s, disagreement between producer and consumer countries, and a prevailing economic ethos of trade liberalization, led to the dismantling of the quota system. Production patterns soon started to change, with **Vietnam**—following advice from the World Bank—investing heavily in the coffee sector and becoming a major new supplier. Vietnam certainly needed the income and jobs, but its emergence as a major player in the coffee market, along with other factors such as new processing technologies that allowed lower quality beans to be substantially improved, soon led to a massive rise in the production of useable coffee. As the basic laws of supply and demand dictate, this was accompanied by a concurrent drop in the price that farmers could get for their crops.

The crisis soon spiralled into a vicious circle. Since many coffee farmers lack the experience, circumstances or capital to produce other crops, many have tried to deal with the price drop by working as hard as possible to produce even more coffee. But this, of course, only helps to build up the stockpiles and drive prices down even further.

The shifting dynamics of the coffee industry are also having **environmental impacts**, with traditional "shaded coffee" grown under a native tree canopy, giving way to "sun coffee." Sun coffee yields more coffee more quickly, but the bushes last for only 10–15 years, as opposed to the 50 years of a shaded bush. They typically also require far more fertilizers and pesticides, which, combined with the forest clearance required to plant the bushes, hugely endangers the delicate ecological balances of highland tropical areas. According to groups such as Conservation International (www.conservation.org), these farming methods are threatening whole ecosystems, from Latin America to Indonesia.

The coffee giants

Even greater than the supermarkets' stranglehold over food retail is the domination of the coffee market by a handful of giant roasters and packagers: **Nestlé** (producers of Nescafé), **Kraft** (owned by tobacco giant Philip Morris and behind Maxwell House), **Sara Lee Corp** (who own Douwe Egberts) and **Procter & Gamble** (the biggest manufacturer of household products in the US).

Since these firms make their money buying, processing and reselling coffee, the drop in farm-gate prices has been to their advantage. Hence Nestlé's Annual Management Report for 2000, in explaining their good profits for that year, pointed to "favorable commodity prices"—business terminology that obscures the people behind the product. The idea of giant companies getting richer while farmers suffer—and in some cases literally starve—has led to a huge amount of resentment.

Starbucks and other cafés: an ethicino?

Some independent cafés have been offering Fair Trade coffee for years, but recently the trend has been boosted—ironically enough—by the kind of chain cafés which have themselves often been the target of campaigner anger. **Dunkin Donuts**, **Borders, Bruegger's Bagel** and **Tully's** all have it available, as does **Starbucks**, which by 2003 ran 20% of the retail outlets in the US where Fair Trade coffee was sold.

While Starbucks started selling it in the whole-bean form in 2000, getting the java to sip on its premises isn't as straightforward. It's usually only billed as available on special days, and though it's the company's policy to brew Fair Trade coffee at a customer's request, many patrons (and, according to some complaints, some Starbucks staff) aren't aware of this provision. It also hasn't been promoted as its brewed "Coffee of the Day," and while that might seem like a small sticking point, campaigners argue it's the only way to ensure real volume for Fair Trade farmers.

For these kinds of reasons, the Organic Consumers Association has accused Starbucks of making only a token gesture, pointing out that only a tiny fraction of the company's coffees were Fair Trade, but, more recently, the company has been praised by none other than Oxfam, which wrote, "It is a welcome relief ... to see Starbucks taking a lead amongst the major coffee companies in addressing the crisis in the coffee market ... it is paying its suppliers around double the open market price and it has independent checks done to see that it carries out its own purchasing guidelines."

This leaves ethical consumers with yet another conundrum. The company's coffee buying policies are clearly progressive, but writers such as Naomi Klein have criticized Starbucks' aggressive expansion policies (forcing out local cafés), its questionable employment practices (keeping employees as temporary workers to avoid benefit and pension obligations), and its contribution to the homogenization of shopping districts globally (with everything from the design to the music prescribed by the Seattle HQ).

Similarly, **McDonald's** recently introduced Fair Trade coffee into about 650 restaurants in New England and New York State, though many socially conscious consumers make McDonald's itself a no-go area.

One option, of course, is to ask your local independent cafés to start serving Fair Trade. An alternative model for socially conscious enterpreneurs to consider is the UK cafe chain **Progreso**—set up, and jointly owned by, two Honduran coffee cooperatives, Oxfam and the UK's leading independent coffee roaster. Though as of this writing they have just two outlets (both in London), the plan is to open twenty  branches over the next few years, targeting "bohemian urban villages" in London, Southeast England and Central Scotland. For more information, see:

Progreso www.progreso.org.uk

Of course, the big coffee firms are only doing what companies always do: buying their raw products from the cheapest seller with the aim of maximizing shareholder value. And it's true that they can't really be blamed for the oversupply. But campaigners have long accused the Big Four of failing even to acknowledge the extent of the problem.

In the last couple of years, there have been some positive developments, with three of the big four launching at least one coffee made from Fair Trade beans—Nestlé in the UK and Kraft and P&G in the US. In the case of Nestlé, this raised plenty of eyebrows, since the company is still the target of a boycott over its alleged marketing of breast-milk substitutes (see p.148).

Fair Trade coffee

Like all products marked bearing the label, Fair Trade coffee is sourced directly from the grower according to ethical trading principles. This gives the farmers a number of advantages (see p.20 for more details), but probably the most important in this case is a **minimum price guarantee**. No matter what happens on the commodity markets, the Fair Trade coffee price will never go lower than a certain level. At the time of writing, for example, despite the fact that Fair Trade coffee is only marginally more expensive than the conventionally traded equivalent, the price received by coffee farmers under the Fair Trade program is three times the international price for robustas and double the international price for arabicas.

Despite the clear benefits of Fair Trade coffee, the organizers of the program are well aware that, on its own, it doesn't provide a long-term answer to the problems caused by coffee oversupply. Other than every consumer increasing their caffeine intake, a structural solution would have to involve drastic measures such as destroying the coffee stockpiles and returning to a quota system. Since this seems relatively unlikely to happen, some right-wing commentators have taken the rather extreme attitude that Fair Trade may be more of a hindrance than a blessing (dragging the problem out and giving "conventional" coffee a bad name) and that the problem would be better left to the free market. For more on this debate, see pp.28–29.

Fair Trade coffees are very widely available in supermarkets and health-food shops—and via the Net. The selection includes instants, beans and ground ranging from End the Embargo on Cuba Dark Roast (grown by cooperatives in Nicaragua, Mexico and Guatemala) and Peruvian Organicto Sumatra Mandheling and Italian-style espresso blend.

For a full list of Fair Trade coffee brands, and where to buy them, try:

TransfairUSA www.transfairusa.org/do/wheretobuy

And for background info about the coffee trade and crisis, visit:

ICP www.ico.org
Oxfam www.maketradefair.com

There's also coffee that has been certified as "shade grown," such as the **Bird Friendly** variety; the Rainforest Alliance also certifies shade grown coffee, as well as bananas, citrus and cocoa. This doesn't go far enough for many Fair Trade champions, however, who point out that these only require a local minimum wage, which might not be enforced or meet living costs. In addition, the programs mostly focus upon larger farms, not the smaller family-run ones that Fair Trade hopes to benefit.

Tea

Whereas coffee is grown mainly by small-scale independent farmers, tea is primarily a **plantation** crop. There are some small tea producers, but the sector is dominated by large estates, many of which include a factory in which the teas are processed and packed. As such, the most pressing issues are those of **workers' rights**—pay, hours, conditions, etc. As with many areas, unions are often discouraged, or disallowed, on tea plantations, leaving the pickers and packers, most of them women, with little bargaining power to demand better conditions. Health and safety is also important, especially the issue of pesticides, which are widely use on (non-organic) tea plantations, in some cases leading to health problems among the workers.

Fair Trade & organic tea

Tea bearing the Fair Trade Certified label (see p.23) ensures decent minimum standards of pay, conditions and labor rights for tea workers. Its strictures also include some environmental policies, but tea that is both organic *and* Fair Trade ensures even stricter standards.

In the last few years, the range of Fair Trade teas has grown enormously, so even connoisseurs and fans of obscure flavors are likely to find something to their taste. As of this writing, more than 50 US brands (and

Fairly traded foods & drinks without the label

It's common to see foods which don't bear the Fair Trade label, but which—according to the packaging or retailer—have been fairly traded. While some such goods may indeed have been produced according to similar standards as those used by the Fair Trade program, they don't offer any official guarantees, and arguably serve to harm the credibility of the Fair Trade system. In such cases, leading Free Trade advocate Global Exchange advises contacting the companies to ask about their purchasing guidelines, though again there's no official body that can certify their claims.

more than a dozen importers) throughout the US were licensed to offer Fair Trade certified tea. Most of them have on-line sites through which it can be purchased, though they're usually widely available at health food stores and (to a lesser degree) supermarkets. For a full list and where to buy them, go to the same TransfairUSA page listing coffee sources: www.transfairusa.org/do/wheretobuy

Other Fair Trade foods & drinks

Though the Fair Trade Mark is primarily associated with coffee and tea, it can be found on a much wider range of products. In addition to fruit, coffee and tea, TransFair USA has also introduced **cocoa** and, more recently, **rice** and **sugar** to the US market. If the US fair trade movement follows trends in other countries where the concept is more familiar and established, that line could soon expand; in the UK, for instance, fruit juice, honey, wines and beers, muesli, and a variety of preserves, condiments, and snacks are also labeled as Fair Trade goods. A few of these—such as **Mexican honey**—raise the question discussed on p.136: is it more ethical to buy Fair Trade or to favor the locally produced equivalent on environmental grounds? Others, however, pose no such dilemmas. Fair Trade **chocolate**, for instance, is not only giving a living wage to small farmers who desperately need it. It's also helping to inject transparency and other

Mäya bars were one of the first US-produced Fair Trade chocolate bars available nationwide, and are stocked in many "high-end" supermarkets and convenience stores across the country. Their parent company, Lärabar, is committed to making foods that are organic, non-GE, and vegan friendly.

ethical standards into an industry which is being increasingly associated with serious human rights abuses. Nearly half of the world's chocolate is grown in Côte d'Ivoire in West Africa, where, according to US government estimates, more than 100,000 child laborers work in hazardous conditions on cocoa farms. Many of these are slave laborers, taken from neighboring Mali. To make matters worse, cocoa farmers—like coffee producers—are currently suffering a low market price for their crop.

Fair Trade **sugar**, on the other hand, allows consumers to support the more conscientious growers in the developing world—which may help them overcome the crippling effect of foreign farm subsidies (see p.22).

Fair Trade foods and drinks can be found in some supermarkets and many health food stores, but also try the the Fair Trade specialist suppliers listed on p. 162. For the most up-to-date range of Fair Trade products, brands, importers, distributors, retail outlets and online shops, see www. transfairusa.org/do/whereToBuy

Food & drink: the big brands
Nestlé et al.: who owns whom?

Food is an increasingly branded world. In the US every day brings, on average, nearly thirty new food products. That's 10,000 new potato chip flavors, sodas—and, indeed, organic peanut butters—each year. Of these, most—with all the ad campaigns, press releases and packaging that went with them—will be junked in the bulging trash can of food-marketing history.

Despite this extraordinary turnover of new products, however, the more popular and widely known food brands—such as Coca-Cola, Nescafé and Pepsi—are remarkably enduring. There are hundreds of such household names, but the number of major companies actually producing them is surprisingly small. Just as food retail is increasingly controlled by just a few giant supermarkets, and pesticides by a few huge agrochemicals firms, branded, packaged food and drink is increasingly dominated by a handful of multinational corporations, each the result of many mergers and takeovers.

These big firms are a highly controversial bunch. Besides specific accusations such as Nestlé's alleged promotion of formula milk in the third world (see p.148) and Pepsi's financial support for George W. Bush, the sector as a whole is associated with the unethical promotion—including advertising to children—of salty, fatty and otherwise harmful foods that are leading to a massive rise in obesity, diabetes and other nutrition-related diseases.

Whether these problems are the fault of the companies or cultural shifts, such as people doing less exercise, is an open question. But the situation is looking increasingly extreme—in both rich and poor countries alike. According to the National Health and Nutrition Examination Survey for 1999–2002, over 30% of the adult population (and 16% of the children) in the US are obese, a rise of more than 50% per decade during the 1980s and 1990s. A 2005 report by the *New England Journal of Medicine* contended obesity could cause the first drop in average life expectancy in modern times.

> **// The school system is where you build brand loyalty. //**
>
> John Alm, president, Coca-Cola Enterprises, quoted in *The Atlanta Journal-Constitution*, April 6, 2003

The big "snack and pop" companies certainly aren't entirely to blame for the obesity boom, yet the firms do spend an astonishing amount of time and money each year lobbying governments against legislation that might do something to solve these problems—banning soda machines in schools, or candy displays at supermarket checkouts, for example, or enforcing compulsory health warnings on the packaging of certain products. Indeed, the major American food brands are A-list political donors, and sugar and food lobbies pressured the US government to reject recommendations from the World Health Organization and FAO to limit sugar consumption and children's exposure to junk food advertising. (Appallingly, the Alliance for American Advertising was formed in 2005 specifically to lobby against government regulation of such marketing to youngsters.)

The big companies consistently describe themselves as being socially responsible "corporate citizens," and yet their trade associations have a tendency to simply refuse to admit that unhealthy foods and drinks cause health problems. A poster supplied to teachers by the National Soft Drink Association (now the American Beverage Association) several years ago, for example, stated that "as refreshing sources of needed liquids and energy, soft drinks represent a positive addition to a well-balanced diet … In your body it makes no difference whether the sugar is from a soft drink or a peach."

A few of the big players

It's well beyond the scope of this book to examine the ethical standards of every major food brand. But following is a quick summary of a few of the most controversial members of Big Food, with a list of the best-known brands owned by each. To find out more, try these online resources: **Responsible Shopper** (www.responsibleshopper.org), **Ideals Work** (www. idealswork.com), **Social Accountability International** (www.sa-intl.org), and **Alonovo Intelligent Marketplace** (www.alonovo.com). In print, *The Blue Pages* (published by PoliPointPress) has specific information about the political contributions of numerous major food and beverage companies, as well as general info about the ethics of companies of all sorts. Unfortunately, there is not yet a US equivalent to the UK magazine *Ethical Consumer* (www.ethicalconsumer.org), which, though oriented toward the UK resident, has information of value to everyone concerned about these issues.

Nestlé

With more than 230,000 employees and control of more than half of the international coffee market, Nestlé is easily the world's largest food company. The company's brands have been marred by two and a half decades of boycotting relating to their marketing of formula milk in the developing world (see box overleaf). And it came under fire in 2003 when it attempted to claim millions of dollars from the the government of Ethiopia for assets seized by that country's military regime way back in the 1970s. Eleven million Ethiopians were facing starvation at the time, but Nestlé still saw fit to call it a "matter of principle," only dropping the claim after a public outcry. Nestlé has also recently been criticized by Oxfam for failing to act to help the farmers hit by the coffee crisis (see p.141). However, rumors that the food giant may launch a Fair Trade range in the near future may soften views on this.

Nestlé brands

▶ **Alpo**	▶ **Fancy Feast**	▶ **Nesquik**	▶ **Sweetarts**
▶ **Arrowhead**	▶ **Friskies**	▶ **Nestea**	▶ **Taster's Choice**
▶ **Calistoga**	▶ **Kern's**	▶ **Perrier**	▶ **Turtles**
▶ **Carnation**	▶ **Libby's**	▶ **PowerBar**	▶ **Willy Wonka**
▶ **Dreyer's**	▶ **Nescafe**	▶ **Stouffer's**	

Altria (Philip Morris)

Tobacco giant Philip Morris is best known for its Marlboro cigarettes. Less well known is the fact that the same corporation—recently renamed Altria—is among the world's biggest food companies, owning the majority of Kraft foods, as well as half the US tobacco market. Philip Morris's ethical record includes such highpoints as denying that smoking is addictive, being fined for failing to disclose political donations, and coming close to the top of the table of George W. Bush campaign contributors (see pp.68–69).

Altria brands (all part of Kraft Foods North America)

- Balance
- Breakstone's
- Breyers
- Cheese Nips
- Cream of Wheat
- Grape-Nuts
- Honeycomb
- Jell-O
- Knudsen
- Kool-Aid
- Kraft
- Maxwell House
- Minute
- Nabisco
- Newtons
- Oscar Mayer
- Oreo
- Philadelphia
- Post
- Raisin Bran
- Ritz
- Sanka
- Shake 'n Bake
- Shredded
- Wheat
- Stoned Wheat Thins
- Tang
- Triscuit
- Velveeta
- Waverly

Coca-Cola and PepsiCo

When the World Health Organization launched an offensive on the global health effects of sugary foods in 2003, soft drinks were at the top of

Coca-Cola brands

- A&W
- Barq's
- Cherry Coke
- Coca-Cola Classic
- Dasani
- Dr. Pepper
- Fanta
- Fresca
- Hi-C
- Minute Maid
- Nestea
- Odwalla
- Powerade
- Schweppes
- Sprite
- Tab

PepsiCo brands

- Cheetos
- Cracker Jack
- Doritos
- Frito-Lay
- Fritos
- Gatorade
- Mountain Dew
- Quaker Oats
- Pepsi-Cola
- Tropicana

Nestlé & infant formula

Since 1977, Nestlé, the world's largest food company, has been the target of the most global, long-standing and highly publicized of all consumer boycotts. The food giant has scores of brands (see p.146), but the controversy focuses on the product that launched the company back in the 1960s: **infant formula**, also called breast-milk substitute, baby milk or bottle milk.

Where breast-feeding is impossible or impractical—as is often the case—infant formula can be a lifesaver, but it also comes with certain health risks. Even in rich countries, babies fed on formula milk during the first few months are more likely to suffer certain health problems, since breast milk provides a perfect combination of nutrients and antibodies. But in **developing countries** the dangers are more acute. Formula milk needs to be prepared with water and served in sterilized bottles, which can be problematic if pure water or fuel are in short supply. And if parents find themselves stuck with it but unable to afford sufficient quantities (a real possibility, because moving back to breast-feeding is often impossible once formula milk has been used) they may over-dilute it, mix it with unsuitable solids or substitute for it with cheaper but completely unsuitable alternatives, such as cows' milk or tea.

These risks have been known for decades. Back in the 1930s pioneering pediatrician Dr. Cicely Williams published and spoke about the hazards of inappropriate bottle feeding. But for much of the twentieth century the formula milk manufacturers—of which Nestlé was and is the biggest—aggressively promoted their products around the world. Pictures of plump "first-world" babies were used on containers and posters, and free samples (sometimes given out by marketing "nurses") were provided for hospitals and given out to new mothers, often making breast-feeding impossible and forcing mothers into months of purchasing the stuff. The result was a huge decline in the exclusive use of breast-feeding and the completely avoidable deaths of hundreds of thousands of babies each year around the world.

Things came to a head in the early 1970s, after exposés by *New Internationalist* magazine and War on Want. The latter's article was translated into German as "Nestlé Tötet Babies" (**Nestlé Kills Babies**) and Nestlé sued for libel. It won the court case on the grounds of this title, but it generated massive negative publicity for itself in the process. Things didn't really improve, so a few years later a consumer boycott

began—first in the US and then internationally—coordinated by the International Baby Food Action Network (IBFAN).

In 1981, the World Health Assembly drew up the **International Code of Marketing of Breast-milk Substitutes**, a set of recommended minimum standards relating to the promotion (or non-promotion) of formula milk. A few years later, Nestlé agreed to implement the Code voluntarily and the boycott was lifted. But four years after that, the campaign was revived, as IBFAN determined that Nestlé hadn't lived up to its promises and was still supplying cheap or free formula milk to hospitals.

A decade and a half on, the situation is still dire: in 2001 the World Health Organization reported that "some 1.5 million children still die every year because they are inappropriately fed … less than 35% of infants worldwide are exclusively breast-fed for the first four months of life." And though there have been many positive developments—explicit formula milk marketing has been almost stamped out, and breast-feeding rates in the developing world are rising—the question remains as to whether Nestlé, who has gone to great lengths to promote itself as an ethical company, is acting responsibly.

According to IBFAN, the answer is unquestionably no, since Nestlé and other firms are "continuing their unethical promotional activities whilst claiming to abide by the International Code." The campaigners continue to document some direct violations of the Code—which they display on their website—though their main accusations today relate to more subtle things such as Nestlé lobbying against regulation relating to infant formula, and refusing to accept that the Code should apply to *all* "breast-milk substitutes"—including those aimed at older babies—not just "infant formula."

Nestlé denies such allegations, pointing to its widespread promotion of breast-feeding, its regular audits, and its internal ombudsman for reporting bad practice. Peter Brabeck-Letmathe, the CEO, even claims to look personally into each reported breach of the Code, while acknowledging that—in a company of nearly a quarter of a million staff—slip-ups are bound to happen occasionally. Nestlé also claims that formula milk products are "legitimate and useful," allowing mothers in poor countries the option of returning to work instead of staying at home—something which women in the West take for granted. And they claim that the only reason why they receive all the negative publicity is because they're the easiest target: while their food and drink brands are household names, the other baby milk firms are pharmaceutical companies, so couldn't easily really be boycotted.

However, criticism of Nestlé's formula milk activities—albeit less fierce than it once was—keeps coming from sources as wide ranging as UNICEF and, in 2003, the *British Medical Journal*. And the boycott continues. For both sides of the story, and more background on the breast-feeding issue, visit:

IBFAN www.ibfan.org
Nestlé www.babymilk.nestle.com
UNICEF www.unicef.org

their hit-list. To defend themselves against such attacks, and ensure that no one restricts their capability to sell soda to kids, the market leaders of this sector—Coca-Cola and PepsiCo—got the US government on their side through proactive lobbying and political donations (both are major George W. Bush sponsors, according, again, to www.opensecrets.org).

Coca-Cola, especially, has also courted controversy on many other levels. During the months in which this chapter was written, for example, they have been faced with public and shareholder criticism regarding their failure to address the murder of trade unionists in a Colombian bottling plant, and also for their factory in Kerala, India, where farmers have complained of their water reserves being bled dry and their fields polluted by dangerous waste which the factory allegedly sold to them as fertilizer.

Unilever

Though often described as among the more benevolent of the food giants, Unilever has also faced heavy criticism. Besides standard transnational behavior—massive fat-cat pay, tax dodging through havens, etc.—the company has been accused of working hard to keep tea prices to a minimum, testing on animals, buying crops harvested by child labor, harming people and the environment at its thermometer factory in India, and actively lobbying for GE crops in Europe while claiming to be "listening to our customers."

Unilever brands			
▶ Becel	▶ Birds Eye	▶ Flora	▶ Lipton
▶ Ben & Jerry's	▶ Boursin	▶ Hellmann's	▶ Magnum
▶ Bertolli	▶ Findus	▶ Knorr	▶ Slim-Fast

Organic goes corporate

While the manufacturers of organic and natural food are usually not part of corporations—often quite determinedly so—buying organic doesn't guarantee steering clear of the giants entirely. With organic/health food such a rapidly growing (if still niche) market, it's unsurprising that many of the big companies are wanting in on the action. A number of organic brands are fully or partially owned by corporations, and that number could grow appreciably in the coming years as organic food increases in popularity, particularly among general consumers who rarely shop anywhere but the supermarket.

As ever, you'll find two sides when measuring the goods and bads of corporate intrusion into the organic and natural marketplace. With their wider and more effective distribution (not to mention more mainstream packaging and advertising), it could be argued that the corporate organic and natural brands will raise awareness of, and increase demand for, organic foods in the overall US population. There's worry, however, that corporate owners won't be nearly as vigilant over quality and processing standards as independents. There's also concern that takeovers of smaller, local companies will result in downsizing, as Ben & Jerry's workers found out after their business was absorbed into Unilever, with one-in-five employees losing their jobs. And if past track records are any guide, there's little reason to expect corporations to be as willing as the companies they bought out to reinvest a portion of their profits into environmental or social causes.

Following is a list of some large corporations and the organic and natural food brands they owned as of April 2004, as researched by the Community Food Co-op in Bellingham, Washington:

▶ **Hain Food Group:** Arrowhead Mills, Bearitos, Breadshops, Casbah, Celestial Seasonings, Deboles Pasta, Earth's Best Baby Food, Garden of Eatin', Health Valley, Little Bear Organic, Nile Spice, Rice Dream, Shari Ann's Organics, Terra Chips, Walnut Acres, Westbrae, Westsoy

▶ **Nestle:** Arrowhead Water, Caligstoga, Perrier, PowerBar

▶ **Nspired Foods:** Cloud Nine, Cool Fruits, Maranatha, Sunspire

▶ **Dean Foods:** Horizon Organic Dairy, Mountain High, Silk Soy, White Wave

▶ **General Mills:** Cascadian Farms, Muir Glen, Nature Valley Granola Bars

▶ **Kellogg's:** Kashi, Morningstar Farms, Natural Touch

▶ **J.M. Smucker Co.:** After the Fall, R.W. Knudsen, Santa Cruz Organic

▶ **Hansen Naturals, Inc.:** Blue Sky, Hansen's Juices, Hansen's Sodas

▶ **Altria:** Back to Nature Cereal, Balance Bars, BocaBurger

▶ **PepsiCo:** Mother's Natural Foods, Near East

▶ **Solera Capital:** Annie's Homegrown, Simply Organic

▶ **Group Danone:** Stonyfield Farm

▶ **Con Agra:** Lightlife

▶ **Mars, Inc.:** Seeds of Change

Supermarkets & alternatives
Where to shop?

The explosive growth of **supermarkets** in the last half century has completely revolutionized the food sector. If the United States ever was a nation of shopkeepers, it's certainly not any more. The top ten supermarket chains account for more than half of the nation's grocery sales, a sharp rise from the one-third share they claimed in 1995. Wal-Mart alone takes about 20% of the pie, a portion projected to rise to as high as 35% by 2010. Along with a few other large chains (Kroger, Albertsons and Safeway being the biggest) and a handful of smaller players, supermarkets account for about two-thirds of grocery sales. And it's not just retailing they've taken over: they've also displaced a huge number of businesses in the import, distribution and wholesale sectors.

Despite the supermarket stranglehold, however, some markets and local shops survive. And a number of alternatives with a distinctly ethical slant—such as **farmers' markets**, **health food stores** and **specialists** in Fair Trade products, free-range meat and so on—are starting to gain popularity across the country. Following is a brief look at the morals of supermarket shopping, followed by a listing of alternatives (from p.156).

Supermarkets

More than almost any country in the world, the US is addicted to supermarkets. Maybe it's their special offers or their dazzling choice. Or perhaps it's their all-under-one-roof convenience. But, whatever the reasons, few Americans buy food anywhere else.

Compared with most giant companies, the big supermarkets have less of a yawning chasm on their ethical resumes. Kroger and Safeway, for instance, both implemented *some* animal welfare policies for its suppliers (albeit under pressure from PETA), while Albertson's has a plan to reduce its annual energy consumption by ten percent. Even Wal-Mart, the favorite whipping boy of social justice crusaders everywhere, participated in an EPA program aimed at cutting harmful carbon dioxide and nitrogen oxide emissions, donated $20 million in cash and merchandise to Hurricane Katrina relief efforts, and underwrites some programming on National Public Radio. And they've been central in bringing certain "ethical foods"—such as **organic** and **Fair Trade** products—into the mainstream, selling almost half of the organic food bought in the US. Arguably, the supermarkets also have a very worthwhile aim: making a wide selection of foods available to the public at prices that people can afford.

But despite all this the supermarket sector is the subject of more resentment than almost any other, with criticism coming from consumers, environmentalists and farmers alike. Some of the objections are standard complaints about big businesses—**political lobbying** (which the supermarkets are famously good at), executive pay, and so on. And some relate to **quality**: food writers and gourmands accuse the big retailers of replacing the US's base of knowledgeable fishmongers, butchers and greengrocers, and countless varieties of local fruit and veggies, with a food non-culture devoid of expertise and variety (see p.134). But there are also a number of more specific accusations...

Damaging communities & small businesses

The era of the supermarket has been the era of the **decline of the local store**. While national grocery sales rose about 30% in the 1990s, the number of small grocery stores shrank by about 35-40% in the same period. More specialized bakeries, butchers and fishmongers have also been hard-hit, as well as other food service providers who have been forced out of business.

Apart from obvious negative effects on neighborhood shopping districts—and on people who for whatever reason are unable to drive to the supermarket—this has also led to a loss of decent **jobs**. According to a study by the University of California at Berkeley's Labor Center on "The Hidden Cost of Wal-Mart Jobs," there's strong evidence "that the jobs created by new Wal-Mart stores generally replace other, often higher-paying jobs, as existing retailers are forced to scale back or go out of business." And those jobs which do get created are usually pretty unsatisfying: working as a check-out clerk can't exactly compare with running a corner produce store.

There are additional, not-so-visible costs of supermarket jobs with low wages and few benefits. The UC Berkeley study determined that Wal-Mart employees earn 31% less than the average worker at a large retail company, but require 39% more in public assistance. Taxpayers also bear the burden of state and local development subsidies given to such corporations, such as property tax rebates and free or cheap land; according to Good Jobs First, Wal-Mart has received more than $1 billion in subsidies from individual states.

Commentators who worry about the effect of supermarkets on local communities also point out that the money spent in, say, a Safeway or Albertson's, bypasses, rather than filters through, the **local economy**. According to sustainable communities advocates the Institute for Local Self-Reliance, one study found that local businesses spend 53% of their revenues within the local and state economies, while so-called big box superstores spend only 14% within the local economy.

Another way in which the supermarkets have undercut local bakers, milkmen, and grocers is by treating basics like milk, bread and canned tomatoes as "**loss leaders**," selling them at less than the wholesale cost and making up the profits from other products. On one level, this seems like good news, meaning that even people on very low incomes—if they can get to a supermarket—shouldn't struggle to afford the basics. However, since the supermarkets often overprice healthier foods, the overall effect may be negative. Loss leaders are even illegal in many countries, but seem firmly entrenched as a retail institution in the US, and the political power of the corporate owners of large supermarket chains would likely lobby hard against attempts to regulate them.

Harming the environment

Though the supermarkets claim to be committed to the environment, there's no escaping the fact that they create a number of environmental burdens. They contribute to global warming, for example, by increasing the distance from "plough to plate" on three different levels: locally (by encouraging out-of-neighborhood shopping), nationally (since produce gets delivered to stores via centralized distribution centers that are often far away from the individual outlets) and internationally (by sourcing goods from abroad when domestic produce is available).

Furthermore, organic exponents have accused the supermarkets of profiteering from their movement while flagrantly ignoring its eco principles, wrapping organic fruit and vegetables in unnecessary plastic packaging and failing to favor local growers.

Which supermarkets are the most responsible?

When it comes to the biggest US chains, many would find the very notion of a socially responsible supermarket something of an oxymoron, but there are differences between the behemoths. Unfortunately, there's been nothing here on the order of a recent UK program, **Race to the Top** (organized by the International Institute for Environment and Development), which

Mass produced fruits are picked under-ripe so they can withstand the voyage to market, and are left to "ripen" in supermarket displays wrapped in semipermeable plastic that lets gasses escape as the living cells break down—not only is the packaging unnecessary, picking the fruit so early in the growth cycle is known to rob them of roughly half their potential sweetness.

sets out to measure the top ten supermarkets' ethical policies and practices. The aim was to help them improve their standards in everything from labor and animal welfare, to their impacts on the environment and local economies, though the project was ended three years later after all the big players jumped ship. While voluntary compliance with such a program in the States might prove equally problematic, at least the Responsible Shopper website (www.responsibleshopper.org) does rate the four biggest chains for levels of social and environmental insight, as well as two of the largest health food chains, Whole Foods and Trader Joe's.

It's not too surprising that the list of criticisms of **Wal-Mart** is about as long as it is for all the three or four next-biggest chains combined. Wal-Mart, after all, is the world's biggest and arguably least popular company. If the whole concept of the modern supermarket is problematic, then Wal-Mart must be the best example, a famously anti-union, political-lobbying, sweat-shop-exploiting, gun-selling multinational whose predatory, expansionist policies are the stuff of corporate legend, and whose considerable donations to the Republican party helped lubricate George W. Bush's journey to the White House. China's *People Daily* once looked into why no unions were recognized among Wal-Mart's Chinese suppliers, but the company soon cleared up the confusion: "A Wal-Mart spokesman explained that there are no trade unions in its branches in other parts of the world either."

On the environmental front, Rainforest Relief has campaigned against the company for distributing furniture made of wood from endangered old-growth forests, and the corporation's been fined millions for numerous violations of the Clean Water Act. As the hard-hitting film documentary *Wal-Mart: The High Cost of Low Prices* was about to start its theatrical run in late 2005, the company—concerned both about its public image and the negative publicity's effect on its stock price—went as far as to sponsor a gathering of top economists to discuss the corporation's economic and community impact, though critics dismissed this as more of a PR move than anything else.

Kroger, Albertson's and **Safeway**, Wal-Mart's nearest competitors, are not in the same league, either in revenue or objectionable policies. They're similar enough in their ethical pluses and minuses, in fact, to make choosing among them something of an academic exercise. All sell at least some Fair Trade products and have unionized work forces, though they were criticized for cutting back on health care during a strike of Southern Californian workers. (In turn, the chains blamed Wal-Mart's expansion, claming they needed to cut corners in order to compete with the giant.) But the companies, as well as most of the dozens of other smaller chains operating throughout the US, have generally been unresponsive or only minimally receptive to campaigns to get them to stop carrying GE foods or improve their animal welfare standards.

Health food chains

Though some might view the term "health food supermarket" as a contradiction in terms, national health/natural food chains do offer considerably better options for the socially conscious shopper if you're going to venture into such establishments at all. They're certainly easier to find, now more than ever, with the small but growing niche dominated by three companies, **Whole Foods**, **Wild Oats** and **Trader Joe's**. Their revenues are still small potatoes compared to those of conventional supermarkets, with the biggest of the three, Whole Foods, only ranking about twentieth overall among US food retailers. Still, together the three chains have more than 500 outlets throughout the US, with Whole Foods recently opening stores in the UK, and Trader Joe's in particular expanding aggressively, recently passing the 200-store mark. Whether Trader Joe's, incidentally, is classified as a "health food" store or "specialist foods" retailer seems to vary according to what source you read, but it certainly does offer much more in the way of health and organic products than you'll find at a typical supermarket, often via its own in-house brands.

In general, all three of the chains score far higher than conventional retailers on the ethical board. Whole Foods had its operations declared "Certified Organic" in 2003, carries Fair Trade products, was named by PETA as Best Animal-Friendly Retailer in 2004, and made *Business Ethics'* "100 Best Corporate Citizens" list the same year. Wild Oats has been praised for working with the USDA to create NOP standards and buying from local farmers and companies, and both Whole Foods and Wild Oats have donated generously to social and environmental causes. While it's less conscious of positioning itself as a progressive operation, Trader Joe's has implemented fairly progressive animal welfare standards, and sources only non-GE ingredients for its store brand products, though they enacted these policies only after pressure from activist groups.

As some of those activist groups would point out, however, the records of these three big-fish-in-a-small pond aren't unblemished. All of them have been resistant to unionization; all Trader Joe's employees remain non-union after an attempt to organize at the flagship store in 2003 failed, and it wasn't until 2002 that the first successful union drive was made at a Whole Foods branch. And Whole Foods took flak from many quarters (including one of the doyens of the socially responsible investment movement, Domini Social Investments CEO Amy Domini) for not labeling its in-house products containing GE substances. The company finally agreed to label them in 2005 after pressure from several shareholder resolutions by **Green Century**, a group of socially responsible mutual funds owned by nonprofit environmental organizations.

Even if these chains are far smaller in scale than their conventional competitors, they too have taken heat for driving some local stores out of business and de-personalizing community centers. It's not just corner bakeries and grocers they're displacing. Independent health/natural food shops have complained that it's difficult to impossible to compete and stay afloat after a health food chain enters the area. Whole Foods generated some concern about its sensitivity to some of the very local growers it supports when it opened a branch on Union Square in New York City, on the other side of the park from the Greenmarket Farmers Market, one of the most popular and best-loved establishments of its sort in the country.

Boosters of these natural supermarkets might counter that they offer a wider selection and lower prices than many independent health food stores, as well as providing at least some vehicle for buying organic food and other healthy products in some towns and neighborhoods where few or no other such options exist. There's some merit to those claims, but it's really not so hard to find independents in many regions of the US, and they're well-established in virtually all urban areas. There are around 10,000 health food stores in the country, in fact, and sites such as GreenPeople (www.greenpeople.org), Happy Cow (www.happycow.net), Organic.org (www.organic.org), the Eat Well Consumer Guide (www.eat-wellguide.org), and Vegetarian-Restaurants.Net (www.vegetarian-restaurants. net) can quickly locate ones near wherever you live or travel.

Food co-ops

The best way to put both your principles and your money where your mouth is may be to join one of the many **food co-ops** throughout the US. Democratically run and member-owned, many of these are oriented toward health foods and organic goods, sometimes exclusively so. Some are supermarket-sized, with multiple branches and thousands of members; others are small neighborhood stores in which members often work as volunteers part-time, which usually entitles them to discounts and other benefits. Whatever their nature, they're usually mostly or  wholly free of corporate influence, and far more open to customer queries and input than even most "conventional" health food chains or retail outlets. Too, you don't have to be a member to shop at most co-ops, though you'll usually have to pay more if that's the case. The **Coop Directory Service** (www.coopdirectory.org) lists natural food co-ops throughout the US, as well as co-op distributors; **LocalHarvest** (www.localharvest.org) also lists food co-ops nationwide.

While it's a little-heard criticism, for all their growing numbers, few of these health food stores, health food supermarkets, or coops serve disadvantaged inner-city minority neighborhoods. Organizations such as People's Grocery (www.peoplesgrocery.org), whose "Mobile Market" truck sells healthy food and produce at a few locations in the people-of-color-dominated West Oakland, California, community several times a week, are rare. As its website points out, such areas have little access not just to health food stores, but to healthy food in general—there's just one super-market for its 25,000 residents, and of the 36 liquor convenience stores in the area, just three "sell fresh produce or adequate food for a balanced meal."

Farmers' markets

Though they still only account for a fraction of a percent (about $1 billion annually) of US food sales, farmers' markets are on the up. The National Farmers Market Directory lists nearly 4000 across the nation, more than double the number just a decade ago. The concept is simple: buy produce straight from the growers or producers, giving them a better deal than they would get via a retailer, cutting down on environmentally harmful food transportation, getting fresher and better quality food (at least one market has even gone GE-free), cutting the big-business machine out of the equation and getting the chance to ask questions directly to the pro-

Reconnecting field and city: a farmers' market in Brooklyn, NY.

ducers. It's also supporting a vital farming sector that's largely overlooked by the federal government—although about 40% of farm income comes directly from government subsidies, no money from the $190 billion, 10-year farm bill signed by George W. Bush in 2002 was appropriated toward farmers' markets.

There are no federal guidelines for what constitutes a farmers market, and the strictures regulating them (if there are any) vary widely from state to state, region to region, and even market to market. Indeed, only a few states even give farmers markets a legal definition. Generally, the vendors have grown, reared, or caught their food within the locality or region, though even that can extend to a pretty wide range. The celebrated Greenmarket Farmers' Market in Union Square in New York City, for example, allows farmers from within a 170-mile radius to sell their goods; the California Farmers' Market Association's rules for certified farmers' markets requires that produce be grown within the state of California, a territory that's bigger than entire nations. It's also usually the custom for someone directly involved with the production process to be minding the individual stall.

If you're set on trying to get a handle on what governs specific markets, the Resources for Farmers' Markets website has a page of state and local programs, at www.nemw.org/farmersmarkets/statelist.html. It's most effective, however, to just check out a few of the markets within your region and ask some questions of the farmers directly. Many markets will even have information booths or at least pamphlets that can tell you under what guidelines or principles they're run.

Farmers' markets are springing up all over the country. To find out more, or locate your nearest one, visit:

AMS Farmers' Markets www.ams.usda.gov/farmersmarkets
LocalHarvest www.localharvest.org
Food Routes www.foodroutes.org

Organic online delivery & community supported agriculture

Even with the growing alternatives for buying health/organic food at supermarkets, independent stores, food co-ops, and farmers' markets, plenty of overworked Americans are finding it harder and harder to find a place in their schedules to shop in brick and mortar outlets. If you're looking to save time, or more practically, if you find it difficult to get to stores stocking organic food—if few or none are in your area (or you lack transportation to them)—numerous **online organic delivery services** have sprung up to meet your needs. While on-line transactions in general still generate less than 5% of all grocery sales in the US, both the number of such organic retailers and the scale of their operations is rapidly increasing.

The way in which online organic food is ordered, assembled and delivered varies so widely, however, that it's impossible to make any general summaries as to what you'll get for your purchase. Some services send a weekly box of organic produce to your door, with both prices and quality differing considerably among competing vendors. One service in the New York area, Freshdirect.com, even aims to be a sort of farmers' market on wheels, dealing directly with the growers who sell in those venues. As a further muddying of the water, some supermarkets also offer online organic ordering and delivery, including conventional giants like Safeway and Albertson's—which rather defeats the purpose of going through this exercise in this first place, if you're trying to go organic and be socially responsible at the same time. Non-organic specialists also offer all sorts of other foods and goods, from bread to liquid cleaners, so it's perfectly possible to save yourself from ever going to the supermarket. Whichever service you use, one benefit usually holds true: even when you factor in

A typical mixed box from Farm Fresh to You (www.farmfreshtoyou.com). Boxes contain 9-10 seasonal fruits and vegetables mostly grown on their family farm in northern California. When the weather shifts, they purchase organic produce from other small, organic and sustainable family farms.

the delivery van, the overall pollution and energy use will in many cases be much smaller than driving to the supermarket.

One feature still lacking in online organic grocery shopping—rather surprisingly, given the medium—is a comprehensive online listing of US companies offering the goods, whether they specialize in delivery exclusively or are an auxiliary service of a standard retail operation. GreenPeople (www.greenpeople.org) does allow you to refine searches for vendors of organic food to those who can take online orders, with brief descriptions that sometimes indicate what they carry and whether they offer home and office delivery, though the list is by no means complete. Here, as with farmers' markets, it's best to try a few in the region and familiarize yourself with their features to find the one that best meets your needs.

Another option for both steering clear of stores and directly supporting farmers is becoming a member of **Community Supported Agriculture** programs, commonly abbreviated as CSAs. For an annual fee (usually $300-$500, though sometimes more), a CSA share gets a weekly box of fresh produce from one of its 1200 or so farms across the country, often priced lower than they are in specialty food stores. There are disadvantages to consider as well: most CSAs don't deliver, instead needing to be fetched at the farm or a designated pickup point; the contents can change drastically from season to season, depending upon the success of certain crops; and the boxes are available only *in* season, usually from late spring through early fall. In addition, although the produce is usually organic, you'll need to check with the individual farms to make sure. While the CSA website (www.nal.usda.gov/afsic/csa) has basic information about the program and participating farms, the CSA page on the LocalHarvest site (www.localharvest.org/csa) actually gives more reader-friendly information about how the deal works.

Fair Trade specialists

Transfair USA's website—www.transfairusa.org—lists all the Fair Trade Certified products available in the US, along with contact details for each of the companies licensed to offer them. Some of these sell directly and others can tell you where to find their products.

You'll often find the best range in a specialist Fair Trade shop—such as those listed in chapter nine (see p.315). Many organic or health food shops also have a decent selection, but in terms of price you might be best buying online (or by phone). Among the best sites are:

Transfair USA www.transfairusa.org

Transfair USA's website lists dozens of sites that offer online Fair Trade goods, dominated by but not limited to food. The current listings are heavy on coffee retailers, though outlets with more wide-ranging stocks are included. You can also suggest retailers for addition to the page, which Transfair USA will do after confirming availability of Fair Trade Certified products.

Global Exchange Fair Trade Online Store store.gxonlinestore.org ▷ 800-505-4410

The Global Exchange organization is at the cutting edge of progressive activism on several fronts, including ecotourism, peace campaigns, human rights and fair trade. The online store branch of their website offers Fair Trade goods of all sorts, the food section including coffee, tea and chocolate. Among their coffees are chocolate-covered espresso beans and an End the Embargo on Cuba brand, organically grown by cooperatives in Mexico, Nicaragua and Guatemala with strong cultural and historical ties to Cuba. The tea line includes chai, and the chocolate page has Swiss and dark flavors. Also available are numerous fairly traded food accessories, such as Cambodian silk wine bags and teacups from Bali.

Equal Exchange www.equalexchange.com ▷ 774-776-7400

The oldest and largest for-profit Fair Trade company in the US sells organic, gourmet coffee, tea, sugar, cocoa and chocolate bars, produced by democratically run co-ops in Latin America, Asia and Africa. Specialties include "very dark chocolate" bars and organic green, Earl Grey and English breakfast teas from India. Brewing tips and recipes are on the website.

Fair Trade Federation www.fairtradefederation.com

The Fair Trade Federation's website links to dozens of online catalogs, including, but by no means limited to, fairly traded food. It also has brief descriptions of the wares each outlet offers, as well as similar pages listing Fair Trade retailers, wholesalers, mail-order catalogs and producers.

Other local, specialist & health foods

Following are a few other sites and organizations that sell food relevant to the issues discussed in this chapter.

Diamond Organics www.diamondorganics.com ▷ 1-888-674-2642

A large online selection of farm fresh organic food, including produce, dairy, meat, wine, raw foods, baked goods and gift baskets and samplers. They have guaranteed nationwide overnight home delivery, though it should be borne in mind—as it should for all sites listed here that ship nationwide—that buying organics in this manner entails a lot more transportation and environmental costs than buying them locally.

Earth & Table www.earthandtable.com

Geared toward "those interested in growing, preserving, and preparing healthy and delicious food," with links to plenty of resources for those wanting to go organic in their backyard. Sample topics covered: seeds, mushrooms, composting, and organic pest, weed and disease control.

The Mail Order Catalog for Healthy Eating www.healthy-eating.com ▷ 800-695-2241

Specifically dedicated to vegetarian eating and cooking, with a big selection of certified organic foods. Carries a wide line of meat substitutes, egg/cheese/diary substitutes and soyfoods, as well as vegetarian pet food and veggie cookbooks. Their $50 organic gift basket has, among other items, vegan microwave popcorn, dip mix, chocolate bars, soy coffee, vegetarian pâtés and miso soup packets.

Only Natural Pet Store www.onlynaturalpet.com ▷ 888-937-6677

Natural cat and dog food, including organic options using ingredients like organic chicken, brown rice, carrots, vegetables and grains, as well as free-range beef and poultry. You can submit questions about natural pet care to their veterinarian through the site, and get a 10% discount if you sign up for delivery of specific items at regular intervals.

Organic Wine www.redjellyfish.com/organic/wine.html

This page of the online progressive community site Red Jellyfish has links and information about organic wine, including links to wineries (some of whom sell products online) in the US and other countries. One of the more established of those wineries, if you're looking for a taster, is the Organic Wine Company (www.theorganicwinecompany.com), which offers a range of organic red, white, vegan, sparkling and dessert wines from France, Spain, Italy, Portugal and New Zealand. When placing your order through www.petamall.com, 5% of the sale will benefit PETA.

Rawfood.com www.rawfood.com ▷ 800-205-2350

This large online catalog of raw (i.e. uncooked, unprocessed) foods includes a lot of unusual organic items, from Japanese Power Wraps and Peruvian pepper powder, to pumpkin seed butter and choclate truffles. It can be expensive, but the site does say that if you find a lower price on the Internet, they'll match it.

Clothes, cosmetics & jewelry

Beauty may be only skin deep, but our clothes, make-up and jewelry raise issues that are less superficial. Besides garment sweatshops, the clothing and shoe industries are associated with certain environmental and (in the case of leather and fur) animal rights issues. Cosmetics, meanwhile, are all too often also the result of animal experiments, and the jewelry trade is only just starting to come to terms with the moral problems that accompany it such as child labor and conflicts funded by the illicit sales of diamonds. This chapter takes a quick look at these three industries, and lists the most ethical—and, in some cases, the not so ethical—companies in each.

Clothes & shoes
Fashion victims

Mention "shopping with a conscience" and the first thing many people think of is the boycotting of exploitative Asian sweatshops producing branded clothes for the West. It's certainly true that labor standards in the apparel sector are bad. But the factory isn't the first step in the making of clothes—and it's not the only one associated with social and environmental problems. First of all, the raw material needs to be grown, killed or manufactured, and dyed the right color.

Cotton

Cultivated by humans for more than 5000 years, and the basis of products ranging from T-shirts to US dollar bills, **cotton** is something of a natural wonder. But much has changed since the ancient Greek historian Herodotus first documented the existence of Indian "tree wool … exceeding in beauty and goodness." Today, cotton lies at the heart of global debates on **agrochemicals, GE** and **organic production**, as well as unfair **international trade rules** and **child labor** (see box on pp. 48–49).

The first three of these issues relate to the fact that "conventional" modern cotton growing relies on a huge quantity of chemical inputs. More **pesticides** are used on cotton than on any other crop: despite covering only a few percent of the world's cultivable soils, cotton farms account for roughly 10% of all herbicide use and an astonishing 20–25% of insecticide use.

US cotton subsidies

Though it's not exactly a consumer issue, any discussion of the ethics of the cotton trade should mention the single biggest problem faced by farmers in the developing world: the massive subsidies given to giant cotton farms in wealthy countries. In the US, partly for historical reasons, and partly due to effective political lobbying from farm groups, around 25,000 cotton farmers receive around $4 billion in support from the government—an average of $160,000 each. This allows them to sell below the cost of production, driving down international prices and making it extremely difficult for growers in poor countries to compete. In the words of Oxfam's Celine Charvariat, "American and European taxpayers are financing the destruction of the livelihoods of millions of cotton farmers in Africa … the cotton barons of Texas and Alabama are getting huge subsidies … and driving more efficient African farmers out of business."

Though they certainly haven't caused the problem, these subsidies have also been linked to child labor, as they hinder the economic growth of poor cotton-growing countries. According to a study by the India Committee of the Netherlands (www.indianet.nl) 90% of all labor in the Indian cottonseed market is carried out by nearly half a million children, mostly girls aged between six and fourteen.

In 2004, however, the World Trade Organization ruled in favor of a complaint by Brazil, who asserted that US cotton subsidies are illegal. The US government promised to appeal, and "defend US agriculture in every forum we need to." But the WTO reaffirmed the ruling in early 2005, and a few months later the Bush administration announced a proposal to eliminate all export cotton subsidies as of this writing. However, neither this nor other measures to end cotton subsidies had passed through Congress; when that might happen, and whether Brazil and other nations might engage in retaliatory actions in protest if they don't, remains highly uncertain. For more information, see:

Oxfam www.oxfamamerica.org

GE cotton: immoral fiber?

As with other areas of agriculture, the organic brigade is not alone in claiming it has the solution to the pesticide problem. The biotech companies—mainly Monsanto— have produced GE cotton designed to be resistant to insects (with Bt toxin built into their leaves) and/or resistant to a powerful herbicide (which in theory allows less of other herbicides to be used). The technology is probably the most successful application of a GE crop, and has, according to the UN, allowed farmers in China, India and elsewhere to reduce their pesticide use substantially and increase yields.

Critics aren't convinced, however, claiming that Bt-resistant insects will inevitably appear (though this has yet to happen) and that GE crops may prove damaging to biodiversity by killing non-target insects. They also point out that, as with any GE crop, releasing it into the environment could have any number of unforeseeable implications.

More than half of the cotton on sale is now estimated to be GE; anyone with an ideological problem with the technology—or, indeed, with the biotech companies—should buy organic.

People can and do argue about whether or not these chemicals—which include strongly carcinogenic and otherwise nasty substances such as carbamates and organochlorines—harm the eventual wearer of the cotton. But the effect on farmers and the environment is much more pressing. There are no accurate global measures but, according to pesticide campaigners, thousands of cotton-farm workers are killed by agrochemicals each year. Research by Pesticide Action Network, for example, showed that one region of the small West African state of Benin alone saw "at least 61 men, women and children" killed by cotton pesticides between 1999 and 2001. And, of course, for every one person who dies, hundreds of others have to put up with the effects of polluted air and water on their health.

Some commentators also worry that the chemicals are entering the food chain, as the vast quantities of cottonseed harvested are fed to animals and made into cottonseed oil for human consumption.

So what's the solution to this chemical overload? According to biotechnologists, it's genetic engineering, which is already widely used among cotton growers (see box). According to greens, on the other hand, consumers should opt out both of the pesticides and biotechnology by choosing **organic cotton** and favoring alternatives such as **hemp** (see overleaf). Just as with food crops, organic fibers can be grown using chemical-free alternatives to pesticides. In Uganda, for example, black ants are collected and set on the cotton fields to eat the pests.

Time for a hemp revival?

While some people advocate organic or GE cotton as the best fabric for the environment and the health of farmers, others are singing the praises of hemp—not the King Size Rizla variety, but its non-psychoactive industrial counterpart. The fact that most of hemp's rather evangelical advocates also seem to be keen smokers of their favorite plant doesn't do the campaign many favors. But with increasing numbers of governments and farmers examining its benefits, it seems they may have a point.

Cannabis sativa has a long and distinguished history, taking in at least 5000 years of use as a source of food, cloth, nets and countless other items. Many products have started out life as hemp, from proper paper—first created in Tibet at roughly the time of Christ—to Levi's jeans. Until the twentieth century, the plant was also the main source for ropes and sails (the word canvas is derived from the Latin cannabis), which made it so central to naval success that both Britain and the US once had laws requiring all farmers to dedicate a proportion of their land to it.

Yet a couple of centuries after George Washington advised Americans to "make the most of hempseed and sow it everywhere," the wonderplant was on the decline, gradually being replaced by cotton for clothes, wood for paper and nylon for rope. Once the first round of the war on drugs got under way, things got even worse, with hemp officially or effectively banned in many countries.

Hemp fans claim that now is the time for a revival. Farmers would gain because the plant is unusually easy, quick, inexpensive and safe to grow, requiring very few agrochemicals (compare that with cotton, see p.166). Consumers would benefit because hemp products, once produced in large quantities, would be cheaper than current materials, and because hemp cloth is many times stronger and more durable than cotton. The environment would benefit through reduced use of chemicals, improved soil structures due to the plant's deep roots, and reduced felling of trees for paper and board, since hemp fiber is far quicker to produce at a sustainable rate than wood fiber and requires less energy input and chemical treatment. The plant could also potentially contribute to reduced fossil fuel use, as it's an ideal bio-fuel and can be used to make biodegradable alternatives to plastics and metals (in the 1940s Henry Ford famously produced a partly hemp-resin car powered by hemp fuel). To cap all this off, the plant's seeds are unusually nutritious, with a blend of amino acids close to perfect for humans.

Not everyone is entirely convinced of all of hemp's supposed advantages, and fiber-processing technology will need to be developed before it becomes commercially advantageous. Still, few deny that the plant could offer some real long-term ecological benefits. So it's no wonder that "ethical clothes" suppliers often sell hemp clothes, sometimes sourced and produced according to some fair-trade principles (though, it's worth pointing out that the world's biggest hemp producer is China, a "category A" oppressive regime).

Hemp products have taken off in a big way in the United States in the last few years. Hemp body care products sell about $40 million annually; hemp food about $12 million a year; and hemp clothing and paper markets are growing as well. Yet while we're the #1 importer of the hemp crop, US farmers are still not allowed to grow

Harvesting the hemp in Russia, 1933.

hemp, as it's classified by the Drug Enforcement Administration as a schedule 1 drug under the Controlled Substances Act (a higher rating than given to both cocaine and methamphetamines). The US, in fact, is the only major industrialized nation that prohibits hemp cultivation, unless you count the permit that's been granted for an experimental quarter-acre in Hawaii since 1999. The DEA even attempted to ban hemp food sales here a few years ago, though this was successfully fought in court by the Hemp Industries Association. The whole ruckus, in the view of hemp advocates, stems from the government's refusal to distinguish low-THC, non-psychoactive hemp from the high-THC variety, THC being the main intoxicant in marijuana. Longtime consumer advocate Ralph Nader went as far as to call the whole imbroglio "bureaucratic medievalism."

It's legal to buy many hemp products, from cereal and T-shirts to soaps, yarn and organic hemp oil. But, as Vote Hemp president Eric Steenstra told the Organic Consumers Association, "Hemp is the only crop legal to import to the United States yet illegal to grow. We have been saying for years that American farmers are being left out of this cash crop ... the federal law banning hemp farming is outdated, irrational and hurting American farmers." That's left an alternative niche market for Canadian growers in particular to exploit, with farmers from our northern neighbors planting about 25,000 acres of hemp in 2005, about three times the acreage they used the previous year.

continued overleaf

When Vote Hemp hired the Zogby political polling firm to conduct a national poll in 2003, at least 66% of likely voters were in favor of allowing US farmers to grow industrial hemp. There's some support for that among lawmakers as well, including not just progressives and liberals, but also Republicans such as Hawaii State Legislator Cynthia Thielen. On the state level, there's been some action: 26 states have introduced pro-hemp legislation, 14 have actually passed pro-hemp legislation, and six have removed obstacles to hemp production or research. But the crop can't be grown anywhere in the US until a federal ban against states regulating hemp farming is removed. The Industrial Hemp Farming Act was introduced in Congress in 2005 (by its chief sponsor, Texan Republican Congressman Ron Paul) and would allow this, but as of this writing it hasn't gotten a hearing.

If you fancy supporting the hemp movement by clothing yourself in cannabis, check out the selection at the following stores. If you really catch the hemp bug, a Google search will also reveal everything from ropes to varnishes and paints produced from the the very same plant.

Hempstores.com www.hempstores.com
Lists almost 300 stores in the US that sell hemp products. Not all sell hemp exclusively or mainly, but some do, and many of them offer online service.

The Hempest www.store.hempest.com ▷ 617-421-9944
Or, if you want to browse through a big hemp online seller just to get an idea of what's out there, this hemp superstore has a large catalog of shirts, pants, skirts, sweaters, jackets, shoes, body care products, bags and accessories, and even a hemp bean-bag chair. But with hooded jackets running to $200 and button-down dress shirts in the $60-70 range, it's not bargain shopping. If you want to get your feet wet gradually, though, basic hemp jeans are reasonable at $40, and there's a wide line of T-shirts for much cheaper than that. The Hempest also has four retail stores located in Massachusetts, Vermont, and southern California.

For more information on the political aspects of hemp farming, head toward:

Vote Hemp www.votehemp.com
Hemp Industries Association www.thehia.org

Organic fabrics are also more eco-friendly in terms of processing. In the manufacture of conventional cotton cloth thousands of synthetic substances are used: chlorine **bleaches**, heavy-metal **dyes**, formaldehyde to lessen creaseability and anti-shrinking treatments. Many of these are highly toxic, and can cause environmental and health problems if not handled and disposed of correctly.

The market for organic cotton is skyrocketing, thanks to orders from specialists and from a few big companies—including Nike and Levi Strauss—who have started buying a small proportion of their cotton from organic sources. The US used to be the biggest producer, but increasingly organic production is spreading to developing countries, which can undercut the West when it comes to low-chemical, labor-intensive production methods. Organic products aren't necessarily Fair Trade, of course, but there are now a number of manufacturers and suppliers selling clothes that are both. For a list of organic clothes sellers, see pp. 186–192.

Silk

Silk thread is made by unravelling the cocoon of silk worms, each of which wraps itself up in a single continuous strand of up to a half-mile in length. Known as **sericulture**, the process of harvesting silk—cultivating the worms, harvesting the threads and winding them into thicker strands for making material—is a big industry in Asia, with China and India by far the biggest suppliers.

Millions of economically marginalized people make a living out of the silk trade but, in some regions, including parts of India, the industry is rife with **child workers**, many as young as five and in "bonded" positions: essentially slaves paying off a family debt. A report from 2000 available from the Indian wing of UNDP, the UN's global development network (www.undp.org.in), makes for grim reading:

> Children are employed in almost all processes of the sericulture industry making it almost a child-based economy ... They are required to work in filature units that are cramped, damp, dark, poorly ventilated ... the handling of dead worms with bare hands, and the unbearable stench is also a cause for spreading infection and illness. Standing for 12–16 hours a day with hardly any break, concentrating on reeling the fine threads, leads to other health disorders. Vapors from the boiling cocoons and the diesel fumes from the machines also contribute to the poor conditions in the units ... found responsible for retardation of the child's normal growth and development.

Other reports describe endemic bronchial ailments, coughs, back pains, asthma and TB among the child silk workers, as well as seriously damaged hands from checking the boiling cocoons.

This isn't true of all countries—nor the whole of India—and a blanket boycott of the sector would hurt millions of impoverished silk producers who don't exploit bonded child labor. Also, a real solution can probably only come from the relevant governments: "the problem," according to a 2003 Human Rights Watch study on bonded labor in the Indian silk industry, "is political will." Still, consumers can opt for **fairly traded** silk products, which are available from some companies that are part of the Fair Trade Federation (see the listings in chapter 9, starting on p.315).

The West, curiously, pays much less attention to the children and adults working in the silk industry than to the **silk worms** themselves, though admittedly they do get a rather rough deal. If a worm eats its way out of its cocoon, the thread is broken, so the cocoons are boiled or baked while the worms are still inside (in some countries the worms are eaten afterwards). It is possible to make raw-style silk without killing the worm, and you may occasionally see this sold, usually labelled as vegetarian or vegan friendly.

Leather vs. veggie alternatives

Vegetarians object to leather for obvious reasons: though it might be only a *by-product* of the meat industry, the hide of an animal adds substantially to its slaughterhouse value, and so subsidizes the **meat industry**, including intensive farms.

But leather—whether it be from cow, pig, sheep or goat—also raises another question: its **environmental impact**. Indeed, though animal skin may be a "natural" material, modern leather is the result of intensive chemical processing, including toxic carcinogenic substances such as salts of **chromium**. This not only makes it surprisingly energy-inefficient to produce but means that it generates massive quantities of waste: treating a ton of raw hide can result in 19,800 gallons of waste water and 220 lbs of dried sludge. And anyone who has been within smelling range of a tannery will be unsurprised to learn that this waste, when not treated properly, can be extremely dangerous.

As environmental regulation has tightened in the West, developing-world tanneries have seen their businesses expanding. This provides much-needed jobs and income, but the human and environmental costs can be high. A study by the Tokyo Institute of Technology found that 62% of the 2.4 million people in Kasur, Pakistan, are suffering from serious ailments—including cancer, tuberculosis and blindness—caused by industrial waste, with tanneries the major contributor. Similarly, in the Bangladeshi capital Dhaka, according to a report cited in the World Health Organization Bulletin, half a million residents are at risk of serious illness due to tannery pollution, with tannery workers there 50% more likely than their peers to die before the age of fifty. In other areas, large areas of agricultural land have been rendered unusable by tannery pollution. Farmers in Tamil Nadu in southern India have recently been compensated for the ruin of their land, but not everyone has been so lucky.

Besides all the chemicals, leather is also very often treated with palm oil, a product linked to widespread destruction of rainforests in Indonesia (see p.196).

You may occasionally come across leathers tanned and dyed with natural substances, but this has yet to catch on. Instead, some people advocate "vegetarian" **leather substitutes**. Being made of polyurethane and other plastics, these aren't exactly the most green products in the world, but they're arguably a more ethical choice—especially if you don't want to support the meat industry. PETA's website (www.peta.org) has pages of links to companies who sell non-leather goods; the best-known suppliers include the following, all of which sell online or via phone/mail order:

Heartland Products www.trvnet.net/~hrtlndp ▷ 800-441-4692

Leatherless footwear and miscellaneous accessories, including non-leather Birkenstock sandals, boots, products from the UK's Vegetarian Shoes company and even baseball gloves made without leather. When we see someone in the major leagues using one of those, we'll know the times are *really* changing.

Moo Shoes www.mooshoes.com
▷ 866-59-VEGAN

A great name and an extensive line of men's, women's and unisex vegan shoes, including sneakers, sandals and biker boots for women. Also offers belts, wallets, bags, purses, T-shirts, sweatshirts and more. Sells online and at its retail store in the Lower East Side of Manhattan.

Photo courtesy of averywham.com

Otsu www.veganmart.com ▷ 866-HEY-OTSU

Vegan belts, wallets, and several dozen varieties of shoes from this all-around, San Francisco vegan boutique, which also has an online catalog. Among their footwear is one of the most elusive of products for which athletic vegan-wearers have been vainly waiting for years: a running shoe that's not only vegan, but also sweatshop-free.

Pangea Vegan Products

www.pangeaveg.com ▷ 800-340-1200

Vegan shoes, belts and "No Bull" jackets, as part of a wide range of vegan products, not just clothes. It's worth noting that they sell "only goods made in countries where labor laws or unions are in place to protect the workers," as well as avoiding products made in China or other sweatshop-heavy nations.

Vegan Essentials www.veganessentials.com ▷ 866-88-VEGAN

Lots of vegan footwear, jackets, gloves, belts, bags, wallets and shirts, along with hemp goods and plenty of vegan body care products, cosmetics and food.

Fur

Compared with most ethical shopping campaigns, the anti-fur movement of the 1980s and 1990s was hugely successful; US fur sales were cut in half between 1985 and 1990. But recently fur sales have bounced back to mid-'80s levels, with sales reaching nearly $2 billion per year in the US, and claims from the industry that fur isn't as cruel as people think. The International Fur Trade Federation, for example, suggests that the farmed foxes and minks that supply around 85% of the world's pelts are "among the world's best cared for farm animals," while Fur Commission USA offers that fur farmers "reduce the environmental impact of the agricultural sector as a whole" and "make an important contribution to wildlife conservation."

Animal rights campaigners aren't convinced, claiming that the fur farms keep their minks and foxes in small cages equivalent to those used for battery chickens. And, for all the claims of respect for animal welfare, there is plenty of very disturbing footage—such as that filmed by PETA (People for the Ethical Treatment of Animals; www. petatv.com)—showing caged fur animals apparently driven mad by their captivity, gnawing their own legs and running insanely round and round. Slaughtering methods—designed to protect the fur—are also contentious, in some cases allegedly including genital electrocution.

Trapping still provides some furs, and is often described as less cruel since animals get to live natural lives until capture. But most traps—such as the leghold models described as "inhumane" by the American Veterinary Medical Association—cause enormous suffering, with animals desperately trying to escape at first and being left exposed and in pain for anything from hours to days. Inevitably, non-target animals are also caught in the traps, which add to the death count for each coat—which even in the case of bigger farmed animals is around 30–40 minks or foxes.

Austria, Sweden, Switzerland, Italy, the Netherlands and New Zealand have taken steps to curtail or eliminate fur farming, and the practice is banned altogether in the UK. No states, however, have banned fur farming in the US. The trade thrives less in some regions than others, however, as some states have laws prohibiting keeping foxes in captivity (albeit more as a measure for checking disease from spreading among wildlife

Garment factories

The garment trade has long been associated with sweatshops. Way back in 1895, the *Standard Dictionary of the English Language* defined a "sweater" as an exploitative employer, "especially a contractor for piecework in the tailoring trade." There are various reasons for the link between clothes manufacture and labor abuse. One is the fact that the infrastructure costs of setting up a garment factory, or "shop," are relatively low, and the training needed to work there is minimal. So middlemen can afford to set up factories and compete for the business of clothes designers and retailers. Unlike the car sector, say, in which the big companies tend to own their factories, and are therefore accountable to their own workers, the various

than as an animal rights statement), and California's housing regulations for minks and foxes makes it too costly to be profitable there.

Just as a leather subsitute industry has arisen for those who want an approximation of the style without using animal products, so in recent years have several "faux fur" products hit the market, including coats, shoes, furniture and other types of clothing and accessories. PETA's website (www.peta.org) links to companies that sell faux fur goods, either as specialists in the field or as part of a larger line of animal-free products.

PETA www.furisdead.com
International Fur Trade Federation www.iftf.com

layers of subcontracting in the garment trade tends to diffuse and dissolve responsibility for workers' rights.

The subcontracted garment sweatshop was invented and first flourished in nineteenth-century Europe and America, but in the era of **globalization** the garment sector was one of the first to relocate to the developing world. It's not difficult to understand why. Clothes are big business, with US consumers spending around $200 billion per year on them—that's almost $1000 per person. Yet, aside from materials, the only major production cost is **labor**, which is required in large quantities: taken together, the apparel and textile industries are the biggest industrial employers in the world, with a workforce of around 25 million.

For a US firm, sourcing from a factory in Asia, Africa or Latin America doesn't just reduce this labor cost—it decimates it. According to the International Labor Institute, the average hourly wage for an apparel worker in Mexico is $1.75/hr, about a third of the US federal minimum wage; in Indonesia, it's only about 25 cents an hour. Tariffs on clothes imports would offset some of the savings the firms make on labor, but the North American Free Trade Agreement (NAFTA) and the more recently adopted Central American Free Trade Agreement (CAFTA, which would expand the policy into Guatemala, El Salvador, Honduras, Costa Rica, Nicaragua and the Dominican Republic) has kept such tariffs low. Too, if the proposed Free Trade Area of the Americas (FTAA) is adopted, NAFTA would be expanded to cover not just North America, but all of Central America, South America and the Caribbean (except Cuba).

The steadily shrinking apparel trade in the US, where more than half a million jobs were lost in the last quarter of the twentieth century, has undoubtedly caused pain for many individuals who have found them-selves out of work. But there's also no doubt that these kinds of jobs are desperately needed in poor countries, where millions have been created. The developing world now accounts for close to three-quarters of the world's clothing exports, with some economies relying almost entirely on the sector. In 2000, for example, textiles and clothing accounted for 84% of exports from Bangladesh (where around two million workers produce more than a billion garments for export each year) and 72% from Pakistan.

This is all good news, many people argue. And, indeed, you might even consider the transfer of European garment jobs to Asia just deserts for Britain's having systematically destroyed India's textile trade back in the Colonial days (which it did with the aim of creating a bigger market for British textiles). However, as Western clothing companies shop around for the best deal from suppliers (just as we do at our shopping centers), coun-tries and factories end up competing to offer the cheapest, most "flexible" workforce. Combine this with individual factory owners hell-bent on extracting every last drop of profit at the expense of their workers, and the result in all too many cases, is abysmal working conditions.

Regardless of whether you see these conditions as a never ending race to the bottom, or the first mile of a poor country's road to greater prosper-ity (for more on this debate, see p.45), there's little doubt that conditions are often extreme. True, some campaigners simplify or exaggerate the situation: jobs in export garment factories are clearly in demand and, with the exception of some cases where workers are locked into their positions through debt to their employer, they're clearly seen as a better option than the alternatives. Yet a range of sources—from workers' accounts to audits commissioned by the clothes companies themselves—have shown that, in return for the privilege of having a position, the mostly female workforce

Home-grown sweat

While the majority of the garment factories that deserve the "sweatshop" label are in the developing world, they certainly haven't vanished in the West. According to the Smithsonian Institute, conditions for garment workers in rich countries improved during the mid-twentieth century, but almost universally fell in the 1980s. By 1996, the US government estimated that at least half of the country's 22,000 garment factories were in "serious violation of wage and safety laws." One particularly heinous violation—the 1995 discovery of 80 Thai immigrants sewing clothes sold at chains like Montgomery Ward for less than $2 hour, in a compound fortified by razor wire and armed guards—was instrumental in forcing the sweatshop issue into the eyes of the general public.

However, many US companies—as well as with European, Canadian and Japanese ones—have gotten around the complications of manufacturing in Western countries with higher standards of worker conditions by setting up just over the border in Northern Mexico. About a million Mexicans work at more than 3000 of these assembly plants, or *maquiladoras*, and while they've been growing in number since the 1960s, they've doubled in number since NAFTA came into effect in the mid-1990s. While some have argued that NAFTA has actually multiplied wages and improved working conditions, many workers still have trouble meeting their expenses, especially as the cost of living in border towns is much higher than it is in the rest of Mexico.

The federal branch of the US government (through its General Accounting Office) does at least define a sweatshop, as "an employer that violates more than one federal or state labor, industrial homework, occupational safety and health, workers' compensation, or industry registration law." But it's often been up to states and cities to pass the toughest anti-sweatshop legislation. In 2000, California made manufacturers legally responsible for minimum wages and overtime pay. San Francisco, Los Angeles, Milwaukee, Newark and Albuquerque have all passed anti-sweatshop laws, and the states of Maine, Pennsylvania, New Jersey and California have recently enacted "no sweat" standards for state clothing they procure (as have numerous cities, counties and school districts). Just as anti-war movements have recently moved into the schools to counter military recruitment, so has the anti-sweatshop campaign moved onto campuses, urging students to pressure their universities to organize for sweatfree licensing of university-sanctioned apparel. While many of these initiatives are geared toward sweatshop practices and products in all countries, not just the US, they could at least lead to further safeguards against sweatshops here as well as abroad. For further information, see:

Sweatshop Watch www.sweatshopwatch.org
Maquila Solidarity Network www.maquilasolidarity.org
United Students Against Sweatshops www.studentsagainstsweatshops.org
Sweatfree Communities www.sweatfree.org

has to put up with inhumanely long hours, widespread suppression of unions, abusive managers and demeaning treatment.

Perhaps the biggest issue in most people's eyes is **child labor**—many Western shoppers have an image in their heads of rooms full of eight-year-olds sewing our branded clothes and sneakers. The problem does exist, often with young teenagers being considered to be "apprentices" or "helpers" and earning even less than the adults, but arguably this problem is slightly exaggerated. In countries associated with bad sweatshops, such as China, there is little documented child labor in export manufacturing. Child workers are much more common in less-discussed areas, such as silk production (see p.171) than in clothes factories.

A more obvious problem is **health and safety**, both in terms of workers getting injured by machines (due to lack of training or unsafe equipment) and the risk of **fires**. Despite minimal coverage in the mainstream media, hundreds of garment workers have been killed by fires and other accidents in factories producing for export to the US and Europe. In late 2000, for example, around fifty died in a garment factory near Dhaka, Bangladesh, where most clothes factories are rented properties not designed for that purpose. Most were killed by fumes and flames, but some were impaled on a fence when they tried to jump from fourth-floor windows: it was reported by local journalists that the exits were locked. In 2005, 64 died when a nine-story building housing Spectrum Sweater Industries and Shahriar Fabrics—from which several European companies were sourcing—collapsed just twenty miles away. Local authorities said the facility was structurally unsound and improperly designed. Six months later, the survivors and victims' families were still awaiting compensation. There are many such examples.

Fumes and dust are another serious health and safety issue. Many workers have been made seriously ill in clothes and shoe factories through exposure to **toxic glues** (for shoe soles), while **airborne fibers** can lead to lung damage when proper masks and ventilation aren't used. In a report on Gap factories produced by the UNITE union, for example, one African worker is quoted complaining that "we can't escape breathing in the fibers and particles from the air. When we cough, if the T-shirt we were working on was made of blue fabric, then our mucous would be full of blue fibers." But the fact that it was Gap was immaterial: according to a "provincial task force" report quoted in the *Washington Post*, 96% of businesses in China's Guangdong province—a center of clothes manufacturing—were in violation of health standards. The number of workers getting sick is rising 70% per year, with more than 2500 deaths from people having died of occupational illnesses since 1989.

But perhaps the most pressing issue of all is the **suppression of unions**. A report on Asian garment industry by CAFOD (the Catholic Agency for

Nike and Gap: demons or demonized?

No companies have taken more flak for the sweatshop issue than **Nike** and **Gap**. Both companies have been linked to some extremely exploitative factories and bad practice, from Nike allegedly petitioning the Indonesian government for exemption from the minimum wage and lying about labor conditions at its contractor factories (see box on p.181) to Gap's exploits at Saipan (see box on p.183). And the comparison between what Nike spends on advertising and what it spends on workers is a frightening and depressing indictment both of world inequality and the power of advertising in modern Western society. According to Sweatshop Watch, an average Nike worker would need to put in no fewer than 72,000 years of work to receive what Tiger Woods got for one five-year sponsorship contract (if he or she had worked a seven day week since homo sapiens first arrived in East Asia, they might be nearly finished today).

But are these companies qualitatively different from the industry as a whole in terms of labor and environmental standards? According to most people working to improve garment sweatshops, the answer is no. In fact, due to the threat of campaigns and boycotts, these two major brands have probably done more to improve things than many of the less-high-profile retailers. Indeed, in a 2006 interview with Rough Guides, campaign group Labour Behind the Label named Gap as one of the most progressive of the big clothes companies (albeit with much further to go). Nike, meanwhile, has signed up to the FLA (see p.182) and improved health and safety by phasing out dangerous solvent-based glue (as well as environmentally problematic PVC). In a move that both surprised and pleased anti-sweatshop activists, both companies recently started to release corporate responsibility reports that make information about the working conditions in their supplier factories accessible to consumers. Nike even went as far as to disclose the names and locations of more than 700 factories around the world that make its products, though the Gap has only gone as far as revealing the countries from which they source.

So why the focus on Nike and Gap? Part of the reason is that they're both huge companies which were early adopters of the outsourcing model. And part of the reason is that they're very much marketing-led firms, whose lifestyle advertising clashes sharply with the daily life of the people who actually cut, stitch and glue their products. But part of the reason is simply that, as major US firms, they've been subjected to the scrutiny of our country's unusually large and tireless anti-sweatshop movement, who've targeted the biggest and most visible players in hopes that if the industry leaders change their ways, big and smaller competitors may fall in line as well. Many other American clothes manufacturers, from Wal-Mart to Liz Claiborne, have also felt the pressure, and as Nike and Gap start to make concessions in their policies, the less compliant giants can expect the heat to turn their way that much more.

Overseas Development) pointed out that efforts by local workers, NGOs and trade unions, "are the most important factor in trying to improve wages and working conditions in Asia." The report noted that "In some countries, such as the Philippines and Sri Lanka, a history of active trade unionism, and state support for some degree of labor rights, have established expectations about acceptable labor standards. In others, such as China, Vietnam, and Bangladesh, the floor is often set by physical endurance; how many hours a day, over how many years, can one ill-nourished human body continue to function." And yet many Western clothes and shoe firms have been slow to demand union recognition in the factories they source from, and organizers continue to be harassed or assaulted. One Bangladeshi women interviewed by CAFOD, for example, had been attacked and slashed with razor blades for being a union activist at a clothes factory. Sadly, this kind of assault and intimidation seems to be relatively common.

Young women applying glue to sport shoes at a Reebok Factory in Zhongshan, China. Companies like Reebok—which today is one of the slightly more progressive of the big sportwear firms—have helped created massive economic growth in China. But many people question whether it can ever be ethical to source from a country with an appalling human rights record, widespread labor abuse and no recognition of independent trade unions.

Clothes & shoes: the big-name shops & brands

With such poor conditions in developing-world garment factories, the most pressing issue for ethical shoppers is what efforts each company has made to ensure their suppliers are sticking to decent minimum standards. Despite the focus on Gap and Nike (see box on p.179), this is a question that applies to all clothes and shoe companies.

Due to increasing pressure from consumers, most of the big brands have at least considered this matter—and certain environmental issues, too. Usually this has meant drawing up a **code of conduct**, which the clothes companies request their suppliers adhere to. They've been a long time coming, but today most major brand names have a code based on key labor standards, including the **right to organize** (join a union).

Worker groups and sweatshop campaigners agree that these codes are very useful: they can help inform workers of their rights, make it more difficult for factory owners to claim they didn't know the rules and provide a yardstick by which to measure a company's progress and failings. But they also shouldn't be taken at face value: as discussed in chapter three, voluntary codes of conduct are not necessarily enforced. And it's often very difficult to tell, because the mainstream companies treat the

Don't believe all you read: Nike vs. Kasky

In 1998, California activist Marc Kasky filed a lawsuit in the US, claiming that Nike had made misleading claims in response to accusations regarding conditions at one of its Vietnamese factories (accusations partly based on Nike's own research). Instead of defending its statements as true—presumably because it couldn't—Nike argued it could claim whatever it liked under US free speech law. In 2003, after various rounds of appeals, the state's supreme court decided, as Kasky contended, that free speech didn't apply, as Nike's statements were "commercial speech," intended to increase sales. The case was sent back to the lower courts, to try and determine whether the statements were lies, which are illegal in commercial speech. But Nike finally settled out of court by agreeing to contribute $2 million to the Fair Labor Association and worker education initiatives.

The folks at Reebok, meanwhile, have gone beyond claiming to be a reasonable employer and reinvented themselves as defenders of human rights, instigating the annual Reebok Human Rights Awards. The view that this was a cynical effort to cash in on the bad publicity surrounding Nike was bolstered in 2002 when prominent labor rights activist Dita Indah Sari rejected the $50,000 prize in protest at the "low pay and exploitation" of Reebok employees in Indonesia and elsewhere.

names and addresses of their supplier factories as a closely guarded corporate secret. If the case of Nike vs. Kasky (see box on p.181) is anything to go by, the big companies also simply lie about their commitment to ethical standards.

The gap between professed policy and enforced action leads many commentators to conclude that the big firms are still all basically the same. **War on Want**, for example, interviewed Bangladeshi garment workers and concluded: "it didn't matter which factory they worked in, who owned it, or whom they supplied—the conditions were always bad." Likewise, according to pressure group Labour Behind the Label: "Much as we would like to recommend good companies over bad ones, we have not come across a single company which we feel comfortable recommending."

This seems like pretty good grounds for avoiding the high-profile names wherever possible and favoring Fair Trade specialists such as those listed from p.187. In reality, however, the range of fairly traded clothes is still pretty small. So what efforts have the individual brands made?

One level up from drawing up a code of conduct is joining the **Fair Labor Association**, or FLA, initially set up by Bill Clinton's administration in response to growing concern about sweatshops among US consumers. The FLA focuses exclusively on garment companies, with the aim of enforcing an "industry-wide Workplace Code of Conduct ... based on the core labor standards of the International Labor Organization." In 2003, the FLA broke ground by making the results of company factory audits—code-breaches, warts and all—available to the public (see www.fairlabor.org). However, questions have been raised regarding the number and quality of the factory audits. One insider told Rough Guides that some of the FLA auditing firms had no significant experience of interviewing workers, and had a financial interest in not offending the company whose factory they are examining. Still, the initiative is certainly much better than nothing. Members include:

- adidas-Salomon
- Asics
- Drew Pearson
- Eddie Bauer
- GEAR for Sports
- Gildan Activewear
- Liz Claiborne
- Mountain Equipment Co-op (MEC)
- New Era Cap
- Nike
- Nordstrom
- Outdoor Cap
- Patagonia
- Phillips-Van Heusen
- PUMA
- Reebok
- Top of the World
- Twins Enterprise
- Zephyr Graf-X

Made in the USA? the Saipan debacle

Saipan is part of the Northern Mariana Islands in the western Pacific Ocean. Having been previously held by Spain, Germany and Japan, it was captured by the US in World War II and later given US territorial status. That makes it basically part of the States—so items produced there for the US market are free from import tariffs and quotas. And yet the minimum wage is lower, customs duties are said to be slacker and foreign workers can be granted renewable one-year work permits. Companies soon realized that they could benefit from these favorable conditions and still write "Made in the USA" on their labels. Trade soared and before long the temporary foreign workers—mainly from East Asia—outnumbered the locals by around fifty percent.

However, alleged labor abuse in the islands' many garment factories didn't take long to surface. There were reports of indentured labor (with workers unable to leave their jobs due to debts imposed by their employers), withheld wages, workers being forced to "donate" unpaid hours on top of their normal shifts and union organizers facing firings and deportation.

Finally, in 1999, a collection of workers, human rights groups and others sued some factory owners and more than twenty major retailers and manufacturers, including **Abercrombie & Fitch**, **Calvin Klein**, **Gap**, **Polo Ralph Lauren** and **Tommy Hilfiger USA**, over the alleged labor abuses. Eventually, all the companies except **Levi Strauss** (which claimed the allegations against it were false) were part of a $20 million settlement to pay withheld wages and set up a monitoring organization co-ordinated with the International Labor Organization.

So what about the rest? Affiliations with sweatshop practices remain so prevalent among non-FLA-aligned companies (and still, to some degree, among many outfits who are part of FLA) that it's difficult to single any out as especially egregious.

There's **Gap**, of course. Sourcing from 3000 factories in more than 50 countries, the company has long been the bête noir of sweatshops campaigners. But it was recently lauded by some of its long-standing critics (see box on p.179) and has become the first major American company to join the UK's Ethical Trading Initiative.

Unfortunately, many other sizable companies have black spots on their resumes long enough to fill (or blot out, if you prefer) several pages. **Wal-Mart** has taken steps to improve its image in this regard, chief executive Lee Scott recently pledging that its "factories in China are going to end up having to be held up to the same standards as the factories in the US." Its credibility was undermined, however, when a former executive for the corporation sued them in 2005, contending he was fired for too diligently reporting workplace violations (including mandatory 24-hour shifts) in Central American apparel factories.

And being smaller and less instantly recognizable than Gap, Nike and Wal-Mart doesn't guarantee a better record. As of this writing, for instance, **Fila** sportswear is under fire for not paying back wages and compensation to workers at an Indonesian factory that was recently shut down, as is the **North Sails** surf sail company for firing more than 200 striking workers in Sri Lanka. **H&M**, the Swedish multinational that recently expanded into the US, has a decent code of conduct but is currently under attack from campaign groups for not cracking down on union busting in its factories.

But upmarketness doesn't necessarily correlate with better or worse behavior. Of the smaller, classier retailers, **Timberland** is often cited as something of a shining example, fully committed to improving standards and auditing not only its factories but also leather tanneries and other suppliers. **French Connection**, on the other hand, has what campaigners

The retailer scorecard

Though anti-sweatshop activism has focused upon manufacturers rather than retail chains, it also matters where we shop, not just what we buy. Co-op America gave eight of the nation's biggest chains a "retailer scorecard," rating the players according to which and how many sweatshop-affiliated suppliers they were using. Here are the results, as posted on www.coopamerica.org/programs/sweatshops/scorecard.cfm

Supplier	Federated	J.C. Penny	Kmart	Kohl's	May's	Sears	Target	Wal-Mart
Tarrant	X		X					X
Anvil Ensembles	X				X			
Daewoosa		X		X		X	X	X
WINS Facilities		X			X		X	
Saipan		X			X	X	X	X
Chentex		X	X	X				X
Leader Garments		X			X	X		
Confecciones Ninos	X	X					X	
Burma	X				X			
Grade	C	D-	D	D+	C	D-	D+	F

While May's and Federated come out on top, their "C" grades are hardly ringing endorsements. Unsurprisingly, it's Wal-Mart who trails the pack, dishonored with the lowest possible "F" rating.

describe as a feeble code, with no reference to monitoring. Labour Behind the Label wrote with reasonable indignation in 2002 that the company "has never, in the course of five years of letter-writing by consumers and LBL, acknowledged our letters and concerns."

If you want to research the fine details on a specific brand, the Clean Clothes Campaign (at www.cleanclothers.org/companies.htm) and Co-op America's Responsible Shopper division (at www.responsibleshopper.org) maintain sites monitoring and evaluating numerous apparel manufacturers' sweatshop connections.

Shoes

Compared with clothes production, shoe manufacture tends to be more industrial and hi-tech—something that usually means longer-term contracts and more leverage over labor conditions for brands and retailers. However, aside from the athletic footwear companies discussed above, the shoe sector has shown very little interest in ethical issues.

There is still not a single company in the Fair Labor Association specializing in non-sporting shoes, so this industry clearly has a long way to go. Right now, just about the only shoe shops that seem concerned with ethical matters are specialists producing non-leather shoes (see p.173).

One contentious shoe company is **CAT**, whose bulldozers have become a favorite tool of the Israeli army. As the *Business Respect* newsletter noted in November 2003, the company "celebrated its inclusion for the third year in the Dow Jones Sustainability World Index, just as protesters in Iowa slammed the company for selling equipment to Israel that would allegedly be used 'to bulldoze Palestinian homes.'"

China & Burma

Regardless of the codes and promises of clothes companies, another ethical question is *where* they do business. The international trade in shoes and clothes is increasingly dominated by just one country: China. The country has no recognition of independent trade unions and its sweatshops are notorious. Yet nearly every clothes company is shifting its production there "to stay competitive," in the words of Gap. Indeed, as of mid-2006, China accounts for slightly over 50% of global production in both the clothes and shoe sectors. Some campaigners call on consumers to avoid Chinese-made clothes and other goods wherever possible, pointing to human rights, sweatshops and the occupation of Tibet as reasons to boycott the country. But the arguments are complex (see pp.45 and 61).

A more extreme case is Burma (p.307), whose abhorrent military dictatorship directly profits from the clothes export industry. However, most of the major brands that were importing from Burma, or Myanmar as it may appear on clothes labels, have pulled out, and as the US has trade sanctions against the country, technically no clothing should be getting in.

More info

To keep abreast of the issues surrounding brands and workers' rights in the rag trade, visit:

Clean Clothes Campaign www.cleanclothes.org
Sweatshop Watch www.sweatshopwatch.org

Organic and fair trade clothes

As the issues covered in this chapter become more widely discussed, growing numbers of **fairly traded** and **organic** clothes are appearing on the market. Traditionally, this section of the clothes industry tends toward flowing dresses, flowery patterns and "ethnic" styles. There's still some of that around, and on the low-price end, organic yoga accessories and T-shirts advocating social justice and environmental causes are rampant. But as the niche market rapidly expands, the hippyish relics are actually getting outweighed by sensible and stylish (sometimes even rather middle-of-the-road) gear—not that you can't have both at once, if you're so inclined.

Fiber product made from certified **organic** fiber materials are certified according to the same National Organic Program labeling requirements that apply to organic food (see p.73). However, while there are federal standards for the agricultural production of raw fiber, there aren't any regulating the process from the time it leaves the farm until it appears in a shirt, skirt or what have you. If you want additional assurances in that regard, the Organic Trade Association has developed a voluntary American Organic Standards certification program for the processing end, which provides companies with an additional label claim to make if they wish.

The US is considerably behind the UK and Europe in the fair-trade clothing stakes. No clothes bear the official Fair Trade Certified label, and if they're billed as "fair trade" through retailers, the labor standards usually have to be taken on trust. Most of the companies listed here are widely respected in the field and most make a commitment to environmental and social justice as part of their mission statement, and you can safely assume that this is genuine in most cases. At the very least, you can be confident that non-exploitative and environmentally sustainable sourcing is more central to the business of these companies than to any of the big-volume outfits.

To get some sort of assurance that the companies you're dealing with are working under Fair Trade standards, sticking to outfits in the **Fair Trade Federation** (www.fairtradefederation.org) is an option to consider, and a couple such companies are included in the following listings. FTF members are committed to guidelines that are something of a laundry list of values important to anyone committed to shopping with a conscience, including fair wages, cooperative workplaces, consumer education, environmental sustainability, respect for cultural identity and public accountability. As of this writing, however, it's far heavier on handcrafts than anything else, and while its website also lists online, retail and wholesale Fair Trade clothes dealers, these goods are usually offered only as part of an operation that carries numerous categories of Fair Trade products, not just wearables. This is likely to change as the fair-trade concept becomes more firmly entrenched in the US. In the meantime, you may want to explore the offerings of some US-made "no-sweat" clothes (see p.191).

Eco and organic

Following is a selection of the top eco and organic clothes brands. For longer lists, visit Eco-Mall (www.ecomall.com/biz/clothing.htm) and Co-op America's National Green Pages (www.coopamerica.org/pubs/greenpages). Also see the veggie-leather list on p.173.

Baby's Enchanted Garden www.babysenchantedgarden.com ▷ 866-802-BABY
There are several organic baby's clothing specialists selling online (see p.194). This one offers not only the expected toddler hats, shorts and shoes, but also some eco-clothes for moms, including a nursing bra and maternity bikinis.

Blue Canoe www.bluecanoe.com ▷ 888-923-1373
"Eco-friendly clothing made carefully in the USA" for women, including lines of solid-color "sheer organics" tops and lingerie, combining organic cotton with "a touch of stretch lyrcra." While much of their wares are marketed for yoga practitioners (they also sell "yoga eco-mats"), the material is suitable for casual use and other exercise activities as well.

CottonfieldUSA www.cottonfieldusa.com ▷ 800-954-1551
Offering men and women's clothing using 100% organically grown cotton in the US and Peru, the styles here are on the more conservative side for the eco-clothing field, though

not stuffy. It's pricey, though, with the likes of a $64 flannel work shirt, though they emphasize they're selling clothes to last, not just for one season.

Esperanza Threads www.esperanzathreads.com ▷ 800-397-0045

Most things made of organic cotton are here, including women's wear, men's wear, kid's wear, sleepwear, sweats and socks (the last available in organic wool), though it's on the staid and expensive side as these things go. Part of the nonprofit Grassroots Coalition for Economic and Environmental Justice, the company's committed to fair wages and teaching job skills to low-income individuals.

Global Mamas www.globalmamas.org ▷ 800-338-3032

The goods produced by the Ghana-based Global Mamas cooperative (sold in the US through a Minneapolis distributor) are among the more florid online organic clothes, using batik and tie dye to color and pattern the fabrics for their compact selection of men, women's and kids' clothes and accessories. Global Mamas belong to the Fair Trade Federation, and its women are provided with a living wage. According to the company's website, this amounts to more than ten times the normal minimum wage in Ghana.

Hip and Zen www.hipandzen.com ▷ 800-HIP-NZEN

Although they sell all sorts of eco-"lifestyle" products, not just clothes, Hip and Zen have a decent online selection of women's apparel, helpfully coded as to whether they're organic, fairly traded, recycled, handmade, natural or some combination thereof. Even by the pricey standards of the niche market, however, these aren't bargains, with an organic fleece sweatshirt going for $90.

Indigenous Designs
www.indigenousdesigns.com

"Natural fiber clothing" for women (jackets, sweaters and casuals) and men (just casuals and

Hip and Zen's felted
flower bag from Nepal.

sweaters), with items constructed with organic cotton, organic cotton blends, and eco-wool (taken only from free-ranging sheep). Simple, classy and upscale, with a mission statement emphasizing training and fair wages for the artisans in Peru and Ecuador with whom they work.

Kasper Organics www.kasperorganics.net ▷ 888-875-2233, pin # 0266

Some of the lowest-priced—though not at all inferior—men's, women's and unisex organic cotton T-shirts, underwear, socks and bras, as well as bandannas and hand-kerchiefs. Maybe it's not high-end fashion, but it's good to see that there's something for student budgets out there as well.

KUSIKUY www.kusikuy.com ▷ 866-KUSIKUY

A member (unlike most of the other companies listed here) of the Fair Trade Federation, KUSIKUY sells organic cotton, llama and alpaca produced by Bolivian communities in the Andes mountains. The sweaters, ponchos, mittens, hats, and other accessories are understandably more "ethnic" in pattern and design than most of what's offered by organic clothing retailers, but you'll be hard-pressed to find a softer, more lightweight material than alpaca for breathable warmth.

KUSIKUY's 100% alpaca yarn.

Lotus Organics www.lotusorganics.com ▷ 641-472-7184

Mid-range in price, selection and style, Lotus Organics offers clothes for men, women, and children made with certified organic cotton, as well as hemp, alpaca and wool. "All garments are produced in non-sweatshop, Fair Trade conditions," according to its website.

Maggie's Functional Organics www.organicclothes.com ▷ 800-609-8593

As the name indicates, Maggie's offers some of the simpler and, yes, less expensive socks, tights, shirts, and camisoles made from organic cotton, linen and wool that you can find online. The cotton camisoles are sewn by women in a worker-owned Nicaraguan cooperative, Maquilador Mujeres, which the company turned to not just out of a sense of social justice, but also out of frustration with the quality of sewing in US mills.

Mama's Earth www.mamasearth.com ▷ 800-620-7388

Some of the most reasonably priced—a catchphrase they use repeatedly in their promotional materials, but a true one—men's, women's and unisex organic cotton and hemp clothing available, for those who can live with something a little less fancy (though perfectly respectable) for a good less many bucks. Nominated as "Green Business of the Year" by Co-op America in 2005, which might be as close as you can get to winning the most valuable player award in this racket.

Patagonia www.patagonia.com ▷ 800-638-6464

High-quality fleeces, jackets and other outdoor pursuits gear made from organic cotton by a company with good environmental credentials. Use the details above to find your nearest retailer or order a catalogue.

Round Belly Clothing www.roundbelly.com ▷ 866-336-1458

Organic maternity clothes for "larger and taller women," with an "eco-sprout" section for children's clothes made from organic cotton and eco-fleece (a soft fabric made from recycled soda bottles).

Under the Canopy www.underthecanopy.com ▷ 800-CANOPY

One of the leading players in the young eco-clothing business; the founder of the company is on the steering committee of the OTA's Organic Fiber Council. They require their vendors and manufacturers to meet fair labor standards, and if you're one to check up on the standards of companies selling goods marked as organic, they'll forward a certification of authenticity upon request. Their women's clothing line is extensive and (for the genre) reasonably priced, though the men's section—pitifully under-exploited by this niche market in general—was only offering T-shirts as of this writing.

Wildlife Works www.wildlifeworks.com
▷ 415-332-8081

Organic cotton women's, men's and children's clothes, heavy on the advocacy T-shirts, but also including (though only for the women) some straightforward pants, skirts and yoga wear, sometimes at way-slashed prices. As one of the conservation projects it aims to launch with its proceeds, it's created a wildlife sanctuary in Kenya, next to which is its "Eco-Factory," employing members of the local community to work on their products. According to the FAQ on its website, "when we do work with another manufacturer we carefully scrutinize their fair trade and labor practices before committing business to them."

Wildlife Works' Mikey Bear is hand-made from organic cotton, and the ear and foot pads are made of tree bark cloth.

Organic wool

Compared to organic cotton, the organic wool market in the US has been slow to take off. Just a little less than 20,000 pounds were grown in the US in 2005, with production only undertaken in six states. Demand for organic wool is expected to grow quickly, however, as overall organic clothing sales continue to rapidly expand, and consumers start to look for a more diverse array of fabrics from which to choose. The recently formed **Organic Wool Network**—a collaborative of eleven retailers, suppliers and support organizations—was formed in hopes of raising the profile for the product in the States. These aren't the only people producing and selling organic wool in the US, and it would help their cause to launch a website, which they didn't have as of this writing. Through an article on the Lotus Organics site (www.lotusorganics.com/articles/OWN.aspx), however, you can link to OWN's members, read some product descriptions (which already include organic wool socks, underwear, sweaters and baby clothes), and find out a little more about wool's inroads into American backroads.

"No sweat" clothes

Though the fair trade concept is becoming more widely understood (and popular) here, there still aren't quite as many fairly trading retailers in the States as there are in the EU, where the movement's more firmly established. As some compensation, and perhaps because of the sheer extent of non-unionized garment factories in the US, another type of company has evolved, mainly selling clothes made domestically but under **guaranteed union conditions**. Note that some of these companies—unlike most fair traders and eco-gear outfits, for example—don't subscribe to a specifically social/environmental/activist agenda, other than staunch union support. Some also push the "made in USA" aspect of their goods as a major selling point, which could be interpreted as either laudable protectionism or taking away jobs from poor overseas communities, depending on one's stance. And most emphasize basic, utilitarian clothes and T-shirts, though that will no doubt change if more companies sign on, the niche grows, and the expanding consumer base starts to demand more options.

That's not to say that some "no sweat" retailers don't have a specific socially responsible cause or two to promote. For instance **Adbusters**, the ultimate anti-consumerists famed for tweaking billboard ads to reverse their meaning, have started selling their own non-sweatshop sneakers. Sold at adbusters.org/metas/corpo/blackspotshoes, they're been designed specifically with Nike founder Phil Knight in mind: "Phil Knight had a dream. He'd sell shoes. He'd sell dreams. He'd get rich. He'd use sweatshops if he had to. Then along came a new shoe. Plain. Simple. Cheap. Fair. Designed for only one thing: kicking Phil's ass." It's unclear whether the garment

100% ORGANIC HEMP UPPER

SWEET SPOT (FOR KICKING CORPORATE ASS)

HAND DRAWN ANTI-LOGO

RECYCLED TIRE SOLE

VEGETARIAN LEATHER

UNION MADE

Earth-friendly, anti-sweatshop, cruelty-free, and pro-grassroots, Blackspots are the only rough-and-ready shoes designed to give toxic megacorporations what they truly need the most: a swift kick in the brand.

UNSWOOSHER

workers of the developing world would be impressed by Adbusters helping their plight by producing sneakers in Portugal, but the idea of a sneaker from an "anti-corporation" undoubtedly has a certain appeal.

Several anti-sweatshop sites maintain lists of links to "no sweat" retailers, several of whom sell online. The one on **Sweat Free Communities** (www.sweatfree.org/shopping) states which company's goods are union made or co-op made, while Co-op America offers a much longer list (compiled by the AFL-CIO) of companies using union labor (www.coopamerica.org/programs/sweatshops/sweatfreeproducts.cfm), and exposes any concerns about their social and environmental practices. A few of the more prominent "no sweat" sellers are listed below.

Two of the companies, by the way, that have received the most press for non-sweatshop production are missing from our list, each for very different reasons. SweatX, launched by Ben & Jerry's cofounder Ben Cohen, went out of business in mid-2004 after just two years of operation in Los Angeles (and despite having its SweatX shirts sold at Foo Fighters concerts) due to, as Cohen frankly admitted to *The Nation*, "some serious mismanagement." American Apparel, on the other hand, is not listed by Sweat Free Communities because its "workers are not organized as a worker-owned cooperative or a democratic union." That company's image has taken some other hits of late as well (see box).

Justice Clothing www.justiceclothing.com ▷ 888-661-0620

A wide selection of men's, women's and unisex shirts, dresses, jeans, socks, athletic gear and cold-weather accessories. Unfussily designed and modestly priced, made in the US and Canada by unionized workers. If you have any doubts about their politics, they spell it out on their home page: "If you don't mind buying clothing made by slaves, children, indentured servants, or workers who are paid pennies a day, we are not your kind of store." They're working on getting organic products into their catalog, which in the "no sweat" field would be a welcome innovation.

No Sweat Apparel www.nosweatapparel.com ▷ 877-992-7827

Though heavy on the sneakers, T-shirts and functional footwear, one of the leading "no sweat" companies has a fairly wide line of shirts, pants, jeans and athletic wear as well, solidly made and very reasonably priced. Note, however, that as of this writing, an independent monitoring report by sweatshop watch-dog Sweat Free Communities (www.sweatfree.org)—posted on No Sweat Apparel's own website—generated concern about the union at the Indonesian factory that produces the company's sneakers. The alert advises consumers that the sneakers "are not necessarily made by workers represented by a democratic union."

Union Jean Company www.unionjeancompany.com ▷ 888-937-8009

Not just jeans, but also denim shirts, khakis, jackets, T-shirts and polo/golf shirts, all American-made and union-made.

Unabashedly American Apparel

Of the businesses that have tried to both make money and a social statement, few have been more successful—and controversial—than American Apparel. Founded by Dov Charney in the late 1990s, the rapidly expanding company sells more than $200 million of clothing annually, focusing on fashionable T-shirts, all manufactured in its Los Angeles factory by a largely Latino workforce. The garment workers receive above-average wages—an average of $13/hr, according to Charney—with benefits (including free on-site English-language and yoga classes, Internet access, and massage therapy) and working conditions similarly above the industry norm. So why isn't it one of the companies anti-sweatshop activists recommend to consumers?

The major sticking point is that American Apparel isn't unionized, a condition that "no sweat" advocates demand, no matter how good things might be on the factory floor. Above and beyond that, however, the Union of Needletrades, Industrial and Textile Employees (UNITE) charged that management intimidated workers during a failed organizing drive in 2003. The National Labor Relations Board ended up requiring the company to sign a settlement agreement to refrain from anti-union meddling in the future.

The flamboyant Charney's also gotten in trouble with his unapologetically sexual advertising campaigns—familiar to readers of alternative weeklies throughout the country—featuring photos of skimpily dressed young women, many of them company employees, the pictures often taken by Charney himself. Using sex to sell fashion is nothing new, but recently the boss has been under heat of a more dangerous sort, getting sued in May 2005 by three former women employees who claimed that he sexually harassed them at work. Charney denied the accusations, but his case wasn't helped by a 2004 article in the women's magazine *Jane* that described him performing oral sex with a female employee and masturbating in front of the writer. Charney didn't deny either of those incidents, but maintained to *BusinessWeek*, "I've never done anything sexual that wasn't consensual." Some former employees added fuel to the fire, however, by telling the same publication that senior American Apparel managers chased after sexual relationships with junior coworkers, rewarding them with promotions, apartments and company cars. "It was a company built on lechery," said one.

In spite of the bad ink, by the end of 2005 American Apparel was a major player in the fashion industry, rapidly expanding into retail with dozens of stores throughout the US, and several others elsewhere throughout the globe. It now runs the largest garment factory in the country, employing over 3000 workers. It hasn't shed its posture as a progressive operation, offering its most popular styles in certified organic cotton and recycling, according to its own count, over a million pounds of fabric scraps every year. Charney, however, has cast some doubt as to whether the company would continue to make a commitment to superior wages and working conditions a major part of its advertising campaigns, calling the sweatshop-free tag "a secondary appeal" in *The Los Angeles Business Journal*. "I'm getting a little bored with it myself," he added. "It's too PC. I'm de-emphasizing it."

Diapers & baby clothes
For principled parents

Babies may account for a small percentage of family biomass, but when fitted with **disposable diapers** they generate roughly half the contents of a household's trash. A typical baby gets through around 5000 disposables during its diaper days; across the US, this adds up to an astonishing 20 billion each year, enough to cover a footfall field with a three-mile-high pile. Most of these end up in landfills where, according to environmentalists, the plastic will take hundreds of years to break down, the super-absorbent granules will soak up groundwater needed for the decomposition of other waste, and the excrement and urine may pose a health hazard.

Even if these worries are overcautious, diapers are still enormously wasteful to make (each one requiring considerable quantities of oil for plastic and wood for pulp, as well as gels and other chemicals) and therefore also to buy (parents spend on average a total of $800 annually per baby on disposables, according to the Real Diaper Association).

The green advice has always been to opt for washable cloth diapers (which are also now promoted by local councils keen to cut down on landfill costs). However, a recent in-depth study from the UK's Environment Agency has left many people wondering whether it's worth the hassle. The report concluded that although a baby's worth of disposable diapers uses more oil than washables (205 lbs. vs. 62 lbs of crude), it leads to less CO_2 emissions (963 lbs vs. 1110 lbs) and less water usage (9000 gallons vs. 22,000 gallons). Cloth diapers from a washing service had the highest CO_2 outputs (1554 lbs), with middle-range figures for oil and water.

These figures have been disputed, however. The Women's Environmental Network, long-standing proponents of the washable option, point out that the study made various assumptions that wouldn't apply to many green-minded people. They claim that, if you have an energy-efficient washing machine, use a 60 degree wash cycle, limit yourself to 24 diapers, and don't tumble dry or iron them, then the cloth option ends up producing a quarter less CO_2 than disposables. This is some way from the claims that have long been made by some environmentalists, but worth considering nonetheless.

Cloth diapers are very widely available, though you may prefer to look into fair-trade and organic options at specialists such as the following, all of which sell online and also offer **clothes** for babies and young children:

BabyBunz & Co. www.babybunz.com ▷ 800-676-4559

Baby's Enchanted Garden www.babysenchantedgarden.com ▷ 866-802-BABY

Babyworks www.babyworks.com ▷ 800-422-2910

Better for Babies www.betterforbabies.com ▷ 877-303-4050

Ecobaby www.ecobaby.com ▷ 800-596-7450

Fuzbaby www.fuzbaby.com ▷ 801-282-6895

Gentle Essence www.gentleessence.com ▷ 845-313-2371

KidBean www.kidbean.com ▷ 954-942-2830

Lil Diaper Depot www.lildiaperdepot.com ▷ 866-417-4949

Pure Beginnings www.purebeginnings.com ▷ 866-787-2229

Sage Creek Naturals www.sagecreeknaturals.com ▷ 866-598-1400

Sckoon www.sckoon.com ▷ 877-671-2145

Cosmetics & toiletries
Because you (and the bunny) are worth it

When it comes to cosmetics, toiletries and perfumes, the major worry for most consumers is **animal testing**. We cover this below, but first it's worth running through a few less-discussed issues. One is the ethical standards of the giant businesses that dominate the "health and beauty" market. There isn't room here for a proper profile of each, but suffice it to say that they're very politically active. According to Open Secrets (www.opensecrets.org), George W. Bush's Republican party has received substantial cash donations from **Bristol Myers Squibb** and **Revlon**. And **Procter & Gamble**, **Colgate-Palmolive** and **Johnson & Johnson** are, among other things, on the board of the National Foreign Trade Council, a lobby group which has actively opposed legislation to stop trade with Burma (and whose website opens with a quote of gratitude and approval from none other than Dick Cheney). To see the many brands these companies own, see the box on p.198.

Another issue is the degree to which cosmetics manufacturers use needlessly risky chemicals, such as **persistent toxins** that may accumulate in the human body or the wider environment, posing risks to health and wildlife. As with household cleaning products (see p.254), there is very little evidence to suggest that standard exposure to cosmetics chemicals causes anything more serious than occasional allergic reactions, though intensive long-term exposure does seem to present risks. In 2002, for instance, researchers from Lund University, Sweden, found that female hairdressers were one-third more likely than a selected control group to give birth to babies with malformations or other serious physical defects (especially heart defects). Extended exposure to everyday hair sprays, dyes and the like seems to be the most likely cause.

There are environmental concerns about the use of **"natural" products**, too. According to the World Wildlife Foundation, between four and ten thousand plant species are threatened with extinction due to the demand for herbal remedies, and the natural ingredients used in certain toiletries and cosmetics inevitably pose similar threats. For example, rainforest campaigners worry about the growing demand for **palm oil**, derivatives of which are widely used in soaps, lipsticks and perfumes, among other products. According to environmental groups such as the World Rainforest Movement (see www.wrm.org.uy) these are helping to wipe out biodiversity and tacitly supporting the forced displacement of forest-based peoples in Indonesia and elsewhere.

Similarly, in 2003, a joint investigation by the Environmental Investigation Agency and Friends of the Earth revealed the extensive damage being done by illegal mining of soapstone for talcum power (used in everything from lipstick to deodorant) in the nature reserves of Rajasthan, India. Subjecting workers to appalling health and safety risks, causing serious pollution, lowering the water table and generally causing environmental wipe-out, these mines have been identified as the single most serious threat to the survival of the endangered Indian tiger (for more, see www.eia-international.org). Several multinationals were shown to be purchasing this talc: Revlon, Johnson & Johnson, Cussons, Avon and Unilever. However, to be fair, many smaller companies were probably also benefiting from this destruction—though the ethics and wisdom of buying talc in any form, no matter how it was produced, should be considered too, as cosmetic grade talc increases the risk of ovarian cancer in women, and has also been linked to lung cancer.

Other issues surrounding cosmetics include the human rights standards of developing-world make-up factories—*New York Times* columnist Joseph Kahn recently reported slave labor conditions in a Chinese false-eyelash plant—and the question of whether ingredients such as cocoa butter are traded according to fair trade principles. Finally, vegans and strict vegetarians should be aware that many cosmetic items contain animal-derived products.

Animal testing

In the late 1980s and early 1990s, under the pressure of aggressive campaigns by animal-rights activists, the list of companies that refused to test on animals grew from less than 50 to more than 300, including such industry giants as Revlon, Avon and Benetton. Still, testing does continue, especially as the US (unlike the EU) is making no moves to ban such tests outright. According to animal-rights campaigners, millions of animals globally are subjected to tests each year, for products ranging from hair dyes to toothpastes. These include notorious experiments such as the **Lethal Dose 50% Test** (animals are gradually poisoned with increasing doses of a substance until half of them die) and the **Draize Eye Test** (chemicals added to animals' eyes and the damage recorded over several days). Safety testing on cosmetic products actually only comprise about 10–20% of the animal testing done in the US, according to the Humane Society, but it's the sector that causes the most public outrage.

Even in countries such as the UK where animal testing has been phased out, production of animal-tested cosmetics elsewhere in the globe can still have a major impact, as most of what's on sale there is imported from, or contains ingredients imported from, abroad. After persistent public and campaigner pressure, an **EU-wide ban** on the sale of animal-tested cosmetics was finally agreed upon in 2003. However, it's not due to become effective until 2009 and there have already been at least two legal actions to try and have it overturned: one directly from a coalition of cosmetics companies, which refuse to reveal their identities, and one from the government of France, home to industry giants associated with animal testing such as L'Oréal. So it remains to be seen whether the legislation will survive.

In the meantime, tests are gradually being developed that don't require animals—often funded, it has to be said, by the same companies that are still actively conducting animal experiments. In the EU, once an alternative test exists, it has to be used instead of the animal version, but in the US alternatives must only be considered. (A California state bill does require the use of scientifically validated, federally-approved non-animal methods by testing facilities, and animal rights groups are trying to get similar legislation passed nationwide.) But until non-animal tests exist for all products and ingredients—which, as *New Scientist* has pointed out, is a matter less of ethics and more of governments deciding "how much taxpayers money should be spent"—the argument really comes down to whether you believe intense animal suffering is a reasonable price to pay for the development of new make-up ingredients.

Clean cosmetics

According to survey after survey, nearly all consumers feel strongly that animal testing for cosmetics should be stopped. But the same people continue to give their support to companies that aren't on the animal-testing clean list. According to animal rights groups, this is partly because many statements on the sides of bottles and tubes are misleading. "No animal testing," "not tested on animals," or "this finished product not tested on animals," for example, mean basically nothing at all, as there are no laws regulating such labels. Anti-testing campaigners also emphasize that while some products might be cruelty-free and labeled as such, that doesn't mean that others manufactured by the same company aren't tested on animals. Clairol's Herbal Essence shampoos state that they weren't tested on animals, for instance, but other Clairol products do use the tests, and organizations such as PETA urge boycotting the entire brand line in such cases. Other phrases on the packaging, such as "we have not carried

Who tests on animals?

At the time of writing, according to PETA's Caring Consumer branch, the following companies manufacture products tested on animals:

▶ **Boyle-Midway**

▶ **Chesebrough-Ponds** Fabergé, Ponds, Vaseline

▶ **Church & Dwight** Aim, Arm & Hammer, Arrid, Brillo, Close-Up, Lady's Choice, Mentadent, Nair, Pearl Drops,

▶ **Clairol** Aussie, Daily Defense, Herbal Essences, Infusium 23

▶ **Clorox** ArmorAll, Formula 409, Fresh Step, Glad, Liquid Plumber, Pine-Sol, Soft Scrub, S.O.S., Tilex

▶ **Colgate Palmolive** Ajax, Fab, Hills Pet Nutrition, Mennen, Palmolive, SoftSoap, Speed Stick

▶ **COTY** adidas, Calvin Klein, Davidoff, Glow, The Healing Garden, JOOP!, Jovan, Kenneth Cole,

Lancaster, Marc Jacob, Rimmel, Stetson

▶ **Del Laboratories** CornSilk, LaCros, Naturistics, New York Color, Sally Hansen

▶ **Dial Corporation** Purex, Renuzit

▶ **Erno Laszlo**

▶ **Helene Curtis Industries** Finesse, Salon Selectives, Thermasilk

▶ **Johnson & Johnson** Aveeno, Clean & Clear, Neutrogena, ROC

▶ **Kimberly-Clark Corp.** Cottonelle, Huggies, Kleenex, Kotex, Pull-Ups, Scott Paper

▶ **L'Oreal U.S.A.** Biotherm, Cacharel, Garnier, Giorgio Armani, Helena Rubinstein, Lancôme, Matrix Essentials, Maybelline, Ralph Lauren

out animal testing since 1990," could mean that the manufacturers simply commissioned the animal testing from other companies.

For some sort of assurance that animal testing has not been carried out, consumers have a few options, even if some of them aren't as convenient as looking at the label in your drugstore. One thing to look out for is the white-rabbit logo of the **Coalition for Consumer Information on Cosmetics** (CCIC), a program supported by many animal rights groups that's also administered in Canada, Europe and the UK.

To use the CCIC logo, the company must exclude all ingredients tested on animals after a fixed **cut-off point** (usually a year in the 1980s or 90s)

Fragrances, Redken, Soft Sheen, Vichy

▶ **Mead**

▶ **Melaleuca**

▶ **Neoteric Cosmetics**

▶ **New Dana Perfumes**

▶ **Noxell**

▶ **Olay Co./Oil of Olay**

▶ **Pantene**

▶ **Pfizer** Ben Gay, Desitin, Listerine, Lubriderm, Plax, Visine

▶ **Playtex** Baby Magic, Banana Boat, Ogilvie

▶ **Procter & Gamble** Cover Girl, Crest, Giorgio, Iams, Max Factor, Physique, Tide

▶ **Reckitt Benckiser** Easy Off, Lysol, Mop & Glo, Old English, Resolve, Spray 'N Wash, Veet, Woolite

▶ **Richardson-Vicks**

▶ **Reckitt Benckiser** Bain de Soleil, Coppertone, Dr. Scholl's

▶ **S.C. Johnson** Drano, Edge, Fantastik, Glade, OFF!, Oust, Pledge, Scrubbing Bubbles, Shout, Skintimate, Windex, Ziploc

▶ **Schering-Plough** Bain de Soleil, Coppertone, Dr. Scholl's

▶ **3M** Post-It, Scotch

▶ **Unilever** Axe, Dove, Lever Bros., Suave

The following currently have a moratorium on animal testing, though they have not permanently banned it:

▶ **Bic Corporation**

▶ **Gillette** Braun, Duracell, Oral-B

and prove this via independent audits. For an up-to-the-minute list, or to request its *Pocket Compassionate Shopping Guide*, visit www.leapingbunny. org/shopping_guide.htm.

The fact that a company isn't CCIC-endorsed doesn't necessarily mean it uses or commissions animal testing. Handmade soap specialist **Lush**, for example, doesn't buy from any companies that currently test on animals, but they don't have a fixed cut-off point. Such policies, according to the likes of CCIC, are a step in the right direction, but since they don't eliminate all long- and short-term incentives for developing ingredients that require animal testing, they remain insufficient.

A similar list is maintained by PETA at www.caringconsumer.com, though they don't have an equivalent to CCIC's bunny logo. The companies here have vouched to PETA that they don't do any non-required animal tests on ingredients, formulations, or finished products, also pledging not to do so in the future. Naturally there's some overlap between the CCIC and PETA lists, but while CCIC is the only one to offer a logo, PETA offers the valuable bonus of a comprehensive list of companies that *do* manufacture products tested on animals (see pp.198–199). Hearteningly, the list of outfits that don't is now much bigger than the roll call of those who do.

Alternative suppliers

Leaving aside the animal-testing question, there are a number of manufacturers trying to be ethical operators on a broader level. Often this doesn't go much further than shunning the plethora of synthetic chemicals used by the big firms. But many of these companies also use organic ingredients and recyclable plastic bottles, and shun animal-based ingredients. And, unlike the big boys, they are small businesses far removed from the ugly world of corporate lobbying and political donations. There are now literally hundreds of companies offering organic and testing-free body care products as all, most or part of their catalog. Some of the more established, wider-ranging and avowedly ethical ones are listed below as a taster, but links to many more can be found at www.greenpeople.org.

In August 2005, incidentally, it was announced that cosmetics can be labeled with the USDA organic seal, using the same National Organic Program standards applied to food. It will be probably be a while before the labels are widespread, and as of 2006, the Organic Consumers Association knew of just three companies (Sensibility Soaps, Dr. Bronner's Magic Soaps, and Vermont Soap Organics) with USDA-NOP-certified organic skin and hair cleansing product lines. But the use of the seals on

The Body Shop

Founded by Anita Roddick in Brighton in 1976, the Body Shop is now a global company, with nearly 2000 shops in 50 countries and shares on the London Stock Exchange. But it claims to be unlike other big companies, placing human rights, environmental sustainability and animal welfare at the core of its operations. Dame Roddick, aka the "Queen of Green," has certainly been a tireless campaigner on a wide range of social justice and environmental issues, using her position at the Body Shop to bring numerous issues to the public's attention, from Amazonian rainforest destruction to Shell's activities in Nigeria. And the company has initiated various progressive projects, working with the likes of Amnesty International and creating a fair trade scheme, called "community trade," for some items, including various beauty-product ingredients.

However, the chain has also received its share of criticism. Sometimes the objections, such as those from London Greenpeace in the early 1990s, have focused on general chain-store complaints: the company's near-identical shops leading to homogenization of public spaces and its promotion of a "buy more" lifestyle fuelling the consumerism that's ravaging the planet. But other critics have been far more specific, notably American journalist Jon Entine, who throughout the 1990s made it a personal mission to expose Roddick and the Body Shop as ethical frauds. His allegations—covering everything from the "theft" of the Body Shop name to animal testing—were laid out in his social audit of the company (see www.jonentine.com). But Entine himself is a controversial figure. An "adjunct fellow" with the influential right-wing think tank the American Enterprise Institute, he's a keen defender of big businesses and critic of environmentalists. He recently gave a speech warning that we should be concerned about NGOs and social investors, whose leaders "are products of the activist community, yet they are different and more dangerous."

More recently, criticism of the Body Shop has come from a less likely source: Roddick herself. In 2001 she described the firm as a "dysfunctional coffin" driven too much by soulless market forces and shareholder profits. But that was nothing compared to the takeover of the company in March 2006 by L'Oréal. The French cosmetics giant promised to keep the Body Shop running as a separate company, with its ethical values "ring-fenced." But animal-rights campaigners weren't convinced. Within days of the sale, groups such as Naturewatch and Uncaged were calling for a boycott of the company, due to L'Oréal's animal-testing activities.

So where does all this leave the only "ethical" company most people could name? Tarnished, perhaps. Yet the Body Shop remains far more progressive than its high-street neighbours. It has expanded its fair-trade efforts to dozens of suppliers; it is HCS-approved for being animal-testing free; it has been praised by Friends of the Earth for its policy on dangerous chemicals and by the WWF on sustainable wood; it has published far-reaching codes of conduct and done much social and environmental reporting; and it uses its stores to raise awareness of green electricity and other issues.

For more information, or to buy online, see:

Body Shop www.bodyshop.com

such products should become steadily more common, as will the "100% organic" label (if the product is wholly organic) and "made with organic" label (if the product is 70-95% organic).

All Natural Cosmetics www.allnaturalcosmetics.com ▷ 888-586-9719 or 888-430-6604

Not the most alternative company in the image department, but the stock is extensive, carrying more than 300 products, including organic ones. And they hit all the right "no" buttons, including no animal testing, pesticides, synthetic chemicals or mammal ingredients.

Beauty Without Cruelty www.beautywithoutcruelty.com ▷ 888-674-2344

Unlike many companies in the field, Beauty Without Cruelty has been around for decades, adopting a "no animal testing" policy back in the mid-1970s. Their wide line of skin/body/health care products and cosmetics includes a number of organic options.

Green Products Alliance www.greenproductsalliance.com

Funded through one of the few companies (Vermont Soap Organics) offering USDA-certified organic skin and hair care products, this consortium of manufacturers and marketers of natural personal care products prioritizes social responsiblity and a sustainable economy and ecosystem. Their code of ethics pledges not just animal-free and organic products, but also fair trade and fair-business practices. You can't order online through this website, but it has links to the sites of its several dozen members, many of whom offer cosmetics and toiletries through the Internet.

New Day Organics www.newdayorganics.com ▷ 877-603-2223

Women-oriented natural/organic body care, worth noting as it features "products created and marketed by womenn entrepreneurs."

Pangea Organics www.pangeaorganics.com ▷ 877-679-5854

Although the body and facial care stock is limited, this company espouses a commitment to "always cruelty-free" and "always organics," and also "always fair trade." There are some more exotic items on offer here than through more mainstream competitors, too, like Indian lemongrass with rosemary lotion and Argentian tangerine & thyme facial toner.

Jewelry
How bad is your bling?

Compared with clothes, say, the ethics of the jewelry industry are rarely discussed—perhaps partly because, unlike T-shirts and jeans, jewelry tends to be non-branded, so there are no household-name corporations to hold to account. Yet both in terms of extraction of materials and manufacture, the production of jewelry is associated with a number of problems, including poverty wages, widespread child labor, dangerous working conditions, environmental degradation and even wars.

In some cases, there are obvious things that consumers can do. If you happen to be buying **diamonds**, for example, you can demand assurances that the stones haven't come from conflict zones (see box on pp.204–205). And **coral** jewelry is a no-no: coral reefs are among the world's most fragile eco-systems, and they're already taking a severe beating from global warming, farm effluent and other pollution. Direct harvesting of coral for pendants can only make things worse.

For the more common materials, however, it's not immediately obvious how ethical shopping can improve standards. For instance, the majority of **precious and semi-precious stones** (though not diamonds) come from small-scale mines in remote regions of poor countries such as Brazil, Madagascar, Mali and India. These mines are associated with desperate and dangerous conditions—with women and children "literally scratching for a living," in the words of campaigner and Fair Trade jewelry retailer Greg Valerio—as well as serious, and often avoidable, environmental impacts. But jewelry shops and importers aren't directly associated with the mines or their workers, so it's unlikely that consumer pressure will result in direct improvements. And, since the mines are very often the only source of employment in a region, simply avoiding precious stones is not going to help.

Similarly, the more industrial mines from which most of our **gold** and **silver** come are linked to environmental hazards such as the contamination of groundwater through "acid-rock drainage"—a phenomenon that takes place when air reacts with sulphide minerals in the rocks. Yet, in most cases, there's no way to know the green credentials of the specific mines from which a bracelet, say, originated.

Then, of course, there's the question of the conditions under which the jewelry is manufactured. Much of the cheaper, mass-produced stuff is made in **sweatshop** conditions in East Asia. As ever, jobs in these factories are in much demand, but the mostly non-unionized workforce is often exposed to serious health and safety risks. Many migrant workers in China, for example, have been left crippled by **silicosis**—also known as "dust lung"—after drilling beads or cutting semi-precious stones such as opal and topaz into hearts and other shapes for use in Western bangles, necklaces and earrings. And child labor is common throughout the smaller developing-world workshops that produce many of the higher-quality pieces for sale.

Conflict diamonds

Granted, diamonds aren't an everyday purchase. But if you're going to spend a fortune on a wedding ring, or treat yourself to a once-in-a-lifetime gift, it's worth bearing in mind that they're directly associated with large-scale human rights abuses. The problem is that, like all valuable natural resources, diamonds have the potential to cause fuel corruption, land appropriation and even full-scale conflict in the countries in which they're found. Only a minority of diamonds come from war zones (an estimated 2%) but that minority has contributed to the drawing out of wars in which millions of innocent people have been murdered, mutilated or tortured. In the last decade alone, at least three brutal African conflicts—in **Sierra Leone**, **Angola** and the **Democratic Republic of Congo** (which has cost more civilian lives than any conflict since World War II)—have been party driven or funded by the exploitation of diamond mines by armed groups.

The victims aren't necessarily limited to those in the countries where diamonds are mined, however. According to Action Aid, the last couple of years have seen a boom in diamond sales—in part because the 9/11 terrorist attacks have reduced the demand for travel, leaving the affluent with more disposable income. But this is sadly ironic considering that **Al Qaeda**—believed to be behind the 9/11 attacks—is thought to have been partly funded by conflict diamonds.

After years of tireless campaigning from groups like Global Witness (www.globalwitness.org), the international community has started to address the conflict-diamond problem through an international initiative called the **Kimberley Process** (www.kimberleyprocess.com). Involving governments, NGOs and the diamond companies, it aims to "Stop conflict diamonds, Promote prosperity diamonds" by imposing a certification scheme that tracks all rough (uncut) stones from mining to cutting. Forty-five countries, including producers, exporters and importers, have now signed up. And while some of the organizations involved have expressed concerns about

Ethical jewelery suppliers

A number of companies are now offering jewelry sourced according to Fair Trade principles. As with all uncertified fair trade, there are no rules and regulations governing exactly what this means, but in general it refers to the retailers working directly with manufacturers, ensuring they get decent working conditions, a decent slice of the profits and long-term trading agreements. Obviously, a few ethical jewelry suppliers can't immediately solve all the problems mentioned above, but they're a growing alternative for socially conscious consumers, if still growing more slowly than the ones for organic food, sweat-free clothing and cruelty-free animal products. Many fair trade shops and online sites, in fact, sell some jewelry as a section of their overall stock, and while it's often a small sideline, in the case of some of the bigger outfits (such as Global Exchange, at

the lack of monitoring, the recent expulsion of Congo from the scheme (in response to its government's failure to combat conflict diamonds properly) has renewed faith in its legitimacy.

For all its positive impacts, however, the Kimberley Process only tracks diamonds to the cutting stage, so it's doesn't help jewelry shoppers to be sure about what they're buying. As such, some people have suggested avoiding African diamonds and opting instead, where possible, for Canadian stones, which are distinguishable through a minute etched hallmark of a polar bear. After all, even developing-world diamonds that *don't* come from war zones raise ethical problems: the expulsion of the Gwi and Gana Bushmen from their lands in the Botswanan **Kalahari**, for example, is seem by many as inseparable from diamond prospecting.

But a boycott of African diamonds would hurt some very poor countries that are economically reliant on these precious stones—in Botswana, for example, diamonds contribute 33% of GDP. So probably a better option is to quiz your jewelers as to where their diamonds are from, and whether their suppliers offer a warrantee that their stones are Kimberley certified. If they give you a blank look (which is highly likely) suggest that they get up to speed on the issue and shop elsewhere. And if they show you some paperwork, check that it isn't a simple gemmological certificate, which relates purely to the diamond's authenticity, not its origins.

In the near future, things may be clearer, since a number of NGOs and big players in the diamond industry agreed on a "fifth C" label in mid-2004 that should appear in the shops. The idea is that conflict and child labor certification is added along with the "four Cs" by which diamonds are currently measured: carat, color, clarity and cut. Bigger stones may even come with a microchip tracing their origin back to the mine. For more information on conflict diamonds, see: www.conflictdiamonds.com

store.gxonlinestore.org/jewelry.html), the selection's both fairly extensive and pretty affordable. The companies listed below are fair trade jewelry specialists; see the sites of the Fair Trade Federation (www.fairtradefederation. org) and Co-op America (www.coopamerica.org) for more comprehensive overviews of websites and shops that carry such products.

Fair Trade Gems www.fairtradegems.com ▷ 800-888-2444

Upmarket designer gemstone rings, pendants, bracelets and earrings from a company that declares a commitment to Fair Trade via fair labor practices and environmental protection, as well as preventing synthetic or treated gems from entering its supply chain.

Jewels of the Trade www.jewelsofthetrade.com ▷ 777-528-9431

Inexpensive bracelets, earrrings, necklaces and bangles from Chile and Indonesia. The company's a member of the Fair Trade Federation, and several of the suppliers belong to IFAT, the International Federation for Alternative Trade. Much of it can be yours for under $10, some of the clearance items going for much lower than that.

Sumiche Jewelry Co.

www.eco-gold.net ▷ 541-896-9841

Specializing in custom-designed gold, silver, and platinum wedding and commitment rings, from the quite pricey to the modestly pricey. What sets it apart from many other such companies, however, is that it uses conflict-free diamonds, and is the only US company using "Certified Green" gold and platinum, sustainably mined and fairly traded in Colombia.

Sumiche's Double Happiness 14k gold ring.

Money matters

Apart from stashes in cookie jars and under mattresses, we generally trust our money to institutions which attempt to increase its worth—both for our gain and their own. They do this by investing the money in shares, bonds and property; loaning it at interest to companies, countries or individuals; or gambling it on currency or commodity values. This goes not only for the cash in our bank accounts, but also for our pension contributions and our investments, as well as the essentially collective pools of money in the power of insurance companies.

So what's wrong with that? Well, that depends whether you care who your money is invested in or loaned to. And unless the financial institution has a transparent investment policy stating otherwise, the companies your cash will be supporting may include those linked to oppressive governments, arms sales, deforestation, animal testing for cosmetics and the rest of the sin list. As for currency speculation, it's a way of making money that can wield economic chaos in developing countries (see box on pp.227).

All these issues are particularly pertinent because financial institutions are so powerful. Indeed, if there's any truth to the maxim "money talks," then these organizations are the most verbal on the planet. The ten biggest US banks alone control nearly half of the bank assets in the country. And the political influence of financial companies is also immense. One director at the World Trade Organization, for example, claimed that the hugely controversial GATS agreement—which aims to open up global "trade" in services such as teaching and medical provision—would never have been created "without the tremendous pressure exerted by the American financial services industry, particularly by companies like American Express and Citicorp."

In response to a gradually increasing public awareness of these kinds of issues, more and more financial service providers—principally mutual funds and banks, pension funds, investment agencies, insurers and some others—are offering "socially responsible" investment services. But how does it all work? And does it have any effect? This chapter deals with these questions, and then gives more specific background and recommendations for **mutual funds** (p.220), **banks** (p.225), **pensions** (see p.232), **insurance** (see p.234), **mortgages** (see p.236), and **financial advisers** (see p.224).

Ethical finance basics
How does it work? *Does* it work?

In the world of money, as in any sector, the term "ethical" has no fixed meaning as such. But most commonly it refers to **socially responsible investment** (SRI): the practice of considering social and environmental factors when deciding which shares to buy and who to loan money to. This concept is nothing new—it's often traced back to Quakers and Methodists boycotting certain sections of the stock market around a hundred years ago. But in the last decade it has become a booming sector. Remarkably, the Social Investment Forum estimated that by the end of 2003, more than one out of every nine dollars under professional management in the country was tied to socially responsible investing—$2 trillion in assets, a sum approximating the 2000 gross domestic products of Canada, Mexico and Italy combined. Indeed, there are now a number of banks and more than 200 US investment funds driven by SRI policies, plus numerous financial advisers specializing in the field. However, socially responsible investment policies vary widely, from the highly strict to the more flexible. Three general principles, however, are generally acknowledged as the core principles of the SRI movement: **screening**, **shareholder advocacy** and **community investing.**

Investment screening

Socially responsible investment policies are traditionally based on both **negative screening** and **positive screening**. Though the language can occasionally change—some prefer the terms "avoidance screening" and "exclusionary screening" for punishing the negative, and "qualitative" screening for rewarding the positive—the concept remains the same. Negative screening involves drawing up a list of unacceptable practices deemed to be harmful to people, the environment or animals and excluding any company found to be involved in these practices. An investment organization might decide upon its own criteria, or it could get some pointers from an external body such as SocialFunds.com (see p.224), but either way the approach involves excluding *entire industries*—nuclear power, arms manufacture and tobacco being a few common examples—as well as any individual company associated with unethical behavior.

Common screening criteria

Here are the kinds of pluses and minuses that an ethical finance organization would be looking out for:

NEGATIVE

▶ **Industries** The blacklist often includes alcohol, animal experiments, arms, fur, gambling, genetic engineering, intensive farming, nuclear power, oil, pornography and tobacco.

▶ **Environment** Association with specific problems such as chemical pollution, C02 emissions or deforestation; or a straightforward lack of any kind of environmental policy.

▶ **Human rights** Lack of a code of conduct on workers' rights; association with human rights abuses of any kind; anti-abortion funding; or links to oppressive governments.

▶ **Management** Excessive directors' pay; lack of financial transparency; political donations; conflicts of interest; use of tax havens.

POSITIVE

▶ **Charity & community** Charitable donations; participation in and support for local events; sensitivity to the business's effect on local people.

▶ **Environment** Clear environmental policies; environmental auditing and reporting; recycling; minimizing pollution and avoidable energy use.

▶ **Labor Relations** Clear codes of conduct on pay and labor conditions, equal opportunities, and staff "development."

▶ **Management** Disclosure of payments to foreign governments; compliance with "corporate governance" protocols.

Positive screening, on the other hand, aims to invest in companies with good enviromental and social records. Above-average marks in those areas are considered a minimum must, and many investors go further by trying to identify companies with so-called best-in-class standards, or the best environmental and social records, not just better-than-average ones.

Most investment screening is done through socially responsible mutual funds, which choose where they invest assets by some combination of both positive and negative screening. Too, it's important to emphasize that screening criteria are not fixed, but change and evolve over time in response to changing geopolitical conditions. For example, as the whole SRI movement was getting off the ground in the 1980s and early 1990s, divestment from South Africa was usually at or near the very top of the list of priorities. With the end of apartheid, that's no longer the case. But other screens are being adopted with increasing seriousness in just the past few years, including ones relating to several of the major issues covered elsewhere in this book: climate change, sustainability, corporate codes of conduct and the use of genetically modified organisms, to name just a few. Environmental screens are among the most popular, with almost 20% of US SRI mutual funds using at least one set of standards to inform their decisions.

Screening criteria can vary from fund to fund, and differ among countries as the SRI movement becomes a global phenomenon. SRI is now also practiced widely in Canada, the UK, Europe and Australia, and while the language might differ, the principles are roughly similar, sometimes nearly exactly so, though environmental and labor screens are somewhat more popular in Europe than in North America. Yet according to the Social Investment Forum's 2003 report on SRI trends, an official at Nikko Asset Management in Japan—the most rapidly developing Asian SRI market—reported that Japanese SRI fund managers and investors don't consider cigarettes, alcohol, gambling, nuclear power or weaponry as "anti-social" issues that should be negatively screened, although they do screen environmental conditions and human rights.

The issue of whether screens based on moral values should be used, incidentally, has far from unanimous enthusiasm in the SRI community, even for oft-used measures such as gambling and pornography. Yet, more contentiously, there are widely accepted "avoidance screens" in place for companies that facilitate access to abortion clinics, contribute to Planned Parenthood, and manufacture contraceptives, though these are among the screens least frequently applied.

Shareholder advocacy

It's one thing to move money around so it steers clears of the bad guys and makes its way to the good guys; it's another to force those bad guys (and, sometimes, even the not-so-bad guys) to better their behavior. The usual way SRI funds achieve this is via **shareholder advocacy**, also sometimes called **shareholder activism**. Using their clout as shareowners in the companies they've invested in, they are able to exert pressure for policy change from the "inside." It's a drawn-out process, and one that might not be as directly satisfying to an average individual investor as directly withdrawing money from the Darth Vaders of financial services and depositing it with the underdog do-gooders. But it's another vehicle, and an important one, for getting big financial players to improve their ways, as they're more accountable and responsive to their shareholders than anyone else—more, some would argue, than to governments and legal regulations.

As the first and mildest means of getting voices heard, **proxy** ballots are sent out to shareholders for voting on proposals brought forth by the company's board of directors (or other major shareowners). Another option is private negotiation, usually called **dialogue** in the SRI community, where investors work behind the scenes with company management to air out policy concerns. A few SRI funds, such as Dreyfus Corporation and Parnassus Funds, use dialogues rather than the more upfront filing of a **shareowner resolution** (publicly announcing revised policy suggestions that would, if approved, change company practices), to address a particularly pressing environmental or social issue. **Divestment**, or removing funds from a company altogether, is the most drastic option, albeit one that SRIs would usually prefer to employ only as a last resort, and one that's become less common now that South African apartheid isn't on the table (though urging the companies themselves to divest from Burma still is on occasion).

Advocates of this approach think that it's morally unacceptable to profit from companies or industries whose activities may cause harm to others—regardless of whether the link is obvious (as with arms manufacturing) or more convoluted (oil consumption contributing toward global warming, for example).

On the other hand, pragmatists argue that working *with* companies through votes, dialogue and resolutions is far more likely to make a difference than simply avoiding their whole sector. It's better to have progressive bankers and investors involved in every industry, they claim, than to leave the most unscrupulous financial backers and most dubious businesses to get on with wrecking the planet. After all, SRIs have a small market share, and there are plenty of other lenders and investors lining up to finance or buy into even the murkiest companies. As Tracy Fernandez Rysavy contends in *Co-op America's Financial Planning Handbook*, "If large groups of SRI investors allow 'borderline' companies into their portfolios, they suddenly have a new form of leverage to demand that these companies improve."

Furthermore, advocates of working within the system to some degree point out that there's an odd logic to "financially boycotting" sectors which we continue to support as consumers and voters. Does it make sense, for example, to object to our money being invested in oil companies while we continue to drive cars? Or shunning arms firms unless we're committed to the total abolishment of US armed forces?

These are all fair points. But does shareholder advocacy actually work? Can investors and bankers really make a difference by "engaging" in "dialogue" with companies? Exponents of this approach claim there have been numerous successes. Friends of the Earth point to **McDonald's** phasing out environmentally problematic polystyrene packaging, for example, and **Ford** pulling out of the Global Climate Coalition (a now-defunct pressure group which argued against the Kyoto treaty and other measures to combat climate change). Others point to the role that shareholders played in the fall of apartheid in South Africa. But, despite all these examples, there are few cases where it can be said definitively that shareholders' ethical concerns have resulted in a company changing significantly for the better.

That's perhaps not too surprising, because the financial "engagers" are only likely to change a company's practices if they can show not just a moral case for improving behavior, but also a financial one. Sometimes this may be possible, but very often it's simply not true that better corporate behavior means more profits. As one financial analyst told *The Observer* in 2002, "On current share trends it pays to be socially irresponsible all the way."

To really *force* a company to change requires the progressive investors—or "shareholder activists," as the more extreme ones are known—to table a resolution at the company's annual general meeting. These are occasionally successful on some issues, such as the 2003 GlaxoSmithKline shareholders' protest against the outrageous pay awarded to the company's CEO, or a Green Century Balanced Fund resolution that influenced PepsiCo to use a lid that saves 25 million pounds of aluminum a year. But when specifically *ethical* resolutions *do* happen, they don't generally achieve landslide support. The Greenpeace-led resolution against BP Amaco's Northstar project in Alaska, for example, was considered a major success when it achieved around 13.5% of the vote, and the Social Investment Forum describes even more than 20% of the vote as a strong show of support for environmental proposals. A 2002 resolution to eliminate sexual orientation discrimination at Cracker Barrel, in fact, was the first social issue proposal opposed by management to get majority support in US shareholder history.

But that doesn't mean the engagement approach is worthless. Such resolutions can force issues not just into the AGM but also into the media. Some shareholder activists feel that resolutions have, in a reversal of the way the process often works, led to behind-the-scenes dialogue that resulted in significant progress. They can also play their part in wider protest, both in the US and abroad. For instance, British construction company Balfour Beatty withdrew from the Ilisu Dam project in Turkey—which would allegedly have displaced thousands of people and have had potentially disastrous environmental consequences—after a wide-ranging campaign against the company. Shareholders were not solely responsible, but they played their part, delivering, in the words of Simon McRae from Friends of the Earth, "a big slap in the face" at the AGM. If you're curious as to what kind of resolutions have been filed lately and how they've fared, go to www.iccr.org/shareholder/proxy_book05/05statuschart.php, on the website of the Interfaith Center on Corporate Responsibility.

Community investing

Community investing, or assets directed to rural and lower-income communities whose needs aren't adequately served by conventional financial services, is a relatively small sector of the SRI market—less than 1%, in cold figures. Nonetheless, it's one of the fastest-growing areas, more than doubling (to $20 billion) between 2001 and 2005. Too, it's a concept that the socially responsible investment community as a whole has devoted more attention to in recent years, as investors grow more aware of the importance of not just putting their money into more benevolent financial institutions, but also in the hands of those who need it most. Admittedly, it demands more commitment and effort from individual investors, whether you're searching for a community development bank to take care of routine checking and savings accounts, or for a mutual fund that allocates some of its assets for CDFIs (community development financial institutions). If you don't want to use a mutual fund for socially responsible investments, depositing in a community investment bank or credit union is probably the route you'll take.

CDFIs try to facilitate construction of affordable housing; creation of living-wage jobs in poor communities; business ownership by women and minorities; and community services such as child and health care. Many progressives and liberals, naturally, would argue that much of this could or should be supplied by the government, not by capital from ordinary citizens. In twenty-first century America, however, the government has failed to come through in many socially progressive arenas, and whether or not you agree it's the job of financial institutions to pick up the slack, community investment is one way of doing so. Plus, if you take the view of being a global citizen as well as an American one, community investment projects can help disadvantaged areas not just here but also in the third world.

CDFIs aren't nearly as widespread as socially responsible mutual funds, particularly if you're set on finding a bank near you providing conventional financial services. However, a growing number of mutual funds are now setting aside a portion, though usually a very small one, of their assets for community investments; for more information on the practicalities of community investment alternatives, see p. 228.

The bigger the better

Ultimately, all of the SRI strategies are valid, and in practice many ethical investment funds favor a **mixed approach**: excluding some industries and giving preference to companies with positive practices; but also taking the engagement path on some issues, and sometimes allocating some assets for community investment. Similarly, rather than boycotting a whole industry, an organization may be more selective. Pax World Funds (the very first American SRI mutual fund, founded in 1971 in opposition to militarism and the Vietnam War), for instance, doesn't explicitly rule out all companies with revenue from Department of Defense contracts, but will exclude any that derive more than 5% of their gross sales from such sources.

Regardless of the approach, the biggest determinant for the impact of ethical finance is simply the size and number of organizations involved. Indeed, when really major investors—such as **CalPERS**, the Californian public pension fund worth more than $100 billion—start throwing their weight around, even governments start taking notice. According to journalist Jon Entine, when Thailand found itself on the CalPERS investment blacklist, "government officials pleaded for time, saying 'there should be

The FTSE4Good series

Launched in 2001, the FTSE4Good is the world's first significant series of share indices (statistical tools which list companies and share prices) designed specifically for socially responsible investors. It's essentially a screened version of normal FTSE indices, in which tobacco, nuclear-power and arms industries are excluded. Other companies only qualify if they meet "globally recognized corporate responsibility standards." These standards, set out by FTSE and the UK-based EIRIS (Ethical Investment Research Service), focus on three areas:

▶ Working toward environmental sustainability

▶ Developing positive relationships with stakeholders

▶ Upholding and supporting universal human rights

There are two indices each for UK, US, Europe and Global: a "benchmark" index listing all the companies that qualify, and a "tradeable" index listing the current top 50 or 100 companies. Numerous ethical investors use the index as a reference tool—they pay a fee, which is donated to UNICEF (the UN's children's fund).

There's no doubt that the FTSE4Good has increased public awareness of corporate ethics. For example, when the index was launched, the exclusion of the massive UK supermarket chain Tesco (for its failure to publish an environmental report) was widely reported in the mainstream press. But not everyone approves of the indices. Some critics see them as yet another tool for promoting corporate social responsibility—which they consider a hopeless substitute for proper regulation (see p.55)—while many in the ethical investment world have criticized the criteria it uses for being too vague or loose.

Presumably in response to these concerns, the requirements have been made more rigorous numerous times since the indices first launched; over the next few years, for instance, they're adding measures for bribery & corruption, climate change, governance of corporate responsibility, and health & safety. But it's still toward the "light" end of the green spectrum, with oil firms and other controversial companies lurking on the list. For more visit: www.ftse.com/ftse4good

FTSE4Good Index Series

sufficient channels in which we are given appropriate opportunities to show that Thailand has complied with good-practice standards, as we have every intention to do.'" So even if socially responsible finance is not revolutionizing the world right now, its impact gets greater with each person who changes banks on ethical grounds, or signs up for an SRI mutual fund.

Ethical finance Q&A

Does "going ethical" mean getting less interest?

In the case of banks (see p.228), having an "ethical" account certainly doesn't need to mean you being poorer. The returns on savings, checking, individual retirement (IRA) and certificate of deposit (CD) accounts at community development banks and credit unions are about the same as those of conventional banks.

Things are a bit more contentious when it comes to SRI mutual funds, where far more socially responsible money gets invested, and more studies have analyzed account performance. But evidence suggests that "screened" mutual funds and non-ethical ones have a similar rate of return. The mutual fund rating firm Morningstar gave more than 40% of SRI funds its highest four- and five-star rankings, —only 32.5% of all existing funds can claim to have performed as well. And respected mutual fund analysts Lipper found that over a five-year period (1997-2001), 29 of 45 SRIs performed better than the average similar mutual fund did. Not everyone's convinced: a 2003 *New York Times* article referred to a study by the Wharton School of Business that concluded SRIs could cost investors as much as 3.6% a year, though some criticized the methodology for its selective fund comparisons.

Other studies—such as a recent Australian survey carried out by AMP Henderson—have even suggested that ethical investments funds are actually *more* profitable than average. As SocialFunds.com reported, the survey found that socially responsible investment funds "outperformed the most relevant benchmark, the S&P/ASX 200, over the one-, two-, three- and five-year periods, through September 30, 2003," despite underperforming in 2002.

Who does the research?

Some investment funds have their own research teams, but many socially responsible investors trust a research service to screen companies on their behalf. The four main services in the US are KLD Research & Analytics,

 Inc.; Innovest Strategic Value Advisors; the Investor Responsibility Research Center; and Institutional Shareholder Services' Social Investment Research Service (SIRS). All of them dig up information about the social and environmental standards of thousands

of companies here and abroad. They're also paying increased attention to what's become known in the trade as **corporate governance**, which includes issues such as accounting practices, director and executive pay, and the composition of company boards. As an individual investor, you're unlikely to use these fee-charging services unless you're pretty well-off—in which case you'd do better using a financial advisor to slog through the data (see p. 224).

You won't find many hard numbers on corporate performance if you're only cruising a monitoring services' website, but if you have a serious interest in the subject, you might want to explore them anyway, as they offer some general info on SRIs that could come in handy. The KLD site, for instance, offers a free downloadable 36-page PDF file of SRI resources (if rather scholarly ones), complete with links to online papers on the subject.

KLD www.kld.com
Innovest Strategic Value Advisors www.innovestgroup.com
Investor Responsibility Research Center www.irrc.org
Institutional Shareholder Services' Social Investment Research Service www
.issproxy.com/institutional/research/sirsresearch.jsp

Who gets the money?

It is sometimes said that socially responsible investment funds and banks do invest in corporate bastards—just slightly lesser bastards. It's certainly true that most SRI funds, while they shun arms, tobacco and the like, nonetheless invest in a list of companies that you might not exactly think of as moral trailblazers. As the box on the next page shows, the most popular shares in ethical portfolios include major banks, supermarkets and retailers that are themselves highly criticized from some corners.

This may not bother you, but if it does, bear in mind that not all ethical policies are alike. There aren't many standard banks (even community investment ones) out there with idiosyncratic criteria, but it's likely more will pop up like Shorebank Pacific (in the Pacific Northwest), which describes itself as "the first commercial bank in the United States with a commitment to environmentally sustainable community development." In the much larger world of SRI mutual funds, there are investment policies out there ranging from **pork products** (exclusion of companies that make a significant amount of their income from the pork business) to what's termed by the Social Investment Forum as an **"anti-family entertainment"** screen (which rules out companies that derive significant revenue from TV programs with sex and violence). Ask a financial adviser for more advice (see p.224).

SRI holdings: where green turns to gray

To some critics, socially responsible funds shouldn't be taken to task merely for investing in *slightly* less evil companies, but for supporting more or less the exact *same* companies as many conventional mainstream financial institutions. Indeed, according to the Natural Capital Institute, they're all but identical. A 2004 report by the environmental restoration and social justice advocacy organization published two lists side by side (see right), one of the 30 US companies that make up the Dow Jones Industrial Average, the other of the 30 top US holdings in North American SRI mutual funds (as compiled by the Institute). "Can you tell which is which?" asked NCI Executive Director Paul Hawken.

The criticism might have stung all the more as it came not from the conservative right or the mainstream press, but by a recognized figure of the sustainability movement. In addition to writing several books on the economy and the environment (such as *The Ecology of Commerce*), Hawken's also hosted and produced a PBS series on starting and running socially responsible businesses, having cofounded several natural food companies relying on sustainable agricultural methods himself. The report he and the NCI authored also stated that SRI funds own shares in 90% of firms on the Fortune 500 list; criticized the Sierra Club Mutual Funds for not owning alternative energy companies, or any "that address the environment in an innovative or proactive way," though they at the same time invest in steakhouses and candy bars; and that many SRI funds had holdings in numerous companies quite a few progressive investors might find odious, including Wal-Mart, Clear Channel, Coca-Cola, McDonald's, General Electric, Monsanto, Exxon Mobil, and Halliburton. Among the findings: "There is a strong bias towards companies that aggressively pursue globalization of brands, products and regulations … the environmental screens by portfolio managers are loose and do little to help the environment." Hawken's also urged SRI mutual funds to "create an association with real standards, enforceability, and transparency."

The report soon sparked heated discussion, and sometimes rebuttal, within the SRI community, some countering that the NCI's methodology was crude and its vision unrealistically utopian. A Sierra Club representative was quick to point out in *The Christian Science Monitor* that Sierra Club funds screen out mining, gas, oil and timber firms. A senior adviser of an SRI fund praised in the document, Joe Keefe of Calvert, noted that none of the nearly dozen especially problematic companies in NCI's "Top 30" chart met Calvert's criteria. "If some of them are held in some SRI portfolios, I suspect this is the exception rather than the rule," Keefe contended on the *dragonflymedia.com* site, adding, "it would be impractical, and self-defeating, for SRI firms to exclude all or even most Fortune 500 companies from their portfolios."

Hawken, meanwhile, might be getting a chance to put his principles to the ultimate market test—in 2005 he began advising a Massachusetts firm that was starting a socially responsible portfolio for investors. The full Nature Capital Institute report on Socially Responsible Investing can be downloaded from www.naturalcapital. org/projects.html.

Natural Capital Institute list of top 30 US holdings in North American SRI mutual funds

▶ Micosoft Corp.

▶ Pfizer Inc.

▶ Johnson & Johnson

▶ Citigroup Inc.

▶ Intel Corporation

▶ Cisco Systems, Inc.

▶ Amgen, Inc.

▶ American International Group, Inc.

▶ Bank of America Corporation

▶ Delphi Corporation

▶ Medtronic, Inc.

▶ General Electric Company

▶ International Business Machines Corp.

▶ Fannie Mae

▶ Home Depot, Inc.

▶ Procter & Gamble Company

▶ Verizon Communications

▶ Comcast Corporation

▶ PepsiCo, Inc.

▶ Wells Fargo & Company

▶ 3M Company

▶ J.P. Morgan Chase & Co.

▶ SBC Communications, Inc.

▶ American Express Company

▶ The Rouse Company

▶ Target Corporation

▶ The Coca-Cola Company

▶ Wal-Mart Stores, Inc.

▶ Hewlett-Packard Company

▶ Exxon Mobil

The 30 companies that make up the Dow Jones Industrial average

▶ Microsoft Corp.

▶ Pfizer Inc.

▶ Johnson & Johnson

▶ Citigroup Inc.

▶ Intel Corporation

▶ Alcoa Inc.

▶ Boeing

▶ American International Group, Inc.

▶ E.I. DuPont de Nemours & Co.

▶ Caterpillar

▶ Honeywell Int.

▶ General Electric Company

▶ International Business Machines Corp.

▶ Walt Disney Co.

▶ Home Depot, Inc.

▶ Procter & Gamble Company

▶ Verizon Communications

▶ United Technologies

▶ McDonald's

▶ Merck & Co.

▶ 3M Company

▶ J.P. Morgan Chase & Co.

▶ SBC Communications, Inc.

▶ American Express Company

▶ Altria Group Inc.

▶ General Motors

▶ The Coca-Cola Company

▶ Wal-Mart Stores, Inc.

▶ Hewlett-Packard Company

▶ Exxon Mobil

SRI mutual funds
Surveying your options

If you have more than a few thousand dollars at your disposal, it's very likely that you'll want to, or be advised to, put the bulk of socially responsible investments into a socially responsible mutual fund, which (like standard mutual funds) pools assets from a group of shareholders to invest in stocks or bonds. A relatively small percentage, incidentally, of all assets in socially screened portfolios come from individual investors; about $2 trillion are in what the Social Investment Forum terms "separate accounts," or portfolios privately managed for institutions (and some individuals). That still left, in 2005, about $180 billion in SRI mutual funds—a large sum by any measure, and a figure that continues to grow.

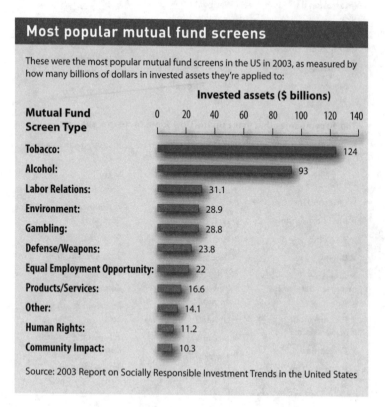

Most popular mutual fund screens

These were the most popular mutual fund screens in the US in 2003, as measured by how many billions of dollars in invested assets they're applied to:

Invested assets ($ billions)

Mutual Fund Screen Type	Invested assets ($ billions)
Tobacco:	124
Alcohol:	93
Labor Relations:	31.1
Environment:	28.9
Gambling:	28.8
Defense/Weapons:	23.8
Equal Employment Opportunity:	22
Products/Services:	16.6
Other:	14.1
Human Rights:	11.2
Community Impact:	10.3

Source: 2003 Report on Socially Responsible Investment Trends in the United States

In such a constantly growing field, and one that (unusually for this business) is accustomed to transparency and accountability, the problem isn't so much finding a suitable SRI fund as sifting through the overwhelming plethora of information available to help you make up your mind. The first step might be, simply, to ask yourself if you have enough money to start one. While the stodgy image of mutual funds might have led some Americans to think you have to be pretty upper-crust to get a piece of the action, in reality it shouldn't be hard to start an account with an SRI unless you're living hand-to-mouth. Most of the account minimums vary from $1000-$5000, usually at the lower end of that scale, and some are even lower—Pax's accounts, for instance, require just $250 to open. A few (though not many) will do it for even less if you choose an automatic monthly investment plan. Similar minimums, and slightly lower ones at that, apply to opening an IRA account with these companies.

The next step is to find a fund, or a few, that most closely align with your own set of values. The best start is to take a look at their screening criteria. If your social consciousness barometer is high, you'll likely want to invest with companies that employ a good number of positive and negative screens of various sorts (see p.209). If you do want a lot of screens in place, you'll have a lot of options: about two-thirds of socially screened mutual funds employ five or more. There are outfits out there that offer only one or two if you're less fussy, though if you're reading this book in the first place, odds are you'll likely be somewhat more finicky. You can generally find out what screens are used at each fund's website, but it doesn't have to be as dauntingly time-consuming a task as that. Several SRI informational websites (see listings at the end of this section) have handy tables laying out the screening policies of numerous companies, coded according to whether certain issues are given positive screens, negative screens, restricted investment or no screens at all.

Screening is just one pillar of the three-legged stool that's socially responsible investment, and depending on your interests, you'll probably also want to check out how heavily the companies you're considering are engaged in shareholder advocacy and community investment. Not all SRI mutual funds are committed to all three strategies by any means; just 30% of the Social Investment Forum's members used all of them, according to its 2003 report on SRI trends (and it gets much lower for non-SIF member SRI mutuals, only 8% of whom use more than one strategy, and zero percent of which use all three). Shareholder activism and community investment aren't as handily charted as screening policies, and you'll need to do more digging into individual websites and prospectuses if you want a lot of details. Community investment in general is lagging behind the other two principles in SRI fund priorities, but that might be changing to some extent with the recent launch of the SIF/Co-op American-initiated "1% or More in Community Campaign," encouraging both individuals and companies to move 1% or more of their assets into that sector. So far ten SRI mutual funds have gotten with the program; check the Community Investment Center website (at www.communityinvest.org/investors/campaign.cfm) for an up-to-date list.

Another important consideration is the financial performance of the fund. While you may not want to boast too loudly about your impending financial good fortune as you're doing your research, you shouldn't feel embarrassed about asking questions concerning your returns. You are, after all, taking a risk, both in terms of the variable returns you can expect from your investment, and because the federal government doesn't insure against losses from a mutual fund. Particularly if you go with a reputable and well-established SRI fund, you shouldn't be worrying much about all your savings going down the drain (though if that's a concern of yours, you should consider a community investment bank or credit union instead, as deposit accounts of up to $100,000 in those institutions are insured by the feds). No matter what kind of account and which fund you go with, there's no guarantee as to how well you'll do—some months you might be whistling The Gold Diggers' Song (We're in the Money), and others you might dread to open your statement, so tiny might the dividend be. Statistics on individual funds' performances are readily available online, again through the sources below.

Just as there are different types of conventional bank accounts, there are also different types of mutual funds. You have the option of putting

Top performers

These are the Top 10 performing SRI mutual funds according to SocialFunds.com, based on three-year percentile ranking statistics:

▶ Calvert Large Cap Growth   ▶ Green Century Balanced Fund

▶ Calvert Social Bond   ▶ Parnassus Fixed Income

▶ Calvert Social Enhanced Equity ▶ Pax World Balanced Fund

▶ Citizens Income Fund   ▶ Pax World Growth

▶ Citizens Value Fund   ▶ Winslow Green Growth Fund

assets into a **money market fund** (which invests in short-term bonds, and doesn't have early withdrawal penalties); **equity funds** (which invest in stocks and have higher return rates over the long-term than money market/bond funds); **fixed income funds** (which invest in bonds issued by companies or governments); and **balanced funds**, which invest in both bonds and stocks. Generally, money market funds are considered the lowest risk, the investments becoming progressively chancier with fixed income funds, balanced funds, and equity funds.

Unless you're already well-schooled in stocks and most matters financial, this might be the point in the process—especially in combination with poring over the multiple return figures for various funds' accounts—where you start to feel overwhelmed by the jargon, percentages and risk/return calculations. At the very minimum, you should order a **prospectus**, or informational booklet, that charts the progress and investment ideology of a specific fund, before whipping out your checkbook; mutual funds are legally required to send you one by law, and these can sometimes be downloaded from their websites. The 20-page booklet *Investing in Socially Responsible Mutual Funds*, which can be downloaded for free from www.socialfunds. com, does a good deal to explain the nuts and bolts of the whole investment process, no matter which fund you choose. If you still feel like you're out of your depth, consider enlisting the help of a **financial adviser** with expertise in SRI accounts (see p. 224). With so many options out there, and new players entering the market all the time, we've decided that a list of funds here would be of little use. Instead we've provided links to resources where you can find the information you need to make an informed decision:

Social Investment Forum www.socialinvest.org

A nonprofit group affiliated with Co-op America, with many institutional and individual professional members. The SIF site has a section on mutual funds (at www.socialinvest.org/areas/sriguide/mfpc. cfm) that charts several dozen funds on financial performance, screening and advocacy, proxy voting, account minimums and fund performance. The site also has a great deal of general information about SRI mutual funds and community investing, as well as plenty of news about the world of socially responsible investing as a whole. At www.socialin-

vest.org/areas/research, you can download (for free) their lengthy biennial report on trends in socially responsible investing, which is much more lucid and readable than the usual such documents, though relentlessly upbeat in tone.

SocialFunds.com www.socialfunds.com

"The largest personal finance site devoted to socially responsible investing" has a wealth of information about SRI mutual funds, community investment and financial services, with downloadable guides to working with each (though only the mutual funds and community investment guides are free). The site also has descriptions of numerous SRI mutual funds, along with charts detailing their performance and policies, complete with thorough lists of their screening criteria, which you can sort by issue if you want to narrow down the choices you're considering. SocialFunds.com is part of the SRI World Group site (www.sriworld.com), which has news on global SRI developments.

ResponsibleInvesting.org www.responsibleinvesting.org

A subset of the Natural Capital Institute, whose executive director, Paul Hawken, might not be the most popular figure in the SRI community at the moment, owing to a report he issued in 2004 that was highly critical of the SRI movement (see p. 220). Still, the ResponsibleInvesting.org site has an extensive database of equity holdings and screening categories of North American SRI mutual funds, allowing you to search for funds that meet varying levels ("no screen," "negative screen," "positive screen," "restricted screen") for 25 criteria, right down to screens for biotechnology and indigenous peoples rights.

Financial advisers

An increasing number of financial advisers are developing expertise in socially responsible investment, so finding advice shouldn't be difficult. There are hundreds (at the least) of such professionals throughout the US, as well as some firms with specialization in the field. SocialFunds.com allows you to search (at www.socialfunds.com) for SRI brokers, financial planners and money managers by state. They also sell (for $9.95) the Working With Social Investment Professionals guide, which explains what to look for in a financial adviser. In addition, the member directory of the Social Investment Forum includes more than 200 SRI consultants, advisors and planners; for a full list, with some descriptions of the services each provides, contact information and links to their websites, check www.socialinvest.org/areas/sriguide/Directory. You can also get much the same information in book form from Co-op America's Financial Planning Handbook ($11.95 through www.coopamerica.org/pubs/fph or 800-58-GREEN), which also has useful articles on finding a financial adviser and other aspects of SRI investing, along with a financial planning worksheet.

Banks & building societies
Your savings, your landmine

The major banks have a pretty unimpressive ethical track record, and though some have improved to a certain extent, they still leave a lot to be desired. And the biggest of them keep getting bigger, and wielding more and more influence, financial and otherwise. The top ten US banks—including such names as Bank of America, Citigroup, J.P. Morgan Chase, Wells Fargo, and Wachovia—now hold nearly half of all bank assets in the country, as opposed to only 17% in 1990. The trend toward consolidation could continue as more giants merge, J.P. Morgan Chase's recent acquisition of Bank One being one example.

The most common criticism they face relates to who they lend to (and offer accounts to). Wells Fargo, for example, has been accused by Rainforest Action Network of funding illegal deforestation in Indonesia by investing in BlueLinx, the biggest importer of Indonesian wood to the US. But all of the big boys have been attacked at some stage by NGOs

Another section of the Amazon is razed to the ground. US banks have long been criticized for lending money to companies involved in destruction of rainforests, which are home to at least half the world's plant and animal species. Besides the collection of valuable wood, deforestation is driven by gold mining, the claiming of farmland for animal feed and palm oil, urbanization and global warming. If current rates of deforestation continue, there will be no tropical rainforest left by 2100.

focusing on areas such as arms exports to—and natural-resource extraction from—countries with oppressive regimes.

Some progress has been made recently in the area of unethical lending, with about 35 banks worldwide—including US lions Wells Fargo, J.P. Morgan Chase, Citigroup and Bank of America—having signed up for the **Equator Principles**, a set of guidelines on socially and environmentally sound financing. Citigroup, J.P. Morgan Chase and Bank of America have all been applauded by Rainforest Action Network for adopting policies to safeguard old growth and endangered forests and protect the rights of indigenous peoples. Bank of America has even joined the Coalition for Environmentally Responsible Economics (CERES), endorsing its 10-point code of environmental corporate conduct. However, as with most voluntary progrmas, campaigners claim that the "EP" framework hasn't stopped banks making irresponsible loans. For instance, in a report called *Principles, Profits, or Just PR?*, pressure group Bank Track noted that "despite the existence of the Principles, many controversial projects such as the Baku Ceyhan oil pipeline went ahead virtually unaltered while other, similarly disastrous projects, such as Sakhalin II oil project in the Russian Far East and the Nam Theun dam in Laos are lined up for financing by the EP banks." For more info, see:

Equator Principles www.equator-principles.com
Bank Track www.banktrack.org

But other problems remain. One of these is **currency speculation**, which is linked to the destabilization of developing-world economies (see box opposite). According to a 2002 report by War on Want, the US's biggest currency gamblers included Citigroup (who topped the list worldwide), with Bank of America and J.P. Morgan Chase not too far behind. Most of the big banks also have offices in **tax havens**, which are associated with high-level tax dodging and money laundering.

Some contribute to conservative political causes: Citigroup donated half a million dollars to Texans for a Republican Majority in 2002, which supported "right to work" laws and opposed gay rights and abortion, and AmSouth Bancorp helped fund American 21, a contributor to Alabama governor Bob Riley and Congressman Spencer Bachus (both on record as opposing gay rights and abortion). And there are the astronomical salaries paid to their top executives, as well as controversial perks such as the $50 million in stock and options Bank of America chief executive Hugh McColl received in 1999, despite below-expected company earnings and a dropping stock price.

Currency speculation

Every day, an estimated $1–2 trillion is traded on the international currency markets. To put this figure in perspective, imagine a couple of hundred dollars for every single person on the planet, or a stack of $50 dollar bills reaching from the earth to the moon. Some of this is related to trade and long-term investment, but the vast majority—probably at least 90%—is the speculative "**hot money**" of banks, investment funds and super-rich individuals aiming to profit from short-term changes in exchange rates. Currency speculation is nothing new, but it has grown out of all proportion in the last decade.

The problem with this potentially lucrative activity is that it can be hugely damaging to economic stability, especially for developing countries whose governments lack the financial weight to protect themselves against the speculators. There isn't space here to go into the details but, in short, when there's a speculation "run" on a particular currency, the economy of that country can be left in tatters, with a devalued currency and a messed-up banking system. It is now widely accepted, for example, that currency speculation played a major role in the recent financial crisis of East Asia, which resulted in massive job losses and increased poverty. To add insult to injury, speculators pay no tax on their winnings, even though the sums involved are massive: according to the book *Globalize This*, Citigroup had an $8.5 trillion volume of foreign exchange transactions in 1998, more than the GDP of the entire United States.

Increasingly, economists and anti-poverty campaigners are calling for the "caging" of speculative money. One suggested means for doing this is the introduction of a minimal tax on all currency transactions, set at perhaps 0.1%: small enough to leave trade unaffected, but big enough to calm speculation, which relies on very marginal changes in exchange rates. According to its proponents, the would-be **Tobin Tax**—named after James Tobin, the Nobel Prize-winning economist who thought up the idea in the 1970s—could stabilize global finances, to everyone's benefit, and simultaneously raise huge sums of money that could be used to tackle global poverty. Even after the shrinking effect it would have on the currency market, it is estimated that a 0.1% tax could raise up to $300 billion each year—roughly six times the combined international aid budget. For more information, visit the War on Want campaign site (www.waronwant.org) or the Tobin Tax Initiative site (ceedweb.org/iirp).

Scores of NGOs and British Members of Parliament have given their support for the Tobin Tax, and Canada and France have taken a lead by committing to implementing it once other countries agree. But it might never happen, as many commentators see it as unworkable due to the practical problems of implementing any system of global taxation.

Unsurprisingly, it's not nearly as easy for the public to research big-bank policies on investment in defense, deforestation and the like as it is to research what positive and negative screens SRI companies use (though there are fee-charging research services that can help, such as

GovernanceMetrics International, "the world's first global corporate governance ratings agency"). The large banks don't have much to gain by airing their laundry in public records, and campaigns targeting their policies often focus on their performance in one specific issue (such as South African divestment back in the 1980s) rather than their ethical resumes as a whole. There's a gap waiting to be filled by a mega-bank watchdog service that would rate the big financial powers across the board on social responsibility standards. Not everyone's ready to switch from their mainstream account to a smaller, lesser-known community investment bank or SRI mutual fund at a drop of a hat, and such a service would do a great deal to both pressure the large outfits to modify their policies, and popularize the notion of socially responsible investing among the general public. If you do already take the view that the big banks are not for you, fortunately, the number of alternatives are constantly growing.

Banking options

Community investment banks & credit unions

If you have a sizable chunk of change you want to set aside for socially responsible investing, it's probably most effective to put it into an SRI mutual fund (see p. 220), as they offer an abundance of screening options, as well some influence on shareholder activism. Even those funds, however, can suggest putting at least some money into other outlets to cover routine checking account needs, particularly as it's much easier and more convenient to deposit and withdraw from standard banks on a regular basis. SRI advocates also usually endorse putting your checking and savings accounts into **community investment banks** if you can, whether or not you have the bulk of your assets in a mutual fund. Community investment banks offer federally insured checking and saving accounts, and other services common to conventional banks, all at market interest rates (which usually vary between zero and five percent). They do put money into low-income and disadvantaged communities, but it must be noted that they don't make positive and negative screening criteria core to their operations, as SRI mutual funds do.

Though the community investment slice of the SRI pie is rapidly expanding, it's still not all that easy to find a community investment bank near you. As of this writing, the Community Investing Center website listed fewer than 50 throughout the US—and none for some heavily populated metropolises, including the San Francisco Bay Area, Dallas-Fort Worth, Phoenix and Pittsburgh. And most of these banks have only a single, local branch, a notable exception being the long-established ShoreBank, which has branches in Chicago, Detroit and Cleveland (as well as its previously cited, environmentally oriented offshoot in the Pacific Northwest, ShoreBank Pacific). As of yet, however, there's no US counterpart to anything on the scale of the UK's Co-operative Bank, which has 140 branches and three million customer accounts throughout the island nation, as well as an Internet-only offshoot bank (the UK's first) and a comprehensive ethical policy regulating investments with numerous positive and negative screens.

Community development credit unions

If there's not a community investment bank in your vicinity, using **community development credit unions**, which are considerably more widespread, might be a more workable alternative. Credit unions are cooperative-style alternatives to the savings accounts offered by standard banks and building societies. The basic idea is that a group of people, who must be connected by a "common bond"—such as sharing a residential area, employer, occupation, trade union or church—join together to form a union. They invest their savings into a pool, from which loans can be made to union members.

Credit unions claim to offer a number of advantages—ethical and financial—over conventional savings options. On the ethical level, the unions can help tackle **financial exclusion**. Banks often refuse finance to the poorest members of society due to their having a credit history tarnished long ago, but credit unions can make a case-by-case decision on who can borrow based on their current ability to repay and savings record with the union. Furthermore, since only members can borrow, there are no loans to dodgy businesses. There are now quite a few credit unions specifically designated as community development institutions, and the odds are good that if you live in an urban area, there will be at least one in your region.

To many, the distinctions between community development banks and community development credit unions (or CDCUs, as they're sometimes called in the trade) might seem virtually nonexistent: they both offer standard banking services (including checking and savings accounts), and both federally insure deposit accounts up to $100,000. The distinctions are a bit academic, but they *are* different: community development banks are for-profit operations, insured by the Federal Deposit Insurance Corporation (FDIC), and their credit union counterparts are nonprofits insured by the National Credit Union Administration. Be aware that a CDCU might still sometimes be partially tied to the very kind of organization from which you've just withdrawn your money; Bank of America, for instance, makes nonmember deposits into community development credit unions that fund consumer loans.

The Community Investment Center's **Community Investment Database** (www.communityinvestingcenterdb.org) offer listings for both community banks and credit unions, sortable by state and services. Also useful is SocialFunds.com's less elaborate **Community Investment Center** (www.socialfunds.com/ci/index.cgi) and, for credit unions only, the **National Federation of Community Development Credit Unions** (www.natfed.org). Finally, you can download a free 20-page *Community Investment Guide* on the homepage of www.socialfunds.com.

If you're worried about the loss of access to ATM machines in every neighborhood when switching from a large bank to a much smaller community develpment bank or credit union, you can still maintain a free savings account at a national bank that lets you access its ATMs anywhere in the country. You can keep enough money in the account to get free use of their ATMs, writing a check from your community bank to the larger bank every month or so to cover your cash withdrawals. Admittedly that's a roundabout processs that doesn't cut the big banks out of the equation entirely, but it's one way of arranging your assets so that you still have widespread ATM privileges while keeping most of your actual money out of the big bad wolves' jaws.

Traditional credit unions

Not all credit unions support community development, and if you're not able to find one (or a community development bank) that does, there's no reason to feel embarrassed about choosing an honorable middle ground and using a standard credit union instead—in which case it's unlikely you *won't* be able to find one nearby, so numerous are they. Credit unions are owned by their members and are **run democratically** within a clear legal framework—including the obligatory training of people elected as officers. They've been around since the nineteenth century, but have become increasingly popular of late: there are now more than 35,000 credit unions in more than eighty countries, with a collective membership of more than 100 million people, including more than 25% of the population in the US,

Canada and Australia. For more information, or to locate a credit union, visit:

National Credit Union Administration www.ncua.gov/indexdata.html
Credit Union National Association www.creditunion.coop/cu_locator/index.html

Credit unions have made an enormous impact in the **developing world**, where rural populations live many miles from the nearest bank, and the poor have few possessions to put down as security. To read more about this, see:

World Council of Credit Unions www.woccu.org/development

Credit cards

None of the major credit card providers—such as Visa and Mastercard—are known for being particularly ethical companies, but there are a wide range of "green" or "socially responsible" credit cards available, which support causes ranging from the National Audubon Society and the Nature Conservancy to the Humane Society.

Usually the credit cards donate half a percentage point from every transaction to the group of your choice, sometimes offering a small sum to the same organization when you sign up or renew. It takes $1000 of spending to generate $5 of charity under this plan, and as some sour souls note, you'll often have to use your card quite a bit each year just to make the flow to your "green" cause celebre equal to the "green" of your annual card fee.

All those pennies are adding up, though; more than $1 million's been raised for the Sierra Club through that route, for instance. Perhaps the most established of these cards, Working Assets Visa, has raised nearly $50 million for a large assortment of nonprofit groups (including Planned Parenthood, Rainforest Action Network, the American Civil Liberties Union and Oxfam America) since 1985, handing over ten cents for every time the card makes a purchase. The credit card industry being the most profitable in the United States, it's perhaps unsurprising that some of these cause-based cards are issued by big players in that business, and some socially conscious companies have been criticized for partnering with them. Working Assets and Nature Conservancy cards, for instance, are issued by MBNA America, the second-biggest credit-card issuer in the US, which has donated nearly $10 million to the Republican Party since 1994, according to the Center for Responsive Politics.

On the less feel-good side of the spectrum, credit card destruction has sometimes been used as a tool for motivating corporations to mend their ways. The most celebrated instance was the 2003 Rainforest Action Network television ad featuring actors Susan Sarandon, Daryl Hannah, Ed Asner and Ali McGraw cutting Citibank cards in half in protest against its environmental behavior. Perhaps partly as a result of that flamboyant campaign, Citigroup has not only adopted policies and joined groups pledging higher environmental consciousness; it's also agreed to consider making non-plastic credit cards.

Pensions
Responsible retirement?

Socially responsible investors are steered, almost without fail, toward mutual funds and community development banks and credit unions. It's important to note, however, that these aren't the only repositories of ethical investment. **Pension funds** and **insurance companies** account for a great deal of the institutional investments in SRI mutual funds, and pension funds in particular wield considerable clout in the financial world at large, comprising over 30% of the New York Stock Exchange. As such, they have the potential to put enormous pressure on companies to improve their ethical standards. And they sometimes have, like when the New York City Teachers Retirement System cosponsored a shareholder resolution with the National Wildlife Federation asking General Electric to disclose its expenditures on *avoiding* the dredging of toxic PCBs from the Hudson River. The muscle can be used for less contentious causes as well, as with the California Public Employees Retirement System (CalPERS), the country's biggest public pension fund, putting some of its investments into economically distressed regions in its state.

Not everyone's agreed that SRI pensions are the best or fairest deals for its beneficiaries. Journalist Jon Entine, for instance, has argued that CalPERS' decision to sell its tobacco shares costs pensioners "who often have little say in what's being done in their name" more than $1 billion, though it would seem unreasonable to expect every such strong ethical stand to be profitable or break even. Such losses still haven't discouraged state and municipal pensions throughout the US from continuing to expand their socially responsible investment practices.

It's beyond the scope of this book to offer outlines of how institutions go about setting up such operations, and if your pension and insurance plans are determined by your place of work, you might have a limited voice (or no voice at all) as to how they're operated. Still, if you do have any input into the process, it's worth speaking up. And just because a company is large and mainstream doesn't mean it isn't responsive to feedback—many pension plans offer ethical investment options, including ones at the Gap, General Motors and Hewlett-Packard.

Considering how much money's involved, angling for your employer to set up socially responsible pension funds, or at least advising individuals on how to investigate what options might be available through their

Greening your pension fund

Friends of the Earth advises using this four-step process for routing your pension monies into social responsible investments:

Step 1: Find out if you have an SRI pension option already.

That's as easy as going to the human resource department and asking. If they don't (or, heaven forbid, don't know what a socially responsible investment option is), go to step 2.

Step 2: Find out how your pension plan is managed.

These fall into "bundled plans," in which your employer contracts just one financial management company, and "unbundled plans" in which it contracts to a few firms for pension management and investment. It's going to be a lot harder to take action if it's a "bundled plan," as you'll have to convince the pension manager to add an SRI alternative, or switch to an entirely different option. Still, that might not necessarily be as hard as it seems, as even large, traditional investment companies are starting to offer investment options with screens (see p.208), though probably due more to market demand than an ethical change of heart. If the plan's "unbundled," it will be easier to add an SRI alternative to the options that already exist.

Step 3: Find out if your plan is employer- or employee-directed.

It's probably going to be a harder, slower road if your plan is employer-directed (or "defined benefit"), doling out regular payments during retirement based on your salary and years of service. If you're up for doing a lot of organizing, though, you can go the shareholder activist route by finding out who's in charge of the pension plan and starting a dialogue with management (see p.211). Friends of the Earth suggests writing a memo to the Chief Financial Officer (CFO) and circulating a petition specifying what you do and don't want your plan to support, and participating in the Investment Committee if employees are represented.

Employee-directed (or "defined contribution") plans work differently, using tax-deferred savings plans for retirement. Here Friends of the Earth suggests having an SRI pension option with a defined contribution plan set up, as per step 4.

Step 4: Take charge of your green.

The most popular defined contribution plan is the 401(k) option, which allows both employer and employee to make tax-deferred contributions, and for you to select a mutual fund in which your money is invested. As Friends of Earth states, "The key to greening your pension investment is to select an SRI fund—one which screens the investment portfolio for non-financial factors—to manage your 401(k)." Another option is opening up an Individual Retirement Account (IRA) managed by a financial adviser specializing in socially responsible invvestment. If you have no 401(k) option, still check with your human resources manages to determine whether there are similar defined contribution plans, as there sometimes are, particularly for municipal government and nonprofit employees.

company plans, seem underplayed by the leading US SRI informational organizations. Friends of the Earth's US branch, however, has started a **"Green Paycheck Campaign"** to push for socially responsible pension investment at the workplace. Their strategy is outlined in the box on the previous page, with fuller details on its website, at www.foe.org/camps/intl/corpacct/wallstreet/greenpaycheck.

Insurance
Peace of mind—at a cost

Like pension companies, insurers have huge assets—it is estimated that at any one time the industry controls roughly 10% of the world's capital. Technically speaking this isn't consumers' money, but for all intents and purposes insurance funds are collectively owned by their policyholders— and, since the money is widely invested, that makes taking out insurance a bit like any other form of investing.

You might expect, therefore, that there would be a range of socially responsible insurance choices available from companies operating screened investment policies (see p.220). Yet the options are surprisingly limited, particularly considering how many US residents need to resort to private (rather than employer or government) coverage for health care and other forms of insurance.

The main reason for this is the interrelated structure of the industry. To be an actual insurer—rather than a small insurance firm selling policies *underwritten* by an insurer—requires an enormous amount of money. Even if you did have the required cash, you'd rely on a **reinsurer** to underwrite you, and there aren't any reinsurers with serious ethical investment policies. Also, according to some insiders in the industry, the culture of the whole sector is inherently at odds with the idea of anything beyond profits—even more so than that of other financial industries.

Quite apart from what your insurance company is investing in, another issue is who and what insurance companies are willing to cover. Indeed, since many environmentally dangerous projects wouldn't be feasible without insurance, the insurance companies collectively wield major influence over what does and doesn't go ahead. As such, they could be a force for good if they imposed industry-wide ethical standards.

Nice motor! Patriot missle launcher at 1997's IDEX Arms Show in Abu Dhab, United Arab Emirates. Arms firms are widely invested in, or receive loans from, US pension funds, insurers and banks.

In 1995, some in the industry made moves toward recognizing their responsibilities by signing up to the UN's *Statement of Environmental Commitment by the Insurance Industry*, also referred to as **UNEP III**. This focuses on sustainable development and includes the statement "we will seek to include environmental considerations in our asset management." However, as with many non-binding agreements, the document has allegedly been largely ignored by many of its signatories. Friends of the Earth's aptly named report *Capital Punishment* (2000) emphasized this, listing some of the environmentally damaging companies, mainly within the oil industry, that big-name insurers continue to invest in.

Despite the failings of UNEP III, it's better than nothing, so as a first step, it might seem logical to ask your insurer if they've signed up. Sadly, in the US that's a moot point, as no insurance companies from this country have yet signed the statement, although almost 90 companies from 27 other nations have done so. If a 2003 corporate responsibility report on the global insurance industry by the Munich-based environmental and social rating agency Oekom is any indication, we shouldn't expect any consciousness-raising soon, as all 26 US companies it contacted declined to participate in the study. A few insurance companies in the States do use social screens, among them some big names, such as Kaiser Permanente and a few branches of Blue Cross—you can find them in an appendix in the Social Investment Forum's biennial report on US SRI trends (downloadable from www.socialinvest.org). But that's really getting down to grasping at straws, and not just because of their limited number; just because an insurance company uses *some* social screens doesn't mean they use criteria you might find necessary. And you'll have to do quite a bit of research into individual insurers to find out which screens they use, and which they ignore.

Mortgages
When eco-warriors become eco-borrowers

The mortgage industry is a huge part of the US economy; in 2002 alone, it financed $2.5 trillion in loans. Considering what a massive business it is—and how the building of "green" or environmentally responsible real estate is itself a rapidly growing field—it's rather astonishing that there are virtually no companies or financial institutions specializing in "ethical" mortgages. As of this writing, for instance, Co-op America's National Green Pages listed just three companies specializing in the field—two of which did not even have websites, and one didn't even mention mortgage specialization in the paragraph-long company description contained in the directory.

One option, of course, is to use a community development bank or credit union, though not all of them offer mortgaging as part of their services. After all, during the lifespan of a mortgage you'll potentially be handing over tens of thousands of dollars worth of profit to whoever lent you the money in the first place. So if, for example, you don't trust the ethical standards of the major banks (see p.225), it would certainly be a logical step to avoid them for mortgages as well as for checking accounts. By their very nature, too, such banks and credit unions are more apt to lend to borrowers of modest means and first-time home-buyers; the Self-Help Credit Union in Durham, North Carolina, for instance, has made more than $2 billion of purchases in affordable mortgages, helping tens of thousands of low-income families in most of the country's states become homeowners. On a smaller scale, the Permaculture Credit Union in Santa Fe, New Mexico, has directed virtually all of its mortgage loans toward sustainable dwellings and projects, though as of late 2005 it had allocated money to less than 30 such mortgages.

Another option is to search for a company that, even if it doesn't subscribe to overt SRI principles, is at least making ethical considerations a part of its way of doing business. **Freddie Mac** (www.freddiemac.com), for instance, is a publicly held corporation chartered by Congress in 1970 that helps mortgage lenders make funds available to homebuyerrs and investors, and considers the initiation of community development lending projects as part of its mission. PMI was praised for starting a program to increase home ownership opportunities for Native Americans nationwide, on and off reservations. If you select this path, however, it's going to be hard—if not impossible—to keep your money out of the hands of some of the less-than-ethical financial powerhouses. PMI's Native American effort, for example, was done in partnership with Wells Fargo, although it could be argued that without the support of such a heavy hitter, such a noble endeavor might have been impossible to pull off in the first place.

There is one company that does make a clear commitment to supporting environmental and social causes as part of its standard operation. **MortgageGreen** (www.mortgagegreen.com), based in Marin County near San Francisco, earmarks 10% of its profits for a dozen organizations devoted to environmental sustainability and progressive social change, including the Rainforest Action Network, Environmental Defense Fund, Earthjustice and Adbusters. As with socially responsible credit cards, this could take a while to add up to a substantial sum, though as the company points out in its literature, if just one in a thousand US mortgages were funded through such a program, $5 million would be generated annually. MortgageGreen says it will beat any mortgage lender's total loan package cost, and contribute $400 to its social and environmental activism fund in the borrower's name if it can't meet that obligation for any reason.

Though some might view it as drifting afield from core SRI principles, it's also possible to qualify for an energy-efficient mortgage, or **EEM**, by buying an energy-efficient home or committing to upgrading a building as per recommendations of a certified Home Energy Rating System inspector. While the inspection might run you a few hundred dollars, the idea is you'll earn that back (and more) by the energy you save. Here again, though, you might be funneling your mortgage through behemoths lacking socially responsible policies—precisely the sort of operations you might hope to avoid. The most prominent outfit offering green EEM Mortgages, Fannie Mae (a Congressionally chartered private company working with lenders to mortgage homes for low-to-moderate income households), is one of the five largest financial institutions in the

US, and has been tarnished by federal investigations into its irregular accounting practices in recent years (along with the aforementioned Freddie Mac). In addition, its lender partners include fellow financial giants like Bank of America, though it's possible to use credit unions for lender partners as well. If you're on the fence, do note that the financial terms on EEM mortgages are not considered to be of notable excellence, as these things go.

For more comprehensive information on mortgages, seek the help of a clued-in financial adviser (see p.224).

Socially responsible student loans

Whether you're a student, parent, or anyone else helping someone through school, student loans represent a huge financial commitment, both during school and for years following graduation. It's not well publicized, but many of the loans end up borrowing from big banks or other financial institutions that some students and their helpers might find objectionable. This is particularly true of one type of the most common student loan, the federally guaranteed **Stafford Loans**, which break down into two categories. The Direct Stafford Loan supplies money to students from the US Department of Education; the second, more worrisome one, the Federal Family Education Loan (FFEL), lets banks do the loaning. With so many college attendees handling large sums of money for the first time, it's to be expected that relatively few of them (or even their parents) might realize that the sums are being channeled through financial institutions they might not favor. In turn, the mega-banks secure the banking habits of young adults, who then stick with them for life.

If you're getting money through FFEL, it might be possible to use, or switch to, a bank with higher standards than the major ones handling most of this stuff, but you must choose a bank from a list your school's guaranty agency accepts. If the list isn't supplied to you by the school, you can call the Federal Student Aid Information Center (1-800-443-3243) to get the guaranty agency's address and phone number, and contact it directly.

If you're nearing graduation, be aware that you can consolidate federal student loans into one larger loan after you receive your diploma, and then switch to a more responsible financial institution. Your interest rate may drop, but more crucially, your former, "unethical" bank will lose interest on your loans for the ten-year FFEL repayment period. For more information, check the "financial alternatives" section of the Rainforest Action Network's website, at:

RAN www.ran.org/ran_campaigns/global_finance/ria_studentloans.html

Household

From the electricity that powers them to the hardwood furniture that adorns them, our homes involve us in all kinds of environmental and social issues. In terms of global warming, the average US household accounts for an estimated twenty tons of CO_2 every year—far more than the average car. And much of this is avoidable. Meanwhile, our soft furnishings, such as bedlinens, curtains or rugs, are linked to many of the same issues of poor labor conditions as clothes and shoes. This chapter takes a look around the home—and garden—and gives some ethical-shopping pointers.

Home energy
From greenhouse to green house

When we flick on a "natural light" 100-watt bulb or turn up our home heating, the first thing that comes to mind is unlikely to be a coal mine, gas field or oil rig. And yet around two-thirds of the US's electricity—and, of course, all of our gas—is generated from these **fossil fuels**, which pose environmental problems on an altogether different scale from other products we consume.

It's not just that fossil-fuel use is driving **global warming**—arguably the most serious issue facing humanity (see p.14)—but also that burning, extracting and processing these fuels releases a whole range of harmful chemicals. "Flaring" (burning off) waste gases, burning coal and refining oil, for example, generate huge quantities of **pollutants**, many of which—such as benzene—can accumulate in the flesh of animals and humans. Other noxious emissions include volatile organic compounds (VOCs), polycyclic aromatic hydrocarbons (PAHs) and hydrogen sulphide.

Most of the other third of our electricity comes from **nuclear power**, which poses its own problems. Even though the risk of Chernobyl-style

What you're plugging into: the bellowing smokestack of a fossil-fuel power station.

disasters is relatively low, there is still no way to dispose safely of the radioactive waste that nuclear power stations generate. This waste, most of which is currently in "temporary storage" while permanent solutions are researched, looks set to end up buried deep in solid rock, where it will remain highly dangerous for tens of thousands of years. Critics of nuclear power point out that the waste is enormously expensive to manage, poses risks to people and the environment (in the case of an accident occurring), and, in the wrong hands, could be a major security threat.

We're likely to use coal, gas, oil and nuclear power for most of our domestic electricity and heating for some time to come. Although some European countries have cut down coal consumption by about 40% since 1990, and the United Kingdom and the Canadian province of Ontario have plans to phase coal power out altogether, it's risen over the same period in the US, where it's responsible for more than half of fossil fuel use. That doesn't look likely to change in the next few years, as the Bush administration supports heavy subsidies for the industry. Coal plants could become much less harmful—in terms of climate change, at least —if they buried the CO_2 they create (a process known as carbon capture and storage) but it would require enormous investment and political will to roll out this technology with the speed necessary to combat global warming.

Natural gas consumption, except for a blip in the wake of Hurrricane Katrina, has increased (as have consumer gas prices), and natural gas power plants are expected to more than double their capacity between 2000 and 2010. And while no nuclear plants have been built since the Three Mile Island accident in 1979, more than 100 continue to operate within our borders. In the meantime, our electric generation capacity needs are expected not to level off, but to grow—by a full third during the next 20 years, according to the Energy Information Administration.

So what can consumers do about all of this? A good first step is to take stock of the energy you use and how you use it. Consider organizing a home energy audit from your local utility or an independent auditor. Or if you'd rather do that yourself, go to Home Energy Saver, which calculates your energy consumption and potential savings, as well as suggesting upgrades.

Home Energy Saver hes.lbl.gov

Once that's done, there are two obvious steps to take. One is to buy electricity from **renewable sources**—or even purchase the equipment to generate your own. People argue about whether the US could be entirely reliant on green sources such as wind, solar, tidal and so on. But no one doubts that the more we generate, the better. Secondly, we can try to simply use less power and/or heating fuels—something we can do surprisingly effectively with a bit of thought.

Green electricity suppliers

The US has unusually strong potential in terms of renewable energy—according to the Union of Concerned Scientists' *Clean Energy Blueprint* report, we could supply 20% of our electricity with renewable energy sources by 2020 if we put our minds to it, reducing CO_2 emissions by two-thirds and saving each family \$350/yr. in the bargain. However, right now only about two percent of our electricity comes from non-hydropower renewable sources, and much of that comes from the incineration of municipal solid waste, which environmental groups claim is polluting and a disincentive to recycling.

These days, however, there are a wide range of **green electricity options** on offer—both from major electricity suppliers and specialist companies which only deal in renewable energy. According to the US Department of Energy, in fact, about 50% of customers are now able to buy green power directly from their suppliers. These offer consumers a way to help support renewable energy, but they work in a few different ways—and some have a far bigger effect that others. Too, the options vary greatly in both number and quality depending upon in which state you live, though everyone in the US can theoretically choose to do their part.

The basic premise of most green, "eco" or other such power plans is that you pay a little bit more and the company supplies you with energy generated from renewable, environmentally friendly sources. It usually doesn't work that directly; most often you're paying for more green power to go into the regional grid, not for door-to-door delivery, as you can't specify which electrons you get. So obviously the actual flow arriving in your plug sockets probably won't come straight from the wind farm. But you can at least support suppliers who are using green-generated electricity to some degree, the hope being this will make the whole business a darker shade of green.

But it's not quite this simple. As much as you might like to just switch over to the greenest company around, and although electricity markets were opened to competition by the National Energy Policy Act in 1992, you can only change to a different supplier if you live in a state where such competition is allowed. As of the latest update, such "restructuring" was allowed in just 17 states (plus the District of Columbia), though more are expected to open up in the future. And just because competition's allowed doesn't mean a green power company's there to serve you: according to the Union of Concerned Scientists website, only Illinois, Maine, Maryland, New Jersey, New York, Pennsylvania, Texas, Virginia and the District of Columbia are offering such "green marketing" options.

Whether you're in those states or not, however, you might be able to opt for **green pricing**. Under that plan you stay with the same provider, but voluntarily pay a premium on your electric bill that will go to the cost of purchasing green, sustainable energy. This most commonly entails paying a higher price per kilowatt-hour, a surcharge that can vary widely, from a half-penny to more than a dime; otherwise, the money will be collected by fixed monthly fees, rounding up bills and some other methods. About 35 states and more than 300 suppliers have green pricing (and more have announced plans to put it in place), though living in a state with such companies is no guarantee that you can take advantage of this with the one you're using: one of the largest (and most notorious) utilities, Pacific Gas & Electric, has no green pricing policies, for instance. For quick info on whether you can buy "green power" and/or "green pricing" in your state, as well as what plans are available through which companies, go to the Green Power Network site, maintained by the US Department of Energy.

Green Power Network www.eere.energy.gov/greenpower

A final choice, though the one that consumers usually find the least satisfying, is buying **green energy certificates**—also sometimes called **green tags**, **Tradeable Renewable Certificates (aka TRCs)**, or **Renewable Energy Certificates (RECs)**—which you can do no matter where you live. The program's usually rather fuzzily explained even by the nonprofit

Green Internet and phone services

If you want to divert yet more of your household expenses toward green power, a few companies are now offering Web hosting, phone and even DSL services that are powered by renewable energy sources. Earthsite and Elfon both offer such Web-hosting plans, and EcoSky offers Web hosting, dial-up Internet access and DSL, though the DSL component is currently limited to just nine states in the Western US (of which California is not one).

Earthsite www.earthsite.net
Elfon www.elfon.com
EcoSky www.ecosky.com

Red Jellyfish has a difference approach. It doesn't draw the actual power from renewable sources, but for each year one of its members uses dial-up Internet access services, it will donate funds to protect 6000 square feet of rainforest.

Red Jellyfish www.redjellyfish.com

organizations that recommend buying them. But essentially, each tag represents the environmental and social benefits associated with a certain amount of renewable electricity generation, usually running about $20 for one kilowatt-hour. *You* won't get that kilowatt-hour delivered to your home, mind you, and often the available options involve paying for green electricity in an entirely different area of the country. So if you have your heart set on impacting your own region, you might find the whole concept of (as one plan would allow you to do) living in California and paying for green electricity in Maine a little weird. But the thinking is that you're at least enabling its production somewhere, and in so putting just a little more green power into the regional or national electric grid. Again, it's easy to find vendors of green tags through the Green Power Network site (www.eere.energy.gov/greenpower/buying/buying_power.shtml). And for those who don't live in states offering either green power or green pricing, it's one small way to to help the overall cause.

How green is it really?

If you're going to be paying a premium to generate green power, whether directly or indirectly, you should be entitled to some sort of assurance that solar, wind, geothermal and biomass options are being substituted for fossil fuels. As yet, however, green power certification programs aren't nearly as robust in the US as, say, those for organic food, or possibly even those for fairly traded food. Here yet again, accountability varies widely according to your state. Many states now have **environmental disclosure policies** requiring electricity suppliers to make information available on their fuel sources, and in some cases their emissions. The policies differ from state to state, however, and about half of the states, hard it as may be to believe, have no requirements at all. The disclosures, such as they are, can be viewed at www.eere.energy.gov/greenpower/markets/disclosure.shtml.

While there are no federal regulations in place for authenticating green power suppliers (or even standards for what constitutes "green" electricity), the voluntary **Green-E** program, run by the nonprofit **Center for Resource Solutions**, does at least verify and certify green energy products, pricing plans and certificates. Under this program, if it's a "green" utility company, at least 50% of the electrical supply has to come from renewable resources. Also, any nonrenewable part of the product has to have equal or lower air emissions than conventional electricity, and the product can't contain any nuclear power. Providers are also required to comply with a code of conduct that obligates them to fully disclose the percentage and type of renewable resources in their product, and reveal all the finery in their pricing plans. The code of conduct's on its website,

Power Scorecard

If you have the option of choosing your electricity provider, you are likely to want some reference that can give you some basis for comparison, particularly as to how high each scores on the "green" voltage meter. Although it's still limited in scope, one measuring stick is offered by Power Scorecard, sponsored by a coalition of six environmental organizations (Environmental Defense, the Natural Resources Defense Council, the Izaak Walton League, the Northwest Environmental Coalition, the Pace University Energy Project, and the Union of Concerned Scientists). Its website rates companies' environmental performance in eight areas of air, water and land impact, on a scale from "excellent" to "unacceptable," as well as grading them by the percentage of electricity obtained from renewable resources sourced from newly built technology. Prices are also noted, as is whether the companies' products are certified by Green-E.

Unfortunately, as of this writing, Power Scorecard rated companies in just four of the states in which competition is allowed: New York, New Jersey, Pennnsylvania, and Texas. (California was included when the program started, but was dropped when the state's Public Utilities Commission put a still-standing moratorium on provider choice in 2001, as a fallout of California's state financial crisis.) The organization does hope to include more states in its survey in the future, and its FAQ section offers some basic, helpful hints about green power in general.

Power Scorecard www.powerscorecard.org

www.green-e.org, which tells you what products, certifications and pricing plans are certified in your state (the site also has a good amount of info on green energy certificates in general).

EcoPower (www.ert.net/ecopower), administered by the **Environmental Resources Trust**, also certifies renewable energy certificates using different standards—in the inimitably bureaucratic language of the Green Power Network website, "under EcoPower certification, RECs convey only the renewable energy attributes of renewable electricity and do not convey environmental benefits." EcoPower, which also certifies "blocks" or large quantities of power (as opposed to entire companies), contends that it takes a more active role in marketing and tailoring clean energy to an organization's specific needs, terming (on its website) Green-E as a more "passive" outfit that merely acts as a certifying stamp and requires products to bear a larger renewable component than many municipalities and corporations can afford. These probably aren't huge differences to the average citizen, and if one or both methods are good enough for you, the Green Network Power site's list of companies reveals which sell green tags certified by either Green-E or EcoPower.

Be mindful, too, that many of the companies that offer "green" power alternatives are sometimes subsidiaries of larger companies that own nuclear and coal power plants, like Southern Califiornia Edison, which offered "Earthsource" through its Edison Source division. And some of the companies with green options are themselves large and notorious financial powers—Enron, for instance, offered a green "EarthSmart Power" plan to California consumers when that state was open to competition, though it was scrapped just a few months later after it proved unprofitable. Standards across the whole green energy field remain so erratically defined and enforced that vigilant customers would do well to heed the Union of Concerned Scientists' advice about dealing with green electric suppliers in general: "Be skeptical and ask questions."

Although we're focusing on household green energy here, it should also be noted that green power is also available to institutions and businesses. And it's not just left-leaning organizations that take advantage of this option: according to the Green Power Network, big purchasers include the usual suspects, like Ben & Jerry's, Whole Foods and Clif Bar, as well as some surprises, such as the United States Army, Safeway and Bonnie Raitt, who had the Green Mountain Energy Company supply wind energy certificates equivalent to all the power consumed during her 2002 summer tour. The Green Power Network's *Guide to Purchasing Green Power* is specifically geared toward organizations, and can be downloaded for free from its website.

For more on green electricity, try these websites:

Co-op America www.coopamerica.org/programs/greenergy
Union of Concerned Scientists www.ucsusa.org/clean_energy

Grow your own power

If you want to put renewable power in your home on a more tangible level, there are a number of options. Most of the renewable energy sources—from wind and solar to hydro and geothermal—can be tapped into on a household level. Some of these make sense not only from an environmental perspective but also from a financial one: you may save money in the long run, and there are numerous grants and tax incentives available to contribute to the price of installation. Under the **net metering program**, you may even be able to feed any extra power back into the utility grid and get paid for it.

That said, a system that will make you anywhere close to self-sufficient in electricity will require massive up-front investment, and in most cases it's far more efficient to start off by improving your heating system (see p.251) and insulation (see p.252). Following is the low-down on each of the main micro-generation options.

Systems, costs & grants

Now, more than ever, there are many tax incentives and grants available to US householders who want to buy some kind of renewable energy source. These can take the form of personal tax credits and rebates, property tax exemptions, personal deductions, sales tax exemptions and utility rebates, and though the grants tend to be targeted toward commercial and institutional buildings, some of those are available for homeowners as well. These tax incentives and grants are so numerous, and vary so much according to your state of residence, that it would be futile to try and list them all, or even generally summarize what you might be able to expect. Fortunately, the Database of State Incentives for Renewable Energy (**DSIRE**, funded by the US Department of Energy) has a user-friendly map allowing you to just click on your state for lists and descriptions of all the programs available.

DSIRE www.dsireusa.org

Net metering

If you're generating more power at home than you need (some or all of the time) you can sell the surplus back to your utility company under the net metering system. As in so many things energy-related, how it works, or if it works at all, depends on where you're living. In the best-case scenario, you can sell the excess back to your utility (via your meter turning backward) at the "retail rate," or the same rate you're paying for the electricity. In some other states, the deal's not as good: you sell it back to the utility at "avoided cost," or what the utility would have to pay to buy electricity on the wholesale market, which can run as much as ten cents less per kWh than the retail rate. In still other states, you won't be able to sell the excess at all; as of this writing, net metering was available in 40 of the 50 states. For more details about net metering and how it might work in your state, go to the net metering section of the Green Power Network, at:

Net Metering www.eere.energy.gov/greenpower/markets/netmetering.shtml.

You might not be able to catch a huge break, but depending on where you live, some of these programs are fairly generous. Idaho, for instance, allows $20,000 of tax deductions (spread over four years), and Pennsylvania offers rebates refunding up to 80% of the system cost. More typical values, though still worthwhile, include Maryland's solar energy grant program, which provides 20% (or up to $3000) of the cost for solar photovoltaic equipment on residential property; similarly, Utah's individual income tax credit for residential renewable energy systems applies to 25% of the cost of installation, up to as much as $2000 per system. Note that much bigger grants are often available for community, nonprofit, school, and commercial projects.

In addition, as of late 2005, California—home of 85% of the solar roof installations in the US—seemed likely to pass a "Million Solar Roofs" program that would unleash about $3 billion of incentives over the next decade. That would quite possibly send the solar roof market through the roof, and would also, as the usually staid *San Francisco Chronicle* editorialized, help establish "a thriving solar industry, driving down prices as well as demand for new power plants."

The kind of renewable energy source that's most suitable for your home will differ considerably according to where you live and what kind of residence you have. Following is some basic information on the major types available, as well as pointers to where you can find out more.

▶ **Solar electricity** Photovoltaic panels generate electricity without any moving parts or chemical emissions. Although the environmental

Solar hot water heaters

With a solar hot water system a **"collector"** panel is placed on your roof, focusing the sun's energy directly into your hot water system. This is not to be confused with a photovoltaic (PV) system for generating electricity (what most people tend to think of by "solar panel").

The technology is much more efficient today than it used to be, so a few thousand dollars will buy a system capable of providing about 70% of your hot water, reducing your utility bills by (according to a study by the Florida Solar Energy Center) as much as 50–85%. However, to get the best from a solar system, you'll need a home in a sunny area with a **south-facing roof** free from too many shadow-casting chimneys or trees. Moreover, installation costs can rise if your roof is difficult to access.

Many companies offer solar hot water systems, often in conjunction with other solar products. Finding one is often as simple as leafing through the appropriate listings in the Yellow Pages, though the Source for Renewable Energy, a big online business directory, can also be useful.

Source for Renewable Energy www.energy.sourceguides.com

benefits of PTV systems are universally acknowledged, they'll take a long time to pay back the initial investment, varying so much according to your individual building, location, sunlight exposure and other factors that government organizations seem deliberately hesitant to offer even ballpark estimates. To be safe, however, you should probably figure on a minimum of ten years or so before you break even—though it could take quite a bit longer, depending on factors such as future electricity prices and how much electricity you use in the day, when the panels are active. The 2003 edition of the Wisconsin Division of Energy's *Consumer Guide to Photovoltaic Systems* asserted that "given current energy prices, the payback period is often longer than the system's life." All in all, then, it's crucial to do lots of research before taking the plunge. **Typical cost**: Entirely depends on the number of panels you buy, though about ten to twenty should supply enough power for a household; it'll also vary a lot depending on your location, weather and available tax incentives and grants. $16,000–20,000 is around average for a two-kilowatt system, which will provide most of a typical household's power consumption. A five-kilowatt system, which will completely cover the energy needs of most homes, can run you $30,000-$40,000. The Department of Energy's *Consumer's Guide to Buying a Solar Electric System*, downloadable for free from www.nrel.gov/buildings/pv/h_add_resources.html, lays out the basics. State-specific guides are also available for California, Arizona, Colorado, and the Mid-Atlantic region (Pennsylvania, Virginia, West Virginia, Delaware, District of Columbia, Maryland and New Jersey) at www.eren.doe.gov/pv/onlinelrn.html.

▶ **Wind** Household wind turbines are these days near silent and also pretty efficient. The electricity can be directed either into batteries or onto the grid. Wind speeds being so variable across the US, however, it's vital to check first whether your site has enough air movement to make this a worthwhile choice. To get the best from a domestic wind turbine, you'll need average wind speeds of at least nine miles per hour—and, of course, to live in an area where such construction is allowed. **Typical cost**: About $1000–5000 per kilowatt installed; according to the American Wind Energy Association, a typical home wind system costs $32,000. Needless to say, the windier it is on your property (and the more tax incentives, etc., you get on the initial investment), the sooner it'll pay for itself, though in some extremely favorable circumstances, that can happen as soon as a half-dozen years after it's up and running. However, current roof-mounted turbines, as opposed to free-standing ones, are unlikely to ever break even. *Small Wind Electric Systems: A U.S. Consumer's Guide* is downloadable for free from www. nrel.gov/learning/ho_wind.html, and state-specific variations of the guides are also available.

The Skystream from Southwest Windpower (pictured below) is the first fully integrated small wind generator specifically designed for the grid-connected home. The unit costs approximately $7,000–10,000, depending on tower height and installation costs, and is expected to produce energy for under $0.09/kWh. Depending on installed cost, average wind speed, local cost of electricity and state rebates, the unit can pay for itself in as little as five years.

▶ **Micro-hydro** systems can provide a reliable and highly efficient source of power—if, that is, you happen to have a fast-flowing river at the bottom of your garden. A ten-kilowatt system can provide enough power for a large home, according to the Department of Energy. **Typical cost**: varies widely depending on positioning. The US Department of Energy's *Consumer's Guide to Energy Efficiency and Renewable Energy* has some information about evaluating potential sites. You can find it at: www.eere.energy.gov/consumer/renewable_energy

▶ **Ground source heat pumps** concentrate heat from the ground and use it to heat water, allowing annual energy savings of 30–60%. **Typical cost**: $7500 for a residence of typical size, or $2500 per ton of capacity. As above, go to www.eere.energy.gov/consumer/renewable_energy for a primer.

Other good sources of information about home-grown power include the following:

Energy Efficiency and Renewable Energy Network (EREN) www.eren.doe.gov

A site run by the US Department of Energy, with lots of basic information about home renewable-energy technologies.

Findsolar.com www.findsolar.com

A joint partnership between the American Solar Energy Society, Solar Electric Power Association, Energy Matters LLC and the US Department of Energy, this site aims to link consumers interested in buying solar power systems with the professionals who can install them. Enter information about your home and location, and the site will supply (for no charge) suitable recommendations, cost/benefit estimates and a suggested list of companies to consider, with customer reviews and ratings to boot. There's also an extensive FAQ section.

Home Power www.homepower.com

A bimonthly magazine about home renewable energy and sustainable living, whose website has free downloadable basic primers on solar and wind power.

The Source for Renewable Energy www.energy.sourceguides.com/index.shtml

An online business directory of nearly ten thousand renewable energy business and organizations around the globe.

Reducing your household energy use

With the exception of those who have spent their life savings going energy self-sufficient, it pays—environmentally and financially—for us to reduce our household power consumption. After all, homes currently account for about 15% of the country's CO_2 emissions, and therefore also a huge chunk of our contribution to global warming and pollution.

Reducing energy use doesn't have to mean drastic lifestyle changes (though that might be ideal). After all, at present a large proportion of our household power is simply wasted, frittered away by the likes of energy-inefficient fridges, drafty windows, uninsulated hot water tanks and TVs

Tax credits for energy savings

Under the Energy Policy Act of 2005, there are various **tax credits** available to help pay for insulation, replacement windows, or a more efficient boiler, central air conditioning unit, furnace, fan, or water heater. For more on these, or any other issue relating to saving energy in the home, visit:

Tax Incentives Assistance Project www.energytaxincentives.org
Database of State Incentives for Renewable Energy www.dsireusa.org

You can also qualify for an energy-efficient mortgage, or **EEM**, by buying an energy-efficient home or committing to upgrades recommended by a certified Home Energy Rating System inspector; see p.237 for details.

on standby. Indeed, according to the nonprofit environmental think tank Rocky Mountain Institute, if every US household replaced its old appliances with more efficient ones, we'd reduce our carbon dioxide emission by almost a ton a person. The same institute has also calculated that we could slash off a similar amount—and save around $200 per household each year—through simple adjustments such as washing clothes in cold water, turning off unneeded lights and moving thermostats a few degrees higher or lower.

Other than the obvious stuff—such as not overfilling the coffee pot, and using surge protectors that allow you to turn off power before it reaches your electrical devices ("standby" often uses almost as much power as "on")—there are four main ways that consumers can increase their energy efficiency. Not all of these involve "shopping with a conscience" as such, but they warrant a mention here nonetheless. Also, bear in mind that the Energy Efficiency and Renewable Energy Network devotes a large section of its website to consumer tips on how to reduce household energy use:

Energy Savers www.eere.energy.gov/consumer/tips

#1 Tweaking your heating

Space and water heating account for the majority of our home energy use—and therefore our household greenhouse emissions—so this is a key area. There are many ways to make your heating more efficient, and in the process you may save a couple of hundred dollars each year. Make sure you insulate your hot water tank, if you have one (though be sure not to cover the thermostat); reduce the temperature of your **hot water**;

make sure the heating only comes on when you want it on and are there to enjoy it; consider programmable **thermostats** so the temperature's regulated when you're not around the house. Finally, if you're fitting a new **boiler**, be sure to get a condensing model—they're still far more common in Europe than in the US, but some dealers do offer them here. They're usually a bit more expensive but they're about 10–15% more efficient than the noncondensing variety.

#2 Insulating

Almost half of heat-loss in the average home goes via the attic or walls. Most people will save 20–30% of their heating bill just by installing decent insulation, which may pay for itself in a few years. Bear in mind that some forms of insulation are more environmentally friendly than others. As a rule, those that use minerals as their raw material use more energy and chemicals in their production, and are less likely to be locally sourced, than those that use natural materials like **wool** or **flax**. The latter—though often more expensive—allow for a greater circulation of air and help to avoid the retention of toxins in a building, linked by some to "sick building syndrome" (see p.269). Draft-proofing **windows and doors**, meanwhile, can have a massive impact for a tiny amount of money. The Department of Energy's Zip Code Insulation Program, gives recommendations for insulation you might need in your home based on your area of residence. See:

ZIP Insulation Program www.ornl.gov/~roofs/Zip/ZipHome.html

#3 Buying energy-efficient appliances

Kitchen appliances are our biggest power eaters. Although federally mandated minimum efficiency standards have cut down on the average household refrigerator electric drain, at the turn of the century, kitchen appliances as a whole were still accounting for about 25% of home energy use. Efficient models often use less than half as much power—and the same is true of other electrical goods such as lamps and TVs. So when buying an appliance, make sure it's rated highly for energy efficiency. Look for the **Energy Star** label, given only to products that meet such standards (see box opposite). The benefits to the environment can be substantial—according to the American Council for an Energy-Efficient Economy, replacing a 20-year-old fridge with a new energy-efficient model will reduce household CO_2 emissions by a ton a year.

Shopping for energy efficiency

Developed by the Environmental Protection Agency and the Department of Energy, the **Energy Star** label marks products that have been identified as the most energy-efficient of their type. The logo can be used on appliances, electrical products, heating and cooling systems, windows and even homes and buildings. The EPA's gone as far as to opine that if everyone chose what they bought by what products and structures bear the label over the next decade, the national energy bill would go down by about $200 billion.

The exact qualifying standards used vary according to what product gets the seal, but if you're curious, you can find them on the www.energystar.gov website. Accredited washing machines, for example, must use 50% less energy than standard models, while computers must use 70% less electricity, going into a low-power 15-watt mode if left inactive. It's not only the most common of household items that get the endorsement; exit signs, vending machines, light bulbs and dozens of other products are covered by the program. The site also lists some of the qualifying models in various product categories, including nearly 300 types of washing machines alone. You won't find any dryers here, however: they're not labeled since most use the same amount of energy and there's little difference between models, though the site does offer some tips to reduce the energy dryers use.

Also look out for the **EnergyGuide** label, which shows typical annual energy consumption and cost, and how a product compares to the best and worst performers in its category.

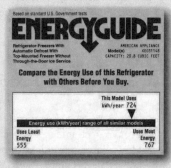

Co-op America advises using additional sources like *Consumer Reports* to zero in on the most efficient products in certain categories. Also useful is the American Council for an Energy Efficient website (www.aceee.org), which rates the most energy-efficient models of several types of appliances; you can also order a hard-copy book with such information, *Consumer Guide to Home Energy Savings*, though the same site.

Another stamp of energy efficiency is supplied by the nonprofit **National Fenestration Rating Council** (www.nfrc.org), which labels windows, doors and skylights. Their criteria takes into account the "U-Factor"—a measure of how well a window insulates—as well as how much solar heat moves though the pane. Their website has a large directory of certified products and detailed (if highly technical) ratings tables.

#4 Choosing low-energy light bulbs

Light bulbs account for around 15% of our electricity usage, yet around 90% of the energy that typical incandescent bulbs use is lost in heat. Energy-efficient **compact fluorescent lightbulbs** (CFLs) reduce wasted energy by about 75% and last around ten times as long. Decent ones cost around $10 or a little more (the cheapest ones tend to produce slightly "artificial" light), but will save you $30–60 in electricity costs during their lifetime. According to the Power Scorecard rating program for electrical product environmental quality, "If every American household replaced one of its standard light bulbs with an energy efficient compact fluorescent bulb, we would save the same amount of energy as a large nuclear power plant produces in one year." Also note that some power companies offer subsidies for CFLs; call your local electric supplier and ask.

What about **halogen** lights? These are a subset of incandescents and tend to be mid-range performers in the efficiency stakes. Better-quality halogen bulbs are around twice as efficient as typical incandescents and half as efficient as compact fluorescents. However, halogen light fittings often take multiple bulbs, raising their overall energy consumption.

Cleaning & laundry products
A green clean?

When it comes to cleaning and laundry, perhaps the most important thing to consider is the energy efficiency of your machines—as discussed above. Some washers, dryers and dishwashers use significantly more power than others to do the same job—in the process creating unnecessary greenhouse gas. But what about cleaning and laundry products themselves? Partly because of the ubiquity of "green" alternatives, most people already have a suspicion that there may be something slightly dubious about conventional surface cleaners, liquid detergents, dish washing powder, polishes and the like. The main issues are what's in them and who makes them—including, of course, whether or not the company in question carries out tests on animals.

The chemical question

Different categories of cleaning and laundry products are based on different types of chemicals. Many of these chemicals are uncontroversial, but some, if environmental and consumer groups are to be believed, pose risks both to human health and to the environment.

The detergents that form the basis of products such as dish soaps are chemicals known as surfactants ("surface active agents"), which do their work by dissolving partly in water and partly in organic substances such as food and grime. Some surfactants—especially those derived from **petrochemicals**—are toxic and relatively slow to biodegrade, and the plant-derived alternatives used by the "eco" companies are less harmful. However, surfactants rarely feature on the list of the most potentially risky chemicals: at the levels used, they're not widely believed to be a serious health hazard to humans, and not everyone is convinced they do that much damage to aquatic life.

More worrying, according to campaigners such as Greenpeace, are the additive substances used, some of which were recently classified as "chemicals of high concern" by the EU. Some of these substances, such as the **phthalates** found in certain multi-surface cleaners, are thought to pose a threat to our hormone systems, while others are known to be **carcinogenic** (cancer causing) in animals. Furthermore, some of the chemicals in question, such as the **artificial musks** widely used as fragrances in laun-

Household toxins: beyond cleaning products

The debate about whether or not the chemicals found in our homes pose genuine risks to people and planet tends to focus almost exclusively on household cleaning products, paints (see p.269) and cosmetics and toiletries (see p.195). However, many of the same chemicals, and numerous others besides, are found in all kinds of household items—from carpets and computers (which may contain substances such as brominated flame retardants) to PVC shower curtains (which may contain phthalates).

Again, there's no pressing evidence to say that, in the quantities we're exposed to them, the chemicals are really that risky. But many people take the view that ethically minded shoppers should avoid any company using bioaccumulative, dangerous and poorly understood chemicals—even if just to reduce the environmental risks of producing them. If you take that view, or you simply want to minimize your exposure to the "chemicals of high concern," visit the Greenpeace International website for the latest reports on toxic substances in everyday products:

Greenpeace Toxins Campaigns www.greenpeace.org/international/campaigns/toxics

dry powders and other cleaning products, are **bioaccumulative**, meaning they can build up in the body tissue of humans and other organisms, and be passed on through the food chain or by birth.

"Babies are born with toxic chemicals already contaminating their bodies," according to Greenpeace, while wildlife groups have raised concerns that bioacculative chemicals are even starting to turn up in the livers of arctic animals such as polar bears, presumably having been passed from plug holes and factories via water treatment systems to plankton, and then up the food chain via crustaceans, fishes and seals, increasing in concentration at each level. They may also pass back to other humans via the consumption of fish.

But how serious are these environmental and health risks? In most cases, we're not exactly sure. In part this is because causal links between specific chemicals and specific effects are almost impossible to prove. Whether you're talking about cancer in humans, or endocrine disruption in arctic birds, there's no simple way to isolate the effect of any single chemical.

But it's also because not a great deal of research has been done. According to *Chemicals in Products,* a recent UK government report from the Royal Commission on Environmental Pollution, "Society might reasonably expect that adequate assessments have been carried out on chemicals that are on the market, and that appropriate risk management strategies are in place for potentially harmful substances. This is not the case..." Hence the EU only recently set out to discover the effects on people and the environment of many of the chemicals already widely used, with an initiative called **REACH**. Passed by the EU Parliament in November 2005, it will require manufacturers to provide health and safety information on tens of thousands of untested, unregulated chemicals. This idea is very popular with anti-chemical campaigners, but not popular with animal rights groups, since it is due to involve a huge number of animal experiments.

There's no similar effort on the horizon in the US, where the 1976 Toxic Substances Control Act defined some standards for new chemicals reaching the market, but where thousands of chemicals already in circulation have never been evaluated in such a manner. REACH could nonetheless have far-reaching implications here, as American companies will need to comply with the guidelines to sell their products in the European market. Unsurprisingly, groups such as the American Chemical Council and the Synthetic Organic Chemical Manufacturers Association are lobbying the US government to oppose the program.

It's worth keeping all this in perspective. Even if the health risks of these chemicals are proven, they are almost certainly many orders of magnitude lower than the risks posed by, say, smoking—or the likelihood of having a car accident while driving. And the environmental impacts of our cleaning products are minute compared with the output of similar chemicals from the oil, gas and coal industries that power our electric sockets and cars, or the plastics industries that produce everything from our plant pots to our computer monitors.

Still, with greener alternatives to most of the potentially risky cleaners available, there is certainly a decent case for adopting the "precautionary principle" and favoring companies that have promised not to use the most worrying chemicals. This basically means opting for specialist green brands (see overleaf), who usually also shun animal-based products as well as chemicals that aren't risky to humans but pose other environmental problems (one example being **phosphates**, which can encourage excessively fast plant growth and clog up water systems).

Animal testing

New ingredients for washing and cleaning products are widely tested on animals, both in the US and elsewhere. According to In Defense of Animals, "the Consumer Product Safety Commission (CPSC)—which regulates products such as detergents and cleaners—does not require animal testing, nor does the Food and Drug Administration (FDA) require animal testing for cosmetics. In reality, many viable non-animal tests exist." Still, awareness of animal testing, and the cruel practices it often involves, remains much higher in the world of cosmetics than that of cleaners.

If you'd rather buy products from companies with strict animal-testing policies, then look for the **Coalition for Consumer Information on Cosmetics** (CCIC) jumping rabbit logo. Used for household cleaning and laundry products as well as cosmetics, it can only be displayed on products made by companies that shun all products tested on animals after a *fixed* cut-off date, and which are audited to prove it. For an up-to-date list of qualifying companies, or to request its *Pocket Compassionate Shopping Guide*, visit:

Leaping Bunny www.leapingbunny.org/shop_household.htm.

What to buy

The vast majority of cleaning and laundry product sales are accounted for by a handful of large companies. Here are the biggest players, and some of their most popular brands:

▶ **Clorox** Glad, Pine-Sol, S.O.S.

▶ **Colgate-Palmolive** Ajax, Fab

▶ **Procter & Gamble** Cheer, Gain, Febreze, Downy, Era, Tide

▶ **Reckitt Benckiser** Lysol, Spray 'N Wash, Easy-Off

▶ **SC Johnson** Pledge, Drano, Windex

▶ **Unilever** All, Surf, Wisk

Perhaps unsurprisingly, none of these multinationals get a clean bill of health on the grounds of chemicals, animal testing or various other measures. So how do the alternatives compare? The best-known and most widely available "green" cleaning range is **Ecover**, which now includes

scores of products, from floor cleaner to fabric softener (for the full list, see www.ecover.com). Ecover claims that "environmentally friendly detergents do not exist," but theirs are about as close as you can get, being almost entirely plant-based and excluding all the "high concern" chemicals discussed above. In 2002, the company even released their own detergent's chemical formula, so that other producers could "improve their impact on the environment." Ecover is widely available in both supermarkets and health-food shops, and often comes up on top in user tests of green household products.

Still, Ecover does have its critics. For years, the company was even on boycott lists, due to the fact that they were part-owned by **Group 4**, the private security firm criticized for violence against anti-road protestors and for its involvement in the controversial Campsfield immigration detention center. Today that link is no longer direct—the two companies just share a significant individual investor—but Ecover continues to be unpopular with the animal-rights lobby. The company claims to be actively "against" animal experiments, and they won't use an ingredient animal-tested in the last five years. However, this kind of **rolling cut-off date** policy—as opposed to picking a fixed cut-off year and sticking to it—leaves open the option of Ecover using ingredients being tested on

Do green cleaners actually work?

They may be kind to baby polar bears, but are "ethical" cleaning products as mean as they are green? It depends on the individual company and product, of course, but these days the eco-options are generally very good. Ecover washing-up liquids and surface cleaners, for example, work almost indistinguishably as well as the big brands, despite the washing-up liquid being forty times less toxic to aquatic life than the market leader (if Ecover's PR material is to be believed).

As for laundry, you probably *will* notice a difference in performance between the green detergents and the big brands for clothes that have oily or greasy soiling. But for day-to-day freshening up they work absolutely fine. So consider mixing and matching.

In truth, however, you can almost get by with no washing powder at all, since sweat and much other dirt is water soluble and removed perfectly well by the warm water and rotating action of a washing machine. Hence the success of products with names such as **eco-balls**, **eco-discs** or **aquaballs** (see www.aquaball.com) that claim to remove the need for detergent by "ionizing" or "magnetizing" the water. Many people swear by them, but few have tried comparing the result to using nothing at all.

animals now or in the future. Granted, they don't necessarily make use of this loop-hole, but in their quest for green-ness they refuse to rule out any eco-friendly ingredient just because it's been tested on animals after a hardwired cut-off date.

Just because a cleaning product makes the CCIC cut, of course, doesn't mean it's necessarily among the lowest in toxicity. The Center for a New American Dream, the flamboyantly named organization devoted to helping US citizens consume with environmental responsibility, cites the following companies as ones whose eco-cleaning-products emphasize both nontoxic ingredients and full disclosure, i.e. a full listing of ingredients on the label:

▶ **Seventh Generation**   ▶ **Ecover**

▶ **Naturally Yours**   ▶ **Shaklee**

▶ **Earth Friendly Products**   ▶ **Seaside Naturals**

▶ **Mountain Green**   ▶ **Citra-Solv**

▶ **Planet**

Of these, the most popular is Seventh Generation—commanding 48% of the natural household products market, according to a 2006 article in *The Utne Reader*—which offers several biodegradable, animal-testing-free cleaning and laundry products, as well as an extensive line of recycled paper and plastic products. Certainly their level of environmental and social commitment is unusual for a company of any sort, and includes the publication of *The Non-Toxic Times* monthly newsletter (available at www.seventhgeneration.com), support for numerous community and nonprofit environmental organizations, and a corporate responsibility report that it doesn't bury deep within its site map, but puts right on the home page. Its 50-page *Guide to a Toxin-Free Home*, downloadable from its site, has helpful pointers about identifying toxic products and lowering household toxins, though naturally this doesn't extend to mentioning any other eco-products by name.

Green cleaners are available in most health-food stores (and, increasingly, conventional grocery stores) and from green websites, such as:

Green Home www.greenhome.com
Kokopelli's Green Market www.kokogm.com

Be wary, incidentally, of products billed as "eco safe," "environmentally friendly," "green" or "nontoxic" that don't disclose all their ingredients or back up the claims with specific information on the package. Unlike the word "organic," the usage of such terms is not regulated by any standards. In fact, all of the above labels are classified as meaningless by the Consumers Union Guide to Environmental Labels. That's not to say that some products billed with these phrases might not actually be among the better choices, environmentally speaking, but that the fine print should be diligently inspected.

Back to basics

Trading in your Ajax for baking soda will be uncomfortably close to green extremism for most folk, but this kind of good old-fashioned, eco-friendly alternative works surprisingly well. As does **lemon juice** as a bleach substitute and **white-wine-vinegar solution** as a descaler and glass cleaner (though it does smell a bit). The more adventurous among the eco-minded community even swear by **tomato ketchup** (organic, of course) as a pot scrubber. For green "recipes" for everything from laundry detergent and dishwashing liquids to oven and toilet bowl cleaners, visit:

Natural Healthy Home Cleaning www.natural-healthy-home-cleaning-tips.com

If you're the kind that hardly ever even has time to clean the house, or if you have any influence over how your place of work is kept tidy, also bear in mind that some **eco-cleaning services** using nontoxic cleaning ingredients are sprouting up around the country. As of now, they're scattered (usually in urban areas), with no national clearinghouse, or any sort of Web locator that lets you punch in a zip code to find one near you. But virtually everything to do with environmentally friendly services and products seems to be expanding and this niche will probably be no exception.

Furniture & DIY
Home improvements

Furniture, timber & other wooden things

Wood is a natural, renewable, recyclable, biodegradable and nontoxic material. It's more energy efficient to produce than metal and most other materials and, in theory, if trees are planted in greater numbers than they're cut down, the timber industry can even help reduce global warming by soaking up CO_2. But, unfortunately, some of the wood we buy—whether it's used for beds, floorboards or candlesticks—comes with serious environmental and social costs. The US still imports large amounts of wood from irreplaceable ancient forests—which continue to be chopped down at the astonishing rate of a football-field-sized area every two seconds. And most of the rest comes from quick-growth plantation forests that are also associated with certain environmental problems.

Sumatra in your sitting room?

Next time you admire the rich, dark grain of a mahogany sleigh bed or eye up a teak table, bear in mind that the Western demand for tropical woods such as these has been a consistent driving force of the clearance of the world's **rainforests**. Though this isn't the headline issue it once was, it is still just as massive a problem, with millions of acres being cleared every year. In fact, recent surveying by the Brazilian National Institute for Space Research found that forest clearance in the Amazon was actually speeding up. This isn't only due to logging—the creation of farmland for cattle feed and palm oil is another major factor, just as urbanization is causing massive deforestation in South East Asia—but logging remains a key contributor.

Such destruction is an environmental disaster. As well as exacerbating global warming and contributing to soil erosion and water pollution (since forests help purify groundwater), it threatens as much as half of the world's biodiversity. A recent peer-reviewed study led by Barry Brook of the Northern Territory University in Darwin, Australia, suggested that deforestation in South East Asia alone looks set to make one-fifth of the world's plant and animal species extinct within the next hundred years. In Indonesia, especially, species are already being lost on a daily basis, with remarkable creatures such as the **orangutan** and **Sumatran tiger** likely to be gone within the next decade or so. According to the Global Trees Campaign, eight thousand species of tree are also currently threatened with extinction.

But deforestation is not only an environmental issue, of course. It's also a human rights one. Many forest-based people have contracted diseases from loggers, and have been forced off the lands where they have always lived, but to which they don't necessarily have any formally recognized rights. From Asia to Latin America, forest-based indigenous people have even been murdered when they've refused to leave. And the wider population can also be affected if the logging—as in the recent case in Liberia—is funding a military conflict. You don't have to take the green groups' word

Sumatran tigers, such as this cub, are the last of the Indonesian tiger subspecies. They are now critically endangered, partly due to habitat loss caused by logging and partly due to hunting. Only a few hundred remain alive in the wild, and many conservationists expect them to become extinct in the wild within ten years.

Of cues, caskets & clarinets

Furniture and timber are the products most widely associated with eco-friendly (and eco-unfriendly) wood. But, naturally, the same issues apply to tree-based products of all shapes, sizes and functions. For instance, the Environmental Investigation Agency reported in 2003 that many **pool cues** and **picture frames** sold in the US were made from "the timber of the ramin tree, a rare species listed under the Convention on International Trade in Endangered Species (CITES). The ramin that reaches us, it's been reported, has been felled and illegally exported from Indonesia's steadily shrinking tropical forests." Over a period of ten months from 2001 to 2002, about $11 million shipments of ramin entered the US from Singapore alone, 80% of which was shown to be illegal. US customs authorities at the Department of Agriculture, in fact, were making more seizures of illegal ramin shipments than any other product.

Of the 200 trees estimated to be used in **musical instruments**, meanwhile, more than 70 are included in the World Conservation Union 2000 Red List of globally threatened trees, according to Fauna & Flora International's SoundWood programme (www.soundwood.org). Some of these so-called tone woods are critically endangered, including species of ebony used in several string and wind instruments (but not any longer on pianos, Stevie Wonder songs notwithstanding).

Even as we leave the earth we may not be treading lightly upon its forests, since some **coffins** are veneered or made out of tropical hardwood such as mahogany. Also widely used are chipboard and plywood, both of which commonly contain illegally sourced wood.

It's currently difficult to imagine the FSC logo becoming a common sight in music shops, sports stores and funeral homes. But pressure from ethically minded consumers—even if it's only asking questions—will at least encourage importers and manufacturers to consider the issues.

As for eco-alternatives, you're unlikely to come across green cues or clarinets (though the respected Martin Guitar manufacturer is exploring the viability of using FSC certifiable wood sources, and, according to its website, "supports the introduction of FSC guitar models as soon as commercially feasible"). But with the first generation of eco-warriors getting on a bit, there have been a growing number of "alternative" coffins made from recycled cardboard, bamboo or wicker on the market in the UK, though they have yet to gain a foothold in the States. These not only avoid hardwood, but also MDF sides made with formaldehyde-containing glues, plastic handles and linings which give off pollution when cremated, and other such green anathemas. This will be taking things a bit too far in most people's eyes. But if you're really keen to ethically shop till you drop, so to speak, there is at least one company, **Belmont Caskets** (www.envirronmentalcaskets.com, 800-914-9145), offering a $3000 solid oak Eco Casket, a minimum of 70% of which comes from forests meeting the Forest Stewardship Council's standards.

Much less expensive, at a little over $400, are the "green eco-caskets" from **Kent Casket** (www.kentcasket.com, 888-534-7239), made from solid pine wood sourced from sustainable forests, and also certified by the FSC.

for it either: a recent European Commission statement reported that "In some forest-rich countries, the corruption fuelled by profits from illegal logging has grown to such an extent that it is undermining the rule of law, principles of democratic governance and respect for human rights."

The US is the world's biggest importer of wood products (nearly $25 billion in 2004), and when it comes to rainforest varieties such as mahogany and teak, a great deal of it has been illegally sourced—that is, cut down or exported in a way that breaks the laws of the country it came from. There are no definitive figures, but according to the Environmental Investigation Agency, $330 million of illegal timber was imported from Indonesia alone in 2000. The timber industry disputes such claims, yet cases keep popping up which suggest that even wood specialists with ethical policies and big budgets are failing to keep their noses clean—as the Royal Family found out in 2002 when the Queen's Gallery was refurbished with wood from endangered forests in Cameroon. In 2003, the President's Initiative Against Illegal Logging (PIAIL) was created to help developing countries combat illegall logging and sale of illegally harvested timber products, but in the view of some environmental organizations, this hasn't been effecitvely followed through, and certainly not come close to eliminating the flow of illegal wood into the country.

Illegally sourced wood from the **West** is much less common, though from the US to Scandinavia campaigners are still having to battle to save the tiny remaining areas of ancient forest. Such forests are under threat of being cleared not only for their hardwoods, but also so that their land can be used for fast-growing softwoods such as pine, from which most of our flatpack furniture and paper is made. Replacing old forests with pine forests is certainly better than slashing and burning for pastureland, but the process of uprooting the old trees gives off more CO_2, according to *The Ecologist*, than will be absorbed by the new trees in their first ten years. Furthermore, herbicides as unpleasant as napalm are often used to get the new trees to grow, and the biodiversity of the new forests is severely limited by the fact that they consist of only one or two types of tree. So "one tree planted for every one cut down" isn't necessarily as good as it sounds.

Good wood

Whether you're buying a salad bowl, a bed or a set of shelves, the only way to be sure that your wood has come from sustainably managed forests is to choose products bearing the logo of the **Forest Stewardship Council** (**FSC**). There are various sustainable wood labeling schemes out there. But many of them—such as the American Sustainable Forestry Initiative—are highly noncommittal efforts of the timber industry, and the FSC remains the only one to take seriously.

An international, independent, nonprofit-making organization, the FSC was founded in 1993 after extensive consultation between "timber users, traders and representatives of environmental and human-rights organizations." It only accredits wood when it can vouch for the entire supply chain—or "**chain of custody**"—from forest to sawmill to processor. The program isn't without its critics: in late 2002 the Rainforest Foundation (www.rainforestfoundation.org) released a report entitled *Trading in Credibility*, accusing the FSC of being "seriously flawed" and "knowingly misleading the public" in terms of the gap between its image and the reality of its operations. But even if these accusations are true—and they're not widely supported—it's still by far the best scheme currently around and the only one recognized by the major environmental groups.

FSC-approved wooden objects—ranging from beds and breadbins to firewood and floorboards—aren't too difficult to come by, though you'll often have to look for a label or ask/take the word of the retailer, as the organization doesn't maintain a list of accredited products. For a list of certified manufacturers and distributors, go to:

FSC US www.fscus.org ▷ 202-342-0413

Reclaimed wood

FSC-certified wood is a good choice, but most environmentalists agree that the ideal solution is to avoid new wood whenever possible and opt instead for **reclaimed (recycled) timber**. After all, for all its recyclable credentials, wood accounts for a significant proportion of our waste: more than 12 million tons in 2000, according to the Environmental Protection Agency. And yet reclaimed wood is usually much better quality, as it contains less water, making it less likely to warp as it dries, and was usually "harvested" before the advent of super-quick-growth forests, which are better at growing fast than delivering really fine woods.

BuildingGreen.com lists sources of reclaimed and salvaged wood throughout the country. Also check out the listings in the relevant page of the **Recycler's World** site.

BuildingGreen.com wwwbuildinggreen.com
Recycler's World www.recycle.net/wood/products

Or if buying new, uncertified wood ...

If buying FSC-certified or reclaimed wood isn't an option, at the very least avoid tropical hardwood such as **mahogany**, **teak**, **redwood**, **rosewood** and **ebony** wherever possible. Such products won't *necessarily* have been logged from virgin rainforests, but it's not unlikely. Also try to avoid suppliers that can't tell you about the origins of their woods.

For more information about the specific woods and the issues they raise, see the "Old Growth" section of the **Rainforest Action Network** website (www.ran.org/ran_campaigns/old_growth), which also lists endan-

Furniture shops & suppliers

The furniture market is increasingly dominated by **IKEA** (www.ikea.com). A true giant, the chain has almost 250 superstores in more than 30 countries, and its founder, Ingvar Kamprad, is one of the five richest people in the world. This, along with its global-domination-style expansion policies, has earned IKEA the usual criticism from anti-corporate groups but, for a business of its size, the company has also received quite a lot of praise. Friends of the Earth have lauded its phasing out of hazardous chemicals, and WWF its commitment to eco-friendly wood sourcing. On the latter issue, IKEA has a long-term plan to only sell wood from certified forests (FSC is currently the only certifier it recognizes). But for now, it only buys some FSC wood and, annoyingly, the label is not displayed on products, since the managers "want the IKEA brand itself to stand as a guarantee of genuine concern for the environment and social responsibility." Still, the company claims to ensure that even its non-FSC-approved woods don't come from intact natural forests, and its code of conduct also covers human and worker rights in supplier factories. Recent research by SOMO (www.somo.nl) suggests that, as usual, breaches to this code are not uncommon. But compared with other companies of its size, IKEA doesn't fare too badly.

The big home improvement centers such as **Home Depot** (www.homedepot.com), the largest US lumber retailer, and its biggest rival, **Lowe's** (www.lowes.com) also both sell FSC-certified products. Environmental organizations are in general agreement that Home Depot's done a lot to improve its policies in this regard, upping its number of FSC vendros from five to 40 between 1999 and 2002—though it took quite a bit of pressure from activist groups such as the Rainforest Action Network to provoke some action. Home Depot has also said it buys cedar from second-and-third-generation forests (as opposed to more at-risk older forests) and has cut its purchases of Indonesian **lauan wood** by 70 percent. The company's record isn't wholly uncontested: a joint report by the Environmental Investigation Agency and the Center for International Policy cited it (along with Ace Hardware, True Value, and K-Mart) for unknowingly stocking illegally imported wood from Honduras, though Home Depot disputed this finding. Lowe's began giving preference to FSC-certified products in its wood purchasing policies in 2000, as part of a five-point program that also promoted recycling and imposed an immediate ban on wood from the endangered Great Bear Rainforest in British Columbia.

gered tree species, the commitments various companies have made to the environment, and sources for "green" construction materials.

To read more about "chainsaw criminals" visit Forests Monitor, or, for the industry's perspective, see the site of the American Forest & Paper Association. Good rainforest primers and more links can be found at RainforestWeb.

Forests Monitor www.forestsmonitor.org
American Forest & Paper Association www.afandpa.org
RainforestWeb www.rainforestweb.org

At the other end of the scale, Rainforest Relief (www.rainforestrelief.org) is currently pressuring a number of retailers to stop selling furniture made from the tropical hardwood **nyatoh**, including Cost Plus, Pottery Barn, Restoration Hardware, Target, Vons (which is part of Safeway) and Linens-n-Things. If you want to extend the line to all retailers (not necessarily furniture/timber sellers) that use wood from endangered forests to build their actual stores, the same organization—which claims credit for convincing Barnes & Noble to cease using mahogany and rainforest wood for this purpose—cites Banana Republic, Tie Rack, Coach, Harvey's New York, The Museum Company and Strawberry Stores as current violators.

If you'd rather support a small, independent furniture company than risk your sanity and/or marriage in a Greenland-sized out-of-town warehouse, you could investigate some of the numerous "eco-furniture" specialists around. They generally produce very high quality, though not inexpensive, pieces. There are a growing number of online sites that offer such merchandise, and many (and likely most) of them will be willing to inform customers as to the details of their wood sourcing policies, whether they use FSC-certified materials or not. A few eco-furniture manufacturers and retailers who sell online are:

Berkeley Mills www.berkeleymills.com 877-426-4557
Cotswold Furniture Makers www.cotswoldfurniture.com ▷ 802-253-3710
Green Culture www.eco-furniture.com
Shopdog Woodworks www.shopdogwoodworks.com
Vivavi www.vivavi.com ▷ 866-848-2840
Gary Weeks & Co. www.garyweeks.com ▷ 888-334-0307
Woodshanti www.woodshanti.com ▷ 415-822-8100

And, though they're fewer and farther between, there are also some furniture makers who only work with **reclaimed wood**. Browse the lists under the "furniture" and "wood" categories at Ecomall (www.ecomall.com) or try:

Celtic Viking Furniture www.celticvikingfurniture.com ▷ 01386 840 438
Whit McLeod www.whitmcleod.com ▷ 707-822-7307
The Wooden Duck www.thewoodenduck.com ▷ 866-848-3575

Bamboo

Bamboo is something of a wonder crop. The central building material of East Asia since time immemorial, it has also served as everything from a foodstuff to jewelry. And today it is hailed by some as the future green alternative to hardwood. It's very strong, and yet doesn't contract as much as wood, and with modern processing it can even be used for "wooden" flooring. It grows incredibly fast—some species can manage two feet in their first day—making it completely sustainable to grow in large quantities, unlike many hardwoods.

Significantly, the way that bamboo grows means that when the plant is harvested it isn't killed: it simply grows back up from where you cut it, so the roots remain in place and the soil isn't damaged or washed away. Furthermore, bamboo doesn't require lots of pesticides, can grow nearly anywhere and is even thought to be capable of sucking pollutants *out* of the water cycle. So, while there's no reason to believe that bamboo furniture and other products have been ethically sourced or made in decent working conditions, the material itself would clearly be a contender for the world's most sustainable hardwood. Were it not for the fact, of course, that it's actually a type of grass.

A small but quickly expanding number of eco-companies are offering bamboo furniture, floors, clothes and other products as all or part of their stock and catalogs. As of yet, however, such items are not FSC-certified, as the organization classifies them under "non-timber forest products." Among the more prominent outfits are:

Eco Designz www.ecodesignz.com ▷ 310-538-3051
Smith & Fong Co. www.plyboo.com ▷ 866-835-9859
Teragren www.teragren.com ▷ 800-929-6333

Paints & other DIY products

Many people dutifully buy their eco-dishwashing liquid, but don't consider environmental issues when shopping for DIY products such as **paint** and **paint stripper, brush cleaner, wood stains** and **preservatives, glues** and **varnishes.** This is a touch ironic, since many of these products, which are mostly derived from nondegradable petrochemicals, are on a different level of eco-unfriendliness from dishwashing liquids and laundry detergents.

One issue is that many paints, varnishes and solvents—both in their manufacture and application—release **volatile organic compounds** (VOCs) into the air, leading to the creation of polluting ground-level ozone, among other things. The EPA has tightened regulations on VOCs in recent years, and paint manufacturers now specify the VOC level on their cans. This development has been widely welcomed, but it doesn't deal with the heavy metals, solvents and other controversial chemicals used in many paints and their DIY products. From dyes to plasticizers, many of these ingredients are fat-soluble, and therefore prone to accumulating in our bodies (and those of animals, being passed up the food chain from low-level aquatic life to fish, birds and mammals). Not all of these are known to be harmful, but some are toxic or carcinogenic.

As with all household chemicals, the direct **health risks** to humans of occasional exposure to DIY products are mostly unproven—and likely to be extremely small. But longer-term use does seem to be harmful. In 1989, for example, the International Agency for Research on Cancer concluded that "occupational exposure as a painter is carcinogenic." Furthermore, paints and varnishes can continue to emit fumes once they're on the door frame or table, and this is thought to be a contributor to sick building syndrome (SBS)—headaches and other health effects which seem to be brought on by a specific building. Though this all sounds a bit New Agey, SBS is an all too real malaise, and has been formally recognized by the World Health Organization since 1982.

As for the effect on the **wider environment,** the amount of VOCs, bio-accumulative toxins and otherwise problematic chemicals released into the atmosphere at the time of application is relatively small with most DIY products. That is, as long as you don't pour any down the sink (instead, give any unwanted half-full paint cans to charities or community organizations; go to www.earth911.org to get a list of some near your area). But the manufacture of a gallon of paint can create ten or more gallons of toxic waste—which, considering that the US goes through more than a billion and a half gallons of paint each year, adds up to pretty staggering total. And paint factories emit a whole range of noxious fumes into the air.

Still, as ever, it's worth keeping this in perspective: most of us account for the release of far greater quantities of problematic chemicals through our cars than we do through our DIY.

Greener DIY products

Due to a gradually increasing awareness of all these issues, an ever-growing range of greener DIY products is available, including a wide selection of paints as well as some varnishes, strippers, waxes, stains and other related products. Co-op America's *Real Money* magazine identified these as the best brands:

AGLAIA (through Environmental Building Supplies) www.ecohaus.com ▷ 800-322-6843
American Formulating and Manufacturing (AFM)/Safecoat
www.afmsafecoat.com ▷ 619-239-0321
Auro USA www.aurousa.com ▷ 888-302-0352
The Old-Fashioned Milk Paint Company www.milkpaint.com ▷ 978-448-6336
Terramed (through Med Imports) www.medimports.net ▷ 866-363-6334
Timber Pro UV wwwtimberprocoatings.com ▷ 888-888-6095
Weather-Bos Stains & Finishes www.weatherbos.com ▷ 800-664-3978

Alternative paints tend to impose a slightly smaller ecological burden on the world. They also give you a chance to avoid the major paint firms, whose parent companies include such controversial companies such as **ICI** (which owns **Dulux**). However, "eco" paints themselves vary widely, from those which include synthetic chemicals but no solvents to more comprehensively "natural" products such as **Auro USA**. In general, the greener the product, the more expensive it is and the smaller the color choice (especially for bright colors).

You can get prices, order color charts and buy online from most of the above suppliers, but for advice you might be better off contacting a store in your area that carries eco-paints, or one of the increasingly sprouting "green" sites that sell paint and other household goods online, such as:

The Environmental Home Center www.environmentalhomecenter.com ▷ 800-281-9785
Green Culture www.greenculture.com ▷ 877-20-GREEN
Green Home www.greenhome.com ▷ 877-282-6400
HealthyHome www.healthyhome.com ▷ 800-583-9523

Green construction

Plenty of design and architectural firms are now billing themselves as "green" builders, as either part of their overall practice or a specialization. How do you know, however, exactly how "green" a structure is, especially if you're contemplating buying a newly built home?

In the near future, you could use the so-called LEED (Leadership in Energy and Environmental Design) rating system, created by the US Green Building Council as a voluntary standard for developing sustainable buildings. For homes, the system measures efficiency in use of water, energy, land and building construction, as well as environmental indoor quality. The buildings are rated on a scale of 0 to (quite oddly, it must be said) 108, with those scoring 30 or better qualifying for certification. Some are in turn marked as "Silver," "Gold," and "Platinum" (the highest rating), depending upon how high they score. As of this writing, though, the Council was just getting pilot testing together, with a rollout of a fully chartered program not expected until early 2007. LEED standards are also in use—or in development—for several types non-residential buildings. For more information (including a large downloadable description of the pilot program for rating homes), go to www.usgbc.org.

For more info, as well as inspiration, tips, links and books, visit the sites below. If you're looking for designers, architects or someone to work on your home, the Sustainable Building Sources site has a large directory of green building professionals. Natural Building Resources gives basic lowdowns, and links to further resources, on constructing with a host of eco-friendly substances, including straw bale, cob, bamboo, hemp and recycled building materials:

Environmental Building News
www.buildinggreen.com
Green Building Supply www.greenbuildingsupply.com
Greener Buildings www.greenerbuildings.com
Natural Building Resources www.strawbalecentral.com
Sustainable Building Sources www.greenbuilder.com

For some products, though, the equivalent might not be quite as green. For example, Timber Pro UV's wood finishes, although they contain no flammable solvents, are actually comprised of 9% hazardous materials— still the lowest, according to the company, in an industry where 50–80% is the average.

Soft furnishings & homeware
Ethical decor

Rugs & carpets

Most of the rugs and carpets we buy are machine-made in the West. About the only ethical problem that anyone has with these is that some of them contain benzene-based flame retardants and other "chemicals of high concern," despite the fact that less potentially harmful alternatives are available. More contentious are the high-quality "exotic" rugs that we traditionally associate with the Middle East, but which are just as commonly made in the Indian Subcontinent. These are usually **hand-knotted** and, with as many as 250,000 knots per square meter, each rug is the result of months of painstaking work.

Carpet making is a venerable tradition that employs millions of poor workers from South Asia to North Africa. However, the sector has become increasingly tarnished by allegations of widespread child labor—including "forced" or "bonded" child labor, with kids being used to pay off debts in conditions roughly equivalent to imprisonment or slavery.

Child workers (sometimes said to be favored for their small fingers) are found throughout much of the rug-producing world, but there are no accurate figures of exactly how many they are in each country, and how many of them are in forced-labor positions (as opposed to supporting their families, perhaps even in between schooling hours). It seems, though, that the problem is particularly acute in **South Asia**, which saw a boom in carpet production from the 1970s, after a crackdown on child labor in Iran. Figures vary widely but it is thought that as many as one million children may be working in the carpet industry in India, Pakistan and Nepal alone.

RUGMARK & fair-trade carpets

As is always the case with child labor, the question of how to solve the problems of the South Asian carpet industry is a thorny one. It goes without saying that a complete solution is going to require the political will of the governments in each country. But what can consumers do?

One option is to buy only rugs bearing the **RUGMARK** label, which identifies carpets made without the use of child labor. Set up in 1994 by a collection of human rights organizations, exporting companies, UNICEF and other bodies, the program also guarantees that a proportion of the price for a rug goes toward providing an education for former child weavers that its inspectors have discovered. RUGMARK currently only covers India, Pakistan and Nepal, but there are plans to extend it to other countries, such as Afghanistan, Turkey and Morocco, if and when funding permits it.

To put the label on their carpets a company has to agree to anti-child-labor policies and allow random inspection of their premises, both by RUGMARK inspectors and other nonprofit child-welfare organizations. And to protect against counterfeit, each carpet is individually numbered, allowing it to be traced back to the specific loom on which it was made. RUGMARK accredits around fifteen percent of registered Indian looms and its inspectors have "rescued" more than 2500 children, nearly all of whom have received education at RUGMARK schools.

RUGMARK lines can be found in more than the 300 stores and showrooms in the US—an important dent in that market, which is the world's largest market for hand-knotted carpets, to the tune of almost half a billion dollars of sales a year. For a list of retailers and more information about the program, see:

RUGMARK www.rugmark.org

Like all such schemes, Rugmark isn't without critics. As evidenced by Mark Tully's recent book, *India in Slow Motion*, some in the carpet industry claim that the labelling organization has exaggerated the extent of bonded child labor and, by publicizing the issue, has reduced the demand for all South Asian rugs, including the majority that are made by adults living in extreme poverty. Such critics also point out that no labelling system can genuinely ensure a carpet is "child-labor free."

On the other hand, RUGMARK has also been criticized for not going far enough—or at least getting its priorities mixed up—since it focuses on illegal child labor rather than the wider social issues that create it. To be fair, RUGMARK does work alongside ethical trade organizations and their inspectors try to keep an eye on wages and health and safety. But it's true that it doesn't claim to be labeling "fair-trade" rugs, as such.

Unfortunately, if you do want fair trade rugs, as with most commodities, TransFair USA does not yet certify any rugs (or any textiles) as Fair Trade goods. The Fair Trade Federation does list a few retail rug and carpet sellers on its online site, but these companies participate in the program as just one part of a handicrafts operation. And Garuda Woven Art (www.garudawovenart.com), which carries naturally dyed Tibetan carpets woven in Nepal, isn't listed by the Fair Trade Federation, but does say on its site that it's committed to providing decent living and working conditions for its employees, and doesn't use child labor.

Other homeware—from bedding to bowls

We increasingly buy our homeware, such as linens, cushions, kitchenware and ornaments, from a few giant companies such as IKEA and Bed Bath & Beyond. But there are now quite a few "ethical specialists" in this field. As with clothes, these companies fall into two overlapping categories: the **fairtraders**, who buy direct from marginalized small-scale producer groups in the developing world; and the **greens**, who attempt to be "non-exploitative" but focus primarily on organic fabrics and other eco-friendly materials. But again, relatively few of the greens subscribe to overt Fair Trade guidelines, and though a few of the companies belong to the Fair Trade Federation, these usually offer fairly small selections of eco-homeware as part of a versatile line of products, rather than specializing in the field.

The following all sell online and/or mail order, but you could also check out your nearest Fair Trade shop—see the list starting on p.315.

A Happy Planet www.ahappyplanet.com ▷ 888-424-2779

Organic pillows, sheets, duvet covers, comforters, blankets and mattresses.

EcoChoices www.ecochoices.com ▷ 415-453-7915

Internet store stocking eco-products for the bedroom, bathroom, pets and more. They aim to advertise the lowest discount prices possible, without lowering the quality of the goods.

Gaiam www.gaiam.com
▷ 877-989-6321

Gaiam is one of the biggest and (relatively speaking) mainstream eco-lifestyle companies, and its large catalog has a healthy selection of organic/ natural home textiles, furniture, linens and apparel. If you're looking for something more offbeat, they have some of that too—ornaments handblown by Guatemalan artisans from 100% recycled glass, and a "sustainably harvested bamboo clock."

GreenSage www.greensage.com ▷ 415-453-7915

Specializing in "sustainable building and furnishing" for the home, with a pretty wide line of towels, bedding, rugs and the like made from organic/natural/recycled-material. They also sell some more unusual items, like soy wax votive candles and glassware made from recycled bottles.

Janice's www.janices.com ▷ 800-526-4237

Organic/natural bedroom, bedding, apparel and household products.

Kwytza Kraft www.kwytzakraft.com ▷ 916-760-4188

As John Cleese used to say in *Monty Python*, "and now for something completely different"—lamps, wastebaskets, magazine racks, CD holders, wine racks, floor mats and even tables made from post-use, single-use, clean-and-sanitized chopsticks, recycled from restaurants in China. If that sounds like making a mountain out of a molehill, the exact reverse could be argued: the company website notes that several billion single-use chopsticks are consumed annually, supported by, according to some estimates, 25 million trees and bamboo plants.

Organic Cotton Alternatives www.organiccottonalts.com
▷ 888-645-4452

Futons, beds, pillows, linens and furniture, all made from 100% certified raw organic materials. They also have organic pet beds for dogs and cats in both rectangular and round shapes.

PurrfectPlay.com www.purrfectplay.com ▷ 219-926-7604

Toys, bedding, collars and more for pet cats and dogs, striving to use "only organic, chemical free, fair-trade materials." The catalog is small but imaginative, with the likes of hemp rope dog toys and cat collars with fairly traded Thai silver bells.

Real Goods www.realgoods.com a 800-919-2400

One of the biggest and oldest names in the home eco-products business, Real Goods has a nice selection of organic bedding, as well as some rather more off-the-beaten-track offerings, like natural fiber shower curtains, an eco-beanbag filled with 100% recycled foam, a storage bench of 100% FSC-certified eucalyptus and recycled scrub sponges. Like several of the more established companies listed in this chapter, Real Goods could be listed in a number of sections, as it also carries nontoxic cleaners and energy-efficient/solar lighting equipment and appliances.

Tomorrow's World www.tomorrowsworld.com ▷ 800-229-7571

Organic towels, sheets, blankets, pillows and mattresses, by a company that also buys handcrafted work from Fair Trade Cooperatives and looks "for businesses and products that encourage equal opportunities and flexibility for women." Also sells nontoxic cleaning products, sustainably harvested/recycled furniture and natural body care items.

Toys
Avoiding PVC playthings

Toys aren't the first things that come to mind when you think of household toxins, but many are made of PVC-laden plastic. This is worrisome not just because PVC contains a "chemical of high concern," **phthalates**, that kids might be inadvertently exposed to if they chew or suck such toys. PVC also releases lead, cadmium and other toxic elements into the environment during its manufacture and disposal. PVC teething toys have been banned since 1999 in the EU, but they remain on the market in the US.

Action figures, teething rings, rubber animals and molding clay are among the products most likely to contain some PVC; look for the word PVC or vinyl in the content listings, or the recycling symbol with the number 3 (which signifies PVC). In addition, Greenpeace USA has a "Toy Report Card" grading major manufacturers on their PVC policies (see box opposite), and ToySafety.net (www.toysafety.net), a project of the National Association of Public Interest Groups, has list of consumer tips and potentially hazardous toys on its website, as well as an annually updated, downloadable toy safety report.

At the other end of the ethical scale is a ballooning market for eco-toys, such as unfinished solid toys made from sustainably harvested wood. Such products are often sold as part of a much wider line of products by environmentally responsible companies, but there are also a few specialists, including:

North Star Elves www.northstartoys.com ▷ 800-737-0112

Nontoxic wooden animals, vehicles, magic wands and puzzles; "recycled materials are used whenever possible," according to its website.

Safe Sand Company www.safesand.com ▷ 415-971-1776

Non-hazardous playsand, without the free crystalline salica (a known carcinogenic) often found in the store-sold variety.

Tree Blocks www.treeblocks.com ▷ 800-873-4960

Wooden blocks, miniature tree houses and furniture, dollhouses, music wands and more from an acclaimed company that uses the discards of managed paper forests.

Worldwide Child www.worldwidechild.com ▷ 800-995-0154

A wide variety of natural toys from producers using nontoxic, sustainable materials, with suppliers chosen based on Fair Trade Federation criteria.

Toy report card

Greenpeace USA issued its first Toy Manufacturers' Report Card at the International Toy Fair in New York, updating it in 2003 to survey company progress. We've reproduced the findings below. For more information, visit www.greenpeace.org/usa/news/2003-toy-report-card.

Grades

A Excellent, will phase out all PVC products, or products contain no PVC
B Above average, will phase out some PVC products
C Average, will eliminate phthalates in toys for children under 3
D Below average, will eliminate phthalates only in toys intended for the mouth
F Fail, no policy change

Manufacturer	2000 Grade	2003 Grade	Comments
Brio	A	A	Keep up the great work!
Chicco	B	A	Good effort.
Discovery Toys	C	B	Could do better.
Disney	D	Inc	No reply after repeated inquiries.
Evenflo	D	A	What an improvement—bravo!
First Years	D	C+	Not living up to potential, but keep trying.
Gerber	A	A	One of the stars!
Hasbro/Galoob/Playschool	D	Inc	No reply after repeated inquiries.
International Playthings (Primetime & Early Start)	A	A	One of the stars!
Kids II	D	Inc	No reply after repeated inquiries.
Lamaze Infant Development	B	A	Hope you can eliminate PVC in those last three products quickly.
Lego Systems	A	A	Still waiting for the elimination of PVC in train wiring.
Little Tykes	A	C	May have been misgraded in 2000, what a disappointment.
Manhattan Baby	F	B	Incredible improvement—keep it up!
Mattel/Tyco/ Fisher Price	C	C	Could do a lot better—keep working at it.
Munchkin Inc.	F	D	Barely improved—need to work much harder.
Safety First	D	Inc	No reply after repeated inquiries.
Sassy	A	A	Please get rid of that one PVC product—the baby photo book.
Shelcore	C	D	Very disappointing.
Tiny Love	A	A	Great work!
Warner Bros.	F	Inc	No reply after repeated inquiries.

Cut flowers

The overwhelming majority—about 70%, according to the US Department of Agriculture—of our cut flowers are imported. The US represents about one-fifth of the global market for buying imported flowers, importing massive quantities from South America in particular, with about 60% of the foreign-grown cut flowers sold in this country coming from Colombia alone (and 15% from Ecuador). (It is no accident that the young Colombian heroine in the recent movie *Maria Full of Grace* works on a flower plantation.) This raises a whole mix of environmental and social concerns. On the environmental side, there's the fact that flowers (due to their short shelf life) are usually **flown** into the US, with the global-warming impact that implies. Furthermore, the demand for cosmetic perfection of the blooms means that huge quantities of **pesticides** are used in their production. This is not only an environmental issue but also a labor one, since these chemicals can be dangerous to workers when not carefully regulated. According to the US-based International Labor Rights Fund (www.laborrights.org), flower workers in Colombia and Ecuador are exposed to up to some hundred different agrochemicals (some of them extremely toxic, and banned elsewhere in the world), and one in five suffers from work-related health problems—from nausea to congenital malformations in their offspring. There are also concerns about worker rights in the industry; less than five percent of Colombian flower workers belong to unions, and *The Ecologist* reported in 2003 that there were only three unionized flower companies (out of hundreds) in Ecuador. In the same country, according to the UN's International Labor Organization, there were nearly 50,000 children working on flower farms in two Ecuadorian provinces alone.

A few companies and specialist food stores now offer **organic flowers**, though it's a tiny part of the overall floral market, with annual sales of about $10 million in a trade that moves $20 billion of flowers a year in the US. There are also some online organic flower sites, the best-known of which are Organic Banquet (www.organicbanquet.com, 877-899-2468), which uses both domestic farmers and foreign growers who stick to certified organic standards, and Diamond Organics (www.diamondorganics.com, 888-674-2642), who buy only from US "family farms." These have environmental advantages, but, as ever, boycotting flowers from the poor world is likely to cause more harm than good for those people who rely on the sector for work.

However, there are a number of plans afoot, or already in practice, to ensure some sort of environmental and/or labor standards. The Green Label, used to certify growers in Europe, South America and Africa—Organic Banquet buys from Green Label-approved South American growers, for instance—is meant as an assurance of good social and environmental practices, though it's not quite as stringent as organic guidelines, as it allows some use of low-impact chemicals. The Veriflora program, which issues a label certifying sustainable agricultural practices and fair labor conditions, is in use by a small group of producers and handlers (listed at www.scscertified.com/csrpurchasing/veriflora). Although it's hardly widespread, it's not wholly unlikely you'll see flowers with the Veriflora label, as they started to appear in some Whole Foods supermarkets as early as 2005. And while flowers are not on the list of Transfair USA's certified products, we may start to see some in the future, as the UK's Fairtrade Foundation now certifies roses. Even that program, however, is in its relative infancy; as of this writing, it was only certifying roses from two Kenyan farms.

Gardening products
Even greener fingers

With so much agricultural land being given over to mono-crop industrial farming, some commentators hope that gardeners could be the saviors of American **biodiversity**. But certain garden products can have the opposite effect, causing harm to the environment either through their toxic contents or their extraction from the earth. Following is a quick look at the most pressing issues.

Pests & weeds

As the abundant health warnings on the packets attest, many garden **insecticides** and **herbicides** contain some seriously nasty substances. Many of these hit not only the target species, but also poison birds and other wildlife, and pollute local water systems. As with many household chemicals, they're also likely to be the result of polluting manufacturing.

Just as with farming, however, pest and weed killers can easily be avoided with a bit of effort. For weeds, this generally means getting down and dirty and pulling them out by hand. But with pests, there are all sorts of techniques, from encouraging **predators** such as birds and ladybirds to **companion planting** (strategically using one plant to attract—or repel— the pests of another). For more information on chemical-free gardening, see the websites of the rather commercially presented Organic Gardening (www.organicgardening.com), which nonetheless has some useful basic starter features, and the funkier, wonderfully named Avant-Gardening (www.avant-gardening.com), which goes into more depth with subtleties like composting for sustainable organic gardening. For organic gardening supplies, go to Extremely Green, which has an almost dauntingly large online catalog, and Seeds of Change, which in addition to selling organically grown seeds has quite a few articles on general organic gardening on its site:

Extremely Green www.extremelygreen.com ▷ 781-878-5397
Seeds of Change www.seedsofchange.com ▷ 888-762-7333

More garden tips

▶ Favor garden centers which either cultivate their own plants and flowers or are sure where their stocks came from.

▶ Look out for the Forest Stewardship Council logo (see p.265) when buying **wooden garden furniture**. This is important, as outdoor furniture is often made from tropical hardwoods.

▶ For low-carbon outdoor lighting, check out the sun-powered options, such as the **Coach-Style Yard Light**, available for $49 from Real Goods (www.realgoods.com, 800-919-2400).

▶ For lounging around in your eco-friendly garden, bag yourself a **fair-trade hammock**. Finding one online in the US takes some digging, and none of the following three sites are Fair Trade Federation members, but all vouch for the fairly traded nature of their hammocks in some fashion. Hammock Jungle (www.hammockjungle.com, 888-529-3497) carries Mayan models from single to super-king size, while Magic Cabin (www.magiccabin.com, 888-623-3655) has a hand-woven one from Colombia "roomy enough for several kids or adults up to 260 pounds." The webstore of the Rainforest Site (part of the "Hunger Site" family of pages, where a click a day benefits various worthy causes) has a $25 "Amazonian Rope Hammock … fair trade imported from Peru."

Transport & travel

Both at home and abroad, we travel farther today than ever before. The average American travels 17,000 miles per year, most of them by car. And, as the price of air travel drops, we also leave the country with growing frequency: about 15% of the miles we travel on long-distance journeys are to international destinations, and overseas trips increased 70% between 1990 and 2000 alone. The main ethical issues surrounding all this extra movement are the environmental impacts—global warming, most pressingly—and the effects of our tourism on the countries we visit. This chapter takes a brief looks at these and other topics that relate to our cars, fuels, air travel and vacations, examining the ethical options in each case.

Cars & fuel
What are you driving?

You might wonder why cars and their fuel are even in this book, assuming them to be a lost cause. After all, our automobiles account for around a fifth of the US's greenhouse gases, contributing to the **climate change** which is already causing massive environmental and human problems (p.14). On average, according to the Environmental Media Association, each car produces its own weight in CO_2 for every 10,000 miles driven. And their emissions also include a cocktail of carcinogens and otherwise **noxious fumes** which are major contributors to the air pollution that causes around 70,000 premature deaths each year in the US alone—as much as the lives claimed by breast cancer and prostate cancer combined.

And there are many more non-lethal hospitalizations tied to air pollution—according to the American Public Transportation Association, high smog levels cause 159,000 emergency room trips and six million asthma attacks each summer.

Road accidents, of course, are responsible for almost as many premature deaths (about 40,000) and hundreds of thousands of injuries annually, as well as costing the economy tens of billions of dollars. Worldwide, according to the World Health Organization, four times as many people died in road traffic mishaps in 2000 than in war and conflict—and many of the victims have been children, pedestrians, cyclists and other nondrivers. You can, alarmingly, watch the global human and financial costs increasing in real time at:

Accident Count www.uk-roadsafety.co.uk/Rs_Documents/accident_count.htm

And that's not all. New roads eat ever further into the countryside and consume huge amounts of resources; buying gas supports the famously ruthless activities of oil companies and countless oppressive governments; and many of the big car manufacturers have highly questionable records on everything from political donations to workers' rights.

But despite all this, for as long as we continue to use cars, writing them off entirely as an ethical no-go zone is counterproductive. All cars consume energy, but some are far more efficient than others. All gas exhaust will cause climate change, but a more ethical oil industry could have an enormous impact on the human rights of millions of people. This section takes a quick look at moral and not-so-moral choices you may come across when shopping for cars, fuel and road assistance organizations.

Gas & diesel

Oil is responsible for much of the West's present-day wealth, powering not only our transport system but also the machines behind modern agriculture and countless other production processes. But its benefits have not come cheaply. Black gold, as it's known, has been responsible for the suffering of millions who have been evicted from their land to make way for drilling, or forced to live under murderous oil-funded regimes. As Christian Aid has observed, oil-dependent poor countries have an unusually high incidence of poverty, corruption, war and unrepresentative government.

Oil has also hit the environment hard, not just in terms of climate change (to which it is the single most important contributor) but also via spills, deforestation for drilling and other types of destruction. And, of course, oil continues to be the driving force behind **international conflict**, both figuratively and literally (at the height of the 2003 Iraq war, Western troops were estimated to be using more oil each day than the entire Indian population of more than one billion).

While it would be absurd to suggest that the giant petroleum firms are solely responsible for these problems—corrupt governments and unconcerned Western consumers deserve large slices of the blame—the big firms do have a pretty shocking history of ignoring human rights, supporting oppressive regimes, damaging the environment, denying climate change and funding pro-oil politicians. For a worrying insight into the politics of the present-day oil industry, see:

Center for Public Integrity www.public-i.org/oil

Recently, however, some of the major oil firms have tried to clean up their image, and while their ethical claims should not be taken at face value, there is a strong case for shopping selectively.

The Exxon boycott

At the time of writing, the Texan-based energy giant **ExxonMobil** (and, overseas, its subsidiary company **Esso**) is the subject of a major consumer boycott, supported by mainstream groups such as Greenpeace, Friends of the Earth, the Sierra Club, MoveOn.org and TrueMajority. The company's record on human rights and oil spills is poor enough, but the impetus behind the boycott is global warming.

Exxon's detractors claim that while most of its competitors have made at least some efforts to address the issue, the world's biggest oil company has done everything possible to persuade people in power that human-induced climate change isn't worth worrying about. This has involved, according to the UK-based StopEsso campaign, a "multimillion-dollar, ten-year campaign of dirty tricks" that has had a real influence on US, and even Russian, global-warming policy. These "tricks" have included massive political donations—Exxon employees donated more than $1 million to Bush's Republicans for the 2000 election campaign, according to their own figures—and the funding of various ultra-conservative climate-change-skeptic **think tanks** and **lobby groups**. A chart in a 2005 *Mother Jones* article traced $8 million worth of donations to more than 40 such organi-

Body artist Rick Mills (right) taking a stand against "E$$o" in May 2002.

zations, and, according to ExposeExxon, the company has spent almost $37 million on lobbying Capitol Hill since 2000.

It would be an exaggeration to say that Exxon was responsible for the US abandoning the Kyoto treaty—which at the time faced widespread cross-party opposition among American politicians. But it seems undeniable that the company has aided the Republican government in its playing down of global warming. For instance, in the autumn of 2003 (within days of World Health Organization scientists suggesting that 160,000 people already die each year from climate change), leaked emails and documents showed that the Bush administration had sought the help of an Exxon-funded think tank—the **Competitive Enterprise Institute**—to try and undermine and dilute the predictions of its own government scientists.

While it is still openly anti-Kyoto, Exxon now officially recognizes the climate-change issue and has made some investment in alternative energy. But critics claim that it continues to spend millions on lobbying via a whole range of groups to ensure that no restrictions are placed on the market for fossil fuels, whatever the human and environmental costs. They've also attacked the company for its support of oil and gas exploration in the Arctic National Wildlife Refuge, Exxon being the only oil giant remaining in the Arctic Power, a group lobbying for drilling rights in the

they are not always put into practice, at the very least makes them much easier targets when they misbehave. BP has also pledged to end donations to any "political activity or party" (it previously gave millions to US presidential candidates), reduce its operational greenhouse-gas emissions to pre-1990 levels (something which many thought would be impossible), and expand its solar power business (still a tiny part of the company, but a big boost to solar power's credibility nonetheless). For its part, Shell has spent about $1.5 billion on solar and wind power research since 1999. As small as these investments might be relative to these corporations' total assets, they stand in stark contrast to their competitors ChevronTexaco (recently added to the Burma Campaign's "Dirty List" for doing business in Burma), ConocoPhillips and ExxonMobil, who have spent little on renewable energy. ExxonMobil, the worst offender, went as far as to term it an "uneconomic niche" when explaining its 2005 decision not to invest in solar or wind energy.

Odd man out **Citgo** got some good press toward the end of 2005 when [it] sold heating oil at discounted rates to poor families in Massachusetts [an]d New York. Primarily for that reason, it was cited as worthy of patron-[ag]e by the progressive group TrueMajority, who also pointed out that [mo]ney spent on Citgo fuel would mostly go to Venezuela, and not Middle [Eas]tern countries without democratically elected governments. Some [crit]ics felt that Citgo's gesture was at least partly motivated by ambitions [to e]mbarrass George W. Bush; Venezuelan president Hugo Chavez, a [criti]c of Bush's administration, went as far as taking out ads in US news-[pape]rs boasting "How Venezuela is keeping the home fires burning in [Mass]achusetts."

[Sho]pping for cars

[Buying] a credible car is a complex business. For one thing, you have [to bala]nce the environmental performance of the specific model with [the soci]al and environmental record of the company you're support-[ing. The]n there's the fact that many smaller car firms are completely or [partly ow]ned by bigger corporations such as **Ford** (Aston Martin, Jaguar, [Land Rov]er, Mazda and Volvo), **General Motors** (Saab and Saturn) and [Daimler-C]hrysler (Jeep, Mercedes and Dodge). Added to this is the fact [that a si]ngle car is likely to be the result of many different factories in as [many diffe]rent countries—seat covers from Indonesia, body panels from [China, w]heel nuts from Mexico.

region. The other three corporations involved (Chevron/Texaco, Conoco/Phillips, and BP) all dropped out in the last few years. On top of all this, Exxon is still appealing a 1994 court ruling ordering it to pay roughly $5 billion for injuries caused by the 1989 ExxonValdez oil spill disaster—a substantial amount, assuredly, but from a company which posted profits amounting to $10 billion in the third quarter of 2005 alone. For both sides of the debate, see:

Exxon www.exxon.com
ExposeExxon www.exposeexxon.com

BP & Shell—greener or greenwashed?

Unlike Exxon, who has until recently seemed relatively unconcerned about being seen as a global villain, other Big Oil companies have spent millions trying to redefine themselves as trailblazers of corporate social responsibility. **BP** (part of BP Amoco) has very much led this trend—swapping its shield logo for a green and yellow flower/sun and deciding that its initials now stand for "Beyond Petroleum." **Shell** (of Royal Dutch/Shell) has followed close behind with numerous CSR initiatives, keen to bury associations with Ken Saro-Wiwa and other anti-Shell campaigners who were executed in Nigeria in the mid-1990s.

Both companies still spend much of their time involved in highly controversial projects. Since "going green," for example, BP has been condemned by leading groups such as Amnesty International for trying to create a "human-rights-free corridor" as part of its **Baku–Tbilisi–Ceyhan** pipeline. It's also been slammed by the World Wildlife Fund in relation to drilling in **Alaska**, and even named as an offender in the UK in the government's *Spotlight on Business and Environment Performance 2002*. Shell, meanwhile, has been widely accused of failing to deal with problems faced by local people near its facilities worldwide (for example, in Friends of the Earth's *Other Shell Report 2002*). While Shell and BP have been better than Exxon in admitting the role that oil plays in climate change, there is still an enormous gap between the rhetoric and reality of these companies.

But despite the high-budget greenwashing, there are signs of some improvement. Both companies have started to be more transparent in their payments to third world governments (though BP is accused of secrecy in its Baku project). Alongside all the criticism, both have gained occasional and previously unimaginable praise from groups ranging from Human Rights Watch to Greenpeace. They have drawn up codes of conduct relating to human rights and the environment, which, even if

Biofuels: a serious alternative?

Biofuels are fuels made from plants—anything from corn to sunflowers. Their primary attraction is simple: the carbon they release when burned is no more than the carbon they soaked up from the atmosphere when growing. This neat cycle isn't entirely "climate neutral," since fossil-fuel energy goes into fertilizing, harvesting, processing and distributing the crops. But the overall carbon footprint of a biofuel is typically substantially smaller than the petroleum equivalent.

The biggest environmental problem for biofuels is demand for land. It would take huge areas of cropland to turn biofuels into a major part of the global energy picture. This could squeeze food production—hence raising the price of the basic crops on which many people survive—or require the conversion of virgin land into farms, something which has implications not just for wildlife habitat but for the greenhouse effect itself—especially if it involves deforestation. All told, the benefits of biofuels depend entirely on how and where the crops they're made from are grown.

There are currently two main categories of biofuel. The first, ethanol (ethyl alcohol) is a substitute for gasoline. It's usually sold in a mixture of 10% ethanol and 90% gasoline (E10). Higher-proportion blends are also available (such as E85, with 85% ethanol), but these can only be used in a flexible fuel vehicle (see p.296). As of 2005, ethanol production in the US was about four billion gallons: about 3% of the fuel swallowed each year by America's cars and trucks. New tax breaks and incentives could nearly double that percentage by 2012. One challenge will be getting oil and gas companies to allow higher proportions of ethanol to be sold at US pumps. Right now many oil companies prohibit it, claiming a lack of quality control.

Most of America's ethanol to date has been derived from corn, which is grown through the sort of farming that makes fairly extensive use of petrochemicals. All in all, corn-based ethanol seems to provide some environmental benefit, but not much. The University of California at Berkeley estimates that corn-based ethanol uses about 74 units of fossil-fuel energy to produce 100 units of ethanol energy. As for emissions, when you factor out the CO_2 absorbed by the corn, a vehicle running on ethanol produces around 30% less carbon than one running on standard gasoline.

A more promising alternative is **cellulosic ethanol**, made from cellulose, which is found in corn husks and various other plants, such as fast-growing grasses. Since many plants high in cellulose can thrive on land that's marginal for regular farming, they're less likely to displace food crops, and the yield per acre can be twice or more than that of corn. Deep-rooted perennials like switchgrass also help stabilize soil and need little if any help from petroleum-based farming techniques. As a result, 100 units of cellulosic ethanol require only about 20 units of fossil energy to produce, according to the Department of Energy. In time, cellulosic ethanol could end up being carbon-neutral or even a net remover of carbon from the atmosphere, according to the Rocky Mountain Institute. The problem is that it costs more to produce than corn-based ethanol. Chemists are working on methods to bioengineer enzymes that lower the processing costs and the playing field with corn ethanol over the next decade.

The other major biofuel is a biodiesel, which is a substitute for petroleum-based diesel rather than gasoline. The idea of running a diesel engine on plant-based fuels isn't

new: when Rudolph Diesel invented his super-efficient combustion engine at the end of the nineteenth century, he famously ran his prototypes on peanut oil. Biodiesel can be almost 50% more climate-friendly than standard diesel, but there is a catch. Though the fuel can be made from sustainably grown crops (or even used cooking oil), it can also be made very cheaply from palm oil, the cultivation of which is a major cause catastrophic deforestation in Indonesia and elsewhere (see p.261). All told, palm-ba biodiesel has the potential to do much more harm than good, but consumers typi have no way of knowing whether palm oil was used to create the biodiesel they're ing. Despite this, the National Biodiesel Board estimates that biodiesel could sup to 10% of the US's fuel in the near future.

Biodiesel can be used in many recently produced diesel cars without modific it's worth checking with the manufacturer before filling up. The fuel is availab form (B100) but blends with petroleum diesel (such as B20, B5, and B2) are m lar. Blends are nowhere near as good from a carbon perspective, but still red harmful emissions and increase engine efficiency. Currently, biodiesel cost petroleum-based diesel, though the price may drop thanks to a federal bi law in late 2004. For a list of pumps at gas stations and field docks, as we information about all things biodiesel, see:

The National Diesel Board www.biodiesel.org ▷ 800-841-5849

So that's biodiesel. But what about all those stories in the press about people filling up with plain old **vegetable oil** in supermarket parking lots (such as Daniel Blackburn, who made the headlines in 2003 by using veggie oil to drive the length of Britain)? Well, it's true that, after a conversion costing about $800, many diesel engines will run perfectly well on standard cooking oil. Many of the 5000 or so car owners in the US who've taken the plunge pay nothing at all for their fuel, obtaining it as a waste product from local restaurants. Since this oil would otherwise be wasted, and because it needs very little processing, the result is perhaps the greenest of any biofuels. The most prominent companies offering conversion kits are:

Grease Car www.greasecar.com
Golden Fuel www.goldenfuelsystems.com

Car companies

Of the various car manufacturers, the US giants **Ford**, **GM** and **DaimlerChrysler**—the first two of which are among the five biggest corporations in the world—have arguably the worst ethical records. For one thing, they're big political donors: all three ranked among George W. Bush's top benefactors in 2000. And they have a pretty appalling record on climate change, not just in terms of promoting gas-guzzling sports utility vehicles (SUVs), but also through seeking to undermine the scientific evidence on human-induced global warming. For example, their detractors point to underhanded tactics such as the funding of the **Coalition for Vehicle Choice**, a significant anti-Kyoto pressure group in the 1990s, which took out ads in the US national press. It claimed it represented the American people and that it was financed by "public support," but allegedly more than 95% of this support actually came from Ford, GM and DaimlerChrysler.

Though none are squeaky clean, the European and East Asian firms have typically courted less controversy. One exception is **Suzuki**, accused at the time of writing of being involved in projects with direct financial links to the Burmese military government. It is beyond the scope of this book to do a full comparison of every brand available in the US, but of the common makes available in the American market, the most recent in-depth report in the British magazine *Ethical Consumer* put the various **VW** companies, **Honda** and **Kia** on its top ten list (see p.329 for subscription and back-issue details for the magazine).

How to buy a greener car

Though the average fuel efficiency of cars in the US has actually dropped in the last quarter century, that's mainly due to the growing popularity of hulking **SUVs**. For anyone who wants to buy a green vehicle, there are plenty on the market and, these days, data on environmental factors such as fuel efficiency (which runs hand in hand with CO_2 emissions) are very easy to come by—in car showrooms, online and in magazines.

One question is whether to go for a gasoline or diesel engine. **Diesel engines** (which are still much more popular in Europe than in the US) are much worse in terms of poisonous emissions—so aren't the most ethical choice for city use—but they're around 40% more fuel-efficient and hence much better in terms of global warming. Another difference is that diesels leave you the option of using biodiesel, while gasoline allows you to use ethanol blends (see p.286) and convert to **LPG** (see p.294).

Cars: the green list & the blacklist

In February 2005, the American Council for an Energy-Efficient Economy rated these 12 cars as the "greenest" available:

	Emissions ranking	City MPG	Highway MPG
Honda Civic GX	(PZEV)	30	34
Honda Insight	(SULEV)	57	56
Toyota Prius	(PZEV)	60	51
Honda Civic Hybrid	(PZEV)	47	48
Toyota Corolla	(ULEV)	32	41
Toyota Echo	(PZEV)	35	42
Nissan Sentra	(PZEV)	28	35
Honda Civic HX	(ULEV)	36	44
Pontiac Vibe/Toyota Matrix	(ULEV)	30	36
Mazda 3	(PZEV)	28	35
Ford Escape Hybrid	(PZEV)	36	31
Ford Focus/Focus Wagon	(PZEV)	26	35

ULEV=Ultra Low Emissions Vehicle (50% cleaner than the average new car in 2003)

SULEV=Super Ultra Low Emission Vehicle (90% cleaner than the average new car in 2003)

PZEV=Partial Zero Emissions Vehicle (Meets SULEV specifications; also has zero evaporative emissions, and has at least a 15-year or 150,000-mile warranty)

The same organization also rated the automobiles below as "2004's 10 Least Efficient Cars":

	City MPG	Highway MPG
Lamborghini Murcielago	9	13
Dodge Ram Pickup 1500	9	15
Land Rover Discovery Series II	12	16
Ford Excursion	12	16
Hummer H2	13	16
Lexus LX 470	13	17
Toyota Land Cruiser	13	17
GMC Yukon XL K2500	13	17
Chevy Suburban K2500	13	17
Toyota Sequoia	14	17

Another question is whether to opt for a fuel-efficient, low-emission "normal" car or for one of the various "alternative" engine types discussed below. The latter are generally more expensive to buy but they're more environmentally friendly and cheaper to run (due to their efficiency and the low tax on their fuels). Also, the government has some tax incentives for owners of hybrid (details at www.fueleconomy.gov/feg/tax_hybrid.shtml) and electric/clean-fuel (www.fueleconomy.gov/feg/tax_afv.shtml) vehicles. The Department of Energy lists other incentives available on the state level at www.eere.energy.gov/cleancities/vbg/progs/laws.cgi.

Besides **biodiesel** and **vegetable oil** (discussed on pp.286–287), the main alternative fuels and engine types include the following.

Electric cars

Recharged via a standard **electrical outlet**, electric cars are the greenest option available. Like most battery-powered devices, they have literally no emissions, and, if charged up with electricity from renewable sources (see p.241), their use creates practically no carbon dioxide. Even if charged up with "standard electricity," they're still much more eco-friendly than gasoline-powered cars, due to their high levels of energy efficiency. The only problems are that most electric cars don't go very fast, that they need to be recharged after a certain number of miles (usually between 50

The electric GEM eL is quickly becoming the standard vehicle used by parks employees in major urban areas.

and 200, depending on the model), and that you need a parking space near an electric socket.

In the past few years, several major automobile manufacturers have produced electric cars—from two-seaters to SUVs and pickup trucks—for the US market, including Honda, General Motors, Daimler-Chrysler, Nissan, Ford and Toyota. To the disappointment of many environmentalists and electric car enthusiasts, however, production for the US had largely ceased by 2005. The reasons for this depend largely upon who you ask, but it's been variously speculated that demand did not meet the industry's expectations; that battery technology was not progressing as hoped (though it's been reported that ones have been developed allowing vehicles to go for more than 200 miles per charge); that companies were putting their chips on hybrid and fuel-cell technologies as the big future winners in the eco-car field; and that oil companies in particular were not keen on an oil-free vehicle making inroads into the market.

The Electric Auto Association's Plug In America coalition has contended that the big automakers made electric cars to help meet California's Zero Emission Vehicle program (which mandated that 4% of new cars sold in the state be "ZEVs"), halting production after that legislation was repealed in 2003 with the help of industry lobbying. There's even a campaign (DontCrush.com) to keep those companies from sending their unsold electric cars to the junkheap, and in the summer of 2006, a popular documentary feature on the controversy, *Who Killed the Electric Car?* But at the time of this writing, the future of the electric car as a widely available option in the US is tenuous, and perhaps nonexistent. Mitsubishi is planning to mass-manufacture an electric car in the future, but it's not set to go on sale until 2010, and then only in Japan.

As another electric car alternative, there are some brands of golf cart-type **neighborhood electric vehicles**, also sometimes called electric mini-cars, such as Daimler/Chrysler's GEM, selling in the region of $10,000. However, these have a top speed of only 25 miles per hour, are not allowed on public roads in some states, and are usually restricted to streets with 35mph speed limits in the thirty-odd states that do allow such use. All told, they're really only of value if you live in a quiet residential neighborhood and drive mostly for short errands and visits.

For for more information on electric cars, try:

The Electric Auto Association www.eaaev.org

Electric hybrids
Electric "hybrid" cars, such as the **Honda Insight**, **Toyota Prius** and **Lexus Hybrid Synergy Drive**, look and drive just like normal cars, yet their semi-electric engines are significantly more efficient than the gasoline-only equivalents. Unlike "proper" electric cars (see above), hybrids never need to be plugged in and charged up. Instead, the car charges its own battery when the brakes are applied (converting the car's kinetic energy into electrical energy) and also when the gasoline-powered part of the engine is powering the car along at high speeds. The battery's energy is then automatically used when lower speeds are required. The result is fuel efficiency of up to 80mpg and very low levels of harmful emissions.

It seems that hybrids will be the primary market for fuel-efficient cars in the next few years—sales increased 80% from 2003 to 2004, and by mid-2005 the Toyota Prius was chalking up almost 10,000 sales a month. (UPS even introduced 50 hybrid delivery trucks in early 2006.) However, hybrids still account for less than 1% of the cars sold in the US. One problem is cost. If buying new, you can expect to pay around $3000–4000 more than you would for an equivalent nonhybrid model.

Keep in mind, however, that not all hybrids are necessarily a big improvement over conventional models. In 2005, the *New York Times* reported that Toyota's Highlander Hybrid and Lexus RX 400h got no better fuel mileage than their nonhybrid cousins, prompting the Bluewater Network (a division of Friends of the Earth) to take out advertising urging Toyota to build more fuel-efficient cars, and stop its opposition (as part of a group of automakers) to Congressional efforts to raise national fuel mileage standards.

The Honda Insight's hybrid gasoline–electric engine makes it one of the greenest "normal" cars on the market.

CNG & LPG

CNG (compressed natural gas) is still a fossil fuel, but of them all it's among the cleanest. When used to power cars, CNG can reduce emissions of carbon monoxide by about 70%, nitrogen oxides by about half, and ozone-causing pollutants by about 90%, as well as nullify most particulate emissions. You can convert your car to run either solely on CNG or on both CNG and gas, though the conversion kit will run you somwhere in the range of $2500–4000.

There are also some natural gas vehicles on the market, such as the Toyota Camry CNG and the Honda Civic GX, the latter of which has topped or almost topped several "greenest vehicle" surveys, such as the one performed in 2005 by the American Council for an Energy-Efficient Economy (see p.290). The big disadvantage is the lack of CNG filling stations, which explains why most of the CNG vehicles in the US are "fleets" (taxis, shuttle vans and the like) run by private companies and government agencies who have their own on-site filling stations.

More common for individuals, though still hardly run-of-the-mill, are vehicles running on **LPG** (**Liquid Petroleum Gas**). LPG is basically **propane**, as used in camping stoves and standalone gas heaters. A by-product of oil refining and natural gas extraction, it's a fossil fuel but has slightly lower greenhouse emissions than gasoline or diesel and much lower poisonous-fume output. Most cars can be converted to run either solely on LPG or on both LPG and gas; conversion costs about $1500–2000, but you'll then get inexpensive fuel.

Fuel cells

Instead of being "charged up," **fuel-cell cars** generate electrical energy on board, using a catalytic process—generally the combination of **hydrogen** and **oxygen**. The hydrogen can be made on the fly from gasoline or methanol, or—more commonly—generated elsewhere and then stored on board in replaceable canisters. Like other electric cars, fuel-cell vehicles help reduce air pollution in towns and cities—water vapor is often the only emission.

However, it's questionable whether hydrogen vehicles will be the environmental panacea that their advocates describe. The main problem is that it takes a lot of energy (most of

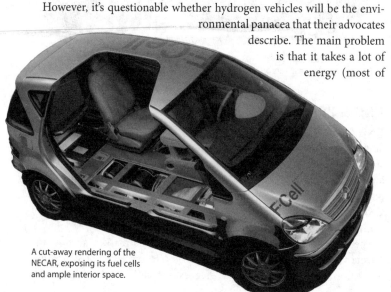

A cut-away rendering of the NECAR, exposing its fuel cells and ample interior space.

which currently comes from fossil fuels) to make the hydrogen in the first place. So it's unclear whether the creation of a hydrogen infrastructure—production plants, distribution channels and refilling stations—would be a major benefit in terms of global warming without a concurrent growth in renewable energy. It's also been contended (notably in *Who Killed the*

Cutting back on cars

If you want to help reduce the number of cars being produced, and the distance they're driven, but you don't want to rely solely on public transport, consider looking into **car sharing** and **carpooling** (especially useful within or nearby major metorpolitan areas). This will not only be environmentally sound, but it will also make sense financially: it is said that if you factor in the time it takes to earn the money to buy, run, insure, tax and maintain your own vehicle, drivers achieve an average speed roughly equivalent to walking.

Under car sharing programs no one person owns the car; instead, you pay by-the-hour for the use of automobiles that have been scattered throughout the area. An Internet search is all that's needed to locate and rent a car for a specific period of time. Obviously this isn't as environmentally pristine a strategy as walking, biking or taking public transportation. But the idea is that if you only drive when you really need to, you're less likely to use up gas and roadspace commuting, or perhaps less likely to even buy a car in the first place. Besides application/membership fees, you only pay for the hours you use (though monthly plans are also available), with rates varying according to the city. It's still a young movement, and as of this writing the most established car sharing company, Flexcar, was only operating in Chicago, Denver, Los Angeles, Portland (Oregon), San Diego, San Francisco and Washington, DC. Another outfit, Zipcar, fills in some of the gaps by covering Boston, Chapel Hill, and New York City/New Jersey, as well as also covering DC. See:

Flexcar www.flexcar.com
Zipcar www.zipcar.com 866-4ZIPCAR

Carpooling—either for a regular commute or a one-off drive—is based on the very sensible rationale that one car carrying four people is four times less polluting, congesting and expensive than four cars carrying one person each. Carpooling's always been popular among neighbors and work colleagues, but a more organized approach is becoming increasingly common, as a growing number of Americans realize that contributing to climate change (and its death toll) and wasting money are more frightening prospects than talking to strangers. The Internet has also helped, providing the ideal way for people to find and organize sharing. So many carpooling organizations are spread throughout the US—many of them online, and some of them government-sponsored—that it would be futile to try and list them all here; get on the web, do a search for carpools in your city/region, and it's likely that several options will pop up. There are even a good number of international carpooling websites if you're so inclined, though you're more likely to make the connections you want through smaller, locally based services.

Electric Car?) that the development of fuel-cell vehicles on a mass scale is much further off in the future than its champions claim.

Trials using taxis and buses have already successfully demonstrated that the fuel cell can work well, however, and commercial models—such as the **NECAR,** designed by DaimlerChrysler, Ford and Ballard—may be available within the next few years, through probably not before 2010. Toyota announced in 2005 that it would release its first commercial fuel-cell vehicle in 2015, with a hefty (even allowing for inflation) projected price tag of $50,000—still quite a bit less than the $1 million it would sell for if it was available today.

Flex-fuel vehicles

Flex-fuel vehicles, or FFVs, operate on a single fuel tank, fuel system and engine. The difference between these and standard models is that they can run on any mixture of unleaded gasoline and alchohol—usually ethanol (see p.286). While the "green" benefits of FFVs might seem mild compared to some of the more adventurous technologies detailed above, they do allow for a substantial cut in CO_2 emissions—25% in a Ford Escape Hybrid research vehicle, according to the company. Nor are they as exotic as they might seem: in 2005, Worldwatch Institute reported that flex-fuel vehicles accounted for more than half of new cars sold in Brazil, where ethanol-fueled vehicles have saved almost $50 billion in imported oil costs since the 1970s.

Although Ford, General Motors and Daimler-Chrysler have produced several FFV models, the big drawback is the same one suffered by CNG drivers: stations that offer flex-fuel (E85, or 85% ethanol, being the most popular kind) are scarce, and some of the stations that do have it only make it available to private fleets. Moreover, E85 gives you lower mileage than unleaded gas, which adds substantially to operating costs.

Before buying an FFV, visit the following website, which lists mileage, annual fuel cost and greenhouse gas emissions for various brands as well as stations nationwide that sell E85.

FuelEconomy www.fueleconomy.gov/feg/byfueltype.htm

More info

A complete environmental comparison of practically all the cars currently available can be found on **GreenerCars.com**, though you have to pay for online access to its full database ($19.95/yr, $8.95 for 30 days). Though its URL is similar, *The Green Car Journal* is an entirely different organization, publishing a quarterly consumer magazine ($19.95/yr) evaluating automobiles from an environmental perspective.

GreenerCars.com www.greenercars.com
The Green Car Journal www.greencars.com

For more on alternative fuels, the US Department of Energy maintains an informative site, and for an international perspective on greener transport in general, check out the annual *Sustainable Transport* magazine, published by the Institute for Transportation and Development Policy, and downloadable for free (including back issues).

DoE www.eere.energy.gov/afdc
Sustainable Tranport www.itdp.org.www.eere.energy.gov/afdc

Roadside assistance organizations

You might use a car but still have some issues with the wider automobile world. For instance, you might be dead against expansion of the road network, for environmental reasons. Or you might feel that, in general, public transport should be prioritized over the needs of drivers. If so, then you should consider which company you use for roadside rescue. **AAA** (the American Automobile Association) may not be the most disagreeable company in the world, but it does have a long history of lobbying for highway expansion and the prioritization of cars over public transport. So you might prefer to check out Better World Club:

Better World Club www.betterworldclub.com ▷ 866-238-1137

Set up specifically as an environmentally sound alternative to the big roadside rescue companies, Better World Club offers a similar service at a similar cost. It boasts a 30-minute average response time in metropolitan areas, 24/7 service in all 50 states, and free maps for members. While it's not anti-car as such, it donates 1% of its revenue to "environmental cleanup and advocacy." It also offers roadside rescue for cyclists.

Air travel
How bad is it?

An ethical flight is something of a castle in the air. Combine their high greenhouse-gas emissions—per passenger, per mile—with the fact that they allow us to travel such vast distances and you have a recipe for environmental disaster. Despite the relatively tiny number of people who regularly fly, aviation accounts for 3–4% of the total human impact on the climate, according to the **Intergovernmental Panel on Climate Change**. That figure may sound small, but it's growing year on year, threatening to offset the cuts in greenhouse emissions being made in other sectors.

The reason air travel is so bad for the climate is not just that airplanes release a great deal of greenhouse gases into the atmosphere—it's the fact that they do so in the upper troposphere and lower stratosphere, where their effect is compounded. The contrails (vapor trails) that planes create

Boeing, Boeing ... bomb!

As if the environmental impact of flying wasn't enough, there is the added concern that most passenger aircraft are produced by arms manufacturers. Next time you fly, instead of ignoring the plane's information and safety sheet, have a look to see who produced your airborne home for the next few hours. With very few exceptions, it will either be **Boeing** or **Airbus.**

Boeing is one of the world's largest arms companies, whose annual turnover of around $50 billion is in no small part generated from selling military equipment to all kinds of governments, including those with very poor human rights records. According to a recent report in the investigative magazine *Mother Jones* (www.motherjones.com), recent Boeing sales include warplanes to Indonesia, Israel, Kuwait and Saudi Arabia; attack helicopters to Egypt; and missiles to Turkey.

Boeing is even "unethical" according to the low moral codes of the arms industry: in late 2003, its chairman, Phil Condit, resigned after, as the Associated Press put it, "months of ethical controversies over the aggressive methods it used to obtain lucrative defense contracts." And it's also a major political donor in the US. According to figures from Open Secrets (www.opensecrets.org), it guaranteed itself a sympathetic president in 2000 by giving nearly a million dollars to both the main parties.

Airbus, meanwhile, is owned by British Aerospace and other major European arms manufacturers. All in all, the tie between commercial aircraft and military equipment is so entrenched that—as Noam Chomsky has written—many passenger planes are actually modified bombers. There's not much that consumers can do about this link, but if you feel particularly strongly about the arms industry it may tip the balance and make you decide to choose another form of transport whenever possible.

It's not just how far they fly—it's how high they fly. At the altitude reached by a modern passenger plane, the effect on climate change is three times worse than the CO₂ output would suggest.

are another factor. The science surrounding this topic is not yet rock solid, but researchers believe that contrails add to the greenhouse effect—especially at night, when their tendency to stop heat escaping from the Earth isn't offset by their tendency to reflect incoming sunlight.

All told, the impact of a flight is thought to be around three times greater than the **CO₂ emissions** would suggest. So two seats on a round trip from San Francisco to London produces the equivalent impact of at least five tons of CO_2—equivalent to around 20,000 miles in a mediumly efficient car.

Super-efficient, low-emission planes may eventually emerge, but there are no promising designs in the pipeline. And even if such planes existed already, they wouldn't replace current fleets any time soon, since passenger planes stay in use for decades. In the meantime, the only way governments could reduce air travel's impact is by cutting down on passenger numbers by making the price of a ticket reflect the environmental costs. But governments have so far been loath to take such steps.

What you can do

For anyone concerned about global warming, cutting back on air travel is an obvious goal. This might mean giving up flying altogether, or it might mean taking fewer flights and making up for it by staying longer each

Carbon offset programs

Anyone who wants to neutralize their effect on climate change will be interested in the various programs that allow you to "offset" your carbon footprint. Whether you want to cancel the CO_2 of a single long-haul flight, a year of car journeys or your entire existence, the process is the same. First, you visit the website of an offsetting organization and use their carbon calculators to work out the emissions related to whatever activity you want to offset. This will be translated into a fee which the offsetting organization will use to soak up a matching amount of CO_2 from the air.

To do this, they fund projects such as the replanting of damaged rainforest or the distribution of long-life, low-energy lightbulbs in developing countries. As a guide, it usually costs around £7/$12 to offset a ton of CO_2. At this price, a seat on a round trip from New York to London costs around $20 to neutralize, while a typical year of driving in a mediumly efficient car clocks in at around $35.

Offset programs have proved popular, not just with individuals, but also with global corporations (HSBC and other office-based giants are going "climate neutral") and celebrities (Pink Floyd, Pulp and the Pet Shop Boys have all neutralized their tours). However, such programs are not without their critics—as evidenced by *New Internationalist* magazine's July 2006 special edition, which had "Do Not Sponsor This Tree!" emblazoned across its cover.

One argument levelled against offsetting is that it's just a plaster on the wound, hiding the inherent unsustainability of carbon-intensive Western lifestyles. There's some truth in this point—offsetting isn't as ideal as not emitting the carbon in the first place. But it's certainly better than doing nothing, and there's no reason why people can't buy offsets and make efforts to reduce their emissions directly.

Another criticism sometimes made is that offset projects may not make the swift, long-term carbon savings that are claimed of them. The major offset services are externally audited to demonstrate that the carbon savings are real, but a key point is timing. Since CO_2 persists in the atmosphere for decades, a carbon saving now is worth more in the battle against climate change than one in the future. And yet some of the offset projects—most notably tree planting—may take more than half a century to fully soak up the carbon you've paid to offset. This is one reason why some offsetting groups, such as Climate Care, are moving towards sustainable energy projects instead of trees.

The most popular offset programs include:

Carbonfund www.carbonfund.org
Climate Care www.climatecare.org
Go Zero www.conservationfund.org

time. It might also mean favoring destinations that are closer to home. Short flights tend to be around 25% worse, per passenger per mile, than long-haul flights (because they have more empty seats and because taking off and landing burns more fuel than cruising) but overall it's still far worse to travel longer distances.

Another approach is to consider alternative ways of travelling. With more than two people on the same itinerary, it can be more climate-friendly to drive than to fly—especially for short distances. Better still are trains and boats, which are typically responsible for many times fewer emissions per person per mile than either cars or planes.

If you do choose to fly, consider offsetting the emissions (see opposite) and try to favor daytime flights due to the issue of contrails already discussed. You may also want to think about which airline you choose. They all lobby for fewer rather than more restrictions on air travel, but some of the big US firms—including **American Airlines** and **United Airlines** (UAL Corp)—are more active political donors, according to data from www.opensecrets.org. And **Japan** and **Austrian Airlines** are on boycott lists at the time of writing for continuing to operate in Burma.

Finally, you might want to consider buying flights via the travel agency of the **Better World Club** (see p.297), which will give you a free carbon offset when you book a flight.

Travel & tourism
Bon voyage

Regularly described as the **world's biggest employer**, even the world's biggest industry, the tourism sector provides more than 200 million jobs and accounts for more than 10% of global GDP. And, despite a brief downturn after the 9/11 terrorist attacks in 2001, the industry just keeps on growing. According to the World Travel and Tourism Council, the number of international trips made each year now exceeds 700 million; by 2010 that's expected to be a billion; by 2020 a billion and a half. The range of popular destinations also continues to broaden, with journeys to **developing countries**—from Bhutan to Botswana to Bolivia—accounting for an increasing chunk of the total. However, while the growth of the travel industry and its economic importance are not in dispute, its overall costs and benefits are hotly contested.

Tourism has the potential to be good for all parties. Tourists get to enjoy themselves and/or increase their knowledge of the world and its people. And the residents of host countries get jobs and money. This can be especially important in the developing countries, where tourists are often the main source of foreign currency—or even, in cases such as the Maldives, the majority of national income.

The very poorest countries sometimes stand to benefit the most. A 2001 report from the United Nations Conference on Trade and Development pointed out that, "International tourism is one of the few economic sectors through which LDCs (Least Developed Countries) have managed to increase their participation in the global economy. It can be an engine of employment creation, poverty eradication, gender equality, and protection of the natural and cultural heritage." Few, however, would claim this ideal exchange of benefits is an accurate characterization of the whole of the modern tourism industry. Tourists, holiday-makers, travelers and trekkers can all unwittingly have damaging social and environmental effects.

Most obviously, while tourism may have the potential to facilitate mutual understanding, in many cases the visitors are unwelcome, imposing or simply **in the way**—unaware of local customs and manners, unable to speak the language and taking up in-demand places on public transport. In poor countries, furthermore, tourists can create resentment by flaunting a degree of leisure time and wealth completely out of reach for most of their hosts. But more serious still are the issues discussed below: the control of land and resources, environmental damage and the possibility that tourists may be propping up oppressive governments. To make things more complicated, all these problems tend to be more acute in precisely the poor regions which have the most to benefit from tourist money.

Land & water

From Peru to the Philippines, there have been many cases of marginalized people being forced—legally, physically or practically—off their **land** to make way for tourist development. Sometimes this has happened to make way for modern beach complexes and other resort-style developments. Tourism Concern, which campaigns for a more ethical travel sector, has reported many such incidents including, a few years ago, that of "a British-controlled company, which was planning a £2.8 billion tourist enclave on the Nungwi peninsula of Zanzibar." Apparently, "the development was to be the biggest in East Africa, with luxury hotels, golf courses and an airport. Shockingly, the plan failed to mention the peninsula's 20,000 residents. Local people hadn't had a say ..." Closer to home, at the time of writing the same organization was calling attention to the construction of a resort/casino just 50 miles off our shores in North Bimini in the Bahamas. Overseen by a Miami-based owner, the project was cutting off residents' access to five miles of the seven-mile-long island, and turning off water supplies to the community in favor of using them for the development.

But, arguably, this kind of flagrant disregard for the rights of local people has been an even bigger problem in the areas popular with **"nature" travelers**, since areas set aside for conservation and wildlife purposes have often been linked to the displacement of indigenous groups. The famous conservationist Bernhard Grzimek once commented that a national park will be effective only if "no men, not even native ones, should live inside its borders," and such views have been responsible for the eviction or even murder of indigenous groups in parks ranging from California's Yosemite and Tanzania's Serengeti to, more recently, Botswana's Kalahari and Tanzania's Mkomazi. Critics of nature travel claim that common tourist expectations—that locals should live a visually exciting "tribal" existence or not be there at all—are a major factor in initiating or maintaining such human clearances.

Just as serious is the appropriation of resources such as water, which is scarce in many of the hot destinations beloved by Western tourists. A single inefficient hotel—especially one with a swimming pool—can require more water than a whole town. And **golf courses** can require up to a million liters a day in some climates (as well as more agrochemicals than even the most intensive farmland). Yet they're now relatively common resort features in even the driest countries.

In poor countries, it's possible that the water demands of rich travelers can speed up the development of reliable water infrastructures that will benefit residents. But it's also possible that hotels can buy a monopoly over, or unsustainable access to, the water, emptying groundwater aquifers and causing serious long-term damage. In fact, this is also an issue in relatively wealthy countries. As *Ergo* magazine recently reported, Mallorca's water table has plunged 295 feet in just 20 years.

Environmental damage

Travel can provide the perfect incentive for countries to look after their environments. If tourists are coming to see beautiful landscapes of wildlife, these very "features" become valuable assets worth protecting. And in

The mixed blessings of ecotourism

The most widely known area of travel to claim to have a socially responsible edge is "ecotourism," which in the last decade or so has grown from a niche market into a major sector, embraced both by tourism industry bodies and the UN, who named 2002 the International Year of Ecotourism, complete with a World Ecotourism Summit in Quebec. But what exactly *is* ecotourism?

According to the International Ecotourism Society, the term refers to "responsible travel to natural areas that conserves the environment and sustains the well-being of local people." Or, as the World Conservation Union put it, ecotourism describes "environmentally responsible travel … to relatively undisturbed natural areas … that promotes conservation, has low negative visitor impact [and] provides for beneficially active socioeconomic involvement of local populations."

Advocates of ecotourism claim that the sector has contributed a great deal both to conservation and economic empowerment of people in remote regions. However, the term has been tarnished by criticism from a range of commentators.

One issue is that ecotourism has no legally binding definition, which means there's nothing to stop an unscrupulous travel agent from slapping the label on any nature-focused holiday, regardless of the damage it may cause. As EcoTravel.com puts it: "an 'eco-lodge' may dump untreated sewage in a river, and still call itself 'eco' simply because it is located in a natural setting." This in itself isn't a reason to avoid travel companies selling "ecotourism" trips, but it is a reason to quiz them carefully on their ethical standards.

However, the vagueness of the term isn't the only problem that critics of ecotourism raise. In all tourism sectors, what starts as a trickle of travelers can often end up as an influx—there's a risk that adventurous ecotourists will inevitably open up the world's most fragile environments to unsustainable tourism. According to a recent report by Conservation International and the environmental wing of the UN, in the 1990s alone, leisure travel to the world's "biodiversity hotspots" (those areas with richly diverse but delicate ecologies) more than doubled, with rises of more than 300% in Brazil, Nicaragua and El Salvador, 500% in South Africa and 2000% in Laos and Cambodia.

countries where few other employment opportunities exist, the travel sector can simultaneously create jobs that offer an alternative to ecologically damaging work such as small-scale mining or tree-felling.

In many cases, however, short-term financial gain wins over long-term ecological protection. From coastal Spain to Goa, whole areas have had their biodiversity decimated by large-scale tourist development. Cruise ships dump sewage straight into the ocean. And in countries that lack decent waste disposal, tourist waste—from sunscreen bottles and food wrappers to toilet paper—may end up in rivers that both people and wildlife depend on for their survival.

Some NGOs, such as Malaysia's third world Network and Thailand's Tourism Information Monitoring, have gone so far as to say that ecotourism's viability is "another myth that needs to be exploded," and that it "will destroy more biodiversity and harm even more local communities." They raise wide-ranging issues such as the low pay of tourism workers and the patronizing phenomenon of "tribe tourism," in which people are encouraged by tour firms to act out a way of life for the cameras that is often long-gone in reality. They even worry about bio-piracy: the patenting of traditional natural remedies by multinational drug companies. "What does it mean," they ask, "when Thailand's National Centre for Genetic Engineering and Biotechnology, which is collaborating with giant biotechnology firms such as Monsanto, gives financial support to ecotourism research projects," such as a university research project entitled "The Exploration of the Different Species of the Birds in Mae Hong Son province and the Promotion of Eco-tourism"? Surely legal protections should be in place, they argue, before we "indiscriminately promote tourism forms that facilitate the stealing and smuggling of local biological resources and traditional knowledge."

Hard-line greens also point out that there's something slightly ironic about flying halfway around the world to look at sensitive environments. And there is an obvious logic to this. For instance, a recent report by the University of Queensland's Centre for Marine Studies suggested that Australia's Great Barrier Reef will lose 95% of its living coral by 2050—the cause is global warming, driven by carbon-intensive activities such as, say, flying from London to Sydney. And that's not to mention the fact—discussed on p.303—that some conservation beloved by ecotourism firms may be the result of land appropriation, or may harm the very animals they're designed to protect.

Some of these accusations are a bit unfair. But what is clear is that the term "ecotourism" does not in itself guarantee any particular ethical standards. The tips for finding an ethical travel operator detailed on p.310 apply to this sector of tourism just like every other.

For more on ecotourism, see:

The International Ecotourism Society www.ecotourism.org

Even where tourism does encourage conservation—such as in game reserves—it needs to be carefully managed. If not, the tourists and their guides may cause harm to the very animals they have come to see. As Philip Seddon of New Zealand's University of Otago in Dunedin recently told *New Scientist*, "Transmission of disease to wildlife, or subtle changes to wildlife health through disturbance of daily routines or increased stress levels, while not apparent to a casual observer, may translate to lowered survival and breeding."

Who gets the money?

It goes without saying that real or potential problems described above have to be balanced both with the enjoyment of the tourists and the economic benefits gained by the people in the visited countries—both of which can be enormous. However, in many cases, the cash tourists spend exits the country as soon as it leaves their pockets, heading straight into the bank accounts of foreign travel firms. The World Bank estimates that 55% of the money from international tourism in the Global South goes to foreign-owned airlines, hotels and tour organizers, or for imported food, drink and other supplies. In some countries, the figure is even higher— 70% in Thailand, according to a study by Sustainable Living.

With package holidays, this economic "leakage" tends to be even higher, or even more for **all-inclusive pay-up-front deals**, where tourists get to consume as much as they like as long as they stay in the hotel complex (and hence give their custom to no one else). In these cases, the main economic beneficiaries are not locals, but foreign companies.

The money spent by **independent travelers** is less likely to disappear overseas. In India, for example, where nonpackage travel is the most popular

The preservation of local culture or a patronizing human "zoo"? A Kikuyu dressed as a Masai selling trinkets to tourists on the east coast of Kenya.

type, around half of total tourist spending is thought to stay in the country. Independent travelers can also choose to favor small businesses, from where money is more likely to trickle down through the local economy—and which also tend to pose smaller environmental burdens. However, there's no escaping the fact that the independent traveller is very often the harbinger of the foreign-owned resort. As tourism academic Brian Wheeller has written, "In the rush to escape the mass tourist [the] individual traveler is forever seeking the new, the exotic, the unspoilt—the vulnerable. Inevitably, however, they are inexorably paving the way ... The sensitive traveler is the perpetrator of the global spread, the vanguard of the package tour."

Perhaps more of a concern than money not benefiting the country in which we spend it is the possibility that it may stay in the country and line

The Burma travel boycott

The Asian state of Myanmar, still more widely known as Burma, has been living under a brutal military regime since the early 1960s. This junta has murdered and tortured tens of thousands of innocent people, imposed slave labor on countless children and adults, spent vast sums on arms while the population lives in poverty, and imprisoned political opponents such as Nobel-laureate Aung San Suu Kyi, who won free elections in 1990 by a landslide but was never allowed to take office. Despite all this, Burma—which, like neighbouring Thailand, is a place of remarkable ancient history and natural beauty—still has an active tourism industry. The human rights abuses are mostly hidden from travellers since the government has a direct financial interest in maintaining the flow of visitors: it owns most of the tourism infrastructure and obliges each person who enters to buy $200 of local currency, providing valuable foreign reserves.

Unsurprisingly, Aung San Suu Kyi and others have called on foreigners to stop visiting the country, and numerous human rights groups have appealed to US travel companies to remove Burma from their list of destinations. Some have refused and, accordingly, groups such as the Burma Campaign UK are encouraging us not just to boycott Burma itself but also these companies, along with all the others still on their "Dirty List." At the time of writing, travel-related firms listed include Japan Airlines; tour operators such as Abercrombie & Kent, Adventures Abroad and Mountain Travel Sobek; and publishers Lonely Planet, Insight Guides, Fodor's (Random House), Nelles Guides (Hunter Publishing), Impact Publications and Let's Go (Pan Macmillan). Some seem simply uninterested in the ethical implications of working and travelling in Burma, for the most part ignoring the political situation in their literature. Others acknowledge the issues but claim that tourism may help rather that worsen the problem. Lonely Planet, for example, hasn't stopped publishing its Burma guide since it would mean "betraying the very principle upon which our company is based: namely that travel CAN make a difference." Campaigners describe this view as naïve, anti-democratic and irresponsible. For more information, see:

Burma Campaign UK www.burmacampaign.org.uk

the pockets of an oppressive, corrupt or otherwise harmful government. After all, governments nearly always benefit financially from tourism. And an oppressive administration can impose tourist development on a population for its own advantage. The most obvious and extreme example of this is Burma, where the military regime has been partly funded by tourism (see p.307).

But while Burma is an unusually clear case, with a boycott call coming from recognized elected leaders within the country, many other countries are less so. Should we avoid travel to China on the grounds of its government's appalling human rights record and its occupation of Tibet (where, incidentally, it is endeavoring to replace Tibetan tourist guides with Chinese ones, in order to keep visitors from getting too many answers about the regime)? What about **Russia** for its activities in Chechnya, or **Indonesia** for its actions in Papua?

Browse recent news reports by country at Amnesty International (www. amnesty.org/library) and you might wonder exactly how many countries you *can* visit with a clear conscience. Human rights abuses abound in many favorite destinations, from **Nepal** ("thousands of cases of arbitrary arrests, unacknowledged detentions, torture and 'disappearances' at the hands of the security forces") and Morocco (where authorities' "uncompromising stance in stamping out any form of dissent on the issue of Western Sahara remains a serious stain on their record") to the **Maldives** ("systematic repression of peaceful political activists"). Whether visiting countries with oppressive governments will exacerbate or lessen human rights abuses is debatable. If a government is eager to promote tourism, it may be less likely to commit day-to-day abuses with foreigners around, or it may be sensitive to complaints from tourists who have witnessed any mistreatment. Foreign visitors may also provide income for people who otherwise would be at the financial mercy of the state, and they may also raise awareness of issues back at home. According to George Monbiot, travelling can even be a disincentive to war: "the people of powerful nations might be reluctant to permit their leaders to destroy the countries they have visited."

As with choosing whether to buy or boycott products from specific foreign countries—discussed on p.30—there are no easy thumbs-up or thumbs-down lists of where and how it's "ethical" to travel. You have to do your own research and make your own rules. You might, for example, decide to avoid big travel companies when travelling in countries whose governments you consider to be problematic, since the bigger firms are more likely to have links to those in power. Or you might decide only to travel to countries with participatory democracies since, with any other system, the people you're imposing yourself upon might not have had the opportunity to vote against tourism development.

"Ethical tourism"

The issues raised above—and the global-warming impact of our flights—shouldn't necessarily make us stay at home. After all, a recent ILO report states that, in the post-9/11 tourism downturn, around 6.5 million jobs are likely to have been lost, mostly in poor countries. But such issues should feature in our decisions of where to go, what we do when we get there and, in the case of non-independent travel, what kind of tourism companies we support.

Certain volunteering projects aside, there's no point in deluding ourselves that we're saving the world by going on vacation; but if tourists and travel companies act and operate with an eye on social justice and environmental sustainability, there's no reason the destination countries can't reap more of the benefits and bear fewer of the costs. This is the rationale behind the various "ethical," "responsible" and—more recently—"fairtrade" initiatives which are growing in the travel industry. In the UK, you can now even get a Master of Science degree in "Responsible Tourism Management" (find out more at this magnificently long Web address: www.theinternationalcentreforresponsibletourism.org).

Self-declared ethical travel took off primarily with **ecotourism**—a loose term for nature travel with a responsible edge (see pp.304–305). But all areas of the travel sector are increasingly being asked to consider their social and environmental impact. This has been in part due to pressure from groups such as **Sustainable Travel International** (www.sustainabletravelinternational.org), though a number of surveys suggest that it also reflects the fact that the traveling public is concerned, though certainly not preoccupied, with the problems.

Research by anti-poverty group Tearfund, for example, found that more than half of holidaymakers would prefer to book a vacation with a company that has a written code covering working conditions, the environment and the support of local charities. And according to a 2003 study by the Travel Industry Association of America, 58.5 million Americans would pay more to use environmentally conscious travel companies. But only when people start asking these kinds of questions of travel agents will pressure for a truly ethical tourism industry be felt.

Finding an ethical vacation

As in any sector, a travel company genuinely committed to acting ethically is very likely to tell you about it. If the promotional literature or website doesn't touch on things discussed above, it's a pretty good bet that they haven't been considered at a very high level. However, that doesn't mean every company claiming ethical credentials is for real, so read their claims carefully and ask questions.

Here are a few pointers for where you can go to find ethically minded travel companies, and some of the various award programs and initiatives that you may come across when shopping for a trip.

Flights & travel companies

Sustainable Travel International www.sustainabletravelinternational.org
▷ 720-273-2975

Sustainable Travel International is an ambitious nonprofit organization whose website addresses many aspects of ethical tourism, and includes an eco-certification program (see entry under "Green Travel Labels" later in this chapter). One of its primary services is an "eco-directory" of travel and tourism providers, "chosen for their commitment to sustainable tourism." The website allows you to search by category (e.g. arts, wildlife/birding, conservation) and/or region/country, and organizations that have qualified for the eco-certification are marked as such. The site also offers carbon offsets, a fair trade online shop and a free Green Travel product database geared toward travel professionals.

Global Exchange www.globalexchange.org ▷ 415-255-7296

The human rights organization Global Exchange has been running "Reality Tours" since 1989, concentrating on social, environmental, political and economic issues. Though it's group travel, the emphasis is very much on both educating through experience and building ties through direct contact with people abroad. Trips to developing and/or tumultuous regions are the focus, with Afghanistan, China, Cuba, Haiti, India, Ireland, Laos, Palestine/Israel, South Africa, and Vietnam among the countries to which they're currently organizing trips; they also put together customized tours to a wide variety of destinations. A tour to Venezuela, for example, is angled toward learning "about dynamic social programs and policies that will rewrite Latin America's regional role in the global economy," while one to India examines the legacy of Mahatami Gandhi, and is led by his grandson. Global Exchange is also very active on several other socially progressive fronts (including fair trade and peace activism), but as the name of the organization indicates, putting their trips together remains very much at its core.

US Servas www.usservas.org ▷ 212-267-0252

Ethical tourism opportunites are ever-more abundant for those traveling in groups and/or package tours, so much so that those who much prefer traveling independently (whether solo, with partners or within family groups) might feel a bit left out in the cold. If you do want to travel both with a social conscience and on your own, one alternative worth investigating is Servas, an international organization founded in 1948 as a means of facilitating direct contact (and thus promoting global peace and cross-cultural understanding) among travelers of different countries. To join, you pay a fee ($85 for a year) and a much smaller deposit for lists of "hosts" in the countries you're visiting. After you successfully qualify for the program (which involves an application and interview with one of the numerous Servas representatives across the US), you can use the lists to stay with residents of the nations in which you're traveling—usually for two or three days, but longer if you and the hosts are getting along well and want to mutually extend the period. More than 135 countries are involved in the program, and while it does take some effort and commitment (both to go through the qualification process and to set up the visits abroad), it's one way to get much more direct, personal contact with people from other regions than you can usually get on a group/package tour. You can also be a "host" to travelers from abroad, whether or not you use Servas accomodations during your own travels.

EcoTravel.com www.ecotravel.com

This searchable directory lists "tour operators, lodges, private guides, nonprofit organizations and ancillary travel services" with a progressive outlook. There's no "screening" as such, but each listing includes the company's response to an EcoResponsibility Survey, asking them to detail their policies, philosophy and the way in which their practices preserve the environment and benefit the local community.

The International Ecotourism Society ecotourism.org ▷ 202-347-9203

Their website has a database of tour operators and travel agents who have signed a code of conduct (also displayed on the website) "stating that they follow the guidelines of responsible ecotourism travel."

International Ecotourism Club ecoclub.com

Another ecotourism website, with members in over 70 countries offering environmentally friendly lodgings, tours and services.

Fair Trade in Tourism South Africa www.fairtourismsa.org.za
▷ 011 27 12 342 8307/8

The concept of "fair trade" tourism is a relatively new one, and there are no global standards to define exactly what it means. Still, this groundbreaking South African initiative could be the start of something much bigger. The idea is to ensure that "the people whose land, natural resources, labor, knowledge and culture are used for tourism activities, actually benefit from tourism." This is done by certifying travel establishments that fulfill criteria relating to six areas: democracy, respect, reliability, transparency, sustainability and, most importantly, "fair share," which means that "all participants involved in a tourism activity should get their fair share of the income, in direct proportion to their contribution to the activity." The Sabi Sabi Game Reserve and the Stormsriver Adventures Co. are among the seven establishments certified at the time of writing. You'll find links to each at the above website.

Responsible tourism awards

Tourism for Tomorrow www.tourismfortomorrow.com ▷ 011 44 20 7481 8007

British Airways has been running the Tourism for Tomorrow Awards, to "recognize and encourage sustainable tourism initiatives across the globe," since 1992. BA admit that it can't run a complete "health check" on the entrants—which include tour and hotel companies of any type and size—so the awards recognize "better" rather than "best" practice. Still, they've been welcomed by the likes of Tourism Concern. You can find information about past winners on the website.

First Choice Responsible Tourism Awards www.responsibletravel.com

A collaborative project between the UK-based ResponsibleTravel.com site (backed by the Body Shop's Anita Roddick), *The Times*, *Geographical Magazine*, and the World Travel Market, these awards recognize that tourism "can and should be operated in a way that respects and benefits destinations and local people." Understandably a lot of the winners are British tour organizers, but there are also a lot of citations given to non-UK operations around the globe in various categories, ranging from hotel/accommodations to poverty reduction and conservation of endangered species.

World Legacy Awards www.wlaward.org

This award program—which so far has only been run in 2002 and 2004—is overseen by *National Geographic Traveler* magazine and Conservation International, with the aim of promoting "environmentally, culturally, and socially responsible tourism practices across a wider spectrum of the tourism industry." You can find details of, and links to, winners and finalists on its website. The 2004 top prizes went to Al Maha Desert Resort in Dubai, Gunung Rinjani region of Indonesia, Anangu Tours in Australia and the Casuarina Beach Club in Barbados.

Green travel labels

EU Eco-label www.eco-label-tourism.com

The European Union's little flower logo is used on energy-efficient washing machines and the like. Recently the program has been extended to take in tourism accommodation. Anyone "from a large hotel chain to a small farmhouse" can apply, and the flower is awarded to those who meet criteria such as the use of renewable energy sources and measures to reduce waste to less obvious things such as offering organic food and using low-emissions paints and cleaning chemicals. Since the program is very young, you're unlikely to come across many accredited hotels for at least a year or two.

The Green Globe 21 www.greenglobe21.com ▷ 011 61 2 6257 9102

The Green Globe 21 environmental certification standard (the number refers to the Agenda 21 Sustainable Development Principles from the 1992 Rio Earth Summit) was established by the World Travel and Tourism Council, a coalition largely made up of CEOs from major hotel chains, large travel companies and airlines. As such, while it's undoubtedly raising the profile of the environmental and social impact of tourism, it's sometimes been accused of having more to do with advertising and greenwash than achieving real results. But it's certainly worth knowing about their three-tier membership policy—an "ABC Pathway" referring to Affiliation, Benchmarking and, finally, Certification. Only level "C" companies that have been externally audited can use the logo with a check on it; "A" and "B" companies, who have had no external assessment, can use the logo, just without the check mark.

Sustainable Travel International www.sustainabletravelinternational.org
▷ 720-273-2975

In addition to being involved in several other areas of ethical travel (see listing under "travel companies"), this nonprofit is developing a Sustainable Tourism Eco-Certification Program™ (STEP). The voluntary system measures standards by "regionally and internationally accepted criteria for sustainable tourism," explained in quite some detail on the organization's site. The program awards points on a scale from 1 to 100 (with 20 bonus points available for especially good practices), those scoring above 80 getting five stars, a score of 60-79 meriting four stars, and so forth. At the time of writing, it was being launched as a pilot program. STEP-accredited organizations will be listed on the site after the launch.

Confused?

The above mixture of issues, programs, logos, claims and groups can make the world of ethical travel seem pretty impenetrable. For this reason, and to encourage global good standards, some groups have called for the establishment of a **Sustainable Tourism Stewardship Council**—much like the Forest Stewardship Council for wood (see p.264) or the Marine Stewardship Council for fish (see p.128). An extensive 2003 report by the Rainforest Alliance concluded that this was a realistic goal, and although the scheme is still in its conceptual stages, it may emerge in the next few years. For more information see: www.rainforestalliance.org

General Fair Trade shops

The previous chapters have listed socially responsible suppliers focusing on specific product areas. But the US also has a number of shops, online stores and catalogues that sell a wide range of fairly trade items. The non-food products they stock are of the uncertified fair-trade variety (see chapter two), but that's not to say everything is entirely based on trust. Stores and websites that are members of the Fair Trade Federation (FTF) must also fulfill a number of criteria in order to become members (see box overleaf).

A few FTF members only sell clothes or rugs, say, and as such some are also listed in the previous chapters. But most of the rest—many of which are listed in the following directory—sell a roughly consistent range of **gifts, cards, foods, jewelry, clothes, hand-made papers, ornaments, quilts, toys** and **musical instruments**. Many of these items tend toward slightly hippyish styles, and goods include all the clichés of ethical shopping such as rainbow textiles and even the dreaded rain-stick. But there are also more fashionably chic items on offer.

All the stores and sites in the following list are members of FTF as this book goes to press. Check the FTF website for additions and deletions, and note that some of the organizations here might be offering services in more areas (either online, mail-order or retail) than are indicated by their FTF listings.

O = Online seller　**M** = Mail-order seller　**R** = Retail seller

A Blue Moon R
416-720-2223, 375 Danforth Ave.,
Toronto, ON M4W 3E2, Canada

A Different Approach O
www.adifferentapproach.com

A Greater Gift OMR
www.agreatergift.org, 800-423-0071,
122 State St., Suite 600, Madison, WI
53711

Across Countries OR
www.acrosscountries.com, 888-395-
4130 or 816-792-8619, 1134 W. Kansas
Ave., Liberty, MO 64068

ALSADU, Inc. R
952-431-2514, 13056 Euclid Ave., Apple
Valley, MN 55124

Ama Servaa Women's Project M
707-569-8171, PO Box 7781, Santa
Rosa, CA 95407

Ananse Village OMR
www.anansevillage.com, 707-964-
3534, 17800 N. Hwy. 1, Fort Bragg, CA
95437

**Marilyn Anderson/Pro Arte Maya
Education Project OM**
www.marilynfanderson.com, 585-271-
4374, 34 Nicholson St., Rochester, NY
14620

Arte Huichol OM
www.artehuichol.com, 301-562-9305,
7416 Piney Branch Rd., Takoma Park,
MD 20912

Artisans' World Marketplace R
941-365-5994, PO Box 5994, 128 South
Pineapple Ave., Sarasota, FL 34277-
5994

ASHRO OM
www.ashro.com 630-515-881, 2748
Wisconsin St., Downers Grove, IL 60515

Asian World Imports R
www.asianworldimports.com, 207-374-
2284, PO Box 1234, Route 15, Pleasant
St., Blue Hill, ME 04614

Asia2You O
www.vietnameseartwork.com

FTF: criteria for Fair Trade organizations

▶ Paying a fair wage in the local context.

▶ Offering employees opportunities for advancement.

▶ Providing equal employment opportunities for all people, particularly the most disadvantaged.

▶ Engaging in environmentally sustainable practices.

▶ Being open to public accountability.

▶ Building long-term trade relationships.

▶ Providing healthy and safe working conditions within the local context.

▶ Providing financial and technical assistance to producers whenever possible.

For more info, see: www.fairtradefederation.com

Baksheesh R

www.vom.com/baksheesh, 707-473-0880, 106B Matheson St., Healdsburg, CA 95448

Baksheesh R

www.vom.com/baksheesh, 707-939-2847, 423 First St. W., Sonoma, CA 95476

Baskets of Africa OMR

www.basketsofafrica.com, 800-504-4656 or 505-323-2315, PMB 260, 12231 Academy Rd. NE #301, Albuquerque, NM 87111

Bean North Coffee Roasting Co. OMR

www.beannorth.com, 867-667-4145, PO Box 20437, Km 9.3, Takhini Hotsprings Rd., Whitehorse, YT Y1A 7A2, Canada

Beyond the Banyan Tree O

www.beyondthebanyantree.com

The Blessing Basket Project R

www.blessingbasket.net, 888-618-1503, 1201 W. First St., Warehouse 3A, Granite City, IL 62040

Blue Summit R

www.bluesummitexperience.com, 402-333-1405, 4101 S. 120th St., Omaha, NE 68137

Bright Hope International OR

www.brighthope.org, 847-519-0012, Bright Hope International, 2060 Stonigton Ave., Hoffman Estates, IL 60195

Cafe Campesino OMR

www.cafecampesino.com, 229-924-2468 or 888-532-4728, 725 Spring St., Americus, GA 31709

Canaan Fair Trade O

www.canaanfairtrade.com

Casa Bonampak OR

www.casabonampak.com, 415-642-4079, 3331 24th St., San Francisco, CA 94110

Circle of the Sun OM

www.circleofthesun.org, 530-798-1484, 2063 E. River Rd., Cortland, NY 13045

Cloudforest Initiatives M

651-592-4143, PO Box 40207, St. Paul, MN 55104

Coffee Exchange Inc. OMR

www.mailordercoffee.com, 401-273-1198, 207 Wickenden St., Providence, RI 02903-4328

Colores del Pueblo OR

www.coloresdelpueblo.org, 713-692-8423, 812 Fairbanks, Houston, TX 77009

Conscious Coffees M

970-453-5353, 229 Continental Ct., Unit 101A, PO Box 4477, Breckenridge, CO 80424

CORAZON OR

www.corazonfairtrade.com, 713-526-6591, 318 Waugh Dr., Houston, TX 77006-1828

The Creative Alternative OR

www.fairtradegifts.org, 541-472-0643, 229A SW G St., Grants Pass, OR 97526

Crossroads Global Handcrafts R

www.fairtradefederation.com/membio/crossr.html, 309-827-0121, 428 North Main St., Bloomington, IL 61701

Crossroads Trade OR

www.crossroadstrade.com, 781-646-3939, 669 Massachusetts Ave., Arlington, MA 02476

Da'Vida R
www.davidafairtrade.org, 607-432-1129, 179 Main St., Oneonta, NY 13820

Dean's Beans Organic Coffee Company OM
www.deansbeans.com, 978-544-2002, 50 R.W. Moore Ave., Orange, MA 01364

dgImports OM
www.pdggallery.com, 616-942-2705, 6137 Chamonix Ct. SE, Grand Rapids, MI 49546-6429

The Earth Friendly Coffee Company O
www.earthfriendlycoffee.com

Eastern Art Arcade O
www.easternartarcade.com

ECO TEAS OM
www.ecoteas.com, 800-839-0775 or 541-482-7745, PO Box 1192, Ashland, OR 97520

El Quetzal OMR
www.elquetzal.org, 206-723-1913, 5224 S. Brandon, Seattle, WA 98118

Equal Exchange O
www.equalexchange.com

Everything Under the Sun R
707-882-2161, PO Box 493, 211 Main St., Point Arena, CA 95468

Fair Trade Quilts & Crafts O
www.fairtradequilts.com

Far East Handicrafts R
www.fareasthandicrafts.com, 206-633-1950, 127 N. 36th St., Seattle, WA 98103

Flavours of Life OMR
www.flavoursoflife.com, 860-961-0741, PO Box 116, West Mystic, CT 06388

Forests of the World O
www.forestsoftheworld.com

Friendship and Peace Society Embroidery Project OM
www.friendship-and-peace.org, 941-922-7657, PO Box 275, Point Arena, CA 95468

Gaia's Fair Trade Gifts R
604-886-7117, PO Box 1124, Gibsons, BC, Canada

Gecko Traders O
www.geckotraders.com

Gifts That Make a Difference R
416-720-2223, 100 King St. West, Toronto, ON M4W 3E2, Canada

Ginger Blossom R
www.gingerblossom.com, 815-678-4015, 3016 Route 173, Richmond, IL 60071

Global Crafts OR
www.globalcrafts.org, 386-424-1662 or 866-468-3438, 2020 A Hibiscus Dr., Edgewater, FL 32141

Global CraftWork OR
www.globalcraftwork.com

Global Exchange OR
www.globalexchange.org, 510-548-0370, 2840 College Ave., Berkeley, CA 94705; 415-648-8068, 4018 24th St, San Francisco, CA 94114

Global Folk Art R
www.globalfolkart.org, 509-838-0664, 35 W. Main Ave., Spokane, WA 99201-0109

Global Handcrafters M
561-499-1818 or 800-244-5099, 13799 Date Palm Ct., #D, Delray Beach, FL 33484

Global Mamas/Women in Progress OR
www.womeninprogress.org, 800-338-

3032 or 612-781-0450, PO Box 18323, Minneapolis, MN 55418

The Global Market R
573-445-6131, c/o Community United Methodist Church, 3301 W. Broadway, Columbia, MO 65203

Global Village R
406-259-3024, 2720 3rd Ave. North, Billings, MT 59101-1929

Global Village Collection R
740-363-6267, 37 N. Sandusky St., Delaware, OH, 43015

Globalcrafts M
800-366-5896, The Catalog of the Christian Children's Fund, PO Box 518, New Windsor, MD 21776

Grounds for Change OMR
www.groundsforchange.com, 360-779-0401 or 800-796-6820, 15773 George Ln. NE, Ste. 204, Poulsbo, WA 98370

Guayaki Sustainable Rainforest Products OM
www.guayaki.com, 888-482-9254, PO Box 14730, San Luis Obispo, CA 93406

Higher Grounds Trading Co. OMR
www.javaforjustice.com, 231-256-9687, PO Box 326, Leland, MI 49654

Holy Land Olive Oil O
www.holylandoliveoil.com

Inka Urpi Galeria OR
www.inkaurpi.com, 207-563-2057, 79 Bristol Rd., Damariscotta, ME 04543

JAMTOWN OM
www.jamtown.com, 206-632-9136, PO Box 31514, Seattle, WA 98103

Jeannette Rankin Peace Center R
www.jrpc.org, 406-543-3955, 519 S. Higgins Ave., Missoula, MT 59801

Jewels of the Trade OMR
www.jewelsofthetrade.com, 727-528-9431, PO Box 7918, St. Petersburg, FL 33704

Jubilee: Global Gifts R
509-548-3508, 723 Front St., 2nd Fl., Leavenworth, WA 98826

Just Coffee OMR
www.justcoffee.net, 608-204-9011, 100 S. Baldwin St., #303, Madison, WI 53703

Just Creations R
www.justcreations.org, 502-897-7319, 2722 Frankfort Ave., Louisville, KY 40206

Kazuri America R
www.kazuriamerica.com, 800-941-2759 or 207-647-5465, 4 South High St., Bridgton, ME 04009

Kindred Handcrafts R
www.kindredhandcrafts.com, 707-579-1459, 605 Fourth St., Santa Rosa, CA 95404

Kusikuy OM
www.kusikuy.com, 866-KUSIKUY or 802-254-4044, 311 Williams St., Brattleboro, VT 05301

Larry's Beans, Inc. O
www.larrysbeans.com

Los Andes Imports O
www.losandesimports.com

Lotus Sculpture OR
www.lotussculpture.com, 866-568-8712 or 203-629-0902, 46 Milbank Ave., Greenwich, CT 06830

Lucuma Designs OR
www.lucuma.com, 877-858-2862, 1144 Tallevast Rd. Suite 107, Sarasota, FL 34243

MacroSun International R
www.macrosun.com, 888-9-NAMASTE
or 314-726-0222, 6172 Delmar Blvd., St.
Louis, MO 63112

Mad Imports OM
www.madimports.org, 718-802-9757,
262 Court St., #3, Brooklyn, NY 11231

**Made By Hand International
Cooperative R**
302-539-6335, Route 1 York Beach Mall,
South Bethany, DE 19930

Mariposa Indigenous Art O
www.mariposaimports.com

Maya Traditions OR
www.mayatraditions.com, 415-587-
2172, 3922 Mission St., San Francisco,
CA 94112-1015

Mayan Hands M
301-515-5911, 12604 W. Old Baltimore
Rd., Boyds, MD 20841-9008

Mayan Traditions O
www.mayantraditions.com

Mayadevi Imports OR
www.mayadeviimports.com, 415-462-
5464, PO Box 1216, North Fork, CA
93643

MayaWorks O
www.mayaworks.org

Mission Traders O
www.missiontraders.org

Moka Joe Certified Organic Coffee O
www.mokajoe.com

Moonflower Enterprises O
www.moonflowerenterprises.com

Mother Earth Coffee Co. OM
www.motherearthcoffeeco.com, 913-
722-5711, 5427 Johnson Dr. #182,
Mission, KS 66205

**Mountcastle International Trading
Company MR**
www.mountcastle.com, 727-360-4743,
107 Eighth Ave., St. Pete Beach, FL
33706

Nicaraguan Cultural Alliance OMR
www.quixote.org/nca, 301-864-5281 or
800-746-1160, PO Box 5051, Hyattsville,
MD 20782

Ojoba Rhythm Collective MR
360-298-1299, PO Box 883, Lopez
Island, WA, 98261

Otavalito R
269-857-7199, 421 Water St., Saugatuck,
MI 49453

Pachamama, A World of Artisans OR
www.pachamamaworld.com, 415-454-
5692, 1925 E. Francisco Blvd. #5, San
Rafael, CA, 94901

PatagonBird O
www.patagonbird.com

Patriot Imports Inc. O
www.patriotimports.com

Peace Coffee OM
www.peacecoffee.com, 612-870-3440
or 888-324-7872, 2105 1st Ave. S.,
Minneapolis, MN 55404

PeaceCraft R
www.peacecraft.org, 859-986-7441,
307B Chestnut St., Berea, KY 40403

Peri Dar Inc. O
www.peridar.com

Plowshare Center R
www.plowsharecenter.org, 262-547-
5188, Plowshare Center, 880 N. Grand,
Waukesha, WI 53186-4823

Pura Vida Coffee O
www.puravidacoffee.com

The Rhythm Inlet R
www.rhythminlet.com, 207-293-2239, PO Box 308, 221 Belgrade Rd., Mount Vernon, ME 04352

Rishashay OM
www.rishashay.com, 406-721-0580, PO Box 8271, Missoula, MT 59807

Rupalee Exclusifs India Imports O
www.rupalee.com

Search Widens O
www.searchwidens.com

SERRV International Gift Shop R
410-635-8711, 500 Main St., New Windsor, MD 21776-0365

Shinkal.com OR
www.shinkal.com, 305-944-9755, 6300 NE Ave., Ste. C, N. Miami Beach, FL 33162

Singing Shaman Traders and Mata Orgiz Originals O
www.singingshamantraders.com

The S.P.I.R.A.L. Foundation M
www.singingshamantraders.com, 310-459-6671, 211 Vance St., Pacific Palisades, CA 90272

Susan Hebert Imports, Inc. OMR
www.ecobre.com, 503-248-1111, 2018 NW Irving St., Portland, OR 97209

Tagua-Ivory Products LLC OR
www.taguaivory.com, 305-852-46761024, Snapper Ln., Key Largo, FL 33037

Ten Thousand Villages R
Numerous retail outlets throughout North America; see www.

tenthousandvillages.com or call 717-859-8100 for info.

Tibet Collection OM
www.tibetcollection.com, 800-318-5857 ext. 13, 5778 Second St. NE, Washington, DC 20011

Traditions Fair Trade OR
www.traditionsfairtrade.com, 206-752-4069, 5102 N Pearl St., Tacoma, WA 98407; 360-705-2819, 300 5th Ave. SW, Olympia, WA 98407

Trails to Bridges OMR
www.trailstobridges.com, 262-364-7788, PO Box 708, Merton, WI 53056

Tribal Fiber OM
www.tribalfiber.com, 888-712-8585 or 303-415-0478, PO Box 19755, Boulder, CO 80308

UPAVIM Crafts OM
www.upavim.org, 301-515-5911, 12604 W. Old Baltimore Rd., Boyds, MD 20841-9008

Venture Imports LLC M
616-656-9353, 4849 Barden Ct. SE, Grand Rapids, MI 49512

Village Imports, Inc. R
www.villageimports.com, 302-368-992, 165 East Main St., Newark, DE 19711

WHEAT's Hand to Hand Project at Paz de Cristo OR
www.hungerhurts.org, 602-241-0372, 4000 N 7th St., Ste. 118, Phoenix, AZ 85210

Winding Road Designs OR
www.windingroaddesigns.com, 303-456-2467, 9081 W 88th Circle, Broomfield, CO 80021; 919-699-4678, 2202-C Duck Pond Circle, Morrisville, NC 27560

World Artz.com OR

www.worldartz.com, 614-448-4060, 815 N. High St., Ste. II, Columbus, OH 43215

World of Good O

www.worldofgood.org

World-Shoppe.com OM

www.world-shoppe.com, 312-933-9227, PO Box 543121, Chicago, IL 60654

World Village Fair Trade Market R

www.fairtrademarket.org, 631-728-7880, 101-2 Montauk Hwy., Hampton Bays, NY 11946

Worldly Goods R

www.worldlygoods.org, 515-233-4568, 223 Main St., Ames, IA 50010-6237

Fair Trade events

As well as permanent Fair Trade shops, you may come across the occasional Fair Trade event. The first **Fair Trade Futures Conference** took place in Chicago in 2005, convened by the Fair Trade Federation and Fair Trade Resource Network with the help of several cosponsors involved in the movement. Focusing on workshops dealing with numerous issues driving the fair trade community, it attracted about 750 attendees from about 20 countries. For information on future conferences, visit:

Fair Trade Resource www.fairtraderesource.org

While it's not a Fair Trade event as such, the **Green Festival**—at which hundreds of stalls sell or tout socially responsible products—has many vendors offering fair trade products, whether certified or trust-based. The festival's been mildly criticized for being a little too oriented toward the selling and buying of eco-conscious goods, but you can always escape to the many workshops and guest lectures (which in recent years have been given by such well-known figures as former presidential candidate Dennis Kucinich, anti-war activist Cindy Sheehan and *Democracy Now!* radio host Amy Goodman). Cosponsored by Global Exchange and Co-op America, the weekend festival is held annually (in separate months) in Chicago, Washington DC and San Francisco.

Green Festival www.greenfestivals.com

There's also the United Students for Fair Trade Convergence. An annual event since 2004 (locations vary), it features workshops, speakers, vendors and more. Finally, many Fair Trade happenings are staged to coincide with World Fair Trade Day every second Saturday of May.

United Students for Fair Trade Convergence www.usft.org
World Fair Trade Day www.wftday.org

Part III

Find out more

- How to research a company
- Magazines
- Books
- Websites

Find out more

Throughout the text of this book, we've included Web addresses and phone numbers that will help you find out more about specific issues and products, from political donations to fairly traded rugs. But there are also scores of publications—online and on paper—that will lead you to info that's either more general (such as news and views about ethical consumerism) or more specific (such as in-depth profiles of the behavior of individual companies). What follows is a short selection of the best sites, magazines and books in both these categories, starting with resources for getting the low-down on whether a specific shop or brand is a member of the mean mainstream or the moral minority.

How to research a company

If you want to find out about the ethical standards of a particular company, there are a number of excellent online sources that might be able to tell you what you want to know. The following is a list of the best. Alternatively, for a detailed, though possibly slightly out-of-date comparison of the various companies within a specific sector, order the relevant back issue of *Ethical Consumer* (see p.329), which though UK-based, examines a good number of multinationals with US branches—its website includes an index specifying which products were covered in which issues.

Business & Human Rights Resource Centre www.business-humanrights.org
A truly amazing resource, this website—run "in partnership with Amnesty International Business Groups and leading academic establishments"—is an index of practically everything on the Web that relates to the effect of companies upon

human rights (including environmental damage). Updated hourly, it points to articles and stories published by newspapers, companies, NGOs and academics alike, and the clear, easy-to-navigate structure makes it simple to view all the links that relate to any one of 2400 individual companies (or to specific industries or issues). All in all, a fantastic, free service.

Corporate Critic www.corporatecritic.org

Corporate Critic is the corporate ethics database maintained by ECRA—the research association behind *Ethical Consumer* magazine (see p.329). It contains thousands of references to good and bad corporate behavior, categorized under environmental, animal and human rights headings. The data set isn't designed for individual users so much as for other research groups and think tanks, and its orientation toward the British market means you won't find your local hemp jeans manufacturer; but all the major multi-nationals are represented. Plus it's expensive for individual use: around $250/month or $1500/year subscription, or around $45 for single-day privileges. Still, Corporate Critic holds a valuable set of data, and if needed, ECRA will write you a report about the ethics of an individual company for around $100.

IdealsWork www.idealswork.com

"What companies do. What to do about it" is the strapline of this site that rates companies up to five stars on everything from labor issues and nuclear energy to women's issues and addictive products. Simply choose a product category and your ethical criteria, and a set of comparative ratings will appear, including the option to send the companies a message (and to buy products online).

ResponsibleShopper www.responsibleshopper.org

Run by Co-op America, this site includes hundreds of companies along with a list of their brands and advice on what they've been "praised for" and "criticized for," along with links to the original sources. It's not comprehensive, but it's still a very useful site, and Co-op America's 2005 Year-End report announced a revamp in which "the new website will focus on the worst offenders in each sector—such as clothing, food, and toys—and provide opportunities for individuals to take action."

For a more comprehensive guide to the dark underbelly of corporate behavior, visit the **CorpWatch** website. In the Research Tools section, you'll find a few pages titled "Hands-On Corporate Research Guide." This gives tips on everything from finding out about corporate structure to digging the dirt on a firm's environmental offenses and military contracts.

The British **CorporateWatch** site, with a slightly different name and URL, provides profiles on a range of big companies. These tend toward the harshly, and occasionally fanatically, anti-corporate, but they're well researched and well written. For more reports, see **PR Watch**, whose work often investigates corporate public relations spin.

Also, Co-op America has a free downloadable 18-page *Guide to Researching Corporations* in the boycotts section of its website. As the report states, they've tried to keep things simple, but it's a good starting point for free and fee-charging sites offering corporate info, and includes clear categories of its resource sources by type and issue.

CorpWatch www.corpwatch.org
CorporateWatch www.corporatewatch.org.uk
PR Watch www.prwatch.org
Co-Op America's Guide to Researching Corporations
www.coopamerica.org/programs/boycotts

Magazines

Many of the magazines listed here publish online as well as in print.

Environmental magazines

E Magazine www.emagazine.com ▷ 815-734-1242 ▷ Published every two months ▷ $4.95 per issue or $29.95 annual subscription

"The environmental magazine," as *E* describes itself, has articles covering all things green. There's strong coverage of alternative energy issues/developments, and a lengthy section in each issue devoted to green living.

World Watch www.worldwatch.org ▷ 888-544-2303 ▷ Published every two months ▷ $4.50 per issue or $27 annual subscription

Published by the World Watch Institute, and a bit more serious-minded than the more general-interest environmental magazines, *World Watch* analyzes trends in climate change, energy consumption, population growth and species extinction. Many of their articles from back issues are available as free downloadable PDF files through their website.

Earth Island Journal www.earthisland.org ▷ 415-788-3666 ▷ Published quarterly ▷ $4.50 per issue or $25 annual subscription

Now closing in on the two-decade mark, this arm of the respected Earth Island Institute has well-researched articles tying together social and environmental concerns, and has done some acclaimed investigative reporting into worrisome industry/government actions. Its website has an archive with issues going back to 1995.

On Earth www.nrdc.org ▷ 212-727-4429 ▷ Published quarterly ▷ $2.95 per issue or $15 or more suggested donation annual subscription

There might not be a mass-distributed eco-consumer magazine for the US market yet, but let it not be said that there aren't plenty of quality environmental publications. Here's another one, exploring climate change, deforestation, chemical manufacturing and more. The Living Green section (also archived on its website) offers "tips on making environmental choices in your daily life."

The Ecologist www.theecologist.org ▷ 011 44 1795 414 963 ▷ Published monthly ▷ $5.99 per issue or $44 annual subscription

Environmental affairs coverage from around the globe, mixing investigative reporting, news, commentary and a Green Pages section in every issue. Though based in the UK, it's international in scope, and available in the US on newsstands and via subscription.

Earth First! Journal www.earthfirstjournal.org ▷ 520-620-6900 ▷ Published every two months ▷ $4.50 per issue or $27 annual subscription

Perspectives on environmental issues of national and global import by the radical  wing of the US ecological movement, with a more avowedly political slant than other widely circulated magazines in the field.

Sustainable living magazines

Co-op America Quarterly www.coopamerica.org ▷ 800-58-GREEN ▷ Published quarterly ▷ $4 per issue or $20 annual subscription (includes membership)

As anyone who's read through this book knows by now, Co-op America is arguably the US organization doing the most to promote socially responsible consumerism. Their quarterly publication has up-to-date news and features on renewable energy, conservation, socially responsible investing, boycotts, sweatshops, eco-activism and more. A membership to Co-op America gets you a subscription to *Co-op America Quarterly*, and to its more financially-minded "green living" newsletter, *Real Money*.

Mother Earth News www.motherearthnews.com ▷ 800 234 3368 ▷ Published every two months ▷ $4.99 per issue or $19.95 annual subscription

Fairly slick, long-established mag that emphasizes the "how-to" aspects of sustainable living, with a consistent stream of articles on making your home greener, growing healthy garden food and the like. There are also profiles of celebrity environmentalists like Robert Redford and contributions from esteemed writers like Barbara Kingsolver.

Plenty www.plentymag.com ▷ 800-316-9006 ▷ Published every two months ▷ $4.95 per issue or $12 annual subscription

With a breezier, chattier style than most of its peers, this young magazine has plenty of short but interesting articles on all aspects of green living, from organic food and alternative fuel vehicles to eco-fashion and environmentally-friendly developments in the corporate world.

Solar Today www.solartoday.org ▷ 800-316-9006 ▷ Published every two months ▷ $4.95 per issue or $29 annual subscription

Published by the American Solar Energy Society, covering the latest in solar energy developments, policies and applications, and some other renewable energy sources as well.

Organic Gardening www.organicgardening.com ▷ Published every two months ▷ $4.99 per issue or $23.96 annual subscription

Plenty of useful information about organic gardening.

Specialist ethical consumerism magazines

Ethical Consumer www.ethicalconsumer.org ▷ 0161 226 2929 ▷ Published every two months ▷ £31 annual subscription (airmail to US, payable via website)

Ethical Consumer describes itself as the "the UK's leading alternative consumer magazine." As it's geared toward the UK market, its appeal in the US might be limited to the hard-core researcher. But since there's no comparable magazine in the US, it is of some value, both because it examines multinational companies doing business here, and because it covers numerous issues relevant to socially conscientious consumers the world over.

Green Car Journal www.greencar.com ▷ Published quarterly ▷ $5.99 per issue or $19.95 annual subscription

A kind of *Consumer Reports* for the "green car" market, evaluating the environmental performance of different models, also running articles on cutting-edge energy-efficient auto technology.

The Green Guide www.thegreenguide.com ▷ Published every two months ▷ $5.99 per issue or $20 annual print subscription, $15 annual e-suscription)

Published by the Green Guide Institute, this 12-page newsletter offers green product reviews/tips and specialized articles of interest to socially/environmentally conscious consumers.

Politics & companies

Business Ethics www.business-ethics.com ▷ 612-879-0695 ▷ Published quarterly ▷ $5 per issue or $49 annual subscription

Dedicated to analysis of corporate responsibility and socially responsible investing, this publication is perhaps a bit more slick and mainstream than many of the more left-leaning ethical shoppers would like. But they do run some penetrating pieces; their fall 2005 issue, for instance, had an interview with a shareholder activist, as well as an article on the question "is it unethical to fight unions"?

Cultural Survival Quarterly www.cs.org ▷ 617-441-5400 ▷ Published quarterly ▷ $5 per issue or $45 annual subscription (includes membership)

Published by the US-based Cultural Survival organization, which promotes "the rights, voices, and visions of indigenous peoples," this magazine often touches upon issues related to socially responsible consumption, such as the effects of fair trade and global warming on indigenous populations.

Ethical Corporation www.ethicalcorp.com ▷ 617-441-5400 ▷ Published monthly ▷ $139 annual subscription

Because of its British base, specialized nature and hefty price, this might be of more use for organizations than individuals. Make no mistake, though; it's got plenty of valuable articles on corporate responsibility, much of it applicable the world over. Plus a subscription gives you access to the substantial member-only portions of its website.

Mother Jones www.motherjones.com ▷ 415-321-1700 ▷ Published every two months ▷ $5.95 per issue or $18 annual subscription

Perhaps the most popular progressive magazine in the US, acclaimed even by establishment types for the depth and color of its investigative reporting.

Multinational Monitor www.multinationalmonitor.org ▷ 202-387-8030 ▷ Published monthly ▷ $4.95 per issue or $29.95 annual subscription

As the name indicates, this magazine is dedicated to examining multinational companies and their effect on the environment the world-over. It also covers labor issues, corporate crime, multilateral banks and consumer activism.

The Nation www.thenation.com ▷ 800-333-8536 ▷ Published weekly ▷ $2.95 per issue or $29.97 annual subscription

The most respected progressive political weekly, with analysis and commentary on the full gamut of contemporary political and social issues.

New Internationalist www.newint.org ▷ 905-946-0407 ▷ Published monthly ▷ $5.95 per issue or $44 annual subscription

While its overall thrust is on global social justice and inequality, *New Internationalist* often covers issues such as socially responsible consumption, fair trade, sustainability and the environment.

Utne Reader www.utne.com ▷ 800-736-UTNE ▷ Published every two months ▷ $4.95 per issue or $19.97 annual subscription

General-interest alternative media magazine that often covers green issues.

Z Magazine www.zmag.org ▷ 508-548-9063 ▷ Published monthly ▷ $4.95 per issue or $33 annual subscription

One of the most prominent magazines of the American Left, with commentary and articles spanning the entire political spectrum, often by leading cultural critics.

The Economist www.economist.com ▷ 800-456-6086 ▷ Published weekly ▷ $4.95 per issue or $129 annual subscription

Unlike virtually every other publication listed here, *The Economist* does not come from a left-of-center perspective. If you want to keep up with more Centrist commentary on all manner of geopolitical issues, however, this international weekly is one of the best available sources.

Books

There isn't space here for a complete bibliography—and anyhow many of the subjects touched on in this book are better covered in magazines, journals and websites than in books. But here are a few particularly relevant recent titles, many of which have been referred to in the text.

Ethical consumerism

The Blue Pages PoliPoint Press, 2006 ▷ ISBN 0-9760621-1-9 ▷ $9.95

This "directory of companies rated by their policies and practices," ranks firms according to factors including political contributions, staff benefits (or lack thereof), lawsuits, community outreach activities and environmental conduct.

National Green Pages www.coopamerica.org/pubs/greenpages ▷ Free with $20 annual Co-op America membership

Co-op America's National Green Pages are viewable for free online, but if you want a hard copy, you'll need an annual membership. While its listings aren't totally thorough, it's the most comprehensive source of contact information for companies and individuals selling socially responsible products and services.

Who's Green? Ecotone Publishing ▷ ISBN 0-9749033-5-3 ▷ $11.95

Initiated in 2006 as an annual publication, "the directory of who's green in the design and construction field" includes contact info and profiles of firms working in architecture, engineering, interior design, green consulting, and green building.

The Editors of E Magazine Green Living: The E Magazine Handbook for Living Lightly on the Earth Plume, 2005 ▷ ISBN: 0452285747 ▷ $16

E Magazine's perspectives and recommendations on many aspects of green living, including socially responsible investments, organic and non-GMO food, nontoxic personal care products and environmentally conscious transportation.

Lisa Harrow and Roger Payne What Can I Do? An Alphabet for Living Chelsea Green, 2004 ▷ ISBN: 1931498660 ▷ $7.95

Slim and basic guide to sustainable living, emphasizing listings and descriptions of websites.

Environmental issues

John McNeill Something New Under the Sun Penguin, 2001 ▷ ISBN: 0393321835 ▷ $17.95

A scholarly yet readable "environmental history" of the last century.

Mayer Hillman How We Can Save the Planet Penguin Putnam, 2006 ▷ ISBN: 0141016922 ▷ $15

An accessible assessment of climate change theory and proposed solutions, including individual action.

James Bruges The Little Earth Book The Disinformation Company, 2004 ▷ ISBN: 0972952926 ▷ $9.95

Pithy, fact-filled mini-essays on everything from water to soil.

Bob Henson The Rough Guide to Climate Change Rough Guides, 2006 ▷ ISBN: 1843537117 ▷ $16.99

A comprehensive overview of climate change science, symptoms and proposed solutions, both international and individual.

Elizabeth Royte On the Secret Trail of Trash Little, Brown, 2005 ▷ ISBN: 0316738263 ▷ $24.95

What exactly happens to our waste after it leaves our house? You might not want to know, but if you do, this book gives you a pretty good idea of both the massive tonnage of US garbage and recyclables produced each day, and the environmental and economic predicaments involved in their disposal.

Paul Roberts The End of Oil: On the Edge of a Perilous New World Houghton Mifflin, 2004 ▷ ISBN: 0618562117 ▷ $14

With ever-more speculation on when oil production will peak, this look at our most prized fossil fuel offers both reason for alarm and renewed urgency for developing alternative energy technologies.

Ross Gelbspan Boiling Point Basic Books, 2004 ▷ ISBN: 0-465-02761-X ▷ $22

A warning bell tolling for the oncoming crisis of climate change, both criticizing the politicians and journalists who aren't acknowledging the gravity of the problem, and calling for internationally funded green technology programs.

Matthew Yeomans Oil: Anatomy of an Industry The New Press, 2006 ▷ ISBN: 159558028X ▷ $16.95

Though it's not the most in-depth study of oil, it might be the most readable, with sections on both the history of the oil business and the need for alternative energy solutions in the near future.

Globalization & trade

Naomi Klein No Logo Picador, 2002 ▷ ISBN: 0312421435 ▷ $15

The book that put branding, world trade, globalization and sweatshops into the public eye.

John Cavanagh & Jerry Mander (eds) Alternatives to Economic Globalization: A Better World Is Possible Berrett-Koehler, 2004 ▷ ISBN: 1576753034 ▷ $18.95

Put together by the International Forum on Globalization, this book advocates localized, centralized governments in developing nations, with 18 prominent authorities weighing in on the subject.

Philippe Legrain Open World: The Truth About Globalization Ivan R. Dee, 2004 ▷ ISBN: 0-349-11529-X 1566635470 ▷ $27.50

A readable defense of globalization, covering poverty, sweatshops, trade rules and brands, and big business.

George Monbiot Manifesto for a New World Order The New Press, 2004 ▷ ISBN: 1565849086 ▷ $24.95

A commentary on globalization that's critical of both the reigning world order and the Left, mooting alternative approaches to world trade.

Sustainability

Greg Pahl Biodiesel: Growing a New Energy Economy Chelsea Green, 2005 ▷ ISBN 1-931498-65-2 ▷ $18

A history of biodiesel, with explanations of biodiesel technology and a look at its potential use of as an alternative fuel of the future.

Daniel D. Chiras The New Ecological Home: A Complete Guide to Green Building Options Chelsea Green, 2004 ▷ ISBN 1-931498-16-4 ▷ $35

An overview aimed at home builders and new home buyers, with chapters on green building materials, energy efficiency, solar heating, green power and more. The publisher, Chelsea Green (www.chelseagreen.com), has a wide assortment of books about specific eco-building techniques, as well as guides to using renewable energy sources and sustainable agricultural methods.

Joshua Tickell Biodiesel: From the Fryer to the Fuel Tank: The Complete Guide to Using Vegetable Oil as an Alternative Fuel Tickell Energy Consultants, 2000 ▷ ISBN 0970722702 ▷ $24.95

Just what it says it is, from a figure familiar in the media from his travels across the country in a "Veggie Van."

Juliet B. Schor & Betsy Taylor Sustainable Planet: Solutions for the 21st Century Beacon Press, 2003 ▷ ISBN 0807004553 ▷ $18

Sixteen essays on various aspects of sustainability, including such noted figures as Seventh Generation CEO Jeffrey Hollander, economist John Cavanagh and New York Congresswoman Nydia Velazquez.

Food

Craig Sams Little Food Book The Disinformation Company, 2004 ▷ ISBN: 1932857036▷ $9.95

A small but juicy look at our food, taking in subsidies, sugar, obesity, organics and more.

Luddene Perry & Dan Schultz A Field Guide to Buying Organic Bantam, 2005 ▷ ISBN: 0-553-38293-4 ▷ $14

Basic explanations of organic foods, cultivation systems and labeling programs, along with shopping tips and price comparisons.

George Pyle Raising Less Corn, More Hell: The Case for the Independent Farm Against Industrial Food Public Affairs, 2005 ▷ ISBN: 1586481150 ▷ $16.50

Pyle argues that industrial farming is not only bad for food quality, but also fosters a system of agricultural mass production that leads to the "dumping" of crops in third world countries, hurting local farmers and workers without necessarily feeding starving people.

Christopher D. Cook Diet for a Dead Planet: How the Food Industry Is Killing Us The New Press, 2004 ▷ ISBN: 1-56584-864-0 ▷ $24.95

A detailed volume on the pitfalls of the modern food industry, encompassing the corporatization of supermarkets and farms, the ills of pesticides, the exploitation of agricultural labor and more, illustrated with both statistics and personal stories.

Ken Midkiff The Meat You Eat: How Corporate Farming Has Endangered America's Food Supply St. Martin's Press, 2004 ▷ ISBN: 0312325355 ▷ $23.95

Another case against big-business farming and for the small local farmers, detailing the costs (environmental and otherwise) of corporate agriculture.

Erik Marcus Meat Market: Animals, Ethics, and Money Brio Press, 2005 ▷ ISBN: 0975867911 ▷ $14.95

While this too criticizes intensive farming, here the emphasis is more on the cost it exacts in animal suffering, contending that activists should focus more on exposing animal cruelty than converting people to veganism.

Jeffrey M. Smith Seeds of Deception: Exposing Industry and Government Lies About the Safety of the Genetically Engineered Foods You're Eating Yes! Books, 2003 ▷ ISBN: 0972966587 ▷ $17.95

Another "case against" volume, the author having assembled a pretty fair one against genetically modified food safety while exposing corporate/government irresponsibility in its dissemination.

Robert S. Devine Bush Versus the Environment Anchor Books, 2004 ▷ ISBN: 1-4000-7521-1 ▷ $12

A damningly detailed examination of George W. Bush's environmental policies during his first few years of office.

Websites

Finally, a few miscellaneous websites that aren't covered elsewhere in this book. Also see the sites listed on pp.325–327.

Eco-Labels www.eco-labels.org

A useful site that examines ethical product labels and descriptions, searchable by both label category and product area.

Co-op America www.coopamerica.org

Co-op America is mentioned numerous times in this book, but it's worth reiterating here that its website is a premier source for information and resources relating to most of the issues covered throughout, including socially responsible investing, renewable energy, sweatshops and consumer activism. Not least among its features are the *National Green Pages*, a database of contact information for, and information about, socially responsible businesses in all categories.

Ecomall www.ecomall.com

Funkier and less comprehensive than the *National Green Pages*, but another useful database linking to socially responsible businesses of all kinds. Includes a *Green Living Magazine* section of articles on the subject.

Good Stuff? www.worldwatch.org/pubs/goodstuff

Articles and links compiled by the Worldwatch Institute, looking at the human and environmental costs behind cell phones, CDs and scores of other everyday products.

EcoTalk www.ecotalk.net

The website of the only nationally syndicated radio program on environmental issues. Check here to find out what affiliated stations are airing the show, or to listen to past broadcasts over the Internet.

Democracy Now www.democracynow.org

Hosted by Amy Goodman and Juan Gonzalez, *Democracy Now* is the most hard-hitting, in-depth, nationally syndicated public radio program examining major national and global political issues from an alternative perspective. You can listen to past and present broadcasts online at this site, which also has a list of stations carrying the show.

Center for a New American Dream www.newdream.org

A somewhat all-over-the-map collection of resources, articles and essays, many of which relate to socially conscientious consumerism.

The Rainforest Site www.therainforestsite.com

Click on this site once a day, and you'll generate a small amount of daily funds toward the purchase of endangered land. Also on this site, you can do the same click-a-day to help out several affiliates raising money to fight world hunger and breast cancer, as well as promote child health, literacy and animal rescue operations. Fair Trade goods are also sold.

Green Map www.greenmap.org

Links to information about several hundred "Green Maps"—i.e., maps emphasizing features such as environmentally conscious/sustainable businesses, buildings, food outlets, transportation and community organizations, as well as scenic land and waterways—from all over the world, including many in the US.

OpenOffice www.openoffice.org

A superb, completely free alternative to Microsoft Office Suite (Word, Excel, etc). It's compatible with pretty much everything and saves you giving your money to Microsoft, who is, among other things, a major donor to George W. Bush. If you're technologically literate, and want to avoid Microsoft altogether, buy a computer without Windows pre-installed and get hold of Linux, a highly powerful free alternative. See: www.linux.org

Index